Celebrated military historian and television presenter Richard Holmes is best known for his BBC series *Battlefields, War Walks* and *The Western Front*. His dozen books include *Firing Line*, and he is general editor of the definitive *Oxford Companion to Military History*. He taught military history at Sandhurst for many years, and is now Professor of Military and Security Studies at Cranfield University and the Royal Military College of Science.

From the reviews:

'Professor Holmes brings great gifts to his task: fine scholarship, the smooth blending of narrative and analysis, and also sufficient humour and irony . . . The result is an enthralling book . . . One of the astounding and cautionary themes throughout is how complex and multifaceted any aspect of our history is, and how – amid the predictable elements – there is always the unexpected and the surprising.'   DENIS JUDD, *Independent*

'Richard Holmes obviously has a deep love of his subject, and writes of it with an infectious enthusiasm which is impossible to resist. Sensibly, he has made great use of contemporary testimonies – letters, diaries, memoirs and autobiographies – which bring the narrative to life.   T. J. BINYON, *Evening Standard*

'Holmes's talent for dramatic reconstruction, as seen on television, is used here to great effect as he paints a portrait in depth of the typical ranker whom Wellington counted on to win his battles. Here you will hear the authentic voice of Private Ezekiel Hobden, Holmes's chosen voice from the ranks, and smell the sweat and burning powder.'
     JOHN CROSSLAND, *Sunday Times*

'A series of literary snapshots of every facet of military life; a vast montage of images culled from memoirs, correspondence and diaries. The sheer bulk of sources that Holmes has mastered is impressive, and his book covers everything . . . Holmes is highly effective in bringing home the realities of the battle and its aftermath . . . Amid the mayhem and slaughter [he] also has a keen eye for the army's endearing oddities and eccentricities.'   JOHN ADAMSON, *Sunday Telegraph*

REDCOAT

THE BRITISH SOLDIER
IN THE AGE OF HORSE AND MUSKET

RICHARD HOLMES

HarperCollins*Publishers*

HarperCollins*Publishers*
77–85 Fulham Palace Road,
Hammersmith, London w6 8jb

www.**fire**and**water**.com

This paperback edition 2002
7 9 8

First published in Great Britain by
HarperCollins*Publishers* 2001

ISBN 0 00 653152 0

Maps by John Gilkes

Chapter heading illustrations are taken from British Military Costume,
coloured etchings by William Heath, 1824, National Army Museum London;
and from 'Camp Scenes, *c.* 1803', coloured etchings by W. H. Pyne,
also in National Army Museum, London

Set in PostScript Linotype Baskerville
with Bulmer and Gresham display by
Rowland Phototypesetting Ltd, Bury St Edmunds, Suffolk
Printed and bound in Great Britain by
Clays Ltd, St Ives plc

CONTENTS

ILLUSTRATIONS

The Duke of Wellington painted by Francisco de Goya. Oil on wood. *The National Gallery, London.*

King George II at the Battle of Dettingen, 16 June 1743. After the original by John Wooton. *Peter Newark Military Pictures.*

William, Duke of Cumberland in General Officer's State coat, *c.* 1750. Oil on canvas by David Morier. *National Army Museum, London.*

Lieutenant General Sir Henry Clinton KB painted in miniature by John Smart, *c.* 1777. *National Army Museum, London.*

General John Burgoyne. Oil on canvas by an unknown artist after Allan Ramsay. *National Portrait Gallery, London.*

Colonel Barnastre Tarleton. Oil on canvas by Sir Joshua Reynolds. *National Gallery, London.*

Lieutenant General Sir John Moore in Lieutenant General's coatee, *c.* 1805. Oil on canvas by Sir Thomas Lawrence. *National Army Museum, London.*

The first Marquess of Anglesey, Colonel of 7th Hussars, 1816. Oil on canvas by Stroehling. *National Army Museum, London.*

Uniform of a Private soldier, King's Royal Rifle Corps, Battalion Companies, 1758. Illustration by P. W. Reynolds from *The Annals of the King's Royal Rifle Corps* by S. M. Milne, 1913.

Bethnal Green Volunteer, *c.* 1799. *Mary Evans Picture Library.*

Uniform of a Rifleman, King's Royal Rifle Corps, 5th Battalion, 1812. Illustration by P. W. Reynolds after Charles Hamilton Smith from *The Annals of the King's Royal Rifle Corps* by S. M. Milne, 1913.

A Private of the 7th or Queen's Own L.D. (Hussars), 1813. Coloured aquatint by I. C. Stadler after Charles Hamilton Smith. *National Army Museum, London.*

An Officer and Private of the 52nd Regiment of Light Infantry, 1814. Coloured aquatint by I. C. Stadler after Charles Hamilton Smith. *National Army Museum, London.*

Ensign of the 9th Regiment of Foot bearing the Regimental Colours, with a Colour Sergeant, 1815. Coloured engraving by I. C. Stadler after Charles Hamilton Smith. *Peter Newark Military Pictures.*

'A View of the Taking of Quebec' 13 September 1759. *Peter Newark Military Pictures.*

The Fight at Lexington Common, 19 April 1775 during the American War of Independence. After the original by Howard Pyle, 1898. *Peter Newark Military Pictures.*

The British surrender at Yorktown, 19 October 1781. *Peter Newark Military Pictures.*

'Steady the Drums and Fifes': the 57th Under Fire at the Battle of Albuera, 16 May 1811. Oil on canvas by Lady Elizabeth Butler. *By kind permission of The Princess of Wales's Royal Regiment.* Photo: Peter Newark Military Pictures.

Wellington at Waterloo. Oil on canvas by Ernest Crofts, 1886. *Bonhams, London/Bridgeman Art Library.*

Quatre-Bras, 18 June 1815. Oil on canvas by Lady Elizabeth Butler, 1875. *National Gallery of Victoria, Melbourne. Courtesy of the artist's estate/Bridgeman Art Library.*

Cuirassiers charging the Highlanders at the Battle of Waterloo, 18 June 1815. Oil on canvas by Felix Phillippoteaux, 1874. *Apsley House, The Wellington Museum, London/Bridgeman Art Library.*

Retreat from Kabul, 1841: 'The Last Stand of the 44th Regiment at Gundamuck.' After the original by William Barnes Wollen. *By kind permission of the Trustees of the Essex Regiment Museum. Peter Newark Military Pictures.*

Battle of Chillienwallah, 1849: The Charge of the 3rd King's Own Light Dragoons. Coloured engraving by J. Harris after H. Martens. *National Army Museum, London.*

Crimean War, 1854. Commissariat Difficulties: the Road from Balaklava to Sevastopol at Kadikioi During the Wet Weather. Coloured lithograph after W. Simpson. *National Army Museum, London.*

'Scotland Forever.' Oil on canvas by Lady Elizabeth Butler, 1881. *Leeds Museums and Galleries (City Art Gallery) UK. Courtesy of the artist's estate/Bridgeman Art Library.*

A Prostitute Drum'd out of the Camp in Hyde Park, 1780. Coloured etching by Paul Sandby. *National Army Museum, London.*

British Recruiting Officers Recruiting Soldiers Outside a Tavern by
W. H. Bunbury. *Peter Newark Military Pictures.*

A Mounted Officer of 18th (Royal Irish) Regiment Takes the Salute,
c. 1840. Coloured lithograph by J. Lynch after M. A. Hayes.
National Army Museum, London.

Camp scenes, 1803. (*above*) An army on the march with baggage-
waggons laden; (*below*) loading the baggage-waggon. Coloured
aquatint by J. Hill and W. H. Pyne. *National Army Museum, London.*

Interior of a Barrack-room with NCOs and Troopers of Life Guards,
Royal Horse Guards and Dragoon Guards, c. 1840. Oil on canvas
by an unknown artist. *National Army Museum, London.*

Florence Nightingale Receiving the Wounded at Scutari, 1856. Oil on
canvas by Jerry Barrett. *Forbes Magazine Collection, New York/
Bridgeman Art Library.*

General Wolfe. *Peter Newark Military Pictures.*

Lieutenant General Sir William Howe. *Peter Newark Military Pictures.*

Bust of Major General Robert Crauford, c. 1810. From *General
Crauford and his Light Division* by Revd. Alexander H. Crauford,
c. 1890. *National Army Museum, London.*

Inscription for the tomb to be erected to the memory of the Marquis
of Anglesey's leg, c. 1815. Coloured etching by Cruikshank.
National Army Museum, London.

Richard Barter, Adjutant of the 75th Gordon Highlanders during the
Siege of Delhi. *By kind permission of Richard John Barter.*

Florence Nightingale. *Peter Newark Military Pictures.*

Hugh, 1st Viscount Gough, in General Officer's frock coat, c. 1850.
Painted in miniature, watercolour on ivory, by an unknown artist.
National Army Museum, London.

Field Marshal Lord Raglan, 1855. Photograph by Roger Fenton.
National Army Museum, London.

General Sir Harry Smith in General Officer's full dress, c. 1860.
National Army Museum, London.

Captain Howell Rees Gronow. From Captain Gronow's *Last
Recollections,* 1866.

Colin Campbell, Lord Clyde, Sir Hope Grant and Sir William
Mansfield. Photograph from a diary kept by Captain P. S.
Lumsden, DQMG, 2nd Division. *National Army Museum, London.*

Battle of Fontenoy, 11 May 1745. The French and Allies confront each other. Oil on canvas by Felix Phillippoteaux. *Victoria and Albert Museum, London/Bridgeman Art Library.*

French and Indian War 1755–1763: the British attack Fort Ticonderoga, 8 July 1758. *Peter Newark Military Pictures.*

The Battle of Mononghala River, 1755: the defeat of General Braddock. Oil on canvas by Edwin Willard Deming, *c.* 1903. *State Historical Society of Wisconsin.*

The storming of Seringapatam, 1799. Stipple engraving by J. Vendramini from the panoramic painting by R. Ker Porter. *National Army Museum, London.*

American War, New Orleans, 1815. 'Defeat of the British Army, 12,000 strong under the commandment of Sir Edward Pakenham, in the attack of the American lines defended by 3,600 Militia commanded by Major General Andrew Jackson, 8 January 1815, on Chalmette Plain, five miles below New Orleans.' Aquatint by P. L. Debucourt after Ladotte. *National Army Museum, London.*

1st Sikh War: the 31st Regiment, Sir Harry Smith's Division advancing to the charge at the Battle of Moodkee, 18 December 1845. Coloured aquatint by J. Harris after H. Martens from a sketch by Major G. F. White, 31st Regt, 1845. *National Army Museum, London.*

Charge of the Light Cavalry Brigade, 25 October 1854. Engraving by E. Walker after William Simpson. *Private Collection/Bridgeman Art Library.*

Crimean War, 1855: the Ordnance Wharf, Balaclava. Photograph by Roger Fenton. *National Army Museum, London.*

Indian Mutiny: Horse Artillery in Action, *c.* 1857. Lithograph after Captain G. F. Atkinson. *Mary Evans Picture Library.*

Indian Mutiny: interior of the Secundrabagh at Lucknow, 1857–8. Photograph by Felice Beato. *British Library, Oriental and India Office Collections.*

Indian Mutiny: 'Heavy Day in the Batteries'. Lithograph after G.F. Atkinson from the series 'The Campaign in India 1857–8'. *National Army Museum, London.*

'Military Leapfrog, or Hints to Young Gentlemen.' Caricature satirising the sale of commissions by the Duke of York's mistress Mary Anne Clarke. Coloured etching after I. Cruikshank. *National Army Museum, London.*

Soldiers drilling: infantrymen in fatigue dress, NCOs and mounted

PICTURES IN THE TEXT

LIST OF MAPS

'Until yesterday I had not seen any British infantry under arms since the troops from America arrived, and, in the meantime, have constantly seen corps of foreign infantry. These are all uncommonly well dressed in new clothes, smartly made, setting the men off to great advantage – add to which the coiffure of high broad-topped shakos, or enormous caps of bear-skin. Our infantry – indeed, our whole army – appeared at the review in the same clothes in which they had marched, slept and fought for months. The colour had faded to a dusky brick-red hue; their coats, originally not very smartly made, had acquired by constant wearing that loose easy set so characteristic of old clothes, comfortable to the wearer, but not calculated to add grace to his appearance. *Pour surcroit de laideur,* their cap is perhaps the meanest, ugliest thing invented. From all these causes it arose that our infantry appeared to the utmost disadvantage – dirty, shabby, mean, and very small. Some such impression was, I fear, made on the Sovereigns, for . . . they remarked to the Duke what very small men the English were. "Ay," replied our noble chief "they are small; but your Majesties will find none who fight so well".'

Captain Cavalié Mercer, Royal Horse Artillery,
describing a review of the British army by the Allied sovereigns,
Paris 1815

INTRODUCTION

I HAVE NEVER really got on with Bertolt Brecht, but cannot deny that he had a point in asking, however rhetorically, whether Caesar crossed the Rubicon all by himself. Of course he did not, any more than Cornwallis surrendered at Yorktown on his own, Wellington won Waterloo single-handed, or Cardigan hacked down the Valley of Death at Balaclava with only his bright bay charger Ronald for company. This is not a book about great, or even not-so-great, generals, though both feature in it from time to time. And it is not about battles either, even if we are rarely very far away from them. Instead, its concern is for the raw material of generalship and the pawns of battle, the regimental officers and soldiers (and their wives, sweethearts and followers of a less defined and sometimes rather temporary status) that served in the British army in a century when it painted the world red.

Hollywood is entertainment rather than history, though its tendency to use the past as a vehicle for story telling blurs fact and fiction so that the latter assumes, however unintentionally, the authority of the former. The redcoat has recently featured on the screen in a role depressingly reminiscent of that assigned to the German army after the Second World War. Brutal or lumpish soldiers are led by nincompoops or sadists with the occasional decent fellow who eventually allows a mistaken sense of duty to win the battle with his conscience. Watch *Rob Roy*, *Last of the Mohicans* or, most recently, *The Patriot*, and you will wonder how this army of thugs and incompetents managed to fight its way across four continents and secure the greatest empire the world has ever seen.

That it was an army born of paradox, forged in adversity, often betrayed by the government it obeyed and usually poorly understood by the nation it served, is beyond question. It drank far too much and looted a little too often, and its disciplinary code threw a long and ugly shadow onto the early twentieth century. It sometimes lost battles: we shall see it ground arms in surrender at Saratoga in 1777 and Yorktown in 1781, wilt under Afghan knives on the rocky road from Kabul in 1842, and quail under Russian fire before Sevastopol's Great Redan in 1855. Yet it very rarely lost a war. In victory or defeat it had a certain something that flickers out across two centuries like an electric current. Little of that was generated by a military organisation which was a characteristically British mixture of tradition wrapped in compromise, and fuelled by the quest for place, perquisites or status. And, important though high command was, this was an army that fought as hard when mishandled by Beresford at Albuera in 1811 as it did when commanded with genius by Wellington at Salamanca the following year. It drew its enormous tensile strength not simply from the fear of punishment and the lure of reward, though both were important, but from that elusive chemistry that binds men together in the claustrophobic world of barrack-room and half-company, officers' and sergeants' messes, smoke-wreathed battle line and darkling campsite. If I deplore its many faults, I love it for its sheer, dogged, awkward, bloody-minded endurance, the quality that inspired its exasperated adversary Marshal Soult to complain after Albuera: 'There is no beating these British soldiers. They were completely beaten and the day was mine, but they did not know it and would not run.'

A word about methodology. The architecture of this book is my own, though there is no doubting the fact that I learnt how to ply my ruler and dividers a quarter of a century ago in the Sandhurst drawing office of Messrs Duffy and Keegan. Sir John Fortescue's venerable multi-volume *History of the British Army* (superseded in many areas but still surprisingly useful in others) helped form a solid foundation. For the book's framework I am fortunate in being able to rely on scholars who have provided me with the academic equivalent of RSJs, those broad, load-bearing studies, which no professional historian can do much work without. These are works by authors like Alan Guy and John Houlding for the army of the eighteenth century, Michael Glover, Ian Fletcher and Philip Haythornthwaite for Wellington's army, and Hew Strachan, Edward Spiers and Donald Huffer for the army of the early nineteenth century.

Individual studies provide the equivalent of ducting and plumbing. Brian Robson has made the swords of the period his own, and Howard Blackmore and Christopher Roads have its small arms at their disposal. The Marquess of Anglesey has charted the fortunes of the British cavalry in his multi-volume history. Elizabeth Longford's biography of Wellington remains unsurpassed, though Christopher Hibbert's more recent personal history is an easier read. I cannot speak too highly of Mark Adkin's study of the Charge of the Light Brigade, and I am grateful that need to amass suitable building materials drew me to Frank McLynn's work on crime and punishment in Georgian England, for it was in a part of the yard not often visited by military historians.

Onto this robust structure I have bolted dozens of personal accounts, letting the men who wore the red coat speak for themselves whenever I can. I had encountered some, like John Kincaid and William Grattan, when an undergraduate, and rediscovering them many years on was like meeting a well-preserved old flame in a King's Parade coffee-shop, and discovering that age has not wearied nor the years condemned. Others were unfamiliar. It is thanks to the Army Records Society that Thomas Browne and John Peebles feature so prominently in these pages, and to Spellmount Publishers that William Tomkinson's Peninsula journal, to name but one of their invaluable books, has escaped from the antiquarian booksellers to which rarity had previously confined it. I have had some pieces of unaccountable good luck: discovering the manuscript Order Book of General Sir William Howe, commander in chief in North America, in the library at the Joint Services Command and Staff College at Watchfield was perhaps the most striking.

So many of the memoirs of the period were written by non-commissioned personnel that I am confident in my denial of the charge that this sort of book is simply epaulette history, giving the officer's view. Robert Waterfield, Thomas Morris and John Cooper of the line infantry, Benjamin Harris and Edward Costello of the Rifles, and John Pearman of the light dragoons are amongst those who remind us what it was like to be 'an atom of an army', as one of their most articulate comrades, Thomas Pococke, actor turned reluctant private soldier of the 71st Regiment, was to put it. And of course there is the incredible John Shipp, twice commissioned from the ranks – once for spectacular bravery in the field. I have tried to provide references for all substantive quotations, and list memoirs and collected letters by the name of their writer rather than their editor: the bibliography, really a working list of books actually used, makes this clear.

My approach is thematic rather than chronological. By and large I start with big issues and move on to smaller ones, first examining the army's size and composition, the character of the society that produced it, and the part it played in the nation's defence policy. Thereafter I review the army's administration and overall structure, its officers and men, and tactics of the combat arms and the effects produced by their weapons. The last two chapters consider the soldier's daily life in peace and war respectively. Such an approach shuns easy categorisation. It is impossible, for example, to separate pay in peacetime from prize money in wartime. Any attempt to place the contribution made by women in a separate chapter might have the benefit of political correctness but would miss the point that they formed an inseparable part of the army, whether getting the Duke of York into trouble with Parliament, consoling the amorous Ensign Lord Alvanley, rising to become inspector general of the medical department while disguised as a man, or simply supporting their own men in rain and shine, and under shot and shell, from Aldershot to Amballa and the Curragh to the Crimea. So you will find them, the Colonel's Lady and Judy O'Grady alike, where you least expect them.

I have not written for what are unkindly termed 'military buffs': indeed, those who go in for the martial equivalent of train spotting will complain that I have paid scandalously little attention to the raising, disbandment, re-raising and renumbering of infantry regiments in the eighteenth century, and so I have. My comments on uniform are very broad: this is not the place to discover which regiments were fortunate enough to wear bastion-ended lace on their tunics. And as to the minutiae of 'off-reckonings' and 'net-reckonings' in regimental accounting, well, if they perplexed the great Sir John Fortescue, they can scarcely do less for me.

The general reader might appreciate some simple definitions, although the British army is not a creature that thrives on simplicity. Officers, 'commission-officers' to the seventeenth century and commissioned officers to later generations, held rank and authority from a commission signed by the monarch. The field marshal, a comparatively rare bird, was their most senior. There were three grades of general officers, general, lieutenant general and major general. Major generals are, confusingly, junior to lieutenant generals, partly because their rank was once 'sergeant major general' and partly because the lieutenant general (as implied by the word lieutenant wherever it appears) stood in for his master when required. Brigadier generals and brigadiers – terminology changed over the period – held a temporary rank from which they might be advanced or not, as the case might be, and were analogous to commodores in the Royal Navy, who were captains temporarily holding a senior appointment.

There were two sorts of colonels. What we may call colonels proper held a substantive rank from which seniority would eventually, provided they lived long enough, elevate them to join the generals. Colonels of regiments, in contrast, were usually not colonels at all but general officers acting as regimental proprietors, dispensing patronage, making a profit, and warning the young, over a glass of port, that standards were slipping. Field officers comprised lieutenant colonels and majors, while company officers were captains, lieutenants and cornets (for the cavalry), ensigns (for most of the infantry), and second lieutenants (for the artillery, engineers and a few infantry regiments). Quartermasters were regimental officers responsible for supplies and quartering, and adjutants (the term was an appointment, not a rank, and its holder would be termed correctly, 'lieutenant and adjutant' or 'captain and adjutant') assisted the regiment's commanding officer in drill, administration – and in the case of Colonel John Wilkes MP of the Middlesex Militia, duelling.

Non-commissioned officers began with sergeant majors, grave and reverend gentlemen of whom there was one per infantry battalion, although the cavalry had one regimental sergeant major and a troop sergeant major for each of its troops. Staff sergeants were senior sergeants on the staff of regimental headquarters rather than one of its subordinate companies, and colour sergeants, a rank introduced into the infantry in 1813, ranked senior to other sergeants and had a very imposing arm badge to prove it. Sergeants were a cut above junior non-commissioned officers, corporals in most arms and bombardiers in the Royal Artillery. The appointment of a chosen man, a private soldier selected by his commanding officer to deputise for a corporal, eventually became that of lance corporal. And as to captain-lieutenants, sub-brigadiers and file-majors: well, I will explain about these worthies when they feature in my story.

The regiment, usually commanded in the field by a lieutenant colonel, was the basic building block in the infantry and the cavalry. As time went on infantry regiments tended to have more than one battalion, and in the British army these battalions, lieutenant colonels' commands, usually fought independently from the other battalions of their regiment. In these pages I follow the convention of showing 1st Battalion 33rd Regiment as 1/33rd, while 1st Battalion 1st Foot Guards is 1/1st Foot Guards. I use 33rd Foot and 33rd Regiment, as contemporaries did, almost interchangeably: do not be concerned, for they are the same creature. The company, a captain's command, was the main sub-unit of the infantry, and the troop was its cavalry equivalent. Cavalry troops were often paired to make squadrons. Infantry battalions and cavalry regiments were formed into brigades, and brigades into divisions, though the precise nature of this combination varied from time to time.

Pay, bounties, prize money and loot played an important part in the motivation of officers and men alike. I am constantly exasperated by authors who give no idea what money was worth in practical and comparative terms. To be told that if an item cost 100 units in 1680 then it cost 123 units in 1750 is unhelpful, and to suggest that a pound then was worth x times more than now is rarely a safe comparator across a broad range of income and expenditure. I far prefer what some have termed the 'Mars Bar Comparator,' which looks at the prices of staple items over the period to provide a practical idea of what money was really worth. There were twelve pence (d) to a shilling (s) and twenty shillings to a pound. A guinea was worth one pound and one shilling. And an Irish shilling, exasperating to those paid in it, was worth a penny less than an English one.

But before we consider what Ensign Alvanley paid for his claret and Rifleman Harris for his bread and cheese, there are a number of important caveats. First, the idea of subsistence wages for agricultural workers may be a misjudgement, as such folk often raised their own pigs and chickens, cultivated cottage gardens, and benefited from a trickle-down income in kind as master's old coat became ploughman Jethro's best, and mistress's worn-out petticoat found a new (and possibly more exciting) incarnation as chambermaid Eliza's drawers. Second, modern ideas of inflation have little relevance to the period in question, where inflation did not rise steadily, but went up and down, sometimes quite sharply: it rose by 36 per cent in 1800 and fell back by 22 per cent in 1802. Prices were generally quite stable except at times of particular hardship, and a pint of decent porter (a more sustaining brew than watery small beer) cost around 2d for most of the period. Finally, there were wide regional variations in pay, and in the prices of goods not easily available locally. The Midlands and the North were the 'Silicon Valley' of the age, where there was good money to be made always provided one was not, like the handloom weavers who formed such an important element of the Wellingtonian army, sidelined by new technology.[1]

For most of our period an infantry soldier was paid a shilling a day, out of which an assortment of stoppages were deducted which might leave him with very much less. He would receive two (later three) meals a day, one of them usually including plenty of beef, bread and small beer. In 1750 a London labourer received 2s a day and a craftsman 3s. A day labourer in Gloucestershire drew 1s 4d but the same man picked up only 9d a day in the North Riding of Yorkshire. A mason or joiner earned 2s a day. In 1760 the weekly poor relief paid to a pauper by the parish was just 1s 6d. In contrast, the aristocrats of labour were respectably paid in 1790, with a chair-carver receiving £4 a week, a London compositor 24s, a London saddler 15s, a Newcastle Collier 13s 6d, a worker in the Worcester potteries 8s 7d, a Lancashire weaver 8s 7d and a woman textile worker 4s 3d.

By 1800 an agricultural worker received 10s a week, rising to 12s in 1812: in 1815 a skilled Lancashire weaver collected £2 4s 6d. In 1817 our farm labourer was receiving only 7s 6d a week, though by 1850 this had risen to 11s. A man robust enough to take work as a heavy clay digger at this time, however, brought home 2s 6d a day, which, at 15s for a six-day week, was good money for a labouring man. In 1820 a village schoolmistress earned £20 a year.

In 1760 a large tot (probably a quarter pint) of cheap gin cost 1d and beer was 2d a pint: if one was drinking simply for effect, as so many were, then liquor was not simply quicker but cheaper. A dozen bottles of claret cost £1. A bread and cheese supper cost 3d, a dinner of cold meat, bread, cheese and beer 7d, and a slap-up meal in a chophouse, with a steak smoking enticingly at its centrepiece was 1s. A cheap room cost 2s a week to rent, a smart town house on Grosvenor Square was £300 a year, and a prosperous merchant in Colchester might house and feed his wife, four children and servants for £350 a year. 6s 6d bought a sturdy gown for a servant girl, and £8 a year, all found, hired her for a year. A clerk's suit cost £4 10s and a gentleman's £8 8s.

In 1762 James Boswell, whose father gave him an allowance of £25 every six weeks, stayed in Queen Street, Westminster – 'an obscure street but pretty lodgings' – for £22 a year. He paid the Jermyn Street sword-cutler Mr Jeffreys five guineas for a handsome silver-hilted small-sword; a 'low brimstone' girl demanded 6d to permit him to 'dip my machine in the Canal', and his surgeon charged him five guineas to cure the resultant gonorrhoea. Lord Alvanley, who had similar weaknesses but more money with which to indulge them, gave five guineas for one night with the blonde and well-upholstered Mrs Dubois in 1808. I hope that she was worth what a working man could only have regarded as absurdly conspicuous expenditure.

A quartern loaf (weighing 4lb 5oz) cost 6d or 8d in 1790 but 15d or 16d in 1801, though it had dropped to 9d in 1830 and was 1s in 1850. In 1796 model cottages cost £58 in wood or £66 in brick. It cost about 30s to £2 a year to rent a cottage in 1790 and £5 to £10 a year in 1824. In 1815 a coat cost £1 7s 1d in Chelsea and shoes were 7s a pair. A lady's good serge suit was £1 in 1850. In 1859, a clean unskilled labourer in London, taking home 18s a week, would spend 4s of it on bread, 1s 2d on beer, 3s 6d on meat and potatoes, 1s 6d on butter and cheese, 6d on wood and candles, 1s on coal, 2s 6d on clothes and shoes, 2s on rent and 10d on soap and sundries. In 1813 the standard infantry musket cost around £2, and it is high time that we turned our attention to these artefacts of walnut, brass and steel and to the men who used them.

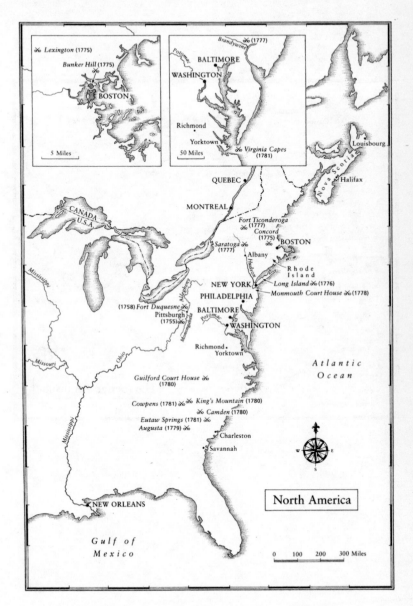

Lexington (1775)

Bunker Hill (1775)

BOSTON

5 Miles

Brandywine (1777)

BALTIMORE

WASHINGTON

Potomac

Richmond

Yorktown

Virginia Capes (1781)

50 Miles

Louisbourg

QUEBEC

Nova Scotia

Halifax

MONTREAL

Fort Ticonderoga (1777)

CANADA

U.S.A.

Concord (1775)

Saratoga (1777)

BOSTON

Mississippi

Albany

Hudson

Rhode Island

NEW YORK

Long Island (1776)

PHILADELPHIA

Monmouth Court House (1778)

(1758) Fort Duquesne

Pittsburgh (1755)

Allegheny

BALTIMORE

Potomac

WASHINGTON

Monongahela

Ohio

Richmond

Yorktown

Atlantic Ocean

Missouri

Guilford Court House (1780)

Cowpens (1781)

King's Mountain (1780)

Camden (1780)

Eutaw Springs (1781)

Augusta (1779)

Charleston

Savannah

W E

N S

NEW ORLEANS

North America

Gulf of Mexico

0   100   200   300 Miles

The Iberian Peninsula

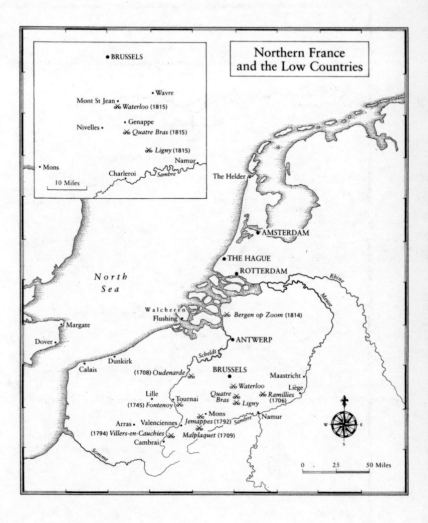

Northern France and the Low Countries

BRUSSELS

Wavre
Mont St Jean •
⚔ Waterloo (1815)

Nivelles •
• Genappe
⚔ Quatre Bras (1815)

⚔ Ligny (1815)
Namur •

• Mons
Charleroi   Sambre

The Helder

10 Miles

North Sea

AMSTERDAM

THE HAGUE
ROTTERDAM

Rhine

Meuse

Walcheren
Flushing •
⚔ Bergen op Zoom (1814)

• Margate

Dover •

ANTWERP

Scheldt

Dunkirk
Calais •   (1708) Oudenarde ⚔   BRUSSELS   Maastricht •

Lille   ⚔ Waterloo   Liège •
Tournai ⚔   Quatre ⚔   ⚔ Ramillies
(1745) Fontenoy ⚔   Bras ⚔ Ligny   (1706)

Arras •   Valenciennes   ⚔ Mons   Sambre Namur •
Jemappes (1792) ⚔
(1794) Villers-en-Cauchies ⚔   ⚔ Malplaquet (1709)
Cambrai •

Somme

0   25   50 Miles

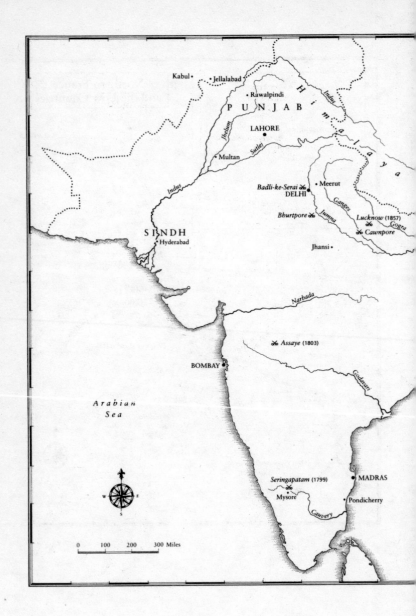

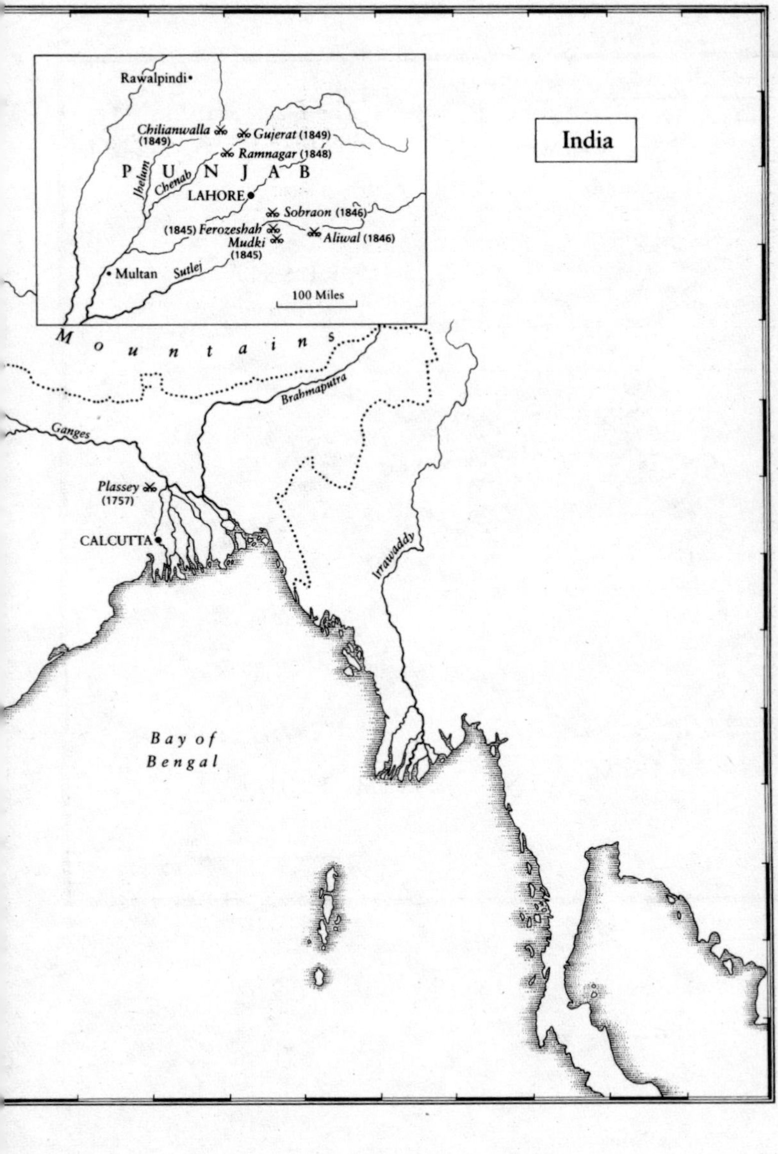

India
Rawalpindi
Chilianwalla (1849)
Gujerat (1849)
Ramnagar (1848)
PUNJAB
Jhelum
Chenab
LAHORE
Sobraon (1846)
(1845) Ferozeshah
Aliwal (1846)
Mudki (1845)
Multan
Sutlej
100 Miles
Mountains
Brahmaputra
Ganges
Plassey (1757)
CALCUTTA
Irrawaddy
Bay of Bengal

The Black Sea and the Crimea

CRIMEA

Eupatoria

Alma (1854)

Alma

Kacha

Belbek

Sevastopol

Inkerman (1854)

Chernaya

Balaclava (1854)

40 Miles

RUSSIA

Odessa

Sea of Azov

CRIMEA

Kerch

Sevastopol

Danube

Black Sea

Varna

Sinope (1853)

CONSTANTINOPLE

Scutari

OTTOMAN EMPIRE

0   100   200   300 Miles

I

THE AGE
OF BROWN BESS

THAT ARTICLE THERE

H E HAS NOT SHAVED this morning. And from the look of things he shaved neither yesterday nor the day before. Ginger stubble sprouts from a sun-tanned face, with red-rimmed blue eyes and a mouth whose teeth stand anyhow, like a line of newly raised militia. Bushy sideburns, ending in a forward sweep just below the ear, emerge from a battered black shako fronted with an oval brass plate and topped with a white over red pom-pom which has seen better days, and many of them. His red coat, waist-length in front, with short skirts at the back, is closed by ten pewter buttons, grouped in twos, with a broad oblong of white worsted lace framing the button holes. Its high collar and deep cuffs are yellow, and trimmed with more white lace. The effect is not improved by the fact that collar and coat-front alike are flecked with small burns made by gun-powder. Around his neck is knotted a piece of material which is now unquestionably black, though it might be that it started out much lighter. Grey trousers, knees and seat patched with cloth which has an uncanny resemblance to that worn by Franciscan friars, hang loose, without benefit of gaiter, over square-toed black boots.

His name is Ezekiel Hobden, Hobden to officers, NCOs and most private soldiers but Zeke to a favoured few. On his attestation form he signified his intention 'to serve His Majesty until I be legally discharged' with a bold cross, alongside which a Justice of the Peace and another witness (who has helpfully included Esquire as part of his signature to make the point) have appended their names. He used to be a plough-boy from the gentle downlands above Alresford in Hampshire, but a row with his master and an evening's drinking saw him take the King's shilling in Winchester. Now his old calling is like some half-remembered dream, although when he sees Portuguese peasants ploughing their red soil he still recalls the plodding team in front and the rich dark earth rolling from the coulter behind. Had he ever heard of Shakespeare he would agree that 'things without remedy should be without regard', but today it will be enough for him to be alive come sunset.

He stands 5ft 6ins tall – taller than many of his comrades – and now he himself is a beast of burden. Broad buff-leather cross belts meet on his chest, with an oval plate at their intersection; thinner buff straps run down from his shoulders and across his chest, and a brown leather strap lies across his right shoulder with the thick canvas belt of a haversack alongside it. We can see, even from the front, the edges of his black canvas pack, and the grey greatcoat strapped on top of it stands well above his shoulders. A black cartridge box hangs at his right hip, and bayonet-scabbard and round wooden water bottle at his left.

His hands have the same worn-leather hue and texture as his face, and their short finger-nails are black-edged. They bear a dozen new cuts and old scars, and his right thumb is thickened with a mighty callous. His left hand hangs loosely by his side, while his right – thumb and forefinger apart – rests lightly on the bright steel barrel of his upright musket. Its 39-inch barrel is tipped with a bayonet, sixteen inches of triangular steel, its point level with his shako-plate.

There is an animal tang about him which even that fine natural deodorant, the pervasive wood-smoke, cannot conceal. In part, it stems from the fact that he has worn the same jacket for six months and it smells powerfully of old sweat laced with the bad-egg stink of black powder, the muddy odour of the pipe-clay which whitens his belts, and the sharper nip of the brick-dust which, dampened by water, brings the metalwork of his musket and the brass of his accoutrements to a shine. It must be said, though, that not much polishing has gone on of late. He has only worn his heavy linen shirt for a week, and so may hope to get another week or more from it yet, but our nose tells us that it is already past its best, and is not much helped by the fact that, long tails tucked in between his legs, it doubles as underwear. Even when clean it was not entirely sweet: the soap used to wash it was made from mutton-fat, and the gentlest scent of roast lamb mingles with the other smells. He cleaned his teeth this morning, using the well-chewed end of a green twig as a brush, but these efforts cannot conceal the facts that there were onions in his supper and rum after it.

To left and right, in a line 250 yards long, stand similar figures. And similar is the word, for they are by no means uniform: there is infinite variety in the injury sustained by shakos and the nature and quality of the patches on clothes. One man has lost his shako altogether, and wears an incongruous round black hat. He does not look his best, and not simply because of this sartorial defect: we may confidently assume that the missing item will not redound to his advantage. The men stand shoulder to shoulder, elbows touching, in two ranks a pace apart, in ten distinct company groups. Each company has about fifty private soldiers and corporals, with three officers, two sergeants and a drummer or two. Some of these worthies stand alongside their companies, while others, the file-closers, lurk behind the second rank. There is some movement amongst the captains, who command the companies: three of them have left their stations on their companies' right and are pacing about in front. One has had a word with the soldier in the round hat, and is stalking down the ranks intent on further mischief.

The officers carry slim, straight gilt-hilted swords and show their status by crimson silk sashes, knotted over their left hips, and their rank by fringed epaulettes. Some have pistols tucked into their sashes or slung in open-topped leather holsters. The sergeants have simpler swords and also wear sashes, but theirs bear a broad central stripe of the same hue as collar and cuffs. They carry half-pikes, whose broad blades tip nine-foot ash hafts.

There is clearly something different about the two companies on each flank. In both cases their sergeants carry muskets and their officers curved sabres. The soldiers wear lace-embellished wings on their shoulders and the officers a more elaborate version in gold

5

braid. The right flank company sports white shako pom-poms, for these are the battalion's grenadiers, and the white commemorates the smoke of the grenades their forefathers threw. They are noticeably bigger men than their comrades in the other companies, and have an unmistakable air to them. At the other end of the line the pom-poms are green: this is the light company, containing the battalion's best shots. Although its soldiers may lack the swagger of the grenadiers, there are several keen-eyed countrymen amongst them, and we may just see – as, indeed, one of the file-closing sergeants already has – that a hare's paw is protruding from one man's haversack. There has already been murder this morning, and there will be more before nightfall.

Behind the file-closers stand the drummers, grouped behind their companies, yellow tunics faced with red and laced with much white worsted. In the centre rear are two mounted officers, a major, the battalion's second-in command, on the right and the adjutant, the commander's personal staff officer, on the left. Further back stand a dozen pioneers, equipped with shovel and axe. The 'band of music' stands to the rear, but today the musicians have laid aside their instruments and are ready to act as stretcher-bearers, although their stretchers are simply sewn blankets looped between two stout poles. The battalion's surgeon and his assistant, in dour anticipation of business to come, have unpacked their instruments from their mule and have blankets and water to hand.

In the centre the battalion's colours jut sharply above the line. Both are of embroidered silk. One, the king's colour, is the Union flag, and the other, the regimental colour, is the now-familiar yellow with the national flag in the upper corner where it joins the staff. The regiment's number, wreathed in laurel, is in the colour's centre. The pike is tipped by a spear point, now ornamental, from which hangs a long double tassel. Although at present the colours rest with their butts on the ground, the two young officers who bear them have broad shoulder-belts, with a strategically situated metal-lined pouch to support them when they are carried.

And young is indeed the word. The ensign bearing the Regimental colour cannot be more than sixteen, and seems in the grip of some powerful emotion. He is as white as a sheet, and though he is standing stiff and straight he is swallowing more than a boy ought. His comrade with the king's colour is altogether more cheery. He is a big lad, and has already outgrown his tunic: lanky wrists and grubby shirt-cuffs protrude from its sleeves, and it is tight across his chest. His beefy face wears an unconcerned grin, and he seems to have enjoyed a whispered joke with the non-commissioned officer to his rear. Behind each officer stands a pike-armed sergeant: the one behind the regimental colour has inched forward till he is nearly touching its ensign, and is whispering, between clenched teeth: 'Steady sir, steady: waiting is the hardest part, and 'twill all be well when the ball opens.'

The officer who we might suppose has something to do with opening the ball is the lieutenant colonel commanding the battalion. He is a surprisingly young man – no more than thirty – on a little chestnut mare, standing on the gentle crest about a hundred yards in front of his men. He looks intently into the valley on its far side and occasionally glances to his left where, 400 yards away, his brigade commander, responsible for another three battalions all tucked in behind the same slope, sits astride his horse with two other mounted officers.

Although Hobden and his five hundred comrades cannot see what is happening on the other side of the hill, they can certainly hear it. For half an hour now the distant popping of musketry has swollen to an almost continuous roar, interspersed with the thump of cannon. There is a good deal of shouting, the occasional anguished yell, and, more particularly of late, the clear notes of a bugle. Some minutes ago a cannon ball skidded over the crest, its force almost spent, sending up a shower of gravel as it bounded its way to a halt away to the battalion's left. Wounded men, in red, dark green and Portuguese grey homespun, have been drifting back over the ridge for some time. Some are going well, limping along with sticks or walking briskly with a bound-up arm, but there are already some chilling sights: one man comes past slowly, wordlessly clutching his belly, and another has lost part of his face to a vicious sword-cut. The noise intensifies, and separate drumbeats soon coalesce into a steady sound. One of the officers present, unversed in musical minutiae of flams and paradiddles, will later describe it as: 'the rum dum,

7

the rum dum, the rum dum dummadum dum dum.' It becomes louder and louder. Old soldiers exchange knowing glances, and some risk a sergeant's ire by muttering 'look sharp, for here comes here comes old trousers,' their nickname for the *pas de charge*, the call beaten by the drummers accompanying French infantry going forward at the quickstep. There are soldiers on the crest-line now, riflemen in dark green, moving in pairs, one kneeling to fire into the valley while his comrade scurries back. The British skirmishers, who have borne the brunt of the fighting so far, have been driven in.

The brigade commander doffs his cocked hat, and waves it unmistakably. The colonel turns his horse, walks it easily back to his battalion, and halts in front of the front rank. 'Thirty-Seventh,' he shouts, and officers and men respond by bracing up, swords and muskets tight in between body and right arm. 'Battalion will shoulder ... Arms!' On the last word muskets are tossed across the body so that their brass butt-plates now rest in the left hand, and the ensigns raise their colours, dropping their staffs into the pouches on their colour-belts. 'By the centre ... March.' And they step off, as one man, with the left foot, boots swinging low over the earth in 30-inch steps at 75 paces to the minute. The drums tap out the step as the line moves forward, men looking in to the centre to get their dressing from the colours, file closers chivvying here and there to ensure that the rear rank stays well closed up.

As the battalion crosses the crest it is greeted by a vision of hell. Clouds of thick smoke, the product of a battle between opposing skirmishers which the enemy seems to have won, cannot conceal the fact that the valley is full of blue-clad French troops, now coming on, up the slope, in thick columns. And they are coming on in the bravest style, their drummers hammering out the *pas de charge*, officers shouting encouragement, and men whooping *'Vive L'Empereur'*. One little spark is actually marching backwards, his shako raised on his sword-point, yelling that the Emperor will reward those who fight bravely. The nearest French column is three full battalions strong, stacked company behind company on a two-company front, fifty yards wide and almost twice as deep. The *voltigeurs* – equivalent of the 37th's light company – have been skirmishing ahead of the column and some now begin to peck away at the British line from close range: with the clatter of a tinker's pack one front-rank redcoat drops his musket, briefly kneels over it and then falls flat. The French grenadiers are leading their regiment, just as their British equivalents would be if the roles were reversed. They are big, stern men with red ornaments to their shakos, a forest of facial hair and the glitter of military dandysim: gold ear-rings, and silver ornaments on their clubbed hair. At least one British soldier is frankly shocked: 'Their hats, set round with feathers, their beards long and black, gave them a fierce look. Their stature was superior to ours; most of us were young. We looked like boys; they looked like savages.'[1] The French are used to winning, and indeed think that they have all but won today. They have brushed aside some British riflemen and Portuguese *caçadores*, and there seems to be very few of the enemy to their front.

Raising his voice against the din, the colonel gives a long drawn-out preparatory command of 'Thirty-Seventh' and follows it three paces later, with 'Halt'. The drums cease on the instant, lending emphasis to the order, and the battalion stands steady, looking down, across open ground speckled with scrub oak and cork trees, at the head of the oncoming column only 300 yards away. The colonel rides round the right flank of his battalion, and takes station just behind the colours. It is not until the French have come another hundred yards, though now, very evidently, a little more slowly than before, as the moral effect of the line's steadiness makes itself felt, that he shouts 'Front rank: Make ready'. The drummers beat the short roll of the 'preparative'; captains step back behind the second rank; the front rank's muskets come up, still perpendicular, but now with the left hand to the walnut fore-end and the right just below the lock, with those callused thumbs resting on the flint-gripping jaws of the musket's cock. The soldiers of the second rank step half a pace forward and to their right, in a movement called 'locking on,' so that, when their turn comes to fire, they will have space to do so.

The column is now less than a hundred yards away. Many features of its members can be clearly seen now. Its colonel has the cross of the Legion of Honour, and is having trouble with his horse, but keeps it going straight with short reins and sharp kicks. His officers and NCOs are desperately urging their men to close up: '*Serrez les rangs, serrez!*' For they know what is coming: it is too late – and too close to that line – to meet fire with fire, and so if they are to succeed the sheer momentum of their mass must not be lost. They are only fifty yards away, close enough now to see now that their enemy's commander has a thin face and a sharp nose, when the command 'Present . . . Fire' rings out. The British front rank fires a volley of shattering precision. Its muskets were carefully loaded in safety behind the crest: their flints and priming alike are fresh. Without delay the colonel orders: 'Front rank: load and prime. Rear rank: Make ready . . . Present . . . Fire.'

In just over thirty seconds each rank has fired two volleys, a total of two thousand musket balls at a range so close that even the unreliable Brown Bess musket is hitting a mass target about once in every ten shots. The head of the column falls like corn before the reaper. Its colonel, an attractive target – not least to the man in the round hat, who has his own views on officers, British or foreign – has half a dozen fatal wounds within seconds. As men in the front ranks fall, their comrades further back are exposed to the winnowing blast of musketry. Men trip over the dead and dying. Some, deaf to the shouts of their own officers and NCOs, who know that if they are to win it will be by shock, not fire, stop to fire back, and others strive frantically to position themselves behind those in front.

A few brave souls get as far as the British line. One thrusts hard, musket flung out to the full stretch of his right arm, with all his weight behind it. His bayonet grazes the side of a front-rank man and jams deep in his pack. Before the Frenchman can recover it, the rear-rank man shoots him in the chest from such close range that his coat smoulders. Although the volleys are still quite regular and accurate, there are signs that this will not last; some men fire at threatening close-range targets as they present themselves, and others fire on the word of command; but, almost dazed by the noise and concussion, they seem to have little regard for where their shots are going.

The colonel's voice and another drum-roll interrupt the firing. 'Now, Thirty-Seventh, I am about to give the word to charge. Three cheers for the king.' There are three harsh, barking cheers: on the word 'Charge . . . bayonets' the muskets come down to hip level, held across the body. Then the men are off down the slope, bounding over the dead and dying. There is a brief flurry of bayonet fighting where line meets the wreckage of the column, but most Frenchmen do not stay to meet the steel. A good number, huddling in a nervous clump, surrender. Most surrenders are accepted with good nature, but one man deliberately bayonets a Frenchman who offers no resistance but, stunned by the horror around him, is slow to drop his musket. The rest are away, running, free of musket and pack, and so much faster than their pursuers.

The colours move quickly down the slope, the pale ensign now wild with excitement, his sergeant, pike thrust out in front of them, again urging steadiness, but this time with a different cause. The action has had its tragedies, even for the victors. The king's colour is now borne by a sergeant and back up the slope, in a thin tide-line of redcoated bodies, its fat-faced ensign lies flat on his back with a blue hole in his forehead and the back blown off his head. There will be a Gloucestershire vicarage for which Christmas will not be the same this year. The surgeon and his mate are busy bandaging and probing. Of the eighteen British wounded five, with bullet-wounds to the abdomen, are probably beyond hope. Three must have smashed limbs amputated, and are more likely to die than survive. The remaining ten have a variety of injuries – one unlucky fellow has had his jaw broken by the French colonel's horse, kicking out in its death-throes as he rifled its saddlebags – but will live to fight another day.

At the foot of the slope the line rallies on the colours and the companies re-form. Private Hobden, face and uniform smutty with powder-smoke, and mouth black with gunpowder from biting open his cartridges, pockets a gold watch and crucifix eased from a Frenchman's pocket. He has also found a buckwheat pancake in someone's discarded shako, and chews it quietly as he picks up his dressing, touching elbows to left and right, and squinting up to see the colours catching the first rays of sun to break through the smoke.[2]

Seven years later, in April 1815, a few weeks before the battle of Waterloo, the Duke of Wellington was walking in a Brussels park with the radical diarist Thomas Creevey. Creevey asked the Duke how he thought the coming battle would go.

'By God! I think Blücher and myself can do the thing.'

'Do you calculate upon any desertion in Bonaparte's army?'

'Not a man, from the colonel to the private . . . We may pick up a marshal or two, perhaps, but not worth a damn.'

'Do you reckon upon any support from the French king's troops at Alost?'

'Oh! Don't mention such fellows! No: I think Blücher and I can do the business.'

Just then a lone British infantryman appeared, walking about the park and gawping at the statues: Hobden, perhaps even Sergeant Hobden, although rather less scruffy then when we last met him.

'There,' said the Duke, pointing at the red-coated figure. 'It all depends on that article there whether we do the business or not. Give me enough of it, and I am sure.'[3]

This book is about 'that article there', the redcoated soldier of the British regular army, like Ezekiel Hobden of the 37th Regiment. And it is about Hobden's father and son as well, for my period opens with the start of the Seven Years' War in 1756 and ends with the Indian Mutiny just over a century later. During it the British infantryman wore a red coat in battle and carried the muzzle-loading flintlock musket known (though the first printed reference to the name is not found till 1785) as Brown Bess. This weapon had several variants. Most encountered today were mass-produced during the Napoleonic Wars, and are the India pattern, introduced into the British service in 1794 by large-scale cession from the East India Company when arms manufacturers, domestic and foreign, were unable to keep pace with the demands of war against Revolutionary France.[4] The first Brown Besses appeared in the late 1730s, and the last were carried – although they were by then long obsolete – by some combatants in the Crimean War of 1854–56 and even the Indian Mutiny of 1857–58.

SCARLET AND BLUE

THE FRAMEWORK INTO WHICH Hobden's army fitted was clear by 1760. It was to change little until the eve of the First World War, and its influence has persisted well into our own times. The army's two main functions were twisted closely together like the strands of a rope. It had a continental role, which it exercised alongside allies and against opponents with both of whom, but for the colour of their coats, it often had much in common. With the continental commitment came a regard for formalism in drill and dress, and an emphasis on the scientific aspects of war like fortification, siegecraft and artillery. In its continental role the British army fought as part of a coalition: two of its greatest generals, Marlborough and Wellington, commanded more non-British than British troops in their biggest battles. But although the British sometimes tugged with a greater weight on the allied chain of command than their numerical contribution seemed to justify, there was no escaping the fact that theirs was a tiny army by the standards of continental war. In the late eighteenth century 'His Sardinian Majesty could boast an army equal in size to that of King George I.'[5]

Into this was wound a colonial thread, in which practicality ranked higher than precedent, dress and discipline tended to be looser, and there were more raids and ambushes than pitched battles. Even when there was no colonial campaigning, the outposts of empire needed garrisoning. In the early eighteenth century several regiments served abroad for twenty-five unbroken years, and the unlucky 38th Regiment spent 1716 to 1765 on the Leeward Islands in the Caribbean. A system of unit rotation was instituted in 1749, and although the demands of war interfered with its measured operation, it was at least a start. Yet it was not to prevent the 67th Regiment from spending 1805–26 in India and then setting off in 1832 for Gibraltar, the West Indies and Canada, where it remained till 1841. Some foreign postings were more lethal than any battle: the 38th Regiment lost 1,068 men, most of them to disease, in seven years in the West Indies, and during the 1740s even regiments in the relatively benign Gibraltar lost seventeen per cent of their strength each year.

The continental and colonial functions were never wholly distinct, any more than they were in the 1960s, when a unit serving in the British Army of the Rhine might find itself sent half a world away to fight an insurgent enemy in paddy-field or rubber plantation. Nor were the techniques and organisations of European and colonial campaigning always separate, as two brief examples show. First, the main impetus for raising light troops was colonial, but such soldiers had a useful part to play in Europe. Second, the export of European military techniques meant that both India and North America witnessed sieges and battles as formal as anything the British army encountered on the continent. Lastly, domestic tasks wove a third skein into the rope. The army had a crucial role in the preservation of public order, all the more so in the absence of an effective police force. It was also repeatedly involved in 'coast duty', assisting Revenue officers in their war on smuggling.

Britain's military policy was determined as much by the physical location of the British Isles as by the wishes of their rulers. As Admiral Earl St Vincent told the House of Lords: 'I do not say the French cannot come: I only say they cannot come by sea.' The dual need to defend Britain from invasion and protect her overseas trade had encouraged the development of a navy which, by 1689, was the equal of the Dutch and the French, and during the eighteenth century the Royal Navy confirmed a predominance it was not to lose till the twentieth. It was able to do so primarily because Britain, with no land frontier with a potentially hostile foreign power, was able to devote the lion's share of her defence expenditure to the fleet. There were no fortress-lines to build, improve and maintain, and no need to sustain a large army in time of peace. The strategist Basil Liddell Hart was later to identify 'a distinctively British practice of war, based on experience and proved by three centuries of success.'[6] Naval dominance 'had two arms, one financial, which embraced the subsidising and military provisioning of allies; the other military, which embraced sea-borne expeditions against the enemy's vulnerable extremities.'[7] Scholars have rightly pointed out that this is strategic theory rather than military history, and that Britain has not always had continental allies to fund, or the liberty simply to engage the enemy's peripheries. Yet if it does rough justice to history, it underscores the great truth that 'all British armies have relied on sea power, even when deployed on the European continent in the main theatre of war.'[8]

This is a major reason for the British ambivalence about soldiers so well summed up by Rudyard Kipling in 'Tommy'. It was often difficult to persuade the electorate that there was any real need for them. Sailors were another matter, for trade depended on secure sea-lanes, and sailors were, for so much of the time, out of sight and out of mind. Not so soldiers, who were an ever-present feature of Georgian and Victorian society. There were times when a sense of real and present danger swung the opinion of the public squarely behind its army. It is sometimes the apparently superficial that makes the point. During the American War, Georgiana, Duchess of Devonshire, threw herself with enthusiasm into helping her husband with the militia of Derbyshire, where he was lord lieutenant. She then raised a female auxiliary corps, and the *Morning Post* reported: 'Her Grace the Duchess of Devonshire appears every day at the head of the beauteous Amazons on Coxheath, who are all dressed *en militaire;* in the regimentals that distinguish the several regiments in which their Lords etc., serve, and charms every beholder with their beauty and affability.'[9] In 1795, with fears of French invasion rife, some fashionable Scots ladies turned out *à l'Amazone* in red coats with military cuffs and epaulettes, and Highland bonnets. English ladies took to velvet dresses of 'rifle-green' and the women of Neath petitioned the prime minister to be allowed to form their own home-defence regiment.

> There are in this town about two hundred women who have been used to hard labour all the days of their lives, such as working in coalpits, on the high road, tilling the ground, etc. If you would grant us arms, that is *light pikes* ... we do assure you that we could in a short time learn our exercise ... I assure you we are not trifling with you, but serious in our proposal.[10]

The Prime Minister himself, Lord Addington, even appeared in Parliament in his militia uniform. Quasi-military dress again became popular during Napoleon's hundred days in 1815, and one of Thackeray's characters, dressed as a pseudo-officer to accompany the formidable Becky Sharpe to Brussels, hastily civilianises himself when he thinks the French have won. But all too often public opinion agreed with the mother of the future Field Marshal Sir William Robertson, who joined the army as a private soldier in 1877. She told her son that she would rather bury him than see him in a red coat.

The Royal Navy's strength made large-scale invasion of Britain all but impossible – although, as we shall see shortly, it could not prevent the occasional French descent on Ireland. It enabled Britain to mount frequent amphibious operations. The first part of Thomas More Molyneux's *Conjunct Operations*, published in 1759, reviewed 68 overseas operations since the days of Sir Walter Raleigh, seven of them great expeditions involving more than 4,000 men. Just over half had failed, and Molyneux devoted the second part of his book to telling his readers how such operations might be managed better in the future. He maintained that Britain's geographical position, large navy and small army gave her a natural proclivity for operations like this, but also argued, as a veteran of Sir John Mordaunt's ill-starred raid on Rochefort in 1757, that amphibious success demanded both specialised troops and equipment.

Amphibious operations were a feature of the age. Some were triumphant, like Wolfe's attack on Quebec in 1759. James Wolfe had blockaded the Marquis de Montcalm in Quebec, but could see

This contemporary map shows James Wolfe's attack on Quebec in 1759, a classic amphibious operation. The British established a base on the Ile d'Orléans, opposite Quebec's strong defences. But a cove west of the city, below the Plains of Abraham, was poorly defended and, on 13 September, Wolfe led a small force which landed there and scrambled up the cliffs. The French counter-attack was decisively defeated and Quebec fell on 17 September 1759.

no way of achieving a decisive result before winter set in. He summoned his brigadiers to ask for their views, and they resolved on an amphibious attack on the Anse du Foulon, west of the city, where a narrow track led up to the Plains of Abraham. On the night of 12–13 September Captain McDonald, a French-speaking Scots officer, bluffed the French sentry on the track, and by dawn Wolfe's ten battalions were drawn up on the plain. Montcalm's men came on in three columns, and were met by an opening volley at a mere 40 yards, one of the most destructive in military history, which stopped them in their tracks. The British fired one more volley and charged, unaware that their youthful commander – he was only 32 – was dying. Montcalm, too, was mortally wounded, and Quebec surrendered on 18 September.

But some other amphibious operations were disastrous. In August 1809 a fleet of 235 armed vessels, 58 of them men-of-war, under Admiral Sir Richard Strachan, escorted 44,000 troops under Major General Lord Chatham to the low-lying malarial Dutch island of Walcheren. The expedition had two aims: first, to capture Antwerp, described by Napoleon as 'a pistol pointed at the heart of England', and second, to provide a diversion by an offensive on the Danube by Britain's Austrian allies. Chatham's army, stuck fast on the island, lost 218 men in action, but 4,000 died of sickness and another 11,000 were ill when they were evacuated: many suffered from recurring fever for years. Ensign William Thornton Keep of the 77th Regiment told his father that Flushing, the island's capital, was 'a most diabolical place'. On 11 September 1809 he reported that 'the increase of sick is beyond all precedent': his regiment alone had 22 officers ill.

> We hear of a change of the Ministry. It is to be expected after so disastrous a result of things . . . had the Ministers been informed of the unhealthiness of this place, different measures would doubtless have been adopted. It seems extraordinary that they were not, as it is proverbially the place of transport for the Military Delinquents of France, and they sent us here at the very time of year in which the fever prevails.

Keep became so ill that he had to resign from the army, though he recovered sufficiently to rejoin, becoming an ensign in the 28th Regiment in 1811.

Without sea power the American War of Independence simply could not have been fought at all, and at its close the Royal Navy's strong grip weakened. It is a measure of the army's understanding of the fundamental importance of seapower that Captain John Peebles of the 42nd Regiment, although only a junior regimental officer, clearly recognised how things stood on 6 October 1781.

> The Fleet are busy making the necessary repairs, and completing their water and provisions, and are expected to be ready about the 12th inst., when the Troops will embark upon board the Ships of War agreeable to a distribution

given out for that purpose, in order to make a Spirited
exertion for the relief of Lord Cornwallis and on which
probably depends the fate of America and the superiority
of the Sea.[11]

His men boarded HMS *London* from their transports with the easy
familiarity that came from having done the same thing half a dozen
times before and with an unswerving Georgian regard for seniority:
'the troops went on board by seniority of Companies, and were
disposed on the middle and lower decks, six to a mess between the
guns.'[12] But on the 24th they took on board a Negro pilot who had
escaped from Yorktown on the 18th. He reported that there had been
an armistice that day, for Cornwallis had asked for terms. Peebles was
to be proved right. Although the war rumbled on, the loss of Yorktown marked the end of major operations, and the Royal Navy's loss
of superiority off the Chesapeake that autumn was just as conclusive
as Peebles had predicted.

Seapower underpinned the Peninsular War in the middle of the
period and the Crimean at its end. In India it was decisive in enabling
the British to seize the coastal bases upon which their future success
was to depend: it was no accident that the three Presidencies comprising British India were governed from the ports of Calcutta, Madras
and Bombay. Well might George Thomas write in 1756 that: 'A fine
harbour ... in the hands of Europeans might defy the force of
Asia.'[13]

Finally, the Royal Navy made its own distinctive contribution to war
on land. Early in the Indian Mutiny, Lieutenant Arthur Moffat Lang
of the Bengal Engineers welcomed the arrival of:

> 100 sailors of the *Shannon* with four 24-pounders. It was
> grand to see Jack Tars again, with their loose large-collared
> blue shirts, loose blue trousers, straw hats with white
> covers, black ribbons and 'Shannon' on the bands; they
> carry musket and bayonet. They seem strangely out of
> place. Rolling about up here, using their sea-language,
> cursing the niggers, driving bullock *gharis* and swearing
> because 'she tacks about and backs and fills so.'[14]

In the same conflict Lieutenant William Alexander-Gordon of the 93rd Highlanders saw one of these 24-pounders breaching the walls of the Secunderbagh at Lucknow 'with a fine fellow of a negro AB [able seaman] ... doing the duty of two or three of the regulation number of gunners.' The gun was manhandled forward under heavy fire, bullets hitting it 'with a noise like that which a crowd of school boys might make throwing stones at an empty saucepan.'[15] The soldiers who painted the globe the colour of their coats did so under the navy's protecting wing.

TO FLANDERS,
PORTUGAL AND SPAIN

URING THE AGE OF BROWN BESS the British army took part in five major wars: the Seven Years' War (1756–63), the American War of Independence (1775–83), the French Revolutionary Wars (1792–1802), the Napoleonic Wars (1803–1815) and the Crimean War (1853–56). It fought the Seven Years' War as an ally of Frederick the Great of Prussia. Operations against the French and their Indian allies in North America began in 1754, absorbed much of Britain's military effort and helped initiate far-reaching tactical change. French possessions in Canada were snapped up, with Wolfe's capture of Quebec in 1759 as the brightest star in a year of victories still remembered in the naval march 'Heart of Oak,' first heard in David Garrick's play *Harlequin's Invasion*

> Come cheer up my boys
> 'tis to glory we steer
> to add something more to this wonderful year . . .

In India, too, there were successes, with Robert Clive's defeat of the pro-French ruler of Bengal at Plassey in 1757 and Lieutenant General Sir Eyre Coote's victory at Wandeswash in 1759 bringing much of India under the control of the British East India Company. On the continent of Europe, where the British always fought as part of a coalition force, their fortunes were more mixed. The Duke of Cumberland, George II's son, was badly beaten at Hastenbeck in 1757, but a British force played a notable part in the victory at Minden in the *annus mirabilis* of 1759.

It is worth pausing to consider just what these battles were like for the men who fought in them. At Minden, Prince Ferdinand of Brunswick with 41,000 Anglo-German soldiers faced Marshal Contades with 51,000 Frenchmen. What made the battle unusual was that it was decided by an attack on a vastly superior force of French cavalry by six British regiments, launched as the result of a linguistic misunderstanding. Hospital Assistant William Fellowes of the 37th Foot wrote that:

> The soldiers and others, this morning, who were not employed at the moment, began to strip off and wash their shirts, and I as eagerly as the rest. But while we were in this state, suddenly the drums began to beat to arms: and so insistent was the summons that without more ado we slip't on the wet linen and buttoned the jackets over the soaking shirts, hurrying to form line lest our comrades should depart without us. There was a keen wind blowing at the time, and with my wet shirt and soaking coat, it was an hour or more before I could find any warmth in me. But the French warmed us up in good time; tho' not, you may be sure, as much as we warmed them![16]

Lieutenant Montgomery of the 12th Foot described the advance, with the redcoats stepping out to the rub-a-dub-dub-dub of the drums, and through:

> a most furious fire from a most infernal Battery of 18 18-pounders ... It might be imagined that this cannonade would render the Regt incapable of bearing the shock of unhurt troops drawn up long before on ground of their own choosing, but firmness and resolution will surmount any difficulty. When we got within about 100 yards of the enemy, a large body of French cavalry galloped boldly down upon us; these our Men by reserving their fire immediately ruined ... These visitants being thus dismissed ... down came upon us like lightning the glory of

France in the Persons of the Gens d'Armes. These were almost immediately dispersed ... We now discovered a large body of Infantry ... moving directly on our flank in Column ... We engaged this Corps for about 10 minutes, kill'd them a good many, and as the Song says, the rest then ran away.

The next who made their appearance were some Regt's of the Grenadiers of France, and as fine and terrible looking fellows as I ever saw. They stood us a tug notwithstanding we beat them to a distance ... we advanced, they took the hint and run away.[17]

Montgomery added a postscript. The noise of battle frightened the regimental sutler's pregnant wife into premature labour: 'She was brought to bed of A Son, and we have christened him by the name of Ferdinand.'

The Seven Years' War was ended by the Treaty of Paris, a triumph for Britain, who gained territory at French expense. But France was soon to have her revenge. A constitutional dispute, focusing on the right to tax, led to war between Britain and her North American colonies in 1775. Although the British won a costly victory that year at Bunker Hill, just outside Boston, and, indeed, won the majority of the war's pitched battles, they were unable to inflict a decisive defeat on George Washington's Continental army, and their strength was eroded by repeated small actions in a landscape that was often decidedly hostile. France, heartened by the surrender of an army under Lieutenant General John Burgoyne at Saratoga in October 1777, joined the war. In 1781 Lieutenant General Lord Cornwallis, commanding British forces in the southern states, was besieged at Yorktown by Washington and his French allies. Admiral de Grasse's fleet prevented the Royal Navy from intervening, and in October Cornwallis surrendered in what was the greatest British military humiliation until the fall of Singapore in 1942. The Peace of Versailles ended the conflict, depriving Britain of many of the gains achieved in the Seven Years' War.

France's victory was dearly bought, for her finances collapsed under the strain of the war. Her government's attempt at reform led to the summoning of the Estates General in 1789 and began the slide into revolution. War broke out between revolutionary France and old monarchical Europe in 1792, and Britain was drawn in the following year. The French Revolutionary Wars saw Britain's Prime Minister, William Pitt, assemble two successive anti-French coalitions, but with little success. Overall the war's pattern was clear enough. There was little to check the French on land, and they overran the Low Countries, scarcely inconvenienced by the intervention in 1793–95 of a British force under the Duke of York, although a French expedition to Egypt ended in failure. At sea, however, the Royal Navy was supreme, and by 1801 the war had run its course, with neither side able to do serious damage to the other, and peace was ratified at Amiens in 1802.

It did not endure for long, and war broke out again the following year. Napoleon Bonaparte, an artillery officer who had risen to eminence by a mixture of stunning military success and deft political opportunism, had become ruler of France, and in May 1804 he assumed the imperial title, gaining popular approval for a new constitution by a plebiscite. By 1812 he had defeated all the major continental powers save Britain, imposing the 'Continental System' designed to prevent British commerce with Europe. But that year he over-reached himself by invading Russia. His former enemies, sensing that the tide had turned, took the field against him, and in 1814 was beaten and forced to abdicate. The following year he staged the dramatic revival of the Hundred Days, but was decisively defeated by the British and Prussians at Waterloo, and abdicated once more, this time for good.

During the Napoleonic Wars Britain's principal theatre of operations was the Iberian Peninsula where a British force, from 1809 under the command of General Sir Arthur Wellesley, later created Duke of Wellington, operated from its base in Portugal against French armies which always outnumbered the British but were constrained by a broader conflict against a hostile population. The British army fought a dozen major battles and endured several painful sieges. The battle of Albuera, on 16 May 1811, came about when a British, Spanish and Portuguese army under Lieutenant General Sir William Beresford blocked Marshal Nicolas Soult's attempt to disrupt his siege of the French-held fortress of Badajoz.

It was one of the hardest infantry contests of the entire period. Soult fixed Beresford's attention by feinting at the village of Albuera, in the Allied centre. He then unleashed a massive attack against Beresford's right flank, where a Spanish division swung round to face the threat and fought gallantly, buying valuable time. A British infantry brigade under Lieutenant Colonel John Colborne – one of the stars of the age, who was to become a field marshal and a peer – moved up to support the Spaniards. It was locked in a firefight with enemy infantry when French hussars and Polish lancers fell on its open flank, at the very moment that a sudden cloudburst drenched the mens' muskets so that they would not fire. Lieutenant George Crompton of the 66th Regiment told his mother of the catastrophe that ensued. It was:

> the first time (and God knows I hope the last) I saw the backs of English soldiers turned upon the French . . . Oh, what a day was that. The worst of the story I have not related. Our Colours were taken. I told you before that the 2 Ensigns were shot under them; 2 Sergeants shared the same fate. A Lieutenant seized a musket to defend them, and he was shot to the heart: what could be done against Cavalry?[18]

Two fresh British brigades then came into line, and Captain Moyle Sherer of the 34th Regiment relates how the powder smoke, so utterly characteristic of these battles, was snatched away for a moment to reveal:

> the French grenadier caps, their arms, and the whole aspect of their frowning masses. It was a momentary, but a grand sight: a heavy atmosphere of smoke again enveloped us, and few objects could be discerned at all, none distinctly . . . This murderous contest of musketry lasted long. We were the whole time progressively advancing and shaking the enemy. At a distance of about twenty yards from them, we received orders to charge; we had ceased firing, cheered, and had our bayonets in the charging position, when a body of the enemy's horse was discovered under the rising ground, ready to take advantage of our impetuosity. Already, however, the French infantry,

alarmed by our preparatory cheers, which always indicate
the charge, had broke and fled.[19]

Perhaps five hundred yards to Sherer's right was Ensign Benjamin
Hobhouse of the 57th Regiment, which was engaged in a prodigious
close-range firefight.

> At this time our poor fellows dropped around us in every
> direction. In the activity of the officers to keep the men
> firm, and to supply them with the ammunition of the
> fallen, you could scarcely avoid treading on the dying and
> the dead. But all was firm ... Tho' alone, our fire never
> slackened, nor were the men in the least disheartened ...
> Our Colonel, major, every captain and eleven subalterns
> fell; our King's Colours were cut in two, our regimental
> ones had 17 balls through them, many companies were
> without officers ...[20]

Lieutenant Colonel William Inglis, hit in the chest by grapeshot, lay
in front of the colours and encouraged his men by shouting 'Die
hard, 57th, die hard'. The 57th Regiment and its post-1881 successor
the Middlesex Regiment, were to be proudly known as Diehards.

Finally, the Fusilier brigade – two battalions of 7th Royal Fusiliers
and one of 23rd Royal Welch Fusiliers – arrived to clinch the victory.
In the ranks of 1/7th was Private John Spencer Cooper, an avid
student of military history who had enlisted in the Volunteers in
1803 at the age of fifteen and transferred to the regulars in 1806.
His book *Rough Notes of Seven Campaigns*, written up when Cooper
was 81, gives a soldier's view of the battle.

> Under the tremendous fire of the enemy our line staggers,
> men are knocked about like skittles, but not a step back-
> ward is taken. Here our Colonel and all the field-officers
> of the brigade fell killed or wounded, but no confusion
> ensued. The orders were 'close up'; 'close in'; 'fire away';
> 'forward'. This is done. We are close to the enemy's col-
> umns; they break and rush down the other side of the hill
> in the greatest moblike confusion.[21]

The word 'moblike' goes to the very heart of the matter. As the
French columns disintegrated, so Soult's army reverted to the shoal

of individuals in which all armies have their origin, and to which, but for the efforts of drillmasters, leaders, and steadfast comrades, they return all too easily. Soult told Napoleon that he had been robbed of victory. 'The British were completely beaten and the day was mine, but they did not know it and would not run.' Well might Sir William Napier, himself a Peninsular veteran, celebrate 'that astonishing infantry'.

Britain's command of the sea, re-emphasised at Trafalgar in 1805, enabled her to mount smaller expeditions. Sometimes these were successes, like the descent on Copenhagen in 1807, and sometimes failures, like the disastrous Buenos Aires expedition of 1806–7. The epoch had a tragic adjunct. An Anglo-American conflict – 'the War of 1812' – had begun promisingly for Britain with the repulse of an American attack on Canada and the temporary seizure of Washington, but ended in British defeat at New Orleans in January 1815, a battle fought before news of a negotiated peace reached North America.

It was not until 1854 that the British army faced its first major post-Napoleonic trial, and the final major war of our period, when an Anglo-French force, with its British contingent under General Lord Raglan, invaded the Crimea in an effort to take the Russian naval base of Sevastopol. The Allies won an early victory on the River Alma in September and beat off two Russian attacks on their siege lines at Balaclava and Inkerman. After a dreadful winter on freezing uplands, they took the outworks that dominated Sevastopol and forced the Russians to withdraw the following summer.

There was sporadic fighting in India throughout the period. In 1764 the British strengthened their grip on Bengal at the battle of Buxar, and in 1799 Tipoo Sultan, ruler of Mysore, was killed when the British stormed his capital Seringapatam. There were three wars against the fierce Mahrattas, whose confederacy sprawled across central India, and in the second (1803–5) they were beaten, with the

---

(overleaf) A British-Indian army on the march, *c.* 1830. Although the British travelled lighter than the armies of Mughal India, which had trailed comets' tails of camp followers behind them, they were usually far more encumbered with baggage than was the case in Europe.

Conveyance for the Wounded.

The Common Cart of the Country.

Spare Ammunition Boxes.

A Sporting Elephant, the Driver and

Foot Artillery.

Cart in which Native Females ride.

his assistant getting up.   The Bazaar Flag.   Washer-Men.

A Regiment of Sepoys.

future Duke of Wellington striking the decisive blow at Assaye (1803). The Pindaris, piratical freebooters who lived on the fringe of the Mahratta armies, were beaten in 1812–17, and a third Mahratta war in 1817–19 saw the British extend their power to the borders of the Punjab and Sind.

In 1838 the governor-general of India, Lord Auckland, decided to install a pro-British ruler, Shah Shujah, on the throne of Afghanistan to provide a bulwark against the threat of Russian expansion. The advance to Kabul went well, but in the winter of 1841–42 there was rising against Shah Shujah. The British and Indian force, weakly commanded, retired from Kabul towards Jellalabad, but was cut to pieces as it did so: only one man, Dr Bryden, managed to reach safety.

Better fortune attended the next expansionist step, and in 1843 the British annexed Sind. This brought them into conflict with the martial Sikhs, rulers of the Punjab. In the first Sikh War (1845–46) the British won hard-fought battles at Mudki, Ferozeshah, Aliwal and Sobraon. When hostilities broke out again in 1848 the British had the better of a scrambling battle at Chilianwallah and a decisive clash at Gujerat, and went on to annex the Punjab.

Brown Bess was now almost a thing of the past, superseded from 1842 by a musket ignited by a percussion cap, which was far more reliable than the flintlock, and from 1853 by a percussion rifle. Ironically it was the introduction of this rifle into the Indian army that helped produce the last conflict of the period. The rifle's paper cartridge was lubricated with grease, and rumours that this was the fat of pork (unclean to Muslims) or cattle (sacred to Hindus) induced some soldiers of the Bengal army to refuse the cartridges and precipitated the Indian Mutiny in March 1857. The mutineers took Delhi, and overwhelmed a British force at Cawnpore, where the survivors were massacred. Lucknow, capital of the princely state of Oudh, held out, and was eventually relieved after the British had taken Delhi by storm in September 1857.

The Mutiny was the last time that Brown Bess was carried in battle by British soldiers. Lieutenant Richard Barter, adjutant of the 75th Foot, – 'the Stirlingshire Regiment, good men and true as ever had the honour of serving their Queen and Country' – describes how a hundred men from his battalion were issued with the new rifle, 'all the rest of the regiment retaining old Brown Bess'. But the new weapon was not deemed a success, and 'the men, with few exceptions, contrived to get rid of their rifles and in their place picked up the old weapons of their dead comrades.'[22] Hobden would surely have approved.

Brown Bess had held sway for more than a century. But within a decade she was as obsolete as the longbow, superseded first by percussion weapons and finally by breech-loading rifles in a process of accelerating technical innovation. There were other major changes too: the purchase of commissions was abolished in 1871, and the regimental system was recast shortly afterwards to produce county regiments, with two regular battalions (the 37th joined the 67th (South Hampshire) Regiment to produce the Hampshire Regiment) linked to form a new regiment which would normally have one battalion at home and another abroad. The process was not popular, and traditionalists demanded the return of 'our numbers wreathed in glory.' In 1884 Colonel Arthur Poole angrily declared that he could not possibly attend a Hampshire regimental dinner. 'Damned names,' he wrote, 'mean nothing. Since time immemorial regiments have been numbered according to their precedence in the Line . . . I will not come to anything called a Hampshire Regimental dinner. My compliments, Sir, and be damned.'[23]

RED COAT
AND BROWN BESS

HODBEN AND HIS COMRADES plied their deadly trade with Brown Bess. This weapon, similar to her cousins such as the Prussian Potsdam musket, named after the great arsenal on the outskirts of Berlin, and the French 1777 pattern, named for the year of its introduction into service, painted the face of battle for more than a century. It was inherently inaccurate and its range was very short, inspiring tactics based on blocks of infantry which fired away at one another at close range in a contest where the rapidity of fire and the steadfastness of the firers were of prime importance. Loading and firing required the infantryman to carry out set actions in the proper sequence, driven home by repeated drilling till they became little less than a conditioned reflex. The efficient movement of large numbers of men, often across difficult country and sometimes under fire, demanded that the individual elements of the mighty whole responded promptly and identically to commands.

The length of paces had to be exact and their frequency precise. 'When men march in cadence,' declared a military writer in 1763, 'it gives them a bold and imposing air; and by the habit they acquire in regulating their pace, we may almost guess what time a body of men will take to traverse a certain length of ground.'[24] Troops usually moved in column, to promote control, and fought in line, to maximise firepower, though there were numerous practical variations. And, most notably from the pens of the French theorists the Chevalier Folard and Baron de Mesnil-Durand, there were assertions that the column was king because the sheer physical and psychological shock it delivered would always triumph over the squibbing musketry of the line.

Deploying from column of march to line of battle was a complex business, which required careful attention to maintaining the intervals between parallel columns so that when each column wheeled through ninety degrees an even, continuous line, without embarrassing gaps or confusing overlaps, was the result. At the 1785 Silesian manoeuvres a Prussian army of 23,000 men approached in column and, on a single cannon-shot, wheeled in seconds into a line two and a quarter miles long. Wheeling required the men on the inner flank to mark time (marching on the spot) while those on the outer flank stepped out briskly. An eighteenth century German writer tells how:

> Whether on horseback or on foot, a regular wheel is just about the most difficult of all movements to accomplish. When a wheel is well done, you have the impression that the alignment has been regulated with a ruler, that one flank is tied to a stake, and that the other is describing the arc of a circle. You can employ these images if you wish to convey to the soldiers a clear idea of what goes on in a wheel.[25]

If repetitious drill and rigid discipline were important in bringing the soldier into battle, they were crucial once fighting commenced. Bad weapon-handling constantly caused accidents. When front rank men knelt to fire and then sprang up to load they were often shot by careless rear-rank men: the Napoleonic Marshal Gouvion St-Cyr reckoned that one-quarter of French infantry casualties in his career were caused this way. Soldiers were terribly burned when cartridge-boxes blew up; eyes were poked out with bayonets as ungainly soldiers bungled drill movements, and ramrods were regularly fired off by men who had forgotten to remove them from the barrel of their musket, causing injuries and broken windows during practice, and difficulty in battle, where a spare ramrod might not be at hand.

Individual nervousness could easily swell to provoke a wider panic, opening a gap that a watchful enemy might exploit. This sort of thing was to the drillmaster what heresy was to the devout: something requiring urgent and extreme correction. A French writer recommended his readers: 'Do not hesitate to smash in the skull of any soldiers who grumble, or who give vent to cries like "We are cut off" . . .'[26] In 1759 Major General James Wolfe famously declared that he would rather have written Gray's 'Elegy in a Country Churchyard' than take Quebec, and he was indeed to be killed capturing it. But there was little echo of the Enlightenment in his regimental orders when he commanded the 20th Foot at Canterbury in 1755 and warned:

> A soldier who quits his rank, or offers to flag, is instantly to be put to death by the officer who commands that platoon, or the officer or sergeant in rear of that platoon; a soldier does not deserve to live who won't fight for his king and country.[27]

The weapon carried by the majority of combatants not only dictated the shape of combat: it helped determine the composition of armies and their conduct off the battlefield as well as on it. Most armies in the age of the flintlock were composed of rank and file drawn from society's lower orders and officered (though the generalisation is broad) by gentlemen. They emphasised uniformity and conformity, and tended to look upon initiative as a potentially dangerous aberration. Their discipline was rigid. In most European armies a mistake in drill would bring immediate corporal punishment: a Frenchman living in Berlin was shocked to see a fifteen year old *junker* thrash an old soldier for a trivial mistake. It was not only tender-hearted civilians who felt uncomfortable with scenes like this. John Gabriel Stedman, an officer in the Scots Brigade in Dutch service, wrote in 1772 that: 'I never remember to have brought a soldier to punishment, if it was not at all in my power to avoid it, while I have known a pitiful ensign, one Robert Munro, get a poor man flogged because he had passed him without taking off his hat.'[28]

Due process of military law (itself usually swift and partial) brought a wide range of other punishments from simple detention, through riding the wooden horse (sitting astride a sharp-backed

These traditional military punishments survived till the late eighteenth century. Victims were enclosed in the whirligig (top), which was spun to make them giddy. Offenders were compelled to ride the wooden horse (below) for set periods, sometimes with a musket or other heavy weight tied to each foot to increase the discomfort.

wooden frame, often with weights attached to the feet to increase the severity), running the gauntlet (the bare-backed offender proceeded between two ranks of soldiers who lashed him as he passed), straightforward flogging to the death sentence itself. Death might be administered by shooting, hanging or breaking on the wheel. In 1776 Stedman watched the latter penalty inflicted on a murderer:

> Tied on the cross, his hand was chopped off, and with a
> large iron crow [bar] all his bones were smashed to

> splinters, without he let his voice be heard ... All done,
> and the ropes slacked, he wreathed himself off the cross,
> when seeing the Magistrates and others, going off, he
> groaned three or four times, and complained in a clear
> voice that he was not yet dead ... He then begged the
> hangman to finish him off, in vain, and cursed him also
> ... He lived from six-thirty o'clock till about eleven, when
> his head was chopped off.[29]

This gruesome penalty was inflicted in the bright noon of the
Enlightenment, with Mozart at his keyboard, Josiah Wedgwood at
his pottery, and Voltaire plying his quill.

Many contemporaries found it easy to reconcile their own liberal
opinions with recognition that the battlefield imposed such severe
stresses that only drill and discipline enabled a man to tolerate them.
The fledgeling United States of America, for all its use of irregulars
and militias, could not have won the War of Independence without
its regular Continental Army, whose drill and discipline owed much
to the efforts of Friedrich Wilhelm von Steuben, an ex-captain in
the Prussian army. He was appointed inspector-general of the Continental Army in 1778, 'bringing to the ragged colonial citizen army
a discipline and effectiveness it had hitherto lacked.'[30] Continental
soldiers may indeed have been fighting for 'inalienable rights', but
they submitted to a discipline scarcely less severe than that suffered
by the men they fought.

What was new about the American Revolution was its recognition
that soldiers were emphatically citizens in uniform. In 1783 George
Washington wrote:

> It may be laid down as a primary position, and the basis
> of our system, that every Citizen who enjoys the protection
> of a free Government, owes not only a proportion of his
> property, but even of his personal service, to the defence
> of it ...[31]

This declaration of principle was a forerunner to another new republic's response to military crisis. The French National Convention,
facing converging attack by the armies of monarchical Europe,
passed the decree of *levée en masse* on 23 August 1793, announcing
grandiloquently that:

Young men will go to battle; married men will forge arms
and transport supplies; women will make tents, uniforms
and serve in the hospitals; children will pick rags; old men
will have themselves carried to the public squares, to help
inspire the courage of the warriors, and preach the hatred
of kings and the unity of the Republic.[32]

The concept of soldier-citizen was to be stamped on the French army
during the Revolution and, indeed, long beyond it. In August 1917
the trench newspaper *Le Crapouillot* warned officers that they often
mistook:

distance for dignity, brutality for firmness, and the propensity to punish for professional zeal. . . . Men are neither
inferior beings, nor simple fighting machines. Our soldiers
are not professional soldiers, but citizen-soldiers. You must
show men that you feel their unhappiness, sympathise with
them, and understand the greatness of their sacrifices.[33]

It was not simply that French soldiers were citizens under arms: they
were soldiers who fought best in a particular way. French theorists
consistently argued that there was something definitively Gallic about
the attack with cold steel. In 1866 one wrote in a military journal
that:

For all Frenchmen, battle is above all an individual action,
the presence of dash, agility and the offensive spirit, that
is to say, the attack with the bayonet; for the German, it
is the fusillade . . . individualism drowned in the mass,
passive courage and the defensive.[34]

French discipline was rarely as rigid as Steuben might have wished.
When Napoleon III met Franz Josef of Austria at Villafranca in north
Italy in 1859, a French officer noted that while the Austrian hussar
escort remained rock-steady, troopers of the *Guides*, crack light
cavalry escorting Napoleon, craned and jostled to get a good view
of the two emperors. They were Frenchmen, and that was just what
he expected.

Important though the concept of the citizen-soldier was, its practical effects were limited. Even the French soon drew back from
democratic notions like electing officers, and although the harsh

disciplinary code of the old regime (which had included beating with the flat of a sword, in an effort to produce a punishment that was painful yet not dishonourable) was jettisoned, its replacement was scarcely benign, and miscreants were consigned to the *boulet*, confinement with a roundshot attached to them by a chain. Napoleon's 'iron marshal', Louis Nicolas Davout, had looters shot, but even this could not restrain his men, and when the French briefly occupied Moscow in 1812 his own quarters were pillaged. However, Napoleonic discipline in general – tough little Davout was something of an exception – was regarded as more relaxed than British. Some French deserters in Spain served with the British (this trade worked both ways, though it was always fatal for a deserter to be captured by his former comrades) but soon re-deserted because they found their new discipline far too severe.[35]

Napoleonic officers sometimes struck their men like the drillmasters of an earlier generation, yet even here the assault might have a distinctively French edge. During the Champagne campaign of 1814, when the Prussians, Russians and Austrians were closing in on Napoleon east of Paris, Captain Charles Parquin of the *Chasseurs à Cheval* of the Guard hit a corporal across the back with the flat of his sabre when he found that he had dismounted against his express orders. The man spun round, pulled open his coat to show his Legion of Honour, grasped his sabre, and said: 'Captain, I have served my country and my Emperor for twenty-two years. I won this cross two years ago and now, in a matter of seconds, you have dishonoured me for ever!' Parquin – 'appalled at having lost my temper with an old soldier' – replied: 'Listen, corporal. If I were your equal in rank I should not hesitate to give you satisfaction, for I am not afraid of you. But I am your captain and I am apologising to you. Will you shake hands?' The corporal, declaring that there was no ill-feeling on his part, shook hands, and Parquin records that: 'Half an hour later he was sharing my modest supper which was, none the less, made all the more appetising by a bottle of brandy.'[36]

The concept of the citizen-soldier made few inroads into the British regular army, although it found more fertile ground when part-time Volunteer and Yeomanry units were raised during the French Revolutionary Wars. Some units balloted the whole corps to select officers, who were then duly commissioned by the lord-lieutenant of their county. It was a common practice for units 'to pool their government remuneration and distribute it evenly among all ranks . . .'[37]

The second major influence on the armies of the period was initially tactical, although, as it questioned many of the assumptions dear to apostles of brick-dust and pipe-clay, it became philosophical, political and organisational too. There were times, especially in forests, woods or on broken ground, when serried ranks and measured volleys were simply inappropriate. European armies discovered the need for light troops in Eastern Europe and the Balkans, and, providentially, discovered some of the men to meet the need in exactly the same place. Having discovered them, they then proceeded to dress them and drill them until they lost some of those qualities that had made them such admirable light troops in the first place.

Hussars, light cavalry introduced into the French army in 1692, were modelled on wild horsemen from the great plain of Hungary. However, the efforts of military tailors speedily made them heavier, first converting the fur-trimmed cap to the towering busby with the cap itself surviving only as the vestigial busby bag hanging down on one side. They then made the dolman (short jacket) and breeches skin-tight, and eventually converted the pelisse, initially an extra jacket handily slung from the shoulders, into a relic as vestigial as the busby bag but a good deal more inconvenient.

The Austrians exacted universal compulsory conscription on the Military Border of Croatia and Slavonia, raising, by the 1790s, seventeen regiments of *Grenzer* infantry. They were traditionally trained as light infantry – or, rather, untrained, for it was believed that much of their value sprang from their experience of hewing a living as free peasants in a tough border area. However, conventionally-minded senior officers increased the amount of formal training given to the *Grenzers*, effectively converting them into second-grade line infantry, leading Major General Joseph Klein to complain that men with less formal training had provided 'a much better light infantry than the present regulated and drilled *Grenzer*.'[38] It is no surprise that the first bout of Austrian military reforms in 1798–9 included withdrawing *Grenzer* regiments from the line and combining small sharpshooter and free corps units into fifteen light battalions. The second reform period continued the movement, but it was clear to promising young commanders that Austrian skirmishers were still too rigidly controlled to take on the French with confidence. Something precious had been drilled out of the army, and as late as 1813 the future Field-Marshal Radetzky admitted that 'fighting *en tirailleur* should be done only in very restricted fashion, because neither we nor the Russians have mastered the *manière de tirailleur*.'[39]

However, at the height of their powers, during the Seven Years' War (1756–63), the *Grenzer* had been formidable light infantry. Hussars and Croats formed a screen which Frederick the Great's intelligence agents found hard to penetrate; they snapped up isolated detachments and cruelly galled the Prussian line if it came within reach of the covered positions they favoured. At Kolin, in 1759, Croats lurking in a cornfield provoked an engagement which soon got out of hand and ended in what was intended as a flanking attack heading, disastrously, for the front of the Austrian line. In 1758 Frederick told General Philip Yorke that 'he was more upon his guard against them than against any other troops ... that it was impossible for them [the Prussians] to oppose anything equal to them in that kind, and that he did not like to be always sacrificing his regular infantry in that kind of war.'[40] Lacking native light infantry of his own, Frederick raised 'free battalions' from disparate regions of his empire, but it was not a happy experiment: one battalion murdered its commanding officer and deserted en masse, complete with its pay chest and a cannon.

The British army first discovered the need for light troops in the forests of North America. Hostilities between Britain and France had begun there in 1754 without formal declaration of war. This was partly because of friction between the thirteen British colonies and the smaller French colonial population, chiefly concentrated in the St Lawrence Valley between Quebec and Montreal. The French had built a string of forts to prevent British penetration, and Major General Edward Braddock made for one of them, Fort Duquesne (now Pittsburgh), at the forks of the Ohio where the Monongahela and Allegheny meet. He had 1,200 men, including regulars from the

44th and 48th Foot – both regiments brought up to full strength by drafting in men from other units and less than cohesive in consequence – and some American irregulars, the young George Washington, of the Virginia Militia, among them.

Near the Monongahela River, Braddock was ambushed by a smaller force of Frenchmen and Indians. The battle was not wholly one-sided, for the French commander was killed by the first volley: most of his men fled and the Indians were only kept in the battle by the courage of the French officers leading them. But after the first shock – and there were rarely times when encountering the rolling volleys of redcoats in line was not a shock – the Indians and remaining French steadied to their task, firing from cover, where they presented poor targets, and they concentrated on the enemy officers. Braddock lost 63 of his 86 officers killed or wounded – with 914 NCOs and men – and was himself hit in the arm and lung. He died four days later, after saying: 'We shall know better how to deal with them another time.'

Shortly after Braddock's defeat, the British raised a new, large regiment, the 60th Foot (Royal Americans), some of whose battalions were trained as marksmen. 'In order to qualify for the Service of the Woods,' ran a contemporary account, they were 'taught to load and fire, lying on the ground and kneeling ... to march in Order, slow and fast, in all sorts of Ground ... [to] pitch and fold their Tents, and be accustomed to pack up and carry their necessities in the most commodious manner.'[41] Each battalion of line infantry was given a light company, whose training emphasised skirmishing and marksmanship, in 1758. These light companies – 'light bobs' – were paired with the pre-existing grenadiers to form what were termed flank companies, with the grenadiers parading on the right of the battalion's line and the light company on its left.

This polarity was as much ideological as ceremonial, with the grenadiers – 'tow rows' – epitomising the wheel and pivot of the old world, and the light bobs the stalk and scurry of the new. In 1763 American Indian tribes in the Great Lakes region rose in a rebellion known from the name of the Ottawa chief who led it, as Pontiac's. Amongst the troops who opposed it were light companies, serving away from their parent battalions, who looked markedly different to

Braddock's redcoats. An officer described the sombre dress of British light infantry.

> The ground is black ratteen or frieze, lapelled and cuffed with blue; . . . a waistcoat with sleeves, a short jacket without sleeves; only arm holes and wings to the shoulders (in like manner to the grenadiers and drummers of the line) white metal buttons, linen or canvas drawers; . . . a pair of leggings of the same colour with their coat which reach up to the middle of their thighs . . . and, from the calf of the leg downwards, they button . . . [The light infantry man] has no lace, but, besides the usual pockets, he has two, not quite so high on his breast, made of leather, for balls and flints . . . His knapsack is carried very high between the shoulders, and is fastened with a strap or web over his shoulder, as the Indians carry their pack . . .[42]

However, the army tended to revert to formal type in peacetime, and light companies disappeared after the Seven Years' War, though they were later reinstated. It was not just that conventionally-minded officers argued that they were of little value on European battlefields, where the fortune of the day would be decided by the volleys of the line, but that whole ethos of light troops was inimical to formal discipline. During the American War of Independence when conditions again made light troops an indispensable component of the army, one British officer described them as:

> For the most part young and insolent puppies, whose worthlessness was apparently their recommendation for a service which placed them in the post of danger, in the way of becoming food for powder, their most appropriate destination next to that of the gallows.[43]

There was a palpable tension between the light infantry ethos, with its emphasis on practical uniform, individual skills and relaxed discipline, and the older notion of unthinking obedience.

By the time the Wars of the French Revolution broke out in 1792 British light companies had little, apart from their shoulder-wings, to mark them out from their comrades in battalion companies. William

Surtees, born in Northumberland in 1781, had always wanted to be a soldier, and in 1799 he joined the 56th Regiment. It was known as the Pompadours because its purple facings were allegedly Madame de Pompadour's favourite colour – or, as some smutty warriors alleged, the colour of her drawers. Surtees was almost immediately posted to the light company, and tells us that: 'I felt not a little proud of my advancement, as I considered it (as I believe the generality of soldiers consider it) an honour to be made a light-bob.' But he wore a red coat like his comrades of the battalion companies, and had little specialist training. His company was combined with ten others into a light battalion commanded by Lieutenant Colonel Sharpe of the 9th Foot and sent on the Helder expedition, dispatched to Holland in September 1799 as part of an Anglo-Russian force commanded by the Duke of York. It fought an inconclusive battle at Egmont op Zee, and, perilously short of supplies, was lucky to be able to negotiate a convention which allowed it to withdraw unmolested.

During the battle, Surtees discovered what it was like to fight real light infantry, *tirailleurs*, some armed with rifles which outranged the musket and all trained to take full advantage of the ground. The French skirmishers 'had greatly the advantage over us in point of shooting, their bullets doing much more execution than ours.' As he followed up the retreating enemy he saw remarkably few dead Frenchmen, and thought that most of the dead must have been carried off, 'but experience has since taught me that we must have done them little harm.'[44] Although he fired almost 150 rounds, he doubted if he actually hit anybody.

The Helder expedition rubbed home the point that light troops were scarcely less valuable in Europe than in North America. Colonel Coote Manningham and Lieutenant Colonel the Hon William Steward were amongst the reformers who demanded the establishment of light troops armed with rifles rather than muskets, dressed in something less conspicuous than the 'old red rag'. We shall see later how an Experimental Corps of Riflemen was raised in 1800, soon to be embodied as the 95th Regiment (later The Rifle Brigade). For the moment, though, it is worth observing that with the Baker rifles and green uniforms of the new riflemen came a new notion of discipline. The new unit's regulations emphasised that trust and

On 3 January 1809, during the retreat to Corunna, Tom Plunket of the 95ᵗʰ Rifles shot the French General Auguste Colbert. To do so, he lay on his back with the sling of his Baker rifle over his right foot, one of the positions taught for accurate shooting. When Colbert's orderly bravely charged to avenge his master, Plunket reloaded in time to shoot him too.

respect were, with discipline, the cement that bound riflemen together.

> Every inferior, whether officer or soldier shall receive the lawful commands of his superior with deference and respect, and shall execute them to the best of his power. Every superior in his turn, whether he be an Officer or Non-Commissioned Officer, shall give his orders in the language of moderation and of regard to the feelings of the men under his command; abuse, bad language or blows being positively forbid in the regiment ... It is the Colonel's particular wish that duty should be done from cheerfulness and inclination, and not from mere command and the necessity of obeying ...[45]

Influential though the linked concepts of the citizen-soldier and the light infantryman were, neither revolutionised the conduct of war. If the Duke of Marlborough, who fought his last great battle at Malplaquet in 1709, was wafted back from the Elysian Fields to watch the battle of Waterloo in 1815 (or even the Alma fifty years later), he would have found many superficial differences but little fundamental change. Shakos were now worn instead of tricorne hats, and long-skirted coats with big turned-back lapels had been replaced by something altogether trimmer. Regiments now had numbers, instead of being known by the name of their current colonel (though if the 37th was no longer Monro's Regiment, it still retained its familiar yellow facings); there were indeed more skirmishers about than he would have remembered, and some of them wore uniforms which might have struck him as disturbingly drab.

Weapons had certainly improved. Marlborough would have observed that reforms like those initiated in the French army by Jean Baptiste Vaquette de Gribeauval had standardised the calibres of artillery pieces and, through improved carriages and better harness, made it possible for them to move faster on the battlefield. The snappy movement of Captain Cavalié Mercer's Royal Horse Artillery would doubtless have merited his applause. Yet most of their projectiles were roundshot, a single solid cannon ball, or canister, a tin container filled with small balls that burst on leaving the muzzle to give the cannon the effect of a gigantic shotgun. Howitzers, still a minority amongst the artillery, fired explosive shells, though, like those in his own day, their effect was uncertain. Sometimes they exploded harmlessly in mid-air, and sometimes they lay on the ground, fuses sputtering, giving ample opportunity for those nearby to escape. Even 'spherical case' – in the British service eponymously named after Henry Shrapnel, its inventor – a shell designed to bust in the air and scatter balls and metal fragments below, was notoriously unreliable.

There had been organisational changes he might have admired. Chief amongst these was the development of the *corps d'armée* system by Napoleon. In 1809 Napoleon had reminded Eugène de Beauharnais of its advantages. 'Here is the general principle of war – a corps of 25,000–30,000 men can be left on its own,' he wrote. 'Well-handled, it can fight or alternatively avoid action, and manoeuvre according to circumstances without any harm coming to it, because an opponent cannot force it to accept an engagement but if it chooses to do so it can fight alone for a long time.'[46] Yet here, as in much else, Napoleon was more adapter than innovator, and his development of the corps harked back deep into the eighteenth century to the ideas of Marshal de Broglie, the Duc de

Choiseul and above all Jacques Antoine, Comte de Guibert. The latter, incidentally, favoured citizen-soldiers, but agreed that 'since we cannot have citizen troops, and perfect troops, [what we must do is] to have our troops at least disciplined and trained.'[47]

What would certainly have impressed Marlborough was the way in which armies, and the populations that supported them, had grown since his day. Nothing in his career could equal 'the Battle of the Nations' at Leipzig in October 1813, where the rival armies put over half a million men into the field. Yet this was exceptional. Just under 200,000 men had met at the bloody and indecisive Malplaquet in 1709, and there were actually rather less at the wholly conclusive Waterloo.

ENGLAND,
HOME AND BEAUTY?

IT WAS AN AGE OF TIPPLING. Captain John Peebles, commanding the grenadier company of the 42nd Regiment in North America, recalled a cheery dinner at which 31 officers drank 72 bottles of claret, eighteen of Madeira and twelve of port, not to mention a little porter and punch by way of skirmishing. He was a serious-minded professional soldier and certainly no drunkard, but his diary is speckled with entries like that for 29 March 1777: 'dined with our light captain and got foul with claret.'[48] Formal dinners as well as more casual gatherings were interspersed with toasts, at which those present drank the health of individuals, institutions or even sudden inspirations. The practice is remembered today in the Royal Navy's toasts, one for each day of the week. Some are patriotic or professional sentiments like 'Our Ships at Sea', or more personal tributes like 'Wives and Sweethearts' (to which cynics add *sotto voce* 'and may they never meet'.) Occasionally the communal drinking was accompanied by a song like 'The Owl', sung as a round, with each drinker taking a line.

> To-whit, to-whoo
> To whom drinks't thou?
> O knave, to thee
> This song is well sung, I make you a vow
> And here's a knave that drinkest now.

By Victorian times, when some of the loucher habits of the Georgian era had been restrained, toasts remained popular, and one of the most common was 'England, Home and Beauty'. It was drunk across the globe in garrisons and outposts summed up by Kipling's ex-Troop Sergeant Major O'Kelly as running:

> From Birr to Bareilly, from Leeds to Lahore,
> Hong-Kong and Peshawur,
> Lucknow and Etawah,
> And fifty-five more all endin' in 'pore'[49]

Attractive as it might be to men surrounded by Khyber rocks, South African kopjes or Chindwin teak, England, home and beauty was a most inaccurate description of the society which had spawned Hobden, his comrades, and many of their officers too.

The word England would not simply have been offensive to many of those round mess table or in barrack-room, but it would have been a poor definition of the army's origins. For, start to finish, it was a British army, its members drawn from England, Ireland, Scotland and Wales. And for most of the period it had a substantial foreign element, whose soldiers were induced to serve King George by financial gain, political opinion, religious belief or simply their ruler's whim.

All major armies recruited foreign troops. Indeed, the notion of nationality itself was still evolving, and in the mid-eighteenth century Voltaire wrote that 'the concept of a fatherland is variable and contradictory. Most of the inhabitants of a country like France do not know what it means.' In 1751 the Prussian army of 133,000 men had only 50,000 native subjects of the king of Prussia, and just 80,000 in an army of 190,000 in 1786. The French army had German, Swiss, Italian, Irish and Scots regiments, and during the eighteenth century 12 per cent of its peacetime and 20 per cent of its wartime strength was recruited abroad. Young men were usually encouraged into foreign service by the prospect of economic betterment, but religion and family tradition also helped establish firm links between, say, Roman Catholic Irish minor gentry families and the French or Austrian armies into which so many of their sons were commissioned. Sometimes, though, enlistment followed a run of bad luck – the penniless Abbé Bastiani signed on into a Prussian regiment and rose to become one of Frederick the Great's closest companions – and sometimes recruits were simply conned, like the young Swiss Ulrich Bräker who thought that he had gone to Berlin to become an officer's servant but finished up 'impressed into the notorious *donner und blitzen* regiment of Itzenplitz.'[50]

In addition to individual recruitment, where young men became officers or signed on as soldiers after making their own way abroad, it was not uncommon for the regiments of one state to be temporarily transferred to the service of another for a suitable fee. For the American War of Independence the British army contracted with the rulers of some German states for the services of their foreign contingents. The diarist Julius Friedrich Wasmus was a company surgeon in the Duke of Brunswick's Lieb-Regiment, which served with the British in North America. In November 1779 Captain Peebles saw two German regiments on parade, 'the Hessian Grenadiers, dressed up and powdered, [and] the Ansbachers the finest looking troops and tallest, I ever saw, and in high discipline.'[51]

There was widespread agreement that France was Britain's natural adversary. In 1759 Sir Thomas Cave of the Leicester Militia told the Marquis of Granby that 'the spirit of the people to oppose the natural enemy of this kingdom is so great, that I had a roll of 50 volunteers offered me, every one a man of considerable property.'[52] Sergeant Roger Lamb of the 23rd Foot, who served in the American War and left a remarkably literate account of his experiences, when writing in 1809 described the French as 'for many ages the professed and natural enemies of Britain.'[53] Indeed, some British politicians welcomed the French Revolution not simply because it represented the overthrow of despotism, but because it apparently did lasting damage to French military potential. William Windham, secretary at war in William Pitt's government of 1783–1801, was happy to see France in 'a situation which, more than at any other period, frees us from anxiety on her account.'[54] The courteous Lord Raglan, commander-in-chief in the Crimea, tended to refer to his Russian enemy as 'the French' because for the whole of his previous active service the French *were* the enemy.

However, until Prussia established herself as the dominant (and thus most-imitated) military nation in Europe during the Seven Years' War, French military fashion held sway. French military terminology was widely used (even in the nineteenth century engineers spoke knowingly of *demi-lunes* and *fausse-brayes*, *tablettes* and *orillons*), and France, with her frequent experience of continental war on a large scale, was the subject of widespread imitation in drill and doctrine.

And there were many Frenchmen in the British army, even when that army's prime function was fighting the French. The first wave arrived after the Revocation of the Edict of Nantes in 1685 forced many Protestants to flee the country, and another wave arrived after the Revolution. During the French Revolutionary Wars a large number of émigré units, composed of French royalists, served under British command. English law was changed in 1794 'to enable the subjects of France to enlist as soldiers' and receive commissions without suffering 'pain or penalty' for professing 'the Popish Religion'. Most of these units had disappeared by the Peace of Amiens in 1802, but some émigrés soldiered on after this, albeit largely in 'British' units. For example, many members of the York Rangers, raised in 1793 and consisting mainly of Germans with French-Irish émigré officers, were eventually incorporated into the 3rd Battalion 60th Foot, which had begun its existence by enlisting Germans for service in North America.

During the Napoleonic Wars foreign corps rose from forming 11 per cent of the army in 1804 to constituting more than 20 per cent by 1813. There was one remaining nominally French unit, the Chasseurs Britanniques, which served with Wellington in the Peninsular War. It generally behaved well in battle, but suffered such an appallingly high rate of desertion – 224 of its men absconded during 1813 – that it was not allowed to post its own pickets in case they seized the opportunity to decamp.[55] Corporal William Wheeler of the 51st Regiment served alongside it in Spain, and was unimpressed, as he told his father in a letter.

> Want of room in my last prevented me from informing
> you that 9 men of the Chasseurs Britanniques Regt. were
> shot for desertion. This Corps was originally formed of
> French loyalists, but the old hands are dropping off and
> they are replaced by volunteers from the French [prisoner

> of war] prisons. A great number of these men enter our service for no other purpose than to go over to their army as soon as an opportunity offers (and who can blame them). The consequence is the major part of the Corps cannot be trusted. I wish they were at the Devil or any where else, so that we were not plagued with them . . .[56]

Other foreign corps included the Calabrian Free Corps, the Ceylon Light Dragoons, the Piedmontese Legion and even the fustanella-clad Greek Light Infantry. In the great Swiss tradition of mercenary service, the Swiss regiments of Meuron, Roll and Watteville served throughout the war. The latter was roughly handled in the siege of Fort Eirie in 1814: on 15 August 83 of its men disappeared when a mine was exploded and another 24 were killed and 27 wounded. Two days later a vigorous American sortie captured another 128 officers and men.

The Brunswick-Oels Corps was known, from the colour of its uniforms, as the Black Brunswickers, or, from their skull and cross-bones badge, as the 'Death or Glory Men'. It was raised in 1809 by the Duke of Brunswick, whose father had been killed commanding the Prussian force at Jena-Auerstadt three years before. After a period in Austrian service it marched across Europe, and was evacuated by the Royal Navy and taken into British pay. It fought in the Peninsula (Wheeler complained that it was 'almost as bad' as the Chasseurs Britanniques) and during the Hundred Days Campaign of 1815, and the duke himself was killed at Quatre Bras.

The biggest and best of the many foreign corps was the King's German Legion. This had its origins in the Hanoverian army, which had fought alongside the British during the eighteenth century – not surprisingly, for since the accession of George I in 1714 kings of England were also rulers of Hanover. The French overran Hanover in 1803, and the Convention of Lauenberg disbanded the Hanoverian army but allowed its members to emigrate and to bear arms against the French once they had been properly exchanged with French prisoners of war. The British government did not accept this provision, and so, instead of incorporating Hanoverian units intact, as it might otherwise have done, it raised a unit known first as The King's Germans and then as The King's German Legion, abbreviated to KGL.

The Legion contained line and light infantry, hussars, dragoons and artillery. It grew rapidly in size, and peaked in June 1812 when over 14,000 officers and men were serving in it. Many of its officers and almost all its rank and file were German, although some British officers joined it, for a young man without money or interest could often gain a commission more easily in the KGL than in a British unit. It was reduced in size after the peace of 1814, as many non-Hanoverians were discharged in preparation for the return of the whole corps to Hanover, where it was to form the nucleus of the new Hanoverian army. However, Waterloo intervened, and the KGL fought there with distinction, with the defence of the farm complex of La Haye Sainte by Major George Baring's 2nd Light Battalion KGL adding fresh laurels to an already distinguished reputation. The KGL was disbanded after the Napoleonic Wars, though many of its officers and men went home to serve in the Hanoverian army while a few transferred to other British units.

The KGL was held in wide respect. On the battlefield its perform-ance was undoubtedly in the first rank. In 1812, at Garcia Hernan-dez, near Salamanca, KGL cavalry broke a French battalion in square, drawn up on ground well-suited to infantry, without the assistance of other arms, one of the few recorded examples of such an achieve-ment. Afterwards Sergeant Edward Costello of the 95th Rifles watched the Germans ride past with their prisoners and testified that their courage was matched by magnanimity.[57]

> I never before saw such severe-looking sabre cuts as many
> of them [the prisoners] had received; several with both
> eyes cut out, and numbers had lost both ears ... The
> escort consisted chiefly of the Germans that had taken
> them prisoners, and it was pleasing to behold these gallant
> fellows, in the true spirit of glory, paying the greatest atten-
> tion to the wants of the wounded.

Off the battlefield, KGL cavalry was renowned for its outpost work. The KGL dragoons developed a warm relationship with the Light Division – which they called the 'Lighty Division' – and it was axio-matic that, while a British dragoon might hurtle through camp with-out occasioning comment, if a German galloped up men stood to their arms and looked to their priming, because it was bound to be a serious matter.

Edmund Wheatley was commissioned into the 5th Line Battalion KGL in 1813, although he came from nowhere more Hanoverian than Hammersmith. He thought that:

> The Germans bear excessive fatigues wonderfully well, and a German will march over six leagues [18 miles] while an Englishman pants and perspires beneath the labour of twelve miles; but before the enemy a German moves on silently but mechanically, whilst an Englishman is all sarcasm, laughter and indifference.

He felt, however, that relations between officers and men were not as good as in the British army, partly because: 'The officers do not hesitate to accompany a reproof with a blow and I cannot imagine any man in so dejected a situation as to bear patiently corporal chastisement.'[58]

Yet there could be no doubting these officers' personal bravery. At Waterloo, Wheatley's commanding officer, Colonel Baron Ompteda, was given a suicidal order by the Prince of Orange. He told his second in command to 'try and save my two nephews', who were serving with him, and led his battalion in a gallant but impossible charge against French infantry in the garden of La Haye Sainte, the farm complex in Wellington's centre. His action was so brave that French officers struck up their men's muskets with their swords to prevent them from shooting him. But he jumped his horse over the garden hedge and laid about him: 'I clearly saw his sword strike the shakoes off,' remembered Captain Charles Berger. Wheatley was knocked out in the hand-to-hand fighting: 'I looked up and found myself, bareheaded in a clay ditch with a violent headache. Close by me lay Colonel Ompteda on his back, his head stretched back with his mouth open, and a hole in his throat.'[59]

KGL cavalry were skilled horsemasters. In the Peninsular War Lieutenant George Gleig of the 85th Regiment watched a party of cavalry ride past:

> consisting of the 12th and 16th Light Dragoons, and two regiments of heavy Germans; nor could we help remarking

that though the 12th and 16th Dragoons are both of them distinguished corps, the horses of the foreigners were, nevertheless, in far better order than those of our countrymen. The fact, I believe, is that an Englishman . . . never acquires that attachment for his horse which a German trooper experiences. The latter dreams not, under any circumstances, of attending to his own comfort till after he has provided for the comfort of his steed. He will frequently sleep beside it through choice, and the noble animal seldom fails to return the affection of his master, whose voice he knows, and whom he will generally follow like a dog.[60]

Captain Cavalié Mercer of the Royal Horse Artillery agreed, writing of the Waterloo campaign that:

Affection for, and care of, his horse, is the trait, *par excellence*, which distinguishes the German dragoon from the English. The former would sell everything to feed his horse; the latter would sell his horse itself for spirits, or the means of obtaining them.[61]

It was entirely typical of the period that during the fighting in Spain the KGL sometimes found itself fighting Germans serving in units of Napoleon's ally, the Confederation of the Rhine. On one occasion a member of the KGL was shocked to discover 'mine own broder' among the enemy dead. And as Napoleon's star fell, some German princelings ordered their men to change sides: in December 1813 Colonel August von Kruse, acting on secret instructions from his sovereign, took his 2nd Nassau Infantry Regiment into the British lines and announced his change of allegiance.[62]

But for all the foreign corps, good, bad and indifferent, the redcoated heart of the army was British. At the time of the American War of Independence, 60 per cent of its rank and file were English, 24 per cent Scottish and 16 per cent Irish. Officers were more evenly distributed, with 42 per cent English, 27 per cent Scottish and 31 per cent Irish.[63] In this context the description English subsumes Welsh as well, and from the early eighteenth century the 23rd Regiment proudly styled itself Royal Welsh Fusiliers (the spelling was letter changed to the distinctive Welch). However, in March 1807 only 146 of its 991 NCOs and men actually hailed from Wales. This did not prevent the regiment from celebrating St David's Day in style, and having a regimental goat traditionally ridden into the officers' mess at the climax of the St David's Day dinner by the smallest of the drummers. Thomas Henry Browne, commissioned into the 23rd in 1805, fought in the Peninsula first as a regimental officer and then on the staff, and died a general in 1855. On 1 March 1808 he celebrated St David's Day at sea on his way to Canada 'in the best manner our situation would permit'. He observed that normally each officer was required to eat a leek:

> The older Officers in the regiment, and those who have seen service with it in the field, are favoured only with a small one, and salt. Those who have before celebrated a St David's day with the regiment, but have only seen garrison duty with it, are required to eat a larger one, without salt, and those unfortunates, who for the first time, have sat in Mess, on this their Saint's day, have presented to them the largest leek that can be procured, and unless sickness prevents it, no respite is given, until the last tip of its green leaf is enclosed in the unwilling mouth; and day after day passes before the smell and taste is fairly got rid of . . . We could not of course, on board our little ship, render all the honours due to the day, but we had every thing dressed in Onions, and drank an extra glass of grog on the occasion.[64]

As far as the Royal Artillery was concerned, over the period 1741–1815 it was only during 1776–79 that a bare majority of artillery recruits came from England. Both before and after this more came from Ireland: 42 per cent in 1795–1810, for instance, at a time when another 21 per cent was Scottish.[65] The high percentage of Irish recruits is surprising when one considers that between 1763 and 1801 there was a separate corps in existence, the Royal Irish Artillery, in which Englishmen were not allowed to enlist. The worsening economic situation in Ireland increased the proportion of Irish recruits towards the end of our period: in 1830 42.2 per cent of the army was Irish and 13.6 per cent Scots. This meant that not only were the fifteen infantry regiments which actually bore

Irish affiliations composed largely of Irishmen, but several 'English' regiments also had many Irish in their ranks. In 1809 34 per cent of the NCOs and men in the 57th (East Middlesex) regiment were Irish, and in the 29th (Worcestershire) the proportion rose from 19 per cent in 1809 to 37 per cent in 1811.[66]

The regional pattern of enlistment changed in the second half of the nineteenth century. After the great famine of 1846 the proportion of Irish recruits began to fall, with emigration to the United States coming to replace enlistment into the British army. In 1870 27.9 per cent of the army was Irish, dropping to 15.6 per cent in 1888 and 9.1 per cent in 1912, roughly proportionate to Ireland's proportion of the population of the United Kingdom. The proportion of Scots – 7.7 per cent in 1879 and 7.8 in 1912 – remained more static, but significantly it fell below Scotland's proportion of the United Kingdom's population. Alongside a shift away from rural Scotland and Ireland as recruiting grounds went a growing tendency to recruit the English urban unemployed, and by the early twentieth century only eleven per cent of recruits were agricultural labourers. The effect was similar in microcosm. The Black Watch (42nd Regiment) drew 51 per cent of its recruits from the Highlands in 1798, but only nine per cent in 1830–34 and just five per cent in 1854. Like other Highland regiments, it was driven to seeking more and more of its soldiers from the Lothians and Glasgow.[67]

Although the definitive swing towards urban recruiting occurred in the second half of the nineteenth century, the robust, malleable and deferential countryman was never as plentiful as recruiting sergeants might have wished. A sergeant major of the 28th Regiment told the 1835 Royal Commission on military punishment that:

> There are no men so good soldiers as the man who comes from the plough. We would never take a weaver while they were there. [Townsmen] require all the means in the power of their officers ... to teach them that subordination is the first duty of the profession into which they have entered.[68]

While around 25 per cent of Royal Artillery recruits gave the trade of labourer on enlistment between 1756 and 1779, thereafter there was a massive jump in the percentage of weavers enlisting, so that they outnumbered even day-labourers.

The army of our period contained a far higher proportion of Scots and Irish officers and men than was to be the case at the end of the nineteenth century, and this was very evident to those who served in it – and fought against it. Highland regiments, recruited from Gaelic-speaking countrymen living north of the Highland line, wore the kilt. Even when it was replaced by trousers on active service in North America – Captain Peebles' journal reveals a constant preoccupation with getting hold of sufficient material to make 'trowsers' for his company – their bonnets marked them out as Scots. Following the Jacobite risings of 1715 and 1745 Scots were unpopular in England: indeed, for much of our period the term 'North British' was used in place of 'Scots' in regimental designations, thus 'Royal North British Dragoons' to describe Scotland's only cavalry regiment, the Royal Scots Greys.

After Culloden (1746) the carrying of arms and the wearing of Highland dress was proscribed by law, but joining a Highland regiment enabled a man to do both – and, indeed, to escape the destitution that threatened his countrymen as sheep drove out men during the Highland clearances. The enlistment of Highlanders also represented a good bargain for the government. It gave legitimate scope to a martial spirit that might otherwise have been used against it, and coincided conveniently with the growing need to find light infantry for North America. As Colonel William Stewart, a leading advocate of light infantry, was to observe, 'being less spoiled and more hardy than [other] British soldiers, [they were] better accustomed for active light troops.'[69]

The senior Highland regiment, the 42nd (Black Watch), gained its baptism of fire at Fontenoy in 1745, the year before Culloden. Other Highland regiments were raised for the Seven Years' War but disbanded after it. More were raised for the American War of Independence, and all but two were disbanded after that. Thus although Highland regiments played a distinguished part in these conflicts, most were unable to trace continuous existence deep into the eighteenth century. The high regimental numbers of the Highland units which eventually became permanent during the French

Revolutionary and Napoleonic wars (like the 71st Highland Light Infantry, the 78th Highlanders [the Ross-Shire Buffs] and the 79th Cameron Highlanders), and consequent lack of seniority in the Army List contrasted with the unshakeable pre-eminence of the 1st Foot – the trousered Royal Scots – recruited, like other lowland regiments, from the largely English-speaking lowlands of Scotland.

This suspicion of Highlanders, useful on active service but less desirable in peacetime, had deep roots in an English population badly frightened by the Forty-Five with a long retained latent fear of a Jacobite revival with French bayonets at its back. When James Boswell went to see 'Love in a Village' at Covent Garden on 8 December 1762 two uniformed officers of Lord John Murray's Scots regiment, just returned from Havana – taken from the Spaniards after a costly siege – were hissed and pelted with apples to cries of 'No Scots! No Scots!' 'I wish from my soul that the Union was broke,' said one, 'and we might give them another Bannockburn.' 'And this is the thanks we get,' added the other, 'to be hissed when we come home . . . If it was the French, what could they do worse?' The first then slipped into a comfortable vernacular which Boswell, a fellow Scot, knew well: 'But if I had a grup o yin or twa o the tamd rascals I sud let them ken what they're about.'[70]

Neither lowland Scots nor Irish regiments were as easily distinguished as kilted Highlanders, though Regimental colours and individual appointments like shoulder-belt plates usually bore a harp for Irish regiments and a thistle for Scots. The 71st Highland Light Infantry went one better: although officers and men wore trousers, its unique head-dress was a blue Highland bonnet, complete with broad diced band, blocked into shako shape. The spread of tartan into all Scots regiments did not come until much later, when a combination of royal interest in Scotland and the novels of Sir Walter Scott meant that Scotland, 'from being a tiresome frontier province, became fashionable'.[71] Most lowland regiments had acquired pipers by the 1850s, and by 1881 they had tartan trews, Highland doublets and an appropriate Scots head-dress. It was the apotheosis of the Highlander: from a potential rebel, useful for dealing with the King's enemies in distant forests, he had become a martial pillar of the Victorian establishment.

Ambivalence also surrounded the far more numerous, though less easily identifiable, Irish. They were accused by Englishmen of being dirty and verminous, 'a standard accusation against those at the bottom of the social heap'. They were resented as a source of cheap labour, suspected because they were alleged to support the exiled Stuarts, and because they owed allegiance to the Pope. Thus they were 'treacherous in all three spheres: economic, political and religious.'[72] They were the butt of frequent jokes. When General William Howe, commander-in-chief in North America, evacuated Boston in 1776, an officer was detailed to scatter crow's feet – sharp four-pronged irons that always lay with one point up – in front of the town gate. 'Being an Irishman,' sniggered an English officer, 'he began scattering the crowfeet about from the gate towards the enemy, and of course had to walk over them on his return, and was nearly taken prisoner.'[73] It was not always safe to chuckle at such jests. The eccentric Lord Hervey entered a coffee-house to find his way barred by a man who ostentatiously sniffed the air and declared: 'I smell an Irishman.' Hervey snatched a carving-knife from a nearby table and slashed off the man's nose, remarking sweetly: 'You'll not smell another.'

The battlefield performance of Irish soldiers, whether serving in Irish regiments or in nominally English units, mocked the cliché. One of the most enduring battlefield descriptions of the period speaks of 1/27th (Enniskillen) lying literally dead in square at Waterloo. In the Peninsula the 88th (Connaught Rangers) had a fighting record which placed it amongst the bravest of the brave. Lieutenant William Grattan (a distant relative of the Irish opposition leader Henry Grattan) watched the 88th getting ready to assault the great breach at Ciudad Rodrigo. The fortress was one of the keys to routes between Spain and Portugal, and Wellington besieged it early in 1812. His heavy guns battered two breaches into its walls, and on the night of 19 January his infantry carried the town by storm at dreadful cost. For a description of experienced infantry preparing for battle Grattan's account can scarcely be bettered:

> . . . each man began to arrange himself for the combat in
> such a manner as the fancy of the moment would admit
> of – some by lowering their cartridge-boxes, others by
> turning theirs to the front in order that they might more

Lieutenant General Sir Thomas Picton was commisioned into the 12th Foot at the age of 13, and having established a fearsome reputation as a disciplinarian, commanded a division in the Peninsula. Famously profane and scruffy, he was killed at Waterloo in a black frock coat and top hat, yelling: 'Come on you rogues, you rascals.'

conveniently make use of them; others unclasping their stocks or opening their shirt collars, and others oiling their bayonets, and more taking leave of their wives and children . . .[74]

Before going forward the regiment was addressed by Lieutenant General Sir Thomas Picton, its divisional commander.

'Rangers of Connaught, it is not my intention to expend any powder this evening. We'll do this business with the

cold iron.' I said before [writes Grattan] the soldiers were
silent – so they were, but the man who could be silent
after such an address, made in such a way, and in such a
place, had better have stayed at home. It may be asked
what did they do? Why what would they do, or what would
any one do, but give the loudest hurrah he was able.[75]

On another occasion Grattan turned round to look at the men of
his company as they advanced on a French regiment, drawn up ready
to receive them, and 'they gave me a cheer that a lapse of many
years has not made me forget, and I thought that that moment was
the proudest of my life.'[76]

Grattan was full of praise for the Irish soldier. 'He can live on as
little nourishment as a Frenchman,' he wrote; 'give him a pipe of
tobacco and he will march for two days without food and without
grumbling; give him, in addition, a little spirits and a biscuit, and he
will work for a week.'[77] There lay the rub, for give him more than a
little and he could become beastly drunk. But even then, suggests
Grattan, he had his advantages: 'The English soldier is to the full as
drunken as the Irish, and not half so pleasant in his liquor.'[78] Captain
George Napier of the 52nd was an Englishman, with none of Grattan's family connections with Ireland, but he still found the Irish
irresistible. A drunken rogue in his company, Private John Dunn,
walked seven miles to see Napier and his brother in his field hospital
in Spain.

> I'm come to see how you and your brother is after the
> wounds ... And sure I thought you was kilt. But myself
> knew you wouldn't be plaised if I didn't folly on after the
> villains, so I was afeard to go pick you up when ye was kilt,
> long life to you!

Napier noticed that Dunn's arm was bandaged.

> Why sure it's nothing, only me arrum was cut off a few
> hours ago below the elbow joint, and I couldn't come till
> the anguish was over a bit. But now I'm here, and thank
> God your honour's arrum is not cut off, for it's mighty
> cruel work; by Jasus, I'd rather be shot twenty times.

Napier then asked after Dunn's brother, a soldier in the same company.

> I seed him shot through the heart alongside wid me just as I got shot myself . . . but, captain, he died like a soldier, as your honour would wish him to die, and sure that's enough. He had your favour whilst he lived, God be with him, and he's gone now.

The incident made a lasting impression on Napier, who told his sons: 'whenever you see a poor lame soldier, recollect John Dunn, and never pass him coldly by.'[79]

A common thread of nationality linked Irish soldiers, and Irish regiments greeted one another with enormous and characteristic enthusiasm. Fanny Duberly was married to the paymaster of the 8th Royal Irish Hussars, and accompanied him to the Crimean War. During operations around Varna on the Black Sea, before the army reached the Crimea, she watched a British division on the march.

> The Rifles marched first, next followed the 33rd, playing 'Cheer, Boys, Cheer' and cheerily enough the music sounded across our silent valley. The 88th Connaught Rangers gave a wild Irish screech (I know no better word) when they saw their fellow countrymen in the 8th Royal Irish Hussars and they played 'Garry Owen' with all their might . . .[80]

Sarah Anne Terrot, a nurse in the same campaign, paid tribute to Irish humour. 'I began operations on the filthy and shattered leg of an Alma Irishman,' she wrote, 'who shouted out "Och!" the blessing of the touch of a woman's hand; she touches my poor leg so tinder and gentle.'[81] Tom Burns, another Irishman, answered a doctor's enquiry as to whether he could feel a splinter of bone being probed for in his leg with: 'Not a bit.' After the doctor had walked off glumly, fearing the worst, he told the nurse: 'If the doctor asks me a fool's question, I am determined to give a rogue's answer, as if he could dig away in my leg, to try to tear out my bones, and I not feel it.'[82] Nurse Terrot compared her patients in national categories:

> There was a great variety of characters among the patients
> – the heavy clumsy English ploughboy, the sharp street-

bred London boy, the canny cautious Scot, the irresistibly amusing Irishman with his brogue and bulls. Certainly estimable as they were the Scotch were in general the least attractive patients – silent, grave, cold and cautious, there were none so winning as the Irish, with their quick feeling and ready wit.[83]

Yet the uncomfortable fact remained that Ireland was a country under occupation by the very army in which Irishmen – officers and soldiers alike – played such an important role. In the last analysis the Irish state rested upon British military power.[84] Prime Minister Lord North wrote in 1775 that the authorities there 'depend so much on the protection and assistance of the military force, who are in constant employment under the command of the civil magistrate for the carrying on of every part of the police of the kingdom, which could not be carried on without it.'[85] We must retain a sense of perspective, because the civil authorities across the whole of the United Kingdom frequently had recourse to military support in an era when violent unrest was frequent. And until the terrifying outbreak of 1798, eighteenth century Ireland was remarkably quiet. In the summer of 1745, when the army was at full stretch, finding garrisons in the Mediterranean, campaigning in Flanders and about to campaign in Scotland, the garrison of Ireland was a mere four battalions of foot and six regiments of cavalry.

Yet there was an added difficulty. Whenever Britain found herself at war with France or Spain, she faced the prospect of a descent on Ireland, in which French or Spanish troops would form the rallying-point for disaffected Irishmen. Regiments were sent to Ireland when the risk of invasion loomed: three regiments of foot went there in early 1727 when Spanish invasion seemed likely, and returned once the threat had passed. In November 1759 the Prime Minister warned the Marquis of Granby, commanding the British contingent in Germany, that the French fleet was at sea, 'to invade this country or Ireland'. Accordingly, Prince Ferdinand, the allied commander was to 'get any Troops he can – Swiss, German deserters or regular German troops – in order to increase and strengthen his Army ... But English we have not to send.'[86]

The most dangerous potential invasion came in December 1796

when a substantial French fleet carrying 12,000 soldiers under General Lazare Hoche slipped past the British blockade, but was prevented by bad weather from disgorging its troops: as the nationalist leader Wolfe Tone put it, England had not had such an escape since the Armada. During the great rebellion of 1798 a much smaller force under the French General Joseph Humbert landed at Killala, on the Mayo coast, and beat Lieutenant General Gerard Lake in an episode which lived on in folklore as 'the races of Castlebar'. But just as co-ordination of operations within Ireland was a major reason for the rebels' failure, so inability to persuade the French that a major and timely invasion might prove decisive was another. Humbert's force was too little and too late, and the rebellion – 'the most violent and tragic event in Irish history between the Jacobite wars and the Great Famine' – was put down with the loss of perhaps 30,000 lives.[87]

Given this background, it is perhaps surprising that Irish regular regiments, and individual Irish soldiers in English regiments, remained as loyal as they did. The one significant lapse came when the 5th or Royal Irish Regiment of Dragoons, which helped suppress the 1798 rebellion, was infiltrated by nationalists, who plotted to murder the regiment's officers. The plot was discovered and the regiment was disbanded at Chatham on 8 April 1799, leaving a hole in the Army List that was not filled until the 5th Royal Irish Lancers was raised in 1858. In 1922 the 5th was amalgamated with the 16th Lancers to form the 16th/5th, the lack of numerical logic being explained by fact that the 5th, despite its senior number, was in fact the junior regiment.

The ambivalent position of Irish soldiers, so many of them Roman Catholics in a Protestant army, and loyal servants of a state against which their countrymen periodically rebelled, was not lost on leaders and comrades alike. Yet the 32nd (Cornwall) Regiment found no difficulty in linking its own motto with that of the Irish rebels in its regimental song:

> *Erin Go Brough* go hand in hand with
> One And All.

And some Irishmen showed their loyalty in the most extreme fashion. When Chef d'Escadron O'Flyn, an Irish officer in French service, was captured by the 16th Light Dragoons near Ciudad Rodrigo in 1811, he was pistolled on the spot by his countryman Private Fitz-Patrick. Lieutenant Thomas Brotherton heard the story from Fitz-Patrick himself: 'The fellow said he was an Irishman, which the dragoon could not hear and allow him to escape alive.'[88] Many Irishmen in the army managed to balance their own instinctive nationalism with a practical loyalty for the army they served in, and saw nothing wrong in singing rebel songs as they marched to do the bidding of a government in which they had no personal interest. And when it came to fighting they had few peers.

So much, then, for England. Our affection for the elegant and well-proportioned artefacts of the Georgian past can all too easily persuade us that British society of the period embodied a similar pleasing symmetry. Yet of course it did not. Georgian society, like that of the Regency and early Victorian age that followed, was marked by tensions between elegance and ugliness, town and country, industry and agriculture. These were reflected in an army which brought together noblemen and the sweepings of the urban gutter; sons of rising bourgeois, who had set the seal on new status by buying their boy a commission, and unemployed weavers; ardent royalists and rabid (though wisely covert) republicans; serious-minded Presbyterians and devout (though necessarily discrete) Roman Catholics.

The contrast was nothing if not visual: between the half-moon silver-gilt gorget, engraved with the royal arms, that officers wore at their throats, and the scarlet tunic, so often sweated to destruction, that it rested on; and between the blue and gilt blade of the sabres carried by the officers of the flank companies and the brain-biting sharpness of their edge. Those gold-laced officers' tunics cost more than guineas, for tailors often went blind:

> of all colours scarlet, such is as used for regimentals, is
> the most blinding, it seems to burn the eyeballs, and makes
> them ache dreadful . . . everything seems all of a twitter,
> and to keep changing its tint. There's more military tailors
> blind than any others.

And the blue and gilt blades caused casualties long before they were drawn in anger: goldsmiths became asthmatic and paralytic because of the fumes of mercury they inhaled at their work.

There can be no better example of the contrast than Brown Bess herself. She was made in the gunmaking district of Birmingham, or the teeming hamlets around the Tower of London. Parts were usually manufactured separately, in hundreds of one-room workshops, where whole families filed away at locks and shaped walnut stocks. Yet even the India pattern, a war economy weapon deemed by modern collectors to lack the grace of earlier models, is more than a simple killing-machine. A double line is chiselled around the edge of the lock-plate; the brass trumpet-mouthed pipes that hold the ramrod have ornamental fluting, and the trigger-guard sweeps out, in front of the trigger itself, into an elegant acorn-shaped finial. In short, it is an artefact in the best of Georgian taste, but designed to impel a lead ball into the body of an enemy.

It was an era of rapid and unsettling change. Britain's population was growing, after setbacks in the 1720s, and its distribution had begun to alter. In 1750 the population was about 5.8 million. It had risen to some 6.4 million by 1770, and almost 8 million twenty years later. By 1831 it was just over 24 million, and was well over 27 million in 1851. Throughout the period just over half the population of Great Britain lived in England, with Ireland containing around half as many inhabitants as England until the mass emigration of the nineteenth century reduced this proportion. Although London contained perhaps 10 per cent of Britain's inhabitants in 1750, the balance was shifting away from the south towards the Midlands and the north as industry expanded and Britain's burgeoning agriculture (about 2.5 times as productive as that of France) enabled the population of these growing towns to be fed.

By 1801 about 30 per cent of the population of Britain lived in towns, a far higher proportion than elsewhere in northern Europe. Towns like Manchester and Glasgow grew fast, with an emphasis on cleanliness and order as medieval centres were pulled down, jumbled lanes making way for straight streets and spacious squares, with piped water and sewerage. London was already bigger than Paris or Naples, and by 1750 it had overtaken Constantinople. Foreign and domestic

visitors alike were astonished at the spacious houses of great mag-
nates, the elegant symmetry of streets and squares, the Royal parks
– Hyde Park, Kensington Gardens, Green Park and St James's Park
– the well-stocked shops of Covent Garden and Ludgate Hill, and
the pleasure-gardens of Vauxhall and Ranelagh.

Yet even the most naive visitor could scarcely have been unaware
of the contrast between polite London and the reverse of the medal.
Simply getting there was not easy. The appalling roads of early
Georgian England were infinitely improved as the century wore
on and turnpike trusts repaired and maintained roads which
could be used on payment of a toll. Provincial centres like Exeter,
Manchester and York, three days away from London in the 1720s,
could be reached in little more than 24 hours by 1780. However,
travel remained uncomfortable and dangerous. Highwaymen were
the aristocrats of crime: when James MacLaine was awaiting hanging
in 1750, 3,000 people visited him in his cell in Newgate prison
in a single day, and John Rann ('Sixteen String Jack') went to
the gallows in 1774 in a new suit of pea-green, fine ruffled shirt
and huge nosegay, and danced his last jig before an appreciative
audience.

Robbers like this were bold and vexatious. Prime minister Lord
North was robbed in 1774, and ten years earlier the Bath stagecoach
was ambushed between Knightsbridge and Hyde Park Corner. In
1771 five ladies and gentlemen on their way back from Vauxhall by
river were boarded by ruffians near Westminster Bridge and had
their watches and purses taken. On a less dramatic scale, shoplifters,
pickpockets and hat-snatchers abounded: an account of 1764 complained that by midnight 'the public streets began to swarm with
whores and pickpockets.'[89] César de Saussure, a French visitor, found
little to chose between sport and riot.

> The populace has other amusements . . . such as throwing
> dead dogs and cats and mud at passers-by on certain festi-
> val days. Another amusement which is very inconvenient
> to passers-by is football . . . in cold weather you will some-
> times see a score of rascals in the streets kicking at a ball
> and they will break panes of glass and smash the windows
> of coaches and also knock you down without the smallest

compunction: on the contrary they will roar with laughter . . .

The English are very fond of a game they call cricket. For this purpose they go into a large open field and knock a ball about with a piece of wood. I will not attempt to describe the game to you, it is too complicated: but it requires agility and skill and everyone plays it, the common people and also men of rank.

Great cities had great slums, sometimes on their fast-expanding fringes, where countrymen arrived in the (generally vain) hope of making their fortune, and sometimes in the gaps between redevelopment. Conditions in these warrens were appalling.

From three to eight individuals of different ages often sleep in the same bed, there being in general but one room and a bed for each family . . . The room occupied is either a deep cellar, almost inaccessible to the light, and admitting of no change of air, or a garret with a low roof and small windows, the passage to which is close, kept dark, and filled not only with bad air but with putrid excremental effluvia from a vault [cess-pit] at the bottom of the staircase.[90]

The rustic who made his way to town had often been dispossessed by the steady enclosure of the countryside, part of it the result of parliamentary enclosure acts in the second half of the eighteenth century, but at least as much resulting from a slower and quieter process which was already long in train. Its general effect was to replace the small yeoman proprietors with a far steeper rural pyramid, in which large farmers, themselves often the tenants of gentry landlords, employed, as landless labourers, men whose fathers had once farmed their own land. This process paralleled a similar development in the towns, as individual artisans were swallowed up in large-scale enterprises, their loss of status being accompanied by dependency on 'new men'. They were sometimes philanthropic, like Robert Owen, who added an institute and community centre to mills built by his father-in-law at New Lanark, but often they were more concerned with their profits than their workers.

Three industries rose head and shoulder above all others: coal, iron and textiles. Between 1750 and 1800 coal production doubled as steam pumps enabled miners to reach deeper, richer seams. Railways, their trucks drawn by horses at the start of our period but by steam engines before its close, took coal to the rivers and canals which carried so much of the country's heavy freight. The construction of a canal from Worsley to Manchester in 1761 initiated a canal-building boom that saw over 2,500 miles built by the time that the railway moved centre stage. In mid-century coke became widely used for smelting iron, and cast iron items, which came straight from the factory and did not require the attentions of finery, mill and smithy, became increasingly popular. In the 1780s Henry Cort patented the processes of puddling and rolling, in which molten iron was first stirred to allow the sulphurous gasses to escape and then rolled to remove remaining impurities. War fuelled the demand for iron: in the decade from 1788 the output of pig iron in Britain doubled, and by 1806 it had doubled again.

But 'textiles were the power which towed the glider of industrialisation into the air.'[91] The wool trade had long been important, as so many stunning English churches built or improved with wool money, and now all too often dwarfing their tiny congregations, show. Cotton was more amenable to machine production, and the growth of slavery in the American south made raw material abundant. From the 1750s a spate of new inventions, like John Kay's flying shuttle, James Hargreaves's spinning jenny, and Samuel Crompton's mule, improved both the spinning of individual threads of cotton and then its weaving into finished cloth. The first inventions made individual handloom weavers more productive, and increased their income at a time of growing demand. But subsequent developments first began to bring individual processes together in small factories, and then, after Edmund Cartwright patented the power loom in 1785, saw the conversion of the whole cotton industry to the factory system. The process was gradual: there were only 2,400 power looms in use by 1814, 45,500 by 1829, and 85,000 in 1833. Similar developments, which often used the same machinery, also revolutionised the woollen industry.

The social impact of this change was enormous. Eighteenth-century Britain grew into a more polarised society. Improvements in literacy and communications made comparisons between rich and poor both frequent and striking: 'The extravagant life-style of a ruling elite which seemed to live in a blaze of conspicuous consumption, and also the more modest but cumulatively more influential rise in middle-class standards of living, made the inequalities of a highly commercial, cash-based economy glaringly plain.'[92] The politics of the seventeenth and early eighteenth centuries had focused on the relationship between monarch and parliament, and latterly on the issue (much more than simply dynastic, for it involved political and religious questions) of the Hanoverian succession and Jacobite claims to the throne.

The dominant political issue of our period, however, was the nature of parliamentary representation. Until the first great Reform Act of 1832 the starkest polarity lay in the mismatch between a House of Commons which reflected the structure of medieval England and the fast-changing nation it ruled. The franchise was limited to men with the appropriate property qualification: only one man in seven had the vote in England, but a mere one in 44 in Scotland. Some constituencies, 'pocket boroughs', were in the pocket of the local magnate and dutifully returned him or his nominee; others, 'rotten boroughs' had a tiny number of electors whose bribery or coercion was facilitated by the fact that they voted in public. There was no relationship between parliamentary representation and population. In 1801 the 700,000 inhabitants of Yorkshire returned two county and 26 borough MPs, while Cornwall, with 188,000 people, had two county and 42 borough MPs. The tiny Cornish boroughs of Grampound and Tregony returned two members apiece, while Birmingham, Manchester and Bradford were unrepresented. The Norfolk constituency of Dunwich had gradually receded into the North Sea, but its fishy inhabitants were duly represented by two members. Few doubted that some sort of reform was essential: the difficulty was how it could be kept within constitutional bounds.

The pressures generated by agricultural and agrarian change found political expression as radicals, within parliament and outside it, demanded reform. The same pressures helped encourage the masses – designated 'the crowd' by sympathetic witnesses and 'the mob' by the more conservative – to riot with frequency and abandon.[93] Often their outbursts had a direct economic cause. The silk-weavers of Spitalfields rioted in 1719–20 in protest against the import of cheap and cool foreign calico, and in 1774 English hay-makers fought pitched battles with immigrant Irish harvest workers.

Innovation provoked physical opposition by those who felt threatened by it. In 1736 a collier was hanged for turnpike-cutting, the 1760s saw several serious clashes between weavers and soldiers, and in 1836 an upsurge of loom-breaking in East Lancashire, as the installation of power-looms gained full momentum, required the commitment of troops and culminated in a pitched battle at Chatterton. Other rioters had political motivates, though they often found themselves seconded by the disadvantaged and by simple opportunists. When John Wilkes, a well-to do journalist, MP and militia colonel, attacked the government over its use of general warrants, which permitted arbitrary arrest, and then demanded that the debates of the House of Commons should be published, he was supported not only by many of 'the middle and inferior' sort of men, but also by rural gentry and urban bourgeoisie. The authorities recognised that such rioters could not be treated as if they were disaffected coal-heavers or weavers. Juries, by definition middle-class, were not only inclined to acquit them, but, worse still from the government's point of view, to convict magistrates who ordered the military to fire and the troops who actually did so.

The Gordon riots of 1780 were far more serious than the Wilkesite disturbances twenty years before. Lord George Gordon gained widespread support, much of it from the 'middling sort' of men, in his demand for the cancellation of the 1778 Toleration Act which had removed some legal constraints imposed on Roman Catholics. After the Commons rejected his petition, the crowd of supporters in Parliament Square was swollen by weavers and others. When a battalion of footguards opened a path to Parliament to allow its harassed denizens to escape, the mob embarked upon an orgy of violence, first burning the Catholic chapels belonging to foreign embassies, the only ones legally allowed to exist. The rioters then turned their attention to the law's visible manifestations, destroying the houses of prominent politicians and magistrates, sacking Newgate jail, releasing all its prisoners, and looting and then burning a large Catholic-owned gin distillery. The government eventually cracked down hard, bringing over 11,000 regular troops into the capital. More than 300 rioters were killed, mainly by gunshot wounds, although some perished from drinking neat alcohol, or when buildings collapsed on them. Twenty-five were hanged on specially constructed gallows near the scenes of their crimes: seventeen of them were eighteen and three under fifteen. 'I never saw children *cry* so,' said one onlooker. Lord George himself, tried for high treason, was swiftly acquitted.

The Gordon riots terrified most middle-class radicals, who favoured political reform but feared the mob. And while the riots can be viewed as an anti-Catholic outburst which ignited the mindless violence often close to the surface of British society, there is indeed a good case for seeing them as 'the nearest thing to the French Revolution in English history.'[94] The mob attacked only *rich* Catholics, and then assaulted the visible symbols of governmental authority.

The French Revolution first attracted those who favoured political reform but swiftly alienated most of them by its growing violence. Its outbreak was widely welcomed in England, for France, a traditional enemy, was widely believed to be the very fount of tyranny. Well might Wordsworth proclaim:

> Bliss was it in that dawn to be alive
> But to be young was very heaven!

But in October 1790 Edmund Burke's pamphlet *Reflections on the French Revolution* warned that the Revolution's growing extremism might spread to England, resulting in the total overthrow of the established order, and the majority of public opinion soon came to regard Revolutionary France with horror and disgust. The government capitalised on this to clamp down heavily on the radicals, although even their 'Corresponding Society' – which did indeed have links with French revolutionary politicians – was 'more foolish and fantastic than violent'. In 1792 the government first prohibited 'seditious writings', and then called up the militia, claiming that insurrection was imminent, and bringing conservative members of the opposition into its camp. The demand for reform was effectively stifled for the duration of the war with France, which lasted, with two brief breaks, till 1815.

Although reform again became a pressing political issue after Waterloo, working-class agitation never really joined hands with parliamentary radicalism, and urban resentment at the Corn Laws (which worked in favour of the landed interest by keeping corn, and thus bread, prices artificially high) was not shared by agricultural workers whose livelihood depended on their employers' prosperity. As a result, the ruling elite never found itself facing a coalition of opposition which might conceivably have brought it down.

Yet there was agitation aplenty. In 1819 soldiers trying to arrest radical leaders at a reform demonstration in St Peter's Fields, Manchester, became violently entangled up in the crowd in the 'Peterloo Massacre'. The following year witnessed a weavers' rising in Scotland and the half-baked Cato Street Conspiracy – a plot to assassinate the Cabinet – in England. In the 1820s the falling price of woven cotton and unemployment amongst hand-loom weavers produced great suffering in Yorkshire and Lancashire. One weaver, William Thom, urged his readers to:

> Imagine a cold spring forenoon. It is eleven o'clock. The four children are still asleep. There is a bed cover hung before the window to keep within as much night as possible: and the mother sits beside the children to lull them back to sleep whenever shows any inclination to awake – the only food in the house is a handful of oatmeal – our fuel is exhausted. My wife and I were conversing in sunken whispers about making an attempt to cook the oatmeal when the youngest child woke up beyond his mother's powers to hush it again to sleep. He fell a-whimpering and finally broke out in a steady scream, rendering it impossible to keep the rest asleep. Face after face sprang up, each saying 'Mother!' 'Mother!' 'Please give us something.' How weak a word is sorrow to apply to feelings of myself and my wife during the rest of that forenoon . . . I look to nothing but increasing labour and decreasing strength in interminable toil and ultimate starvation. Such is the fate of nine tenths of my brethren.[95]

In 1826 a serious outbreak of rioting amongst handloom weavers in Lancashire was put down by troops. Six civilians were shot during the disturbances, eight rioters were transported to Australia for life, and 28 more received various terms of imprisonment.

In 1830, during a wave of agrarian unrest, the diarist Charles Fulke Greville wrote that:

> London is like the capital of a country desolated by cruel war or foreign invasion, we are always looking out for reports of battles, burnings and other disorders. Wherever there has been anything like fighting, the mob has always been beaten, and has shown the greatest cowardice. They do not, however, seem to have been actuated by a very ferocious spirit, and it is remarkable that they have not been more violent and rapacious.[96]

Like so many of his ilk he feared revolution, and was clear that the struggle was defined on class grounds. 'On Monday as the field which had been out with the King's hounds were returning to town, they were summoned to assist in quelling a riot in Woburn, which they did: the gentlemen charged and broke the people . . .'[97]

The passing of the great Reform Bill in 1832 did not end agitation. Although it removed many of the defects of the unreformed parliamentary electoral system, there remaining glaring anomalies – the 349 electors of Buckingham returned as many MPs as the 4,172 electors of Leeds – and the House of Commons remained dominated by landed interests. There was widespread support for the People's Charter, a petition which demanded manhood suffrage, the secret ballot, equal electoral districts, the abolition of property qualifications for MPs, payment for MPs, and annual parliaments. Chartist feeling ran high in the late 1830s and early 1840s, and gained much of its strength from Ireland, where the granting of Catholic Emancipation in 1829 had only blunted nationalist demands. The economic upsurge of the mid 1840s drew most of Chartism's teeth, and its last revival, a monster petition delivered in 1848, fell miserably flat when it emerged that thousands of signatures were faked.

The British army in the age of Brown Bess was the product of a society showing all the strains of population explosion coupled with radical changes in both industry and agriculture. Crime was common and its punishment potentially savage, with the pillory and the gibbet as spectacles of popular entertainment. As time went on society became more orderly: Robert Peel's reorganisation of the London police in the 1820s was followed by improvements in policing outside the capital, and the growth of street numbers for houses made it easier for wanted men to be tracked down. Sanitation, too, improved, but it remained sporadic and epidemics were rife: the cholera outbreak of 1832 probably killed 31,000 people in Britain, and A.C. Tait, a future archbishop of Canterbury, lost five of his seven children to scarlet fever in 1856.

The men who filled the army's ranks came increasingly from an urban working class whose living conditions were only latterly improved by the burgeoning of the nation's wealth. They were led by scions of the ruling elite, although, as we shall see, the officer corps showed a flexibility which characterised society more generally: if the period ended by emphasising the importance of the prosperous middle classes, so too did the army. And while the army's most spectacular achievements were on foreign fields, it was always in demand to extinguish home fires, ignited by King Mob in the towns and Captain Swing in the countryside. For instance, while Sergeant Thomas Morris of the 73rd Regiment wrote with feeling about Waterloo, he was scarcely less concerned about a riot in Birmingham two years later, which highlighted the problem faced by soldiers called to act in support of the civil power.

> The high constable went with us, and proceeded to read the riot act. On some brickbats and stones being thrown at us, our brave captain gave orders to load, and then gave direction that we should fire among the mob, when the high constable interposed, and said. 'There was no necessity for that yet.' 'Sir,' said our officer, 'if I am not allowed to fire, I shall take my men back.' The constable's patriotic answer deserves to be recorded. 'Sir,' said he, 'you are called out to aid and assist the civil power, and if you fire on the people without my permission, and death ensues, you will be guilty of murder, and if you go away, without my leave, it will be at your peril.'[98]

Above all it was an army born of paradox. It fought hard, and generally with success, in defence of an order in which most of its members had scant personal interest, and which showed as little regard for them once they had returned to civilian life as it did before they first donned red coats. Though it was not immune from political sentiment and genuine patriotic fervour, it fought because of comradely emulation, gutter-fighter toughness, regimental pride and brave leadership, laced with a propensity to drink and plunder, and buttressed by a harsh disciplinary code.

It overcame the most brutal trials. When Wellington stormed Badajoz in 1812 his success cost him 4,000 British and 1,000 Portuguese, and the carnage in the breach beggars description. Lieutenant Robert Blakeney of the 28th Regiment tells how:

> gallant foes laughing at death met, fought, bled and rolled
> upon earth; and from the very earth destruction burst, for
> the exploding mines cast up friends and foes together,
> who in burning torture gasped and shrieked in the air.
> Partly burned they fell back into the inundating water,
> continually lighted by the incessant bursting of shells.

He went on to describe the ladders some of the stormers had ascended as 'warm and slippery with the blood and brains of many a gallant soldier.'[99] In wondering how men were able to endure experiences like this, we must remember that they had been forged in the crucible of social change, endemic violence and economic deprivation: this harsh background bred hard men.

II

ALL THE KING'S HORSES AND ALL THE KING'S MEN

SWORD AND STATE

BY ALL APPEARANCES it was the monarch's army. The red and blue so prominent in its uniforms originated in the Tudor livery; the royal cipher was embroidered on regimental colours, engraved on sword-blades and musket-locks; officers' commissions bore the monarch's personal signature, and orders were issued in his or her name. The monarch was commander-in-chief of the army, 'unless the office is granted away,' which was often the case.[1] Royal birthdays and accession anniversaries were marked with appropriate ceremony, even on active service. On 18 January 1777 John Peebles recorded:

> This being the Anniversary of the Queen's Birthday (or the day that is kept for it) a Detachment of 300 British fired 3 vollies on the parade at 12 o'clock Proceeded by 21 guns from ye Battery & the like number of Hessians on the Green behind the Church, and at 1 o'clock the navy fired, each ship 21 guns . . .

Unfortunately the frigate HMS *Diamond*, which had recently been in action, 'had not taken sufficient care in drawing the shot, & discharged a load of Grape[shot] into a Transport ship close by them, & killed 5 men and wounded 3 . . .'[2]

The guards – horse and foot – were troops of the Royal Household, and their officers came into frequent social contact with the royal family. William IV, Duke of Clarence before his accession, regularly dined with the officers of the company on duty at St James's Palace and when at table expected no more deference than one gentleman might normally show another. He once asked whether officers still got 'chocolate', slang for a wigging, which derived from General Sir David Dundas's practice of inviting offenders to breakfast and then giving them a talking-to over the hot chocolate. Young Ensign 'Bacchus' Lascelles of 1st Guards (whose nickname arose from altogether different potations) piped up that he had got 'goose' from the adjutant for having too little powder on his hair that morning, adding 'it is quite immaterial whether a rowing be denominated "chocolate" or "goose," for it is all the same thing.'[3] However, things were not always this genial. When Ensign Gronow went on duty with his hair unpowdered, George III's seventh son, Adolphus Frederick, Duke of Cambridge, threatened him with arrest for 'appearing on parade in so slovenly and disgraceful a condition.'[4] Shortly after his accession, William IV was furious when the guard at St James's failed to turn out because the sentry had not recognised him in plain clothes. He also upset the guards' bandsmen by making them play for him every night, thus depriving them of fee-paying engagements elsewhere.

The first two Georges were 'soldier-kings in the German tradition.'[5] George II identified closely with his army, keeping a brown coat for civil business and a red one for military, and maintaining a notebook in which he recorded officers' characters and achievements. He was the last English monarch to command an army in battle, at Dettingen in 1743. When his horse bolted he dismounted and spent the day on foot, stumping about bravely enough but doing little to control things. Frederick the Great described him standing in front of a favourite Hanoverian regiment with his sword out in front of him like a fencing-master demonstrating a thrust: 'He gave signs of courage, but no order relative to the battle.'[6] But he was certainly in the forefront of the action. Late in the day he said to Sir Andrew Agnew, commanding Campbell's Regiment, that he saw 'the cuirassiers get in amongst your men this morning, Colonel.' 'Oh aye, your Majestee,' replied the broad Sir Andrew, 'but they dinna get out again.'[7] Lieutenant General Lord George Sackville was court-martialled for disobeying Prince Ferdinand's orders to charge at Minden, and the king, who had a high sense of duty and discipline, regarded his sentence of cashiering as too lenient. He personally struck Sackville's name off the roll of the Privy Council, and penned an addendum to the sentence, which was read out at the head of every regiment in the service:

> that others may consider that neither high birth nor great achievements can shelter offences of such a nature, and that seeing they are subject to censure much worse than death to a man who has any sense of honour, they may avoid the fatal consequences arising from disobedience to orders.[8]

William Augustus, Duke of Cumberland, George's second son, was wounded at Dettingen and narrowly defeated at Fontenoy. He had greater success against the Jacobites at Culloden, but was retired after his defeat in Germany 1757. Cumberland was a martinet, with what might be called a Germanic approach to giving orders, and took no care that they should be 'softened by gentle persuasive arguments by which gentlemen, particularly those of a British constitution, must be governed.'[9] His elder brother Frederick, Prince of Wales, and his political allies maintained that he was a dangerous militarist, and after Frederick died in 1751 there were even suggestions that he coveted the succession.

George III, no soldier himself, had a martial brood. His fifth son, Ernest Augustus of sinister repute (he was said to have fathered a son on his sister Sophia) was created Duke of Cumberland in 1799. He lost an eye at Tournai, commanding Hanoverian cavalry, in 1794, and was badly injured by his own sabre in a murderous attack by his valet in 1810. He commanded the Hanoverian army, and in 1837 became king of Hanover. His brothers Edward Augustus, Duke of Kent and Adolphus Frederick, Duke of Cambridge, both became field-marshals, and Kent served as Governor of Gibraltar during the Peninsular War, being recalled after his severity provoked unrest.

George III's second son, Frederick, Duke of York and Albany, took the profession of arms seriously, though fortune did not smile on him in Flanders in 1793 or at the Helder in 1799. He was an efficient and wholly useful commander-in-chief of the army from 1798 till his death in 1827, with a brief interlude between 1809 and 1811 after he was accused of allowing his mistress, the 'gaily-disposed' Mary Ann Clarke, wife of a bankrupt stonemason, to dabble in the commissions trade. The duke had set Mrs Clarke up as his mistress in 1802 with a handsome £1,000 a year, but she supported her extravagant lifestyle by conning tradesmen who trusted her because of her royal connections, and taking bribes to secure the duke's patronage for civil, military and even clerical appointments.

The duke, warned of what was afoot, ended the relationship in 1806, pensioning off Mrs Clarke on £400 a year provided she behaved discreetly. Two years later, however, she threatened to make matters public unless her full pension was restored and arrears paid. When the duke refused, her current protector, Colonel Gwylym Lloyd Wardle, a former officer of the Ancient British Fencibles who had been denied rank in the regular army by the duke's reforms and was now a radical MP, raised the question in the House. A committee of enquiry could find no clear link between Mary Ann Clark's acceptance of bribes and the granting of commissions, but the duke, duly acquitted of selling them, was urged, in treacly tones, 'to exhibit a right example of every virtue, in imitation of his Royal parent'. He had to resign as commander-in-chief, but was re-appointed in 1811 and remained in office till his death in 1827.

His younger brother Clarence joined the navy in 1779 and served in the American war. Peebles saw him in New York and thought him 'a very fine young man, smart and sensible for his years, & sufficiently well grown, a strong likeness of the King . . . he was in a plain Midshipman uniform, & took off his hat with a good grace . . .'[10] He was promoted steadily, becoming admiral of the fleet in 1811. Denied much active service in his naval capacity, he managed to accompany the army on an expedition to the Netherlands in January 1814. Displaying more pluck than prudence, he got up amongst the advanced skirmishers at Merxem, and was saved from capture by Lieutenant Thomas Austin of the 35th Foot in a brisk action in which he behaved very well. As a naval officer he had a sharp eye for detail, and this did not bode well. In March 1834 he conducted a minute inspection of the guards, horse and foot, and then 'had a musket brought to him, that he might show them the way to use it in some new sort of exercise that he wanted to introduce: in short, he gave a great deal of trouble and made a fool of himself.'[11] He believed that sailors should wear blue and soldiers red, and instituted a brief and unpopular deviation from the custom by which light cavalry regiments wore blue. They reverted to blue in 1840 with the exception of the 16th Lancers, which earned it the nickname 'Scarlet Lancers'.

William's illegitimate son, George Fitzclarence, served in the 10th Hussars in the Peninsula, and went on to become deputy adjutant-general: the king made him Earl of Munster, with rather a bad grace, in 1831. Lieutenant John 'Scamp' Stilwell of the 95th, believed to be a natural son of the Duke of York, was killed at Waterloo. Another of the duke's alleged by-blows, Captain Charles Hesse of the 18th Hussars, was wounded there. Charles Greville described him as 'a short, plump, vulgar-looking man,' but he was a famous Lothario and had affairs with both Princess Charlotte and the Queen of Naples. He was killed in a duel in 1832, ironically by Count Leon, an illegitimate son of Napoleon by Eleonore Develle, a young lady-in-waiting of Napoleon's sister Caroline. In 1840 the disreputable Leon challenged his cousin Louis, the future Emperor Napoleon III, then in exile in London, but the duellists and their seconds were arrested on Wimbledon Common.

The late Victorian army lay under the conservative shadow of the queen's cousin, George William Frederick Charles, Duke of Cambridge, son of George III's seventh son. Given command of 1st Division in 1854 at the age of 35, he was the only divisional commander in the Crimea not to have served in the Peninsula, and some of the misfortunes suffered by his men in their untidy advance at the Alma sprang from his inexperience. 'What am I to do?' he asked Brigadier General 'Gentlemanly George' Buller, an unreliable fount of advice. 'Why, your Royal Highness,' replied Buller, 'I am in a little confusion here – you had better advance, I think.'[12]

He was in the very thick of the fighting at Inkerman, where his division bore the brunt of the battle. The duke laconically ordered the Grenadier Guards to clear the Russians from the sand bag battery: 'You must drive them out of it.' The Grenadiers did as they were told, and the duke then halted them, but part of the 95th, in another division, surged on past, led by a huge Irish lance-corporal shouting: 'We're driving them, sir, we're driving them.'[13] Captain Richard Temple Godman of the 5th Dragoon Guards thought that he had been marked by the battle. 'He is said to be in an extraordinary *state of excitement* since Inkerman,' he wrote on 12 November 1854. 'He seems much liked by the soldiers. I hope there is nothing wrong with his mind.'[14] All was certainly not well with his body, for he was apparently as verminous as his men. When the surgeon of the Scots Fusilier Guards complained to his servant that his shirt was full of lice, the servant replied: 'The Duke of Cambridge is covered with them, sir.'[15] He became commander-in-chief of the army in 1856, and had to be bullied into retiring at the age of 76 in 1895. He set his face firmly against military reform, fearing that tradition would be undermined, and arguing that the army's success had been repeatedly demonstrated on the battlefield and could be ensured by a repetitious round of field-days and inspections.

Queen Victoria, disbarred by her gender from military service, none-the-less appeared, when a young woman, in a fetching uniform of a round black hat with a red and white plume, a general's tunic (turned down at the collar to show white blouse and black cravat) and dark blue riding habit. She rode side-saddle on a horse with field-marshal's badges on its saddle-cloth and holsters. Victoria took her military duties very seriously, presenting medals with evident pride and, at the very end of her life, doing her best to sign commissions personally despite failing health and a burgeoning of temporary appointments to meet the demands of the Boer War. Her alleged partiality for the Scots Fusilier Guards caused resentment in the Guards Brigade, and when the regiment fell back in some disorder at the Alma as the result of a misunderstood order, the Grenadiers and Coldstream, coming on steadily through the fire, chorused: 'Shame! Shame! What about the queen's favourites now?'[16] Her husband, Prince Albert, took a lively interest in military affairs. He attended the allied Council of War, held in London on 16 April 1855, and helped dissuade Napoleon III from going to take personal command in the Crimea. He was Colonel of the 11th Hussars and the Rifle Brigade, and both retained his name as part of their regimental titles until the amalgamations of the 1960s.

Many officers found comfort, then as now, in claiming to serve the monarch rather than the government, although it was not always an easy distinction to make in an age when officers often sat in the House of Commons, usually returned for a seat where their family or friends had a controlling interest. In 1775, William Howe, then a major general and MP for Nottingham, assured his constituents that his political principles precluded him from accepting a command in North America. When he did agree to serve there, an aggrieved elector told him frankly: 'I don't wish you to fall, as many do, but I cannot say I wish success to the undertaking.' Howe replied that 'my going thither was not of my seeking. I was ordered, and could not refuse, without incurring the odious name of backwardness to serve my country in distress.'[17]

A generation later, John Fitzmaurice of the 95th believed that a soldier should have no politics, and Francis Skelly Tidy, who commanded a battalion of the 14th at Waterloo, told his daughter that he was neither Whig nor Tory: 'I am a soldier and one of His Majesty's most devoted servants, bound to defend the crown with my life against either faction as necessary.'[18] General Sir Charles Napier, conqueror of Sind, had radical political views, and when in charge of Northern Command in England hoped that the 'physical force' Chartists did not attempt an armed rising, for their own good. 'Poor people! They will suffer,' he wrote. 'We have the physical force not they . . . What would their 100,000 men do with my hundred rockets wriggling their fiery tails among them, roaring, scorching, tearing and smashing all they came near?'[19] He was perfectly prepared to take extreme action to defend the state, though he had little time for its government. Sergeant Samuel Ancell of the 58th Regiment a veteran of the siege of Gibraltar, summed up his own allegiance in words reminiscent of those put by Shakespeare into Henry V's mouth, the night before Agincourt:

> Our King is answerable to God for us. I fight for him. My religion consists in a firelock, open touch-hole, good flint, well-rammed charge, and seventy rounds of powder and

ball. This is the military creed. Come, comrades, drink
success to British arms.[20]

Yet for all the royal iconography on its uniforms and royal interest
in its activities, the army belonged to the government and was controlled by Parliament. The Mutiny Act, first passed in 1689, established military law in time of peace, and was renewed annually. The
system of governing troops on active service by Articles of War issued
under the prerogative power of the crown continued, on an
occasional basis, even after 1689, but was finally superseded in 1803
by a revised form of Mutiny Act which made the Articles of War
statutory. From then until the passage of the Army Discipline and
Regulation Act in 1879 the Mutiny Act and Articles of War formed
the basis for army discipline. The principle of Parliamentary
supremacy was, however, firmly asserted. The Army Act, which
replaced the Army Discipline and Regulation Act in 1881, 'has of
itself no force, but requires to be brought into operation annually
by another act of Parliament . . . thus securing the constitutional
principle of the control of Parliament over the discipline requisite
for the government of the army.'[21]

Parliament also exercised control through the power of the purse.
Army Estimates were published annually, and passed by Parliament.
Central government spent little on areas like poor relief, public
health or the maintenance of roads, and defence accounted for a
high proportion of the money it did spend. In 1803, for example, of
a total government spend of £38,956,917, the regular army received
£8,935,753, the navy £10,211,373, the militia £2,889,976 and the
Ordnance £1,128,913. Subsidies to allied nations were also costly,
amounting to nearly 7.7 per cent of the Treasury's revenue in 1800.
Expenditure fell sharply in peacetime, and governments strove to
economise by disbanding regiments and laying up warships, sending
the officers of both home on half-pay.

There were complaints both inside and outside Parliament, about
the way this money was spent. During the French Revolutionary and
Napoleonic period criticism 'was concerned more with the manner
with which the war was waged than with doubts about the wisdom
of waging it.'[22] William Cobbett, sergeant-major of the 54th Regiment

turned radical politician, lambasted the Peninsular War in his *Weekly Political Register*, complaining that 'we do, indeed, cause some expense and some mortality to France, but we, at the same time, weaken ourselves in a degree tenfold to what we weaken her.'[23] Support for wars flagged when they dragged on, or seemed hard to relate to the national interest: the American War was generally unpopular by its close. Yet there was often the paradox that made casualties harden opinion in favour of war, as Greville acknowledged on 16 November 1854 when reporting the death of his brother's 'youngest and favourite' son, the eighteen-year old Lieutenant Cavendish Hubert Greville, Coldstream Guards, killed in his first battle at Inkerman. Grief-stricken, he wrote:

> But the nation is not only as warlike as ever, but if possible more full of ardour and enthusiasm, and thinking of nothing more than the most lavish expenditure of men and money to carry on the war; the blood that has been shed appears only to animate the people, and to urge them to fresh exertions.[24]

The problems of controlling the army and of its integration into the national framework were either solved directly, 'or by the more British method of procrastination and evasion.'[25] Despite a growing tendency towards centralisation, the high command of the army displayed a very British mixture of checks and balances, shot through with odd historical survivals and a whole host of offices, great and small, which played their part in a wider system of patronage characteristic of the age. Until the Act of Union with Ireland in 1801, there were two distinct armies, with an Irish establishment of 12,000 officers and men (15,325 from 1769), with its own commander-in-chief, paid, administered and commanded from Dublin Castle. Although there was also a commander-in-chief in Edinburgh, Scotland had lost its independence with the Act of Union in 1707, and this officer reported directly to his superiors in London.

LINE OF BATTLE

I F THE ARMY HAD A HEART, then this organ beat away, very steadily indeed, in Horse Guards in Whitehall, and the expression Horse Guards became synonymous for the army's high command. A spacious first-floor office, looking out across Horse Guards Parade to the trees, ponds and greensward of St James's Park, housed the commander-in-chief. The first recorded commander-in-chief was General George Monck, Duke of Albemarle, described as 'Captain General and Commander-in-chief of all Forces' in a commission issued in 1660, and the Duke of Marlborough held the office twice. Its importance decreased in mid-century, and the office was vacant from 1778 to 1793, when the 76-year old Jeffrey, Lord Amherst, was appointed to it with the title 'general on the staff'. He was so far past his best that even the deeply conservative General Sir David Dundas, author of the army's principal drillbook and himself commander-in-chief 1809–11 reckoned that he produced nothing but mischief.

It was only with the Duke of York's appointment in 1798 that the post recovered some of its earlier importance. However, its accession to the level of real authority suggested by its title was effectively blocked because of a typically British piece of constitutional evolution. The commander-in-chief's clerk, the secretary at war, had grown rapidly in status. Even in the late seventeenth century, he was an official of considerable importance and by 1688 he 'issued orders of almost every description for paying, mustering, quartering, marching, raising and disbanding troops, and also upon the various points of discipline, such as the attendance, duty and comparative rank of officers and regiments.'[26] In 1704, the post was held by a politician, the Tory Henry St John, later Viscount Bolingbroke. He dealt with the monarch on a regular basis, led on military matters in the cabinet, and spoke for the army in the House of Commons. And when one commanding officer wrote about the misconduct of officers direct to the prince consort, nominally com-mander-in-chief, he received a sharp reprimand from St John. Although not all St John's successors claimed such powers – or, more to the point, wielded such clout within their party – they were a key instrument in the exercise of parliamentary control.

The secretary at war, however, shared his influence on military affairs with the cabinet's two secretaries of state, whose responsibili-ties were divided geographically. In 1794 Pitt created a Secretary of State for War, adding responsibility for the colonies four years later. The first incumbent of the combined post was Pitt's associate Henry Dundas, later Viscount Melville, who held office until the change of ministry in 1801 and in 1806 was unsuccessfully impeached for misappropriation of public funds. Although the importance of the Secretary at War declined after the establishment of a Secretary of State for War and the Colonies, the post was not abolished but responsibilities were shared: thus while the Secretary of State for War and the Colonies controlled the overall size of the army, the Secretary at War was responsible for its finances and for the introduc-tion of the annual mutiny act.

The misfortunes of the British army in the Crimea provoked enormous popular and political discontent, in part because of the war reporting of William Howard Russell of *The Times.* He was a man of courage, humour and great personal charm: William Makepeace Thackeray remarked that he would give a guinea any day to have Russell sitting with him at dinner at the Garrick Club. He painted a grim (if not always objective) picture of the impact of administrative incompetence on the British soldier. Early in the campaign, before the Allies had even reached the Crimea, he told his readers that:

The men suffered exceedingly from cold. Some of them, officers as well as privates, had no beds to lie upon. None of the soldiers had more than their single regulation blanket ... The worst thing was the continued want of comforts for the sick. Many of the men labouring under diseases contracted at Malta were obliged to stay in camp in the cold, with only one blanket under them, as there was no provision for them at all at the temporary hospital.[27]

He later wrote of the British base at Balaclava that 'words could not describe its filth, its horrors, its hospitals, its burials, its dead and dying Turks, its crowded lanes, its noisome sheds, its beastly purlieus, or its decay . . .'[28] If Russell was subjective he was certainly not inventive: he told the truth. A medical officer also described the appalling conditions for the wounded, this time recalling the hospital at Varna.

No words can describe the state of the rooms when they were handed over for the use of the sick; indeed, they continued long after, from the utter inability to procure labour, rather to be fitted for the reception of cattle, than sick men. Myriads of rats disputed the possession of these dreadful dens, fleas were in such numbers that the sappers employed on fatigue refused to work in the almost vain attempt to clean them . . .[29]

In 1854, in response to the outcry inspired by Russell's articles, the government appointed a specific Secretary of State for War, the Duke of Newcastle. Newcastle's successor, Lord Panmure, combined the offices of Secretary of State for War and Secretary at War, paving the way for substantial reform. The Board of Ordnance was abolished and its military functions transferred to the commander-in-chief. Its civil functions went to the Secretary of State for War, whose War Department was now responsible for the whole of army administration, including the Commissariat and Medical departments. This reforming zeal soon lost its impetus, and in many areas it did not go far enough. But as far as the army's central administration was concerned, it had ended the worst abuses of the system that had prevailed throughout the age of horse and musket.

The paymaster general survived. Originally a subordinate official, he was primarily responsible for issuing money to regiments to pay the officers and men held on their strength. It had once been easy for commanding officers to maintain fictitious soldiers on their regiment's rolls by inventing spurious recruits known as 'widow's men' or by failing to report deaths, and in the early eighteenth century muster-rolls were approved by the commissary-general of the musters before being passed to the paymaster general for payment. These abuses had become rare by the mid-eighteenth century, but they undoubtedly continued. On 27 July 1778 John Peebles complained: 'I signed for an effective drummer that I know nothing about, the Col. caused him to be inserted.'[30] Just as the Secretary at War evolved from official to politician, so too did the paymaster general, and by the time of the American War he was a member of parliament who assisted the Secretary at War in drawing up the army estimates and shared his responsibility for the yearly parliamentary approval of accounts.

Yet if the paymaster general was eager to stamp out financial irregularities within the army, he was often able to reap the considerable rewards of his own office. Fees could be charged for making payments, and, as a parliamentary commission reported in 1781, the fact that the Treasury gave the paymaster general his money in bulk, often without scrutinising his demands, enabled him to make enormous sums on the interest. The paymaster general was able to continue to use the money after leaving office until his accounts were finally passed. Henry Fox resigned in 1765 but his accounts had still not been audited in 1780, enabling him to draw an income of £25,000 a year on the paymaster general's money.

The commander-in-chief was assisted by three senior officers. The adjutant general was responsible for personnel and the quartermaster general for the quartering and movement of troops. The military secretary, a civilian under Amherst, a field officer under the Duke of York and a general by the close of the period, initially dealt with the commander-in-chief's correspondence, but his routine involvement with patronage meant that he assumed responsibility for officers' careers. Lord FitzRoy Somerset, the future Lord Raglan, held the post from 1827 to 1852. He dealt with about fifty letters a day, on matters so varied as Major Champain's claims to be 'second lieutenant colonel' of the 9th Regiment, a plea (sadly unsuccessful) from Lieutenant W. I. B. Webb's mother for his reinstatement follow-ing cashiering for fraud; and the application (rather more fruitful) by 'a poor officer' of the 43rd for a post for his boy, 'a junior clerk in a public office'.[31] Although Somerset was affable and engaging, his was not an easy job, and his office was the scene of many a painful interview. Interestingly, when in 1837 Lieutenant General Sir Latimer Widdrington, who had failed to obtain the colonelcy of a regiment, protested to the Secretary at War that the military secre-tary and commander-in-chief had not treated him fairly, the Secre-tary at War replied that army patronage remained a matter for the commander-in-chief.

There was, though, one area where the commander-in-chief held no sway. The master-general of the ordnance commanded the ord-nance corps – officers and NCOs of the Royal Artillery, officers of the Royal Engineers and other ranks of the Royal Sappers and Miners – whose personnel were financed by a parliamentary vote distinct from that of the army of a whole, and whose separateness was empha-sised by its blue uniforms. The corps maintained its own medical department, paymaster-general and transport service. The civil side of the ordnance department supplied weapons and much equipment to army and navy alike, was responsible for defence works, barracks and military prisons, supervised the Royal Observatory at Greenwich, the Royal Military Academy at Woolwich, the Royal Laboratory and the Royal Carriage Works, and was charged (hence the Ordnance Survey) with military mapping.

The master general, generally a peer and a professional soldier, sometimes chaired the Board of Ordnance which met three times a week in summer and once in winter, in the ordnance office in Westminster, and later in Pall Mall. The Board of Ordnance – whose ambiguous initials BO were stencilled on a variety of equipment – responded to instructions issued by the king, privy council or one of the secretaries of state. The master-general often sat in the cabinet, providing the government with military advice. The board was jealous of its authority and notoriously 'obnoxious and obstructive'. It once took three years for the Board to organise transport to England for a company of artillery in the Bahamas. In the interim, knowing that the unit would be coming home, the Board thoughtfully provided it with no new clothing. Its dead hand lay even on matters as minor as fences at Woolwich.

> A fence happened to require repairs in front of the barracks, and its dangerous state was repeatedly pointed out by the Commandant. But not until years had passed and an officer had killed his horse, and broken his own collarbone, did any steps occur to the Board to remedy it. Even then, while they were brooding, accidents continued, coming to a climax one night when the Chaplain in walking home fell in and broke the principal ligament of his leg . . .[32]

Supply and transport were primarily the responsibility of the Treasury, and were in the hands of its officials, civilians holding appointments in the Commissariat, described by Wellington as 'gentlemen appointed to their office by the king's authority, although not holding his commission'. No qualifications were required of commissaries till 1810, and only in 1812 was an examination in English and arithmetic required. Although they were eventually uniformed, in sober blue, for many years they wore what suited them. Quasi-uniforms were popular, and one Peninsula commissary was unkindly described as wearing 'an hermaphrodite scarlet coat'. Some were admirable: Assistant Commissary Brooke was killed at Talavera leading an ammunition convoy to the front line, and Assistant Commissary Dalton was to win a Victoria Cross at Rorke's Drift in Zululand in 1879. Others were incompetent: Wellington complained that his commissariat was lamentable because 'the people who manage it are incapable of managing anything outside a counting house'. And many were dishonest. Deputy Assistant Commissary General Thomas Jolly was court-martialled (officials of the commissariat were subject to military law when on active service) and cashiered for embezzlement in Spain in 1814. In Dominica in 1796 Commissary General Valentine Jones was estimated to have made £9,789 17s 6d on a single fraudulent transaction. It required great honesty to resist the temptation offered to commissaries. Havilland Le Mesurier, a West India merchant ruined by the collapse of his trade in the French Revolutionary War, gained a commissary's post through his friendship with Pitt and was sent to establish a provision magazine at Bruges in 1793. He told his wife:

> I am obliged to fight venality and corruption through all ranks, and overcome my feelings every day by turning out men who have large families and who have been negligent or corrupt in their duty. To convince thee, my love, of the necessity for this rigorous discipline, I need only say that the day before yesterday a man had the audacity to mention that as I took so much trouble about his contract he could not do less than acknowledge it, and begged that I would accept a 100 Louis . . .[33]

He admitted that 'I did not kick him or knock him down,' but spoke so sharply as to 'prevent my being again insulted in the like manner'.

What irritated many soldiers was the Commissariat's insistence on a bureaucratic exactness seemingly at variance with the demands of the field. In 1854 Sergeant Timothy Gowing of 7th Royal Fusiliers was sent to Balaclava with a working party to draw blankets. After:

> trudging through mud for nine miles I presented my requisition to the Deputy-Assistant-Quartermaster-General, who informed me that it was not signed by the Quartermaster-General of the Division, and that I should not have an article until it was duly signed. I informed him that the men were dying daily for the want of blankets. He ordered me to be silent and . . . informed me he did not care – a correct return or no stores . . . I was ordered out like a dog.[34]

A military transport service was tried briefly in 1794, and in 1799 a Royal Wagon Train was raised for the campaign in Holland. By 1814 it numbered almost 2,000 men with their own wagons. The unit was unkindly known, from the colour of its coats and the supposed origin of many of its members, as 'The Newgate Blues', and in 1814 Commissary August Schaumann wrote scornfully of 'Fat General Hamilton . . . with his useless wagon corps.'[35] Yet it was not without its own remarkable achievements. At Waterloo, when the garrison of the crucial farm complex at Hougoumont, in Wellingon's right centre, was running short of ammunition, Private Joseph Brewster of the Royal Wagon Train drove a tumbril of ammunition down to the farm complex, under fire the whole way. Wellington regarded retention of Hougoumont as fundamental to his success, and Brewster's achievement can scarcely be over-rated.

Even when at its maximum strength, the Royal Wagon Train could not provide for all the army's transport requirements, and most draught and pack animals, carts and drivers were hired locally. In 1776–80 the British army in North America employed an average of 739 wagons, 1958 horses and 760 drivers, some of them procured in England as a result of a contract with a Mr Fitzherbert. Muleteers and ox-cart drivers were hired in the Peninsula, and followed the army like a comet's tail of disorder and dishonesty. The carts themselves had fixed wheels and rotating wooden axles, 'making the most horrible creaking sounds that can be imagined ... almost sufficient to make anyone within reach of the sounds pray to be divested of the sense of hearing.'[36]

The army's medical services plumbed the depths of administrative chaos. There was nothing approaching what would today be termed a medical corps. A physician-general and surgeon-general – both civilians with private practices in addition to their military duties – had existed since the time of Charles I, and an inspector-general of hospitals had been established in 1758. In 1794 an army medical board, on which these worthies sat, was set up, largely at the instigation of the Duke of York, in an effort to give more coherent direction to the medical services. Beneath them came the inspectors and deputy inspectors of hospitals, the physicians, surgeons and their mates who served in the hospitals, and the administrative officers who ran them. Each regiment had its surgeons and two mates, later termed assistant surgeons. In the eighteenth century they were essentially the colonel's employees, who purchased their positions, received an allowance collected by captains from their company funds, and were given a grant from which they were expected to purchase all their medical necessities.

Their status improved with reforms introduced after medical catastrophes in Holland in 1793–94. However, it was not until the more far-reaching reforms after the Crimean War that the army's medical services were put on a proper footing, with the creation of the Medical Staff Corps, forerunner of the Royal Army Medical Corps, in 1855. The keen but unqualified Sergeant Roger Lamb served periodically as assistant surgeon to the 9th and 23rd Regiments in the American War. Even the great James McGrigor, who became Wellington's surgeon-general and was to do so much to improve the medical services and the lot of those in their care, joined the 88th as a surgeon in 1793 without having completed his degree. Dr Hugh Moises declared that: 'I have known men who have served not many months behind the counter of a country apothecary . . . admitted to a regimental practice . . . Mere apprentice boys were appointed as surgeons and mates without exhibiting the proper testimonials of their knowledge or abilities.'[37] A London surgeon observed that military medicine was no place for 'a man of superior merit', who would 'soon abandon the employment for the more lucrative the more respectable and the less sordid work of private practice.'[38] It was not impossible to combine private practice and military employment: the London-based John Leslie remained surgeon to the 3rd Foot Guards until advancing age and a successful private practice persuaded him to resign.

The medical profession was dominated by physicians. It was not until 1754 that the Company of Surgeons at last severed its connection with the barbers, and only in 1800 that the Royal College of Surgeons was founded. Military doctors, whether physicians or surgeons, were poorly regarded: Moises complained that when the king reviewed his unit in 1788 'no surgeon was allowed to kiss his hand'. Things improved, albeit only slowly. In 1796 surgeons were given captain's status when quarters were allocated, their assistants became commissioned officers, ranking as lieutenants, and both were to be regularly paid and provided with medicines (though not their medical equipment) by the government. In 1798 it was ordered that physicians must hold a medical qualification, while assistant surgeons were required to pass a medical examination before being appointed. However, regulations accorded them 'no claims whatever to military command'. It was not until 1850 that medical officers were at last eligible for admission to the military division of the Order of the Bath. *The Lancet* believed this 'great triumph – for triumph it is – to be the greatest step ever made by our profession towards obtaining its just recognition by the state . . . It is the removal of a professional stigma.'[39] The low status of military doctors was mirrored by the limited resources placed at their disposal throughout the period. Many would have agreed with William Gibney, surgeon to the 15th Hussars at Waterloo, that many men died who might have been saved had time or resources been available. It was the hardest part of their job 'to be obliged to tell a dying soldier, who had served his king and country that day, that his case was hopeless.'[40]

Military surgeons, like commissaries, ran the whole gamut from the idle and incompetent to the zealous and committed. And most, as we shall see, were often so busy that they overlooked the obvious. In 1812 Lieutenant William Grattan of the 88th was helped to a field hospital by Dan Carsons, his batman, and the doctor only looked at the entry wound made by the musket-ball which had hit him. Carsons insisted that his officer should be turned over, and the doctor was able to extract a large piece of cloth from his coat, driven into his body by the bullet: 'The doctor looked confounded; Dan looked ferocious . . .'

Some doctors became so fond of the military life that they laid scalpel and bone-saw aside and took up combatant commissions. William Grattan (another member of the widely-branching Irish family) studied surgery in Dublin and became assistant surgeon of the 64th on the eve of its departure for the American War. While overseas he decided to become a combatant officer, and purchased an ensigncy and then a lieutenancy. In the words of the admiring Sergeant Roger Lamb, a fellow Irishman, he:

> lived with economy and frugality, and in the course of a few years, he purchased a company [captaincy]. Captain Grattan possessed a strong understanding, sound judgement, and deep penetration; these, with a perfect knowledge of his profession, made him an invaluable officer. He became the soul of his regiment, which he never exchanged for another. Merit like his could not be hid.[41]

Wounded in America, he died in Ireland during the rebellion of 1798, catching a chill after bathing in a cold river after a long hot ride. The adjutant of the 73rd at Waterloo was Ensign Patrick Hay who, as Sergeant Thomas Morris of his battalion observed, was 'a fine-spirited fellow who had been our regimental surgeon, but, through the interest of the colonel, exchanged to ensign and adjutant.' At Waterloo he saved one of the 73$^{rd's}$ companies from being cut off by French cuirassiers, shouting to its useless commander: 'Captain Robinson, what are you about? Are you going to murder your men?' He ordered the company back just in time for it to help the battalion form square.[42]

Many doctors shared the risks of the men they tended. Few did so as spectacularly as Surgeon William Bryden, seconded to Shah Shujah's medical services in Afghanistan, who accompanied the army on its retreat from Kabul in 1842:

> I with difficulty put my pony into a gallop, and, taking the bridle in my teeth, cut right and left with my sword as I went through them. They could not reach me with their knives . . . One man on a mound over the road had a gun, which he fired close down upon me and broke my sword, leaving about six inches in the handle. But I got clear of them, and then found that the shot had hit the poor pony, wounding him in the loins, and he could hardly carry me.[43]

Bryden was the only member of the entire force to reach safety in Jellalabad after cutting his way through the Afghans.

Without doubt the most remarkable medical officer of the age was James Miranda Barry, who entered the army as a hospital assistant in 1813, was appointed assistant surgeon two years later, and rose to become inspector-general of the Army Medical Department in 1858. It was only after Dr Barry's death in 1865 that it was discovered that she was a woman, who appeared to have given birth to a child: she had concealed her gender throughout her military service. While serving at the Cape she was described as the most skilled of physicians but the most wayward of men, and her quarrelsome temper had led her to fight a duel.

The theme of 'the female drummer', the woman who passes herself off as a man, was a familiar one in the period, and the song 'Polly Oliver' describes a girl who decided to 'list for a soldier and follow my love.' Very few women actually accomplished this feat in the British army (though the Russians had Nadezda Durova, who served in the Napoleonic Wars as 'Cornet Aleksandrov') but Barry's officer status would have given her far more privacy than a private soldier could have attained in barrack-room or bivouac.

The best-documented female soldier is Hannah Snell, who seems (though it is hard to separate fact from fiction) to have served four and a half years in the marines and been discharged in 1750. She subsequently made a living by appearing on the stage in her regimentals to perform arms drill, and selling buttons, garters and lace. The diarist Parson Woodford saw her at the White Hart, at Weston, near Norwich. He believed her assertion that she 'was 21 years as a common soldier in the Army, and was not discovered by any as a woman' and, kindly soul, 'took 4 pr of 4d buttons and gave her 0.2.6.'[44] As we shall see, women routinely accompanied the army and some were killed or died of illness or exposure. One of them, the wife of Sergeant Reston of the 94th Regiment, carried ammunition and supplies to the front line, at the siege of Matagorda Fort at Cadiz in 1810, and received no official recognition of her heroism despite the efforts of her regiment. But Mrs Reston made no attempt to conceal her gender, and Dr Barry's sustained achievement is all the more remarkable.

Lastly, the Home Office had a voice in military policy, for it controlled the non-regular forces of the crown until they were actually embodied into service and came under military command. The oldest reserve force was the militia, liable for limited training in peacetime and embodiment in grave emergency. Parish constables kept 'fair and true lists' of men between the ages of 18 and 45, and militiamen were selected from these rolls by ballot to serve for five years. County militia lists throw fascinating light on village society. In 1777, the village of Yardley Gobion in Northamptonshire listed four farmers and two farmers' sons, each dignified by 'Mr' in the roll, two bakers, two tailors, a butcher, a horse-dealer, a hog-dealer, five servants, two men who maintained (apparently unsuccessfully) that they had already performed militia service, and nine labourers. Seven men were exempted as unfit, among them William Holman, who was 'very near sighted', Thomas Bignall, 'very bow legged' and

William Robinson, who 'saith he has fits'. Literary consistency was not the constables' strong suit. Those of the Chipping Warden Hundred of Northamptonshire managed to spell Thorpe Mandeville, where appeals against listings were determined, as Thorp Mundville, Thrup Mandivil, Thrupmandeveill and Throp Mandevile.[45]

The militia was organised in county regiments, officered by gentlemen selected by the lords-lieutenant of those counties. Sometimes their martial zeal caused marital upset. In 1759 Lord Robert Manners, colonel of the Nottinghamshire Militia, told the Prime Minister, the Duke of Newcastle, that:

> Mr Martin Bird wants his name scratched off the Militia List, as his wife, on hearing he had taken a commission, was so affected that he thought she would have died! I suppose the Lady's condition will be sufficient plea with Your Grace to let the gentleman off.[46]

Because the militia was funded by the land-tax, country gentlemen had a proprietary interest in the force:

> For this reason they felt a pride in furnishing it with officers; and indeed the militia lists of the period are simply a catalogue of the names of the leading county families ... [Lords lieutenant] were to some extent petty Sovereigns, with the Militia for their army. They were attached to the force, frequently spent very large sums upon it, and easily grew to regard it as their own. The officers shared their views, and hence in many cases a regiment of Militia became a very exclusive country-club, with a just pride in itself which was not of little value.[47]

In February 1793, 19,000 militia were called out, but individuals were allowed to provide substitutes, and the demand for volunteers to act in this (relatively safe) capacity deprived the regular army of many potential recruits. Subsequent attempts to use the militia in direct support of the regular army – for instance by drafting the flank companies of militia regiments into battalions under the command of regular officers, granting regular commissions to militia officers who persuaded their men to volunteer for regular service (the so called 'raising for rank'), and finally by raising the Army of Reserve, whose members could be drafted into the regular army (conscription by any other name) – were deeply unpopular in the shires.

There was no militia in Scotland until 1797, not least because of the risk of distributing weapons to a society that had only recently been disarmed. In order to meet the demands of home defence during the Seven Years' War and American War, Fencible regiments were raised, composed of regulars enlisted for home service for the duration of the war. In 1793 nine new Fencible regiments were raised, and more followed. Lastly, although there had been a short-lived plan to raise volunteers for home defence in 1782, in April 1794 an Act of Parliament authorised the formation of Volunteer units which would be subject to military discipline and eligible for pay when called out.

An explosion of volunteering ensued: the five Associated Companies of St George's, Hanover Square, actually formed up before the act was passed. Lord Winchelsea's three troops of 'Gentlemen and Yeomanry of the County of Rutland' were the first units of the new Yeomanry Cavalry. The Yeomanry's home defence role was to be overtaken, in the nineteenth century, by a growing emphasis on the preservation of internal security in a struggle which often pitted town against country, Yeoman against worker. Volunteers and Yeoman who could produce a certificate of regular attendance at drills were exempted from service in the militia. There were repeated suggestions that the congenial part-time soldiering enjoyed by these worthies induced those who could afford it – for Volunteers and Yeoman had to provide some of their own necessities, and the latter required access to a horse – to join the Volunteers or Yeomanry in order to avoid the militia.

In a book whose chief concern is with the army's combatant teeth rather than its administrative tail I have little time to delve more deeply into the labyrinth. But a labyrinth it was, with dark corridors of boards and officials. The Board of General Officers, established in 1705, had some thirty members, of whom five constituted a quorum, met irregularly and reported to the king, through the secretary at war, on a wide range of issues such as misbehaviour, grievances and abuses. The Clothing Board agreed regulation patterns of uniform, approved contracts and examined the clothing supplied. The Board of Commissioners of Chelsea Hospital regulated the affairs of the hospital, a home for old soldiers known as 'in-pensioners', founded by Charles II. They decided who might be admitted to the hospital as in-pensioners, or, as 'out-pensioners', and who might receive an annual pension in lieu of residence at Chelsea.

The judge advocate general, a civilian appointed by letters patent under the great seal, was responsible for advising both monarch and commander-in-chief on the administration of military law, submitting the sentences of courts-martial with recommendations for confirmation or rejection. He attended some trials himself, sometimes as prosecutor but more usually to assist the court and to ensure that the law was obeyed. The apothecary general, another civilian, was responsible to the secretary at war, and supplied the army with medical and hospital stores.

At the start of the period this system worked ponderously, as one example shows.

> In 1758 Lieutenant General Bligh was selected to go on foreign service in command of a body of cavalry. Lord Barrington [secretary at war] first wrote to him, by command of the king, that he was appointed to that service. He then wrote to the Commissioners of the Treasury to tell them that five regiments of cavalry were to go on foreign service, that their lordships might give orders to the Victualling Board for a supply of bread and forage. He next sent orders to each regiment to hold themselves in readiness to embark. He then wrote to the Paymaster-General, signifying to him the King's pleasure, that he should issue subsistence to the men, and twelve months off-reckoning to the Colonels; and lastly, to the Apothecary-general, desiring him to send immediately a supply of medicines for the expedition.[48]

Had the detachment included artillery or engineers the Board of Ordnance would have required a separate approach, and getting the force to its destination would demand the co-operation of the Navy Board, which would furnish and, if necessary, escort the transports. It is small wonder that the historian Sir John Fortescue was to call the entire apparatus, characterised as it was by overlapping, duplication, and decentralisation, as 'a hopeless organisation for war'.

The army's fighting strength lay in its regiments of infantry and cavalry, self-contained enterprises with their own administrative and financial structures, which provided officers and soldiers with a focus for their loyalty: a small, compact, self-regarding world in which they lived and, all too often, died. The most senior were the Household troops, horse- and footguards. Most European armies maintained bodies of Household troops – Austria was a notable exception – in which birth and breeding were prized. Regiments of the Russian Guard maintained 3–4,000 supernumerary NCOs on their lists, all from the higher nobility, and the French *Maison du Roi* cavalry was entirely composed of noblemen.

British guards regiments, quartered in and around London, shared some of the characteristics of European Household troops with, as we have just seen, a close relationship with the royal family. They also enjoyed a rank-structure which ensured that guards officers ranked higher in the army than they did in their regiments. When John Aitchison of 3rd Foot Guards was promoted lieutenant on 22 November 1810 his commission granted him 'the rank of captain in our army,' and guards captains ranked as lieutenant colonels of the line. The three regiments of foot guards – the 1st (subsequently Grenadier) 2nd (Coldstream) and 3rd (later Scots Fusilier Guards and later still Scots Guards) – were officered by gentlemen but recruited from men who differed little from recruits into the remainder of the army. But in the eighteenth century the Household Cavalry still included units with gentlemen serving in their ranks, and whose corporals were commissioned officers. In 1760 the Life Guards comprised two troops of Horse Guards and two of Horse Grenadier Guards, and a full regiment of Royal Horse Guards Blue, or Blues for short. In 1788 the Horse Guards and Horse Grenadier Guards were restructured into two regiments, 1st and 2nd Life Guards: most of the gentlemen serving in their ranks were discharged, although some became officers in the new regiments. The three regiments of Household Cavalry – two of Life Guards and the Blues – retained a peculiar terminology for their NCO ranks, with their sergeants being styled 'corporal of horse' and sergeant-majors 'corporal major'.

There was never any doubt that the guards, regardless of military seniority and social standing, took their share of fighting. Although they did not serve in India, they fought in North America, the Peninsula, during the Hundred Days and in the Crimea, and certainly felt war's rough edge. The Hon John Rous, who joined the Coldstream Guards as a volunteer in Spain before being commissioned ensign in December 1812 cheerfully reported that 'I am bitten all over by fleas and bugs'. After Vitoria he told his mother that 'we went through some very severe work owing to the wet weather and not having any rations of biscuit; we were five days in arrears, but there were scarcely any grumbles amongst our men who seemed to be aware of the consequence of pushing on and the impossibility of the Commissariat department keeping up with us.' Yet he retained a young gentleman's sartorial aspirations, asking for 'two pairs of short boots with buckles at the sides (Kennett, 39 Silver Street, Golden Square) made some for me that I brought out and I believe he has my measure.'[49]

There were moments when guards officers' resolve to take their campaigning as comfortably as possible conflicted with a more austere high command. In 1813 when Wellington saw several guards officers using umbrellas he sent Lord Hill over with a message: 'Lord Wellington does not approve of the use of umbrellas during the enemy's firing, and will not allow the gentlemen's sons to make themselves ridiculous in the eyes of the army . . .' Yet there was no doubting the distinctive contribution the guards made to the battles of the era, as this account by Private Bancroft of the Grenadiers in which he describes the desperate fighting around the Sandbag Battery at Inkerman demonstrates:

> I bayoneted the first Russian in the chest: he fell dead. I was then stabbed in the mouth with great force, which caused me to stagger back, where I shot this second Russian and ran a third through. A fourth and fifth came at me and ran me through the right side. I fell but managed to run one through and brought him down. I stunned him by kicking him, whilst I was engaging my bayonet with another. Sergeant-Major Algar called out to me not to kick the man that was down, but being dead he was very troublesome to my legs; I was fighting over his body. I returned to the Battery and spat out my teeth: I found only two.[50]

The infantry and cavalry of the line formed the bulk of the army. Renumberings, the raising of new regiments which took the numbers of disbanded units and, in the cavalry, changes in terminology as fashionable lancers and hussars replaced the less fashionable light dragoons, make the charting of regimental lineage a science bordering on the occult, but the trends are clear. The army's establishment varied with the ebb and flow of national security. Junior, more recently-raised regiments faced disbandment with the onset of peace, with their officers sent on half-pay and their soldiers discharged or sent to strengthen regiments that were to be retained.

Enterprising officers who sought long-term careers strove to obtain commissions in senior regiments. Conversely, in 1763, James Boswell, lobbying as persistently as unsuccessfully for a commission in the London-based guards, told Lord Eglinton that he would not 'catch at any string'. Any other commission, which might involve posting to some distant garrison, would be 'a rope wherewith to hang myself; except you can get me one that is to be broke [eg disbanded], and then I am not forced from London.'[51] In contrast, his friend Captain the Hon Andrew Erskine, who wanted to serve on, had the bad luck to hold a commission in the 71st, disbanded that year along with all regiments junior to the 70th: he remained on half-pay till 1765.

In 1783, as the American war ended, the 106th Foot was transferred to the Irish establishment (where the authorised strength of units was much lower and their cost, in consequence, smaller), and a dozen regiments of foot were disbanded: another ten followed the next year. There was no blood-letting on quite this scale after the Napoleonic wars. In 1817 ten infantry regiments were disbanded, but there were still 95 on the establishment on George III's death in 1820, and 100 on William IV's death in 1837. The cavalry was no less vulnerable to peacetime economies: four regiments of light dragoons were disbanded in 1783 and in 1818–19 three more regiments of light dragoons and one of lancers followed suit.

Infantry regiments were generally raised with a single battalion, although most obtained further battalions subsequently. The practice of raising second and subsequent battalions was unusual at the start of the period, but 1st Foot Guards and the 1st Foot or Royal

Regiment (later the Royal Scots) had two battalions. Second battalions were either taken into the line as regiments in their own right, or disbanded altogether. In 1755–6, for instance, fifteen regiments were authorised to raise second battalions, but in 1758 these became the 61st to 75th Foot. Extra battalions were raised on a large scale during the French Revolutionary and Napoleonic Wars. The 60th Foot (Royal Americans) was granted a 5th Battalion on 30 December 1797 'to enable His Majesty to Grant Commissions to a certain number of foreign Protestants who have served abroad as Officers or Engineers,' and in 1809 it boasted seven battalions. The post-Waterloo reductions took their toll of junior battalions, leaving the regimental structure largely intact, but vexing officers in second battalions of senior regiments, many of whom found themselves shunted off on half-pay while their comrades in the first battalions of junior regiments soldiered on.

In contrast to continental practice, where the different battalions of a single regiment usually served together, it was uncommon for the battalions of a British regiment to find themselves side by side, and they were generally treated as if they were separate units. There were of course exceptions. The practice of keeping Guards units together on active service meant that at Waterloo, for instance, 2/1st and 3/1st Guards fought side by side in Maitland's Brigade. Both battalions of the 42nd served together in North America during the Seven Years War. Two battalions of 7th Royal Fusiliers and two of the 48th fought at Albuera in 1811. At the end of that dreadful day Houghton's brigade was commanded by Captain Cimtière of the 48th, a French émigré commisioned from the ranks in 1794, and 1/48th was commanded by a lieutenant.

A regiment was headed by its colonel, and until 1751, when the official numbering of regiments was introduced, bore his name as its title and might carry a badge from his armorial bearings on his colours, harking back to the days of the English Civil War when, for example, Sir Bevil Grenvile's fine regiment of Cornish foot wore the blue and silver of the family livery and carried his griffin badge on its colours. The colonel of the regiment, perversely, was usually not a colonel at all, but a general officer for whom the colonelcy represented not simply a personal honour but the opportunity to wield patronage and make money into the bargain. However, for most of the period, despite the occasional nod to political interest, officers appointed to colonelcies were men of experience and probity.[52]

George III himself told General William Picton, brother of the better-known Sir Thomas, and entirely lacking in influence or powerful friends, that for his appointment as colonel of the 12th Foot 'you are entirely obliged to Captain Picton, who commanded the grenadier company of the 12th Regiment in Germany [during the Seven Years' War].'[53] Picton held the post for 32 years, but still fell short of the record set by the 1st Marquess of Drogheda, colonel of the 18th Light Dragoons from 1759 until its disbandment, as part of the post-Waterloo reductions, in 1821. It was unusual for a colonel to resign voluntarily, but the 2nd Duke of Northumberland gave up the colonelcy of the Royal Horse Guards in 1812 when the Duke of York refused to give him a free hand in the appointment and promotion of its officers. Only one colonel was dismissed, the unlucky John Whitelocke of the 89th Regiment, because his sentence of cashiering, imposed when he was court-martialled after the Buenos Aires fiasco, debarred him from serving in any military capacity whatever.

However, there were increasing complaints about the quality of colonels and the growth of political influence. In 1842 an officer wisely using the pseudonym of Colonel Firebrace wrote that:

> Last year, there was a considerable distemper amongst the generals of Cavalry; regiments became vacant so rapidly that they were obliged to hunt in all forgotten nooks and corners for officers who might by chance have been in the cavalry forty years ago, in order to bestow on them nine hundred pounds a year. In such a scarcity of deserving cavaliers, I should like to know why a deserving General Officer of Infantry might not be trusted with a regiment of dragoons?[54]

In 1861 there was a fierce dispute in the military press when Major General Morton Eden (of rapid promotion but allegedly limited capacity) was appointed to a colonelcy. The editor of the *United Services Magazine* declined to argue *ad hominem*, but observed that:

> The subject has been treated as if the whole power of filling up these colonelcies and the whole responsibility were vested in the General Commanding-in-Chief . . . The fact is that . . . the Ministry of the day now has a preponderant voice in the disposal of them, exercised through their colleague, the Minister for War; and we shall generally find that when an objectionable one is made, the fortunate officer possesses a strong Ministerial connection. The family of the recipient on this occasion has long been conspicuous for its faithful alliance with the party now in power, and has thus obtained such a lion's share of good things that its members have come to be described, in a general way, as being born in the garden of Eden.[55]

In some continental armies the colonel was literally the proprietor of his regiment, and 'he owned the regiment as a whole in much the same way that the captains owned the individual companies' but in the British service his powers were more limited.[56] Nevertheless, they remained considerable. His interest was crucial in obtaining a commission, especially for a man who lacked the funds to purchase one, as young Boswell admitted to Lady Northumberland. 'You know, Madam,' he said, 'that there is a delicacy in talking to a colonel when a man is not to purchase, as he gets the profits of commissions that are sold.' The countess observed that purchase was a more certain avenue to a commission, but Boswell lamented that 'my father is rather averse to the scheme and would not advance the money.'[57] A colonel with influence, or whose judgement the king respected, was 'easily able to advance the careers of able officers in the regiment of which he held the command.' This was far more important than it might seem, especially, as we shall see later, because non-purchase appointments were far more common, especially in wartime, than is often supposed.[58]

A good colonel could play patronage like a musical instrument. Lieutenant General Sir Adolphus Oughton was appointed colonel of the 31st Foot in 1762. He had married Mary Dalrymple, widow of a dragoon captain, in 1755, and duly looked after the interests of her brother John Ross, who followed in his slip-stream. His step-son, Hew Dalrymple, became an ensign in the 31st at the age of 13 while still at school, and went on to become a general. Dalrymple was knighted as a major, gaining the honour by standing proxy for his step-father when he was installed as a Knight Companion of the Bath in 1779. Oughton was known by contemporaries to look after his regiment well by ensuring that promotions did not go to outsiders. In December 1774 Lieutenant John Barker of the 4th (King's Own) Regiment wrote:

> This evening died Captain [Gabriel] Maturin of the 31st Regt ... it's reported Lt Rook of the King's Own ... is recommended for the Company but I don't think it probable that he will succeed, as Genl. Oughton is a man of too good interest to allow that in his Regiment.

He was absolutely right. The three captains' vacancies arising in the 31st that year were all filled from within the regiment. One of the new captains was Charles Green, son of Lieutenant Christopher Green, a commissioned ranker who had been killed serving as Oughton's adjutant at Minden, where Oughton had commanded the 37th.[59]

The colonel was responsible for his regiment's clothing, apart from great-coats, which were supplied by the Ordnance, and received a government grant to purchase it. There were repeated assertions that colonels skimped on uniforms – for example by buying poor-quality cloth which shrank dramatically – and in 1798 the *Morning Chronicle* suggested that a colonel could make between £400 and £800 a year on his regiment's clothing, and recommended that it should be provided by the government. Colonels were paid: when their pay was abolished in 1856 it amounted to £900 a year in the cavalry and £600 in the infantry. Until the late eighteenth century the colonel theoretically commanded one of the companies in his regiment, and drew a captain's pay for doing so, although the work was actually done by an officer holding the hybrid rank of captain-lieutenant, who ranked as his regiment's junior captain. Before condemning the system as yet another example of jobbery, we should remember that unless they were employed in field command or the governorship of a fortress or colony, generals received no pay apart from the pay or half-pay of their regimental rank, and a colonelcy was often the only recompense that could be given a general in peacetime.

The colonel appointed a regimental agent, who acted under authority of his power of attorney. In 1811 the agent's functions were described as:

> To ask, demand and receive of and from . . . the Paymaster-General for the time being, all such sum or sums of money as now or may hereafter become due and payable unto me or the aforesaid regiment under my command, as well officers as soldiers thereof, either for pay, off-reckonings, arrears allowances or any other account whatsoever; and also to contract for the clothing, accoutrements, etc, of the said Regiment . . . and to do and to execute all and every other matter, act or lawful thing needful and necessary to be done in or about the premises . . .[60]

The pay office issued the agent monthly, in advance, with sufficient money for pay and subsistence for all ranks. The agent made deductions from this to defray his expenses and retain a contingency fund. The bulk of the residue ('off-reckonings') went to captains to pay their companies, and the balance ('net-reckonings') formed the clothing fund. The colonel pocketed the money left once the clothing bills were paid.

However, by the beginning of the nineteenth century probably few colonels made much of a profit from their regiments. A colonel who took his regiment's welfare seriously, as many did, could spend large sums of his own money on it. On 10 April 1762 the genial Marquis of Granby, colonel of the Royal Foresters (a regiment of light dragoons raised in the Seven Years' War) happily paid £105 5s 6d for dinner for the whole regiment in the Half Moon Inn at Hertford. Later, Wellington reckoned that the colonelcy of the 33rd Foot actually cost him money, while Sir Thomas Graham spent some £10,000 of his personal fortune raising the 90th Perthshire Volunteers in 1794. Graham had been travelling back through France from a Mediterranean tour on which his young and beautiful wife had died when French Revolutionaries, searching for concealed arms, broke open her sealed coffin. Shocked and infuriated, he not only raised a good regiment but took, late in life, to the profession of arms, becoming a general and a peer. In 1823 Lieutenant General the Hon Sir Alexander Hope's agents reckoned that he should make an annual profit of £1,200 on the regimental clothing account of the 47th Regiment but regretted to inform him that in fact he was heavily overdrawn.

There were fifteen army agents in 1831 but only three by 1878, with the business dominated by Cox and Co. A French observer, Francois Dupin, described the agent as 'the man of business and banker of all the officers whose personal interests, both public and private, are attended to by him.'[61] Agents sent cheques to officers on half-pay, claimed and distributed prize money, remitted funds to officers abroad and looked after their business at home. They sought to match vacancies to applicants for commissioning or promotion, and often lent money to officers or their relatives to enable them to buy commissions.

These loans were not always repaid promptly. In 1813 Cox's reminded Brigadier John Murray that it was still owed £800 borrowed by his father to purchase the son's promotion to major in the 108th Regiment in 1795. But it was not until 1822, twenty-seven years after the original debt, that the now Major General John Murray at last settled up, inducing the grateful agent to thank him for: 'taking upon yourself the discharge of so large a sum which would otherwise have been lost to our house.'[62] For junior serving officers, though, the mailed fist lurked inside the velvet glove. Paymaster J. S. Derby of the 2nd Foot was warned that: 'Unless some arrangement be forthwith made for our reimbursement, a representation will be made to the Commanding Officer on the subject, but we shall be glad to be relieved from so painful an alternative.'[63]

The task of commanding the regiment devolved on its commanding officer, the lieutenant colonel, whose title derives from the fact that he was the colonel's 'place-taker', just as, at a lower level, the lieutenant might deputise for the captain of his company. Cavalry regiments and single battalion infantry regiments usually held two lieutenant colonels on their establishment, though only one generally served with the regiment at any one time. Thus Richard Pattoun, junior lieutenant colonel of the 32nd Foot was killed commanding it in the storming of the Sikh fortress of Multan in January 1849, while his senior, Frederick Markham, was commanding a brigade elsewhere. There were inevitably exceptions, and the 16th Lancers had no fewer than four lieutenant colonels on its books in 1833, one of whom had not served with the regiment in living memory. Sickness and battle casualties often led to the command of a regiment ending in comparatively junior hands. After the Peninsular battle of Barossa in 1811 the 28th Regiment had only two officers left on their feet at the end of the day. That evening the junior of them, acting as vice-president of their two-man mess, proposed the loyal toast with the words 'The King, Mr President,' since the traditional toast of 'Gentlemen, the King' would clearly have been inappropriate.

Although establishments varied throughout the period, an infantry battalion generally comprised eight battalion companies, known as 'hatmen' in the eighteenth century because their tricorne hats set them apart from the 'light bobs' of the light company and the 'tow-rows' of the grenadier company, who initially wore a low 'jockey' cap and a taller bearskin cap respectively. When these distinctive head-dresses disappeared with the adoption of the shako in the early nineteenth century the flank companies showed their status by wearing coloured shako pom-poms, white for the grenadiers and green for the light company, with shoulder wings for all ranks. It was common practice to take flank companies from their parent battalions and combine them into grenadier or light battalions. On 14 May 1776 Howe created two battalions of grenadiers and two of light infantry, each containing nine or ten companies. John Peebles became adjutant of a grenadier battalion in 1777, and at once took pains to remedy slovenliness: 'Orders for a more frequent Visitation of the Mens Quarters. A Subn per Compy should at least visit the Barrack thereof 5 or 6 times a day to fulfil the orders . . .'[64]

At Waterloo, the farm complex of Hougoumont was held by light companies from 2/ and 3/1st Guards, 2/Coldstream Guards and 2/3rd Guards. The defence of the farm was entrusted to Lieutenant Colonel James Macdonell of the Coldstream. Private Richard MacLaurence of the Coldstream light company, saw how reinforcements sent down during the battle found the lure of plunder irresistible.

> No sooner were the Guardsmen fairly within the chateau
> gardens than the temptingly ripe cherries drew their atten-

tion and the soldiers were to be seen plucking them off
the wall trees by handfuls, quite regardless of the shot and
shells which were incessantly pouring in amongst them.
'You scoundrels!' roared out Major [sic] James Macdonell.
'If I survive this day, I will punish you all.'[65]

In battalion headquarters were the lieutenant colonel and two
majors, each of whom might command half the battalion if it was
divided into two 'wings'. The adjutant, an ensign or lieutenant acting
as the commanding officer's personal staff officer, had a particular
responsibility for drill and discipline, and was often commissioned
from the ranks, for an ex-sergeant major generally had a better grip
of the intricacies of the drill-book than a young officer. A good
adjutant could be expected to give the commanding officer a helping
hand where the complexities of drill were concerned. Lieutenant
Colonel Frederick Sherwell, who commanded the 8th Hussars at Balaclava, lost track of the right word of command while trying to lead
his regiment from the Russian guns as the Light Brigade ebbed back
after its charge. Private William Pennington remembered how:

> Colonel Sherwell shouted, 'Threes about!' There was some
> hesitation shown, for the withered ranks had kept together
> well, but lost their count by threes. His able subordinate
> [Lieutenant Edward] Seager interposed, 'Excuse me, sir,
> 'tis right about wheel.' The Colonel then cried: '8th right
> about wheel.' The regiment responded as if on home
> parade . . .[66]

The quartermaster, responsible for supplying the battalion with all
its requisites from ammunition and accommodation to food and
fuel, was always an ex-ranker: for most of this period held the commissioned appointment of quartermaster, and was eventually granting formal rank – as in lieutenant and quartermaster. Quartermasters
were not regarded as combatant officers. William Surtees, who spent
most of his long career in the Rifle Brigade, having started in the
56th Regiment, was ordered by his commanding officer not to go
into action 'except for the purpose of bringing ammunition, etc,
and when my duty required me.'[67] However, the post was anything
but risk-free, as Surtees testifies: 'Early in the action [at Barossa in

1811] my horse was killed, being shot in the head, which ball, had the head not stopped it, would in all probability have entered my body.'[68] Quartermasters then cut little ice outside their own departments. Surtees saw a French soldier captured on the Bidossa:

> Poor fellow, he came out sloping his shoulders, and, putting on a most beseeching look, begged we would spare him, as he was only a 'pauvre Italian.' Of course no injury was done him, but his knapsack was immediately taken. I thought it cruel, and would have prevented it, had my voice been of any weight.[69]

The regiment had a surgeon, ranking as a captain, and two assistants, who ranked as lieutenants. Surgeons might be appointed with or without purchase: James McGrigor, Wellington's surgeon-general in the Peninsula, paid £150 for a surgeon's commission in the 88th Regiment in 1793. At the Duke of York's insistence surgeons dressed in a modified version of regimental uniform, scarlet for the army as a whole and blue for the light dragoons, but there remained exceptions. When McGrigor transferred to the Blues at Canterbury in 1804 he was required to dress in the full splendour of a heavy cavalry officer:

> I burst into laughter at my own appearance, equipped as I was with a broad buff belt, jack boots that came high up my thighs, stout leather gloves which reached nearly to my elbows, with a large, fierce looking cocked hat, and a sword of great weight as well as length.[70]

He was luckier than Douglas Arthur Reid, who was appointed an Acting Assistant Surgeon on the staff in 1854 and provided himself with scarlet full dress, blue undress and an assortment of accoutrements. Less than six weeks later he was posted to the 90th Light Infantry, then in Crimea, and discovered that he needed a completely new uniform, together with 'portable bed and bedding, bullock trunks, water-proof rug, canteen supply of warm clothing and a Dean and Adams revolver . . . The bill for all this was a heavy one, and my pay was only 7s and 6d a day. It took quite a year's pay to clear me of debt.'[71]

Cavalry regiments, from 1796 onwards, were entitled to a veterin-

Wellington sat to Goya in Madrid in 1812, after his victory at Salamanca, and his face shows something of the strain of campaigning. Orders and decorations were added subsequently: Wellington usually dressed simply in the field.

ABOVE George II took his military duties seriously, and was the last British monarch to command his army in person, at Dettingen in 1743. He cut a rather less stylish figure than this formal painting suggests, as his horse ran away with him and he spent most of the day on foot.

LEFT George's second son, William Augustus, Duke of Cumberland, had a patchy military record. Wounded at Dettingen, he was beaten at Fontenoy in 1745, defeated the Jacobites at Culloden in 1746, and retired from active service after concluding an ignominious convention with the French in 1757.

General Sir Henry Clinton succeeded Howe in command of the British army in North America in 1778. He developed the strategy for campaigning in the South, and took Charleston in May 1780, but then returned to New York. His subordinate Cornwallis surrendered at Yorktown in October 1781. After resigning his command, Clinton fought vigorously in defence of his reputation.

ABOVE Lieutenant General 'Gentleman Johnny' Burgoyne made his reputation as a dashing leader of light cavalry, and was a man about town and talented playwright. In 1777, he led a column from Canada into the rebellious colonies, but receiving no assistance from Howe, his commander in chief, he was forced to surrender at Saratoga. John Fox Burgoyne, one of his four illegitimate children, later became a field marshal.

LEFT This glorious painting by Reynolds catches the flair of Colonel Banastre Tarleton, who raised and commanded the British Legion of American loyalists and was an outstanding (if controversial) leader of irregular light troops. He is wearing the fur-crested helmet named after him, which was sported by light dragoons, Royal Horse Artillery and many Yeomanry units.

Lieutenant General Sir John Moore was commissioned into the 51st Foot in 1776 and not only campaigned widely but represented a family borough in Parliament. In 1803, he commanded a brigade at Shorncliffe and did much to develop the training of British light troops. Given command in Spain, he retreated before superior French forces and was mortally wounded covering the evacuation from Corunna in 1809.

BELOW The Marquess of Anglesey was a talented cavalry commander who, when Lord Paget, beat the French at Benavente and Sahagun. Unfortunately he ran off with Wellington's sister-in-law, and could not be re-employed in the Peninsula. As Lord Uxbridge he lost a leg at Waterloo.

TOP LEFT A private of the 60th Foot in 1758, wearing the tricorne hat and long red coat so characteristic of the British infantryman of the second half of the eighteenth century.

LEFT The 60th Foot raised numerous battalions, some of them comprising riflemen like this soldier of about 1812. He wears a uniform of dark green with the bugle-horn badge favoured by light troops, and is priming his Baker rifle.

ABOVE A member of the light company of the Bethnal Green Volunteers, c.1799.

ABOVE A private of the 7th (Queen's Own) Hussars in 1813, brandishing his 1796 pattern light cavalry sword, with a Paget carbine hanging from his crossbelt.

ABOVE RIGHT Officer and private, 52nd Light Infantry, 1814. Light infantry retained the 1800 pattern stovepipe shako after line regiments had adopted the 'Belgic' shako with its false front from 1812. Officers of the 52nd carried a stirrup-hilted sabre.

RIGHT An ensign of the 9th (East Norfolk) Regiment carrying the Regimental colour, partly furled to make it more manageable. His covering colour sergeant is armed with the half-pike carried by sergeants of battalion companies.

Amphibiosity in action: Wolfe's landing at Quebec, 1759.

Lexington Common 1775: an American view of the British line.

The surrender at Yorktown, 1781. Ceremonies like this were often elaborately choreographed. Here, the defeated British march on armed, pause to ground arms (*centre*) and march off as prisoners. Their bands played the popular tune 'The World Turned Upside Down', an expression of the genuine shock of this capitulation.

BELOW Albuera (1811) was one of the most vicious battles of the Peninsular War. Elizabeth Butler's romantic painting shows the drummers of 1/57th, their coats in the regiment's yellow facing colour, under fire. But it does not depict the sheer ferocity of musketry which killed both ensigns, riddled the colours, and left the battalion with 61 per cent casualties and the nickname Diehards.

ary surgeon apiece. It was initially intended that commanding officers who were unable to find a vet should send a farrier-sergeant to the Royal Veterinary College for further training. It soon became clear that this would not work, and from September 1796 veterinary surgeons received the king's commission and seven shillings a day, and the improvement in both pay and status made it much easier for suitable candidates to be found.

In the eighteenth century regiments were authorised to have chaplains, holding the monarch's commission but, like surgeons at that time, paid regimentally. At the beginning of the century the system worked well, and attracted some men of real merit, like Marlborough's chaplain Dr Francis Hare and his contemporary the diarist Chaplain Noyes. There were some admirable chaplains in the American war. The plucky Lady Harriet Acland accompanied her husband Major John Acland, who commanded the grenadiers of Burgoyne's advance guard. When their pet Newfoundland dog upset a table, knocking over a candle which burnt their tent and all their belongings: 'It altered neither the resolution nor the cheerfulness of Lady Harriet.' And when he was seriously wounded and captured she crossed the American lines to join him, with Mr Brudenell, chaplain to the artillery, accompanying her to arrange the passage of the sentries. They came close to being shot, but Brudenell duly delivered Lady Harriet to her wounded husband.

But chaplains were already becoming scarcer. Only one clergyman could be found to accompany the 1793 Netherlands expedition; none at all to go to the notoriously unhealthy West Indies with Sir Ralph Abercromby in 1795; and in the following year the Reverend Peter Vataas of the 14th Light Dragoons had been on unpaid leave for 52 years. In 1796 regimental chaplains were abolished, and a Chaplain's Department was set up under the energetic John Gamble. General chaplains were attached to troops in foreign garrisons or the field, whilst at home selected civilian clergymen in garrison towns were given £25 a year to perform divine service for regiments.

Despite the fact that their pay steadily improved – in 1808 it was 16/- a day, the same as that of a major in the infantry – there was a shortage of chaplains throughout the Peninsular War, and some of those that did appear were of poor quality. William Wheeler of the 51st, wounded as a corporal in 1814, lamented that in his hospital there was 'no minister of religion to cheer the dying sinner'. He went on to complain that:

> It is true that there are chaplains with the army who some-times perform divine service, but of what use are they, the service they perform has no effect, for their mode of living do not agree with the doctrine they preach. I have often heard the remark 'That a Chaplain is no more use to the army than a town pump without a handle.' If these Reverend Gentlemen were stationed at the sick depots and made to attend the hospitals, they would be much more usefully employed than following the army with their brace of dogs and gun, running down hares and shooting partridges etc.[72]

There were honourable exceptions. When the Reverend John Owen was warned that if he persisted in moving up with the advancing troops he would undoubtedly be killed, that steadfast gentleman replied: 'My primary duty is now to those departing this life.'[73] Happily he survived, and in 1810 succeeded Gamble as chaplain general. Mr Heywood, chaplain at Cadiz, was a notorious hypochondriac, but he rose to the occasion when the devout Sir Thomas Graham, who had arrived late for service, asked him to repeat it, remarking: 'few divines have enjoyed like myself, the satisfaction of having their sermons encored.'[74] A chaplain who preached to the Light Division in 1811 cut a poor figure by riding up on a thin, ungroomed pony, with his vestments and prayer books on the back of a mule. 'This spiritual comforter,' wrote an officer, 'was the least calculated of any that I ever saw to excite devotion in the minds of men who had seen nothing in the shape of a divine for a year or two.'[75]

The brightest star in the ecclesiastical firmament was the Reverend Samuel Briscall, fellow of Brasenose College, Oxford, who arrived in Portugal in 1808. He had a rude introduction to soldiering: 'My second night, we had thunder and lightning and torrents of rain. I and my poor blanket were in a completely soaked condition, but I suffered nothing. In this state I have done nothing but read prayers to the wounded, for Sunday is as much a marching day as any other.' However, when he reached Lisbon he reported that 'the custom of turning out into the street for a certain necessary purpose has been of serious consequence to me, for in my great bustle and confusion I made use of some paper in which I had wrapped a £20 note, and the note is lost to me, for ever I suppose.'[76] Briscall was described by Wellington as 'an excellent young man'. He spent a year on sick leave in England, and when he returned in 1813 Francis Seymour Larpent, Wellington's judge-advocate general, attended his first service which was 'short, plainly read, but tolerably well: the sermon homely and familiar, but good for the troops, I think but fair and useful for anyone.'[77] Briscall was appointed Wellington's domestic chaplain in 1814, but although Wellington was meticulous in attending his services, he warned: 'Briscall, say as much as you like in five and twenty minutes. I shall not stay longer.'[78]

Briscall served at Waterloo (the Duchess of Richmond described him as Brixall on the list for her pre-battle ball) and was curate of Strafield Saye, a post in Wellington's gift, from 1816 to 1836. He was anything but a prude, writing from Vizen in 1810 that:

> There is a convent to which I sometimes resort here, but it is crowded with the lads of the army . . . When no one is there Colonel Fuller of the Coldstream and myself go in a quiet way and sit by the grating, where a very pretty girl does the favour to sing and talk . . . She is the daughter of a woman of rank by a *clerigo*, who being a very clever man has educated her very well. She is not to come out except to be married or perhaps she would accept an establishment for she is rather frisky . . . If you saw me at one side of the gate and Antonia at the other you would think we were lovers, but no such thing. I shall never be in love again: the widow has done my business![79]

Wellington continually pressed to be sent more 'respectable and efficient clergymen,' fearing that Methodism was spreading steadily in the army. On 6 February 1811 he warned Major General Calvert that: 'The meeting of soldiers in their cantonments to sing psalms, or hear a sermon read by one of their comrades is, in the abstract, perfectly innocent; and it is a better way of spending their time than the many others to which they are addicted; but it may become otherwise . . .'[80] He feared that discipline could become subverted, and soldiers might soon be exhorting their officers to lead more virtuous lives. There were indeed soldiers who disliked the close association between the established church and military authority, and who, despite their own religious sentiments, resented the formality of church parades. The literate and observant Private Robert Waterfield of the 32nd Foot wrote from India in 1848, in terms that confirm Wellington's fears.

> I will leave it to any thinking person to describe what benefit there can be derived to the course of religion as morality, by marching men to church (if there is such a place in the station) once a week to hear prayers read, and perhaps a sermon preached, when it is well known to the men that neither the officers, nor nine out of ten of the clergymen in India, practices what the one listens to and the other preaches. And again, if there is not a clergyman, or a church, within the station, the reading of the service devolves on the commanding officer. Why, it is a mockery, and an insult to the Almighty, to allow a man to come forward to mock his name by calling upon him to send his blessing upon them and their hearers, when perhaps not five minutes before that the same man was damning his men, now his congregation to all intents and purposes, and himself, suffering from his last night's debauchery.[81]

Sergeant John Pearman of the 3rd Light Dragoons, serving in India at the same time, largely shared Waterfield's opinion.

> And the thing I was very sorry to see oftimes when out on night patrol in the officers' lines and in our barracks we would come across our parson dead drunk. We would have him carried to his bungalow or dwelling house. The blacks would laugh and say as they carried him back to his bungalow . . . 'White man's padre very good man and very nice lady.' She was very pretty and fond of life, and this couple never missed a dance or spree at the officers' mess . . . At length he was sent to another station, and we got an old Parson, a very good man, a Mr Whitehead. The men were very fond of him as he would sit in the hospital

for hours with the sick and pray with them and never find
any fault with our ways, only exhort us to pray to God.[82]

The recruitment of chaplains improved after the Napoleonic wars,
especially after Roman Catholic chaplains were appointed after 1836.
These gentlemen did not simply meet the spiritual needs of an army
that had long had substantial numbers of Roman Catholics in its ranks,
but were often welcomed by those who did not share their religious
views. Nurse Sarah Anne Terrot wrote of the Crimea that:

> We had only one chaplain belonging to the Church of
> England with the General Hospital. [Hospital Assistant]
> Sam [Gammon] admired the devotion of the Roman Cath-
> olic priests, though regarding the value of their minis-
> trations with strong Protestant feeling. They were more
> numerous than our chaplains, and seemed very zealous
> in the discharge of their duties, grave and polite to us.
> They used to bow and say 'God Bless you' to us in passing
> in the passages and wards, which I felt very kind, and
> unlike the conduct of the Roman ecclesiastics I had met
> . . . in England.[83]

Yet despite attempts to give each unit its own chaplain, there were
often too few to go round. On occasion this did not matter unduly:
at one mass burial in Spain an infantry officer stepped forward and
recited the burial service from memory. In the Indian Mutiny, the
Reverend John Edward Wharton Rotton was one of few chaplains
to the British force on Delhi Ridge, with fourteen hospitals to visit
'in all weathers and at all times of the day and night'. He wrote
admiringly of his counterpart:

> Father Bernard, a pattern Roman Catholic priest, whose
> services have been justly recognised – not by the Govern-
> ment, perhaps; for judging by its acts, the clergy, and
> particularly the self-denying portion of it belonging to the
> Roman Catholic church, seems to have been regarded as
> a necessary inconvenience; but by his own Vicar Apostolic,
> Dr Persico, in terms not by any means too flattering . . .[84]

Despite the reservations of men like Waterfield and Pearman, there
was a widespread feeling amongst officers and soldiers alike that a

good chaplain enabled men to face death more easily. Richard Barter remembered the Reverend Mr Ellis preaching a sermon on the text 'I am now ready to be offered' shortly before the assault on Delhi, finding it 'curiously applicable to our situation and received by myself and many others as a good omen.'[85] And when the 75th was formed up ready to advance, Father Bertrand appeared and asked the commanding officer for permission to bless the regiment, saying: 'We may differ some of us in matters of religion, but the blessing of an old man and a clergyman can do nothing but good.' The colonel at once agreed, 'and Father Bertrand lifting up his hands to heaven blessed the regiment in a most impressive manner, offering up at the same time prayers for our success and for mercy on the souls of those so soon to die.'[86]

If the chaplain was rarely seen at regimental headquarters, his colleague the paymaster was an altogether more regular feature. Initially the regiment's funds proceeded, as we have seen, from the government, in the person of the paymaster-general, to the regimental agent and thence from him to the paymaster, a regimental officer appointed by the colonel to act as such in addition to his other duties. The paymaster paid out the captains of companies: 'Each captain then accounted with the regimental paymaster, the paymaster with the Agent, and the Agent with the Secretary at War, on whose certificate the final account between the Paymaster-general and the Agent was closed.'[87] In 1797, however, paymasters were appointed specifically to the post and (save in occasional emergencies in the field) concerned themselves wholly with pay, and in due course received it directly from the government, bypassing the agent. Like regimental surgeons, they gravitated steadily towards their own specialist department in the post-Crimea reforms, though it was not until 1878 that the Army Pay Department was formed.

Paymasters were commissioned, with or without purchase, usually in the ranks of lieutenant or captain. The best-known paymaster of the age is Captain Henry Duberly of the 8th Hussars, who has earned his place in history because of his wife. Pleasant but unambitious, in 1850 he married Fanny Locke, the youngest daughter of a wealthy Devizes banker, and she accompanied him on campaign in the Crimea and the Mutiny. Bold, pretty, enterprising and an accomplished horsewoman, she was a great favourite with officers, old and young: but unlike the version of her portrayed by Jill Bennett in the film *The Charge of the Light Brigade*, she seems not to have had affairs with any of them. Her letters and journals give a witty insight into the campaigns she took such pride in accompanying. In June 1858 she accompanied the charge in which the Rani of Jhansi (with whom, had they met, she might have found much in common) was killed. 'The impulse to accompany the cavalry was irresistible,' she wrote, 'and I shall never forget the throbbing excitement of that gallop, when the horse beneath me, raging in fierce strength, scarcely touched the ground . . .'[88]

Last, but by no means least, came the senior non-commissioned officers at regimental headquarters. Things were different in the cavalry, but as far as the infantry was concerned there was only one sergeant major in the battalion. It was not until the amalgamation of eight small companies into four large ones on the eve of the First World War that the rank of Regimental Sergeant Major was introduced to mark out this dignitary from the newly-designated company sergeant majors. The sergeant major was the senior non-commissioned member of the regiment, and his status was later to be enhanced when he became a warrant officer, with an Army Board warrant to give him a rank of which he could not be deprived by summary proceedings.

The sergeant major usually wore a coat of officer's cut and quality with braid epaulettes on both shoulders and, though badges of rank varied over the period, for much of it he bore four braid chevrons on his sleeve. He wore a sergeant's sash of crimson striped with his regiment's facing colour – some regiments, like the 42nd, emphasised his status by giving him an officer's plain crimson sash – and carried cane and sword. When Benjamin Harris was in the East Kent Militia his sergeant major was: 'Quite a beau in his way; he had a sling belt to his sword like a field officer, a tremendous feather in his cap, a flaring sash, his whistle and powder-flask displayed, an officer's pelisse over one shoulder . . .'[89]

In a military manual of 1766, Bennet Cuthbertson warned his readers that 'the choice of a sergeant major must never be influenced by any consideration save that of real merit,' and almost a century later the standing orders of the King's Regiment proclaimed: 'A high sense of honour and respectability is indispensable to his situation.'[90] The sergeant major was selected as much for his literacy and numeracy as his bearing or skill at drill, for the post involved much of the administration now carried out by the adjutant or chief clerk. William Cobbett enlisted into the 54th Foot in 1784 and, as he wrote in good hand, was appointed copier to the local garrison commander, who encouraged him to study and lent him a Lowth's Grammar. He was soon promoted corporal, 'a rank which, however contemptible it may appear in some people's eyes, brought me a clear twopence per diem, and a very clever worsted knot [the NCO badge of rank, later replaced by chevrons] upon my shoulder too.'[91] His clerical skills saw him promoted straight to sergeant-major, 'which brought me in close contact, at every hour, with the whole of the epaulet gentry, whose profound and surprising ignorance I discovered in a twinkling.'[92] Aware that 'being raised from corporal to sergeant major at once, over the heads of thirty sergeants,' was likely to make him unpopular, he took to rising early and working hard, so that 'every one felt that what I did he had never done and never could do.' He was at his desk, dressed and shaved, with his daily report ready for completion as soon as returns arrived from the companies, and could get the regiment on parade 'in such time as the bayonets glistened in the rising sun' enabling the men to get their duties done so that 'they could ramble into the town or into the woods, go to get raspberries, to catch birds, to catch fish; or to pursue any other recreation . . .'[93]

Cobbett's experiences as sergeant-major helped turn him into a political radical. He swiftly familiarised himself with the new drill-book – probably Dundas's *Principles of Military Movements* – taught the officers what to say on parade and gave them crib cards showing the regiment's dispositions. And then, he wrote with disgust: 'There was I, at the review, upon the flank of the grenadier company, with my worsted shoulder-knot and my great high, coarse, hairy cap; confounded in the ranks among other men, while those who commanded me to move my hands or my feet, thus or thus, were, in fact, uttering words which I had taught them and were, in everything except authority, my inferiors . . .'[94] Although he despised his officers 'for their gross ignorance and their vanity, and hated them for their drunkenness and rapacity,' he knew that a false step might see him 'broken and flogged for fifty different offences.'[95] Cobbett left the army in 1791 on the regiment's return to England from Novia Scotia and pursued a vigorous campaign against military abuses, argued strenuously and often wrongheadedly against Britain's involvement in the Peninsula (he preferred to believe Napoleon's inaccurate bulletins to Wellington's more objective dispatches), and in 1810 was imprisoned after leading a campaign against flogging. He became a radical MP in 1832, three years before his death. Despite his experiences, he remained devoted:

> To the army, to every soldier in it. I have a bond of attachment quite independent of any political reasonings. I was a soldier at that time when the feelings are most ardent and when the strongest attachments are formed. 'Once a soldier, always a soldier' is a maxim, the truth of which I need not insist on to anyone who has ever served in the army for any length of time.[96]

Timothy Gowing, a sergeant in the Crimea, became sergeant major of 7th Royal Fusiliers, and was more fortunate in his officers than Cobbett. His battalion was commanded by 'noble' Lieutenant Colonel Lacy Yea, and he knew the acting commanding officer of the 97th, 'that noble-minded man, Captain Hedley Vicars ... He was very affable and kind, and his men seemed very fond of him. He appeared cool, determined ... sure to win the respect of all classes and will lead them at anything ...'[97] However, he agreed with Cobbett that many officers simply did not know their business.

> *Punch* might well put it that the Crimean army was an army of lions led by donkeys. More than half the officers did not know how to manoeuvre a company – all, or nearly so, had to be left to non-commissioned officers – but it would be impossible to dispute their bravery for they were brave unto madness. The writer has seen them lead at the deadly bayonet charges and at walls and bloodstained parapets of Sevastopol, as freely as they would have led off in a ball room ...[98]

Gowing declined a commission on the grounds that he could not support himself in the style befitting an officer, but many sergeant-majors did not, and there was a clear *cursus honorum* which led from sergeant-major to adjutant.

Other NCOs in regimental headquarters included the quarter-master sergeant, the quartermaster's principal acolyte, the pay staff-sergeant (so called because he was on the staff of the battalion, rather than in one of the companies), the drum-major, the sergeant armourer, the pioneer corporal and his ten pioneers. The latter were military navvies who wore buff leather aprons to protect their uniforms, and carried shovels and axes. For ceremonial occasions the aprons were whitened and the axes polished, and some regiments copied the French practice of using the pioneers to form the regiment's *tête de colonne*, marching proudly at the head of the band.

Many regiments spent a good deal of money on their 'band of music', which usually included both professional musicians and serving soldiers. 2nd Foot Guards hired its band in Hanover, and $2/78^{th}$ enlisted German prisoners from a prison-hulk. 'Turkish music' was popular, and cymbals and 'jingling johnnies' were often played by bandsmen in oriental costume: the West Middlesex Militia was amongst the regiments managing to secure a 'real blackamoor' to play the cymbals. Bands frequently played in action. The band of the 87th struck up the incomparable 'Garryowen' after the French repulse at Tarifa, and in 1791 the 52nd was played into the assault of Savandroog with 'Britons Strike Home'. Sometimes music was borrowed from the French. French deserters in the $31^{st's}$ band taught it a tune which became known as 'Bonaparte's March', and, in the most celebrated example of borrowing, the 14th adopted the popular French tune 'Ca Ira' after their commanding officer had enjoined his band to 'beat them at their own damned tune'. In both the Sikh Wars and the Indian Mutiny enemy bands sometimes played British tunes, whether as a deliberate compliment – the Sikhs were given to echoing 'God Save the Queen' – or an accidental insult – the playing of 'Cheer, Boys, Cheer' by Indian bands was especially resented.

Bandsmen routinely acted as stretcher-bearers to carry in the wounded and, in extreme cases, fought as infantry. Lieutenant

Colonel Herbert of the 75th wanted to leave his band behind before the march on Delhi, 'but the men came up in a body and pleaded so hard to be allowed to go with their comrades as duty soldiers in the ranks' that they were allowed to go, and 'all the best players were killed or disabled'. One man had his right hand shot off and, hit by another eight or nine bullets, miraculously survived. He begged to be allowed to soldier on: 'I could play the trombone, sir. I could fix a hook to my stump and play it first rate.'[99]

The battalion's companies were commanded by captains, each assisted by a lieutenant and an ensign. In some units, like the 95th Rifles, the rank of ensign was replaced by that of second lieutenant. While detailed establishments varied, there were usually two sergeants, three corporals, a drummer or fifer and up to 100 rank and file in a company. A General Order of 6 July 1813 established the rank of colour-sergeant, with an establishment of one per company: Lieutenant Colonel Steevens of the 20th tells us that he 'conferred Colour badges on the ten most meritorious sergeants in the regiment' at Lesaca in Spain. In line regiments the badge initially consisted of a crowned union jack above crossed swords, above a braid chevron. The drummers were by no means all the boys of popular imagination. Of those in the 23rd at Waterloo whose ages are known, only one was under 18 but two were over 50 – the oldest of them 62. Just under half were under 18 when enlisted.

Companies were not subdivided into platoons as they now are: at this time the term platoon referred to a body of men designated for a specific task, such as firing as part of the battalion's sequence of volley-firing. The actual strength of companies varied greatly. In 1775 the 23rd Royal Welsh Fusiliers averaged 38 'private sentinels' in its battalion companies. In 1809 the average battalion strength of the infantry as a whole was 980 officers and men, but units on active service were often significantly under-strength. For example, the companies of 5/60th attached to Hill's 2nd Division in the Peninsula averaged 47 all ranks apiece, and the strength of battalions in the same division ranged between 2/31st at 271 and 1/39th at 565. The 75th began the Indian Mutiny in May 1757 with 928 privates, but on 13 September 1857, even before the assault on Delhi, had only 398.

From the 1660s there had been two sorts of cavalry, horse and dragoons, the latter originally little more than mounted infantry, whose horses, at the time of the Civil War, cost half as much as those of cavalry proper. As time went on the distinctions between dragoons and the rest of the cavalry became blurred, but until around 1800 dragoons were still expected to be able to fight on foot as well as on horseback. The old regiments of horse began to disappear in 1746 when the government, to save money on horses and pay, started to convert them to dragoons. They were given the title dragoon guards (although they had nothing to do with real guards) to cushion their pride. In 1756, in response to a growing demand, experimental light troops were added to eleven cavalry regiments, and three years later the first four regiments of light dragoons were raised, establishing a distinction between heavy cavalry – dragoons and dragoon guards – and light cavalry – light dragoons and, later, hussars and lancers. Even though the tactical roles of light and heavy cavalry became blurred, there were sharp sartorial distinctions, and a measure of creative tension, between them. When Captain Anstruther Thompson of the 9th Lancers discovered in 1841 that his regiment was to be posted to India he told his best friend (who, like many swells, also wished to avoid the unfashionable rigours of the subcontinent) that he proposed to exchange into the 6th Dragoon Guards. 'Oh, damn it, no,' replied his comrade. 'Don't be a heavy and wear a brass hat.' The two duly arranged exchanges into the 13th Light Dragoons.[100]

In 1760 there were seven regiments of 'dragoon guards and Irish horse', thirteen regiments of dragoons and eight of light dragoons. There were fluctuations in the cavalry establishment as regiments were disbanded in peacetime, paralleling reductions in the infantry. The process was complicated by the gradual transformation of light dragoons into hussars: three regiments of light dragoons were remodelled as hussars in 1806 and another in 1807, while three more regiments of light dragoons became lancers in 1816. It was not until after the Crimean War that light dragoons disappeared entirely, with the conversion of the last regiment to hussars.

Cavalry regiments, like their infantry counterparts, had proprietary colonels who entrusted routine administration to regimental agents. Regimental headquarters comprised a lieutenant colonel commanding, two majors, an adjutant, a surgeon with his two assistants, and, from 1796, a veterinary surgeon. Regimental riding-masters were added after Waterloo. They were generally promoted from the ranks and were unable to rise above the rank of lieutenant. In July 1858 Riding Master Brown of the 16th Lancers, ordered to put the 16 year old Prince of Wales through an equitation course, felt unable to speak to the prince directly, so criticised his equerry, Colonel Keppell, for the prince's mistakes.

The troop, commanded by a captain, was the standard administrative sub-unit in the cavalry, the equivalent of the infantry company. Establishments varied, but in 1800 most regiments were allowed ten troops, two of them remaining at the regimental depot and the others forming the regiment's fighting strength. The post-Waterloo reductions saw the decrease of troops to eight in 1815 and six in 1822. The troop's officers included the captain, a lieutenant and a cornet. Until 1810 there was a troop quartermaster: thereafter the senior non-commissioned member of a troop became the troop ser-geant-major, and a single commissioned quartermaster was estab-lished at regimental headquarters. The troop had three sergeants, four corporals, a trumpeter, a farrier and fifty to sixty rank and file. Private soldiers in line cavalry regiments were styled 'private' rather than 'trooper' until as late as 1922.

Cavalry regiments had bands, and, as Sergeant-Major George Loy Smith of the 11th Hussars remembered, even in the 1840s the old practice of seeking black percussionists had not died out. E Troop had:

> The only three black men in the regiment: viz Trumpeter Murray, Roderick the cymbal player and McKinley the big drummer. Roderick had a black wife but no children; McKinley was also married and had a large family. Murray and Roderick were West Indians while McKinley was an East Indian.[101]

Although troops of cavalry retained their administrative integrity until the 1880s, from the eighteenth century they were grouped into squadrons on active service. There were usually two troops to each squadron, and squadrons would be commanded by the regiment's field officers (the second lieutenant colonel where one existed, and the majors) or the senior captain of the troops comprising them.

Like infantry regiments, cavalry regiments soon dropped below their authorised strength on active service. Although the 1808 establishment gave most heavy cavalry regiments 905 officers, NCOs and men, they would be fortunate to field half this total even early in a campaign: the 1st King's Dragoon Guards had 556 officers and men on strength at the beginning of the Waterloo campaign, and the 2nd Royal North British Dragoons only 420. The Light Brigade embarked for the Crimea with an average regimental strength of 314 officers and men, but on the morning of the charge the brigade's five regiments totalled only some 673 fit for battle. Its two weakest regiments had only 126 officers and men apiece. Furthermore, two regiments were commanded by captains that day.

'Gunners are a race apart,' ran a piece of First World War doggerel, 'hard of head and hard of heart.' During our period they were indeed a race apart, creatures of the Ordnance Department, not the commander-in-chief, and were controlled from their headquarters at Woolwich, which housed their depot and the Royal Military Academy where officers were trained. The corps was small and professionally distinct – its commissions were never granted by purchase – with just 274 artillery officers in 1791 rising to 727 in 1814 at the height of the Napoleonic wars. Artillery terminology is more than usually confusing. At the start of the period it maintained the junior rank of mattross, ranking below a gunner. Thus on 14 June 1756 Cadet Gunner James Wood recorded in his journal that: 'Edward Hurst, sergeant, was broke to mattross and received 400 lashes by order of a Regimental Court martial for striking Lieutenant Barrett of the RA.'[102] The rank of bombardier equated to corporal in other arms, and that of lieutenant-fireworker, which disappeared towards the end of the eighteenth century, was the junior commissioned rank.

The Royal Regiment of Artillery was divided into a varying number of battalions, two battalions from 1757, six in 1799, and seven in 1801 when the hitherto-separate Irish Artillery was fused with the Royal Artillery, rising to ten battalions in 1808. Artillery battalions, like those of the infantry, were composed of several companies. But for active service companies of gunners were brought together with members of the separate Corps of Artillery Drivers. This had been formed in 1794 in an effort to remedy the problems caused by contracting civilian drivers and horses to pull guns on campaign. These gentlemen had a disturbing tendency to decamp in moments of crisis, leaving the gunners unable to move their pieces. The Corps of Drivers was something of an improvement, although one officer called it an 'Augean stable' and another 'a nest of infamy'.

The artillery company with its attached drivers was known as a brigade. In 1808 a brigade of foot artillery, whose men marched on foot, had an establishment of two captains, two 1st lieutenants, one 2nd lieutenant, four sergeants, four corporals, nine bombardiers, three drummers and 116 gunners. In 1793 horse artillery was formed to provide fast, mobile artillery support for cavalry. All officers and men rode horses or the unit's vehicles. Horse artillery brigades were styled troops, and in 1808 each troop had two captains, three lieutenants, two staff sergeants, three sergeants, three corporals, six bombardiers, a farrier, a carriage-smith, two shoeing-smiths, two collar-makers, a wheelwright and a trumpeter, with 80 gunners and 60 drivers. Foot artillery brigades or horse artillery troops generally had six pieces each, which might be divided into three 'divisions' of two guns, each gun forming a 'subdivision,' a description echoed in the contemporary British army definition of a single gun and its detachment as a 'sub.'

Captain Cavalié Mercer commanded a horse artillery troop in the Waterloo campaign. He wrote that:

> Perhaps at this time a troop of horse artillery was the completest thing in the army; and whether broken up into half-brigades under the first and second captains, or into divisions under their lieutenants, or subdivisions under their sergeants and corporals, each body was a perfect whole.[103]

In the eighteenth century the infantry was provided with 'battalion guns,' usually light 6 pounder fieldpieces, which were manned by infantry personnel and were expected to provide immediate fire support in the style of infantry mortars of a later generation. The practice lurched on till the Napoleonic period, with the Buckingham-shire militia taking its two privately-purchased brass guns to Ireland in 1798 and having them on hand when in aid of the civil power in 1811–12. However, it was deeply unsatisfactory because the guns were less mobile than the infantry they were meant to accompany, giving the latter the choice of moving painfully slowly or pressing on without their guns.

The Corps of Royal Engineers, also controlled by the Ordnance, consisted of officers only, and had fewer even than the Royal Artillery, with only 73 in 1792, rising to 262 in 1813. They were invaluable in conducting siege operations which remained a major feature of the period, and their casualties in the Peninsula were terrible: 25 of the 102 engineer officers who served there died. They suffered heavily in the Crimea, and the blowing in of the Kashmir Gate at Delhi by Lieutenants Home and Salkeld with eight British and Indian sappers was a typical engineer task. They rushed the gate, carrying explosives, under point-blank fire: Salkeld was hit as he applied a slow-match to the fuse, but Corporal Burgess picked up the match and lit the fuse: the charge blew up, destroying the gate, as he fell mortally wounded.

Engineer rank and file were provided by the Royal Military Artificers and Labourers, raised in 1722 and given full military status in 1757. It became the Royal Military Artificers in 1797 and the Corps of Sappers and Miners in 1812. It was not until 1856 that the officer and non-commissioned elements of the arm were brought together with the reformation of the Corps of Royal Engineers, incorporating the sappers and miners. Lieutenant Arthur Moffat Lang of the Bengal Engineers testified the importance of trained personnel and the impossibility of improvising them. He wrote from Delhi that:

> Last night I was out for instruction in platform-laying; it is a great bore having to instruct all these raw Sikh recruits in the duties of sappers; however fine a corps the Punjab sappers may be some day, they are undisciplined, stupid recruits now, and a sapper can't be formed under a couple of years.[104]

Each of the Indian presidencies – Bengal, Madras and Bombay –

maintained its own engineer establishment, and there was much professional rivalry between Indian and Royal Engineer officers, as Lang admitted:

> Major Goodwin drew down the odium of all our corps by resigning his appointment in a huff: so a Lieutenant Lennox of the *Royal* Engineers (hang them all, what do they mean by coming here?) is our Chief Engineer: a very pleasant fellow, but fancy an RE Chief Engineer in an army in Bengal![105]

So there we have them: horse, foot and guns, guard and line, creatures of the commander-in-chief and gentlemen of the Ordnance. Let us now peer more closely into their regiments and see, as Daniel Defoe had put it in 1726, what 'kind of poverty and distress [were] necessary to bring a poor Man to take Arms, and list in the Army, and run the risk of Life and Limb, for so mean a Consideration as a Red Coat and 3/- a week.'[106]

III

BROTHERS OF
THE BLADE

SCUM OF THE EARTH

T HE ARMY'S APPETITE for manpower was almost insatiable. Finding soldiers for a force that peaked at 233,852 officers and men in 1815, was never easy: supply rarely kept pace with demand. During the Napoleonic Wars annual wastage never fell below 16,071 (in 1806) and reached 25,498 in 1812. Recruiting in the British Isles never exceeded the 1808 total of 15,308, and in 1810 was a dismal 7,367. Even in the 1840s, with a much smaller peacetime army of around 130,000 – about 1 per cent of the adult male population – simply sustaining it in the face of annual wastage caused by death, incapacity or routine discharge required the enlistment of 11–12,000 men a year. For most of the period enlistment was for life, which in practice meant 25 years, although shorter enlistments were offered in wartime. Thomas Morris, who enlisted into the 73rd in 1812, reported to its major in Colchester, and was sent, in the care of a sergeant,

> to the doctor, by whom I was examined and pronounced
> fit for service. The same sergeant then went with me to
> the town-hall, to witness my attestation before the magis-
> trate ... They sadly wanted me to enlist for life, but I
> thought seven years quite long enough for a trial.[1]

Given the impossibility of finding sufficient British soldiers by conventional means, wartime governments resorted to a variety of

expedients. One, as we have already seen, was the large-scale recruitment of foreigners. Another was to encourage enlistment into the
regular army from the militia. This required a radical change of
policy, because it was initially a criminal offence for a man to join
the regulars from the militia, and county hierarchies disliked having
'their' armies whittled away. And in the first few years of the Napoleonic wars, service in the militia was more attractive than that in
the regular army. Although the militia was embodied for full-time
service from 1803, it was not compelled to serve abroad (although
some militia units did provide overseas garrisons from time to time),
and the families of militiamen were eligible for support from the
parish while those of regulars were not. By 1803, private individuals
who wished to avoid the militia service for which they had been
balloted were prepared to pay a substitute a fee of up to £25, three
times the enlistment bounty then offered by the regulars, and by
1812 militia substitutes were pocketing the then considerable sum
of £60.

In 1803 the Additional Forces Act created a new Army of Reserve,
distinct from the militia but, like it, raised by locally-administered
ballot. However, battalions in the Army of Reserve were affiliated to
regular regiments in the hope that regiment's reservists would be
attracted by the bounty offered if they transferred to the regulars.
Benjamin Harris, a young shepherd from Dorset, was caught by the
ballot and drafted into the 66th Foot.

> My father tried hard to buy me off, and would have per-
> suaded the sergeant of the 66th that I was of no use as a
> soldier, from having maimed my right hand (by breaking
> a forefinger when I was a child). The sergeant, however,
> said I was just the sort of little chap he wanted, and off
> he went, carrying me (amongst a batch of recruits he had
> collected) away with him.[2]

This smacked of conscription, and the scheme was bitterly unpopular, and the first ballot raised only 45,492 men from a target of
50,000, and no fewer than 41,198 of them were substitutes. Of these,
5,651 deserted in the first ten months (thus rendering themselves
liable to compulsory transfer into the regular army if apprehended)

and 17,307 joined the regulars. A second ballot, in 1805, generated only 7,683 of the expected 29,000 men, and while 3,041 deserted 8,562 transferred to the regular army. Thereafter the scheme was quietly shelved, and remaining men of the Army of Reserve were formed into garrison battalions, most of which served in Ireland.

As one scheme foundered, another flourished. From 1805 onwards the authorities had increasing success in persuading militiamen to join the line. Regular regiments were allowed access to militia units on specified occasions, always provided they did not 'disturb the discipline' of the units they visited by being too liberal with drink. It was a carefully calculated application of stick and carrot.

> The Militia would be drawn up in line, and the officers or non-commissioned officers from the regiments requiring volunteers would give a glowing description of their several regiments, describing the victories they had gained and the honours they had acquired, and concluded by offering a bounty. If these inducements were not effective in getting men then coercive measures were adopted: heavy and long drills and field exercises were forced upon them; which became so oppressive that, to escape them, the men would embrace the alternative and join the regulars.[3]

So many did indeed embrace the alternative that from 1805, the year that recruiting from the militia was officially authorised, about half British recruits came from that source.

Lieutenant John Colborne of the 20th, who had some recently-enlisted militiamen in his company in the 1799 Helder expedition, heard one confidently announce 'Well, I'll stand as long as the officer stands' and observed that they did remarkably well. Many had not even had time to change their uniforms, inducing Major General Ralph Abercromby to lead them forward with a shout of: 'Come along! You are as safe here as if you were in Norfolk!'[4] Several of the non-commissioned authors of memoirs of the Napoleonic period had begun their careers in the militia. In 1809 William Wheeler was a private in the 2nd Royal Surrey Militia, where his service was made miserable by the tyranny of Major 'Bloody Bob' Hudson and the eccentricity of his commanding officer, Lieutenant Colonel Lord Cranley. In April he wrote:

I have at length escaped from the militia without being flayed alive. I have taken the first opportunity and volunteered together with 127 of my comrades into the 51st Light Infantry Regiment. I had made up my mind to volunteer but into what regiment I cared not a straw, so I determined to go with the greatest number . . . Upwards of 90 men volunteered for the 95th Rifle Regiment. I was near going into this Regt. myself for it was always a fancy Corps . . . and another cause was that Lieut Foster a good officer and beloved by every man in the Corps I had left volunteered into the 95th . . .[5]

Here we see several of the key ingredients of volunteering: dissatisfaction with the militia, peer-group pressure, the lure of 'a fancy corps' and the impact of a popular officer. When Wheeler reached the 51st he found that it contained only about 150 old soldiers: the rest were volunteers from 'the Stafford, South Gloucester, 1st and 2nd Surrey together with some half dozen Irish militias.' Edward Costello of the 95th reckoned that recruits from the militia recruits were excellent material.

It is justly due to the militia regiments to say, that in the knowledge and exercise of their military duties, during the war, they were very little inferior to the troops of the line. The men who joined our battalion were in general a fine set of young fellows, and chiefly the elite of the light companies of the different provincial corps.[6]

All regular recruits were, at least in theory, volunteers, although many were offered the choice of serving the monarch in a military rather than a penal capacity, like the eight convicted felons described in *The London Magazine* in 1762, who 'have been pardoned, on condition of serving in the West-Indies'. Death rates in the West Indies and West Africa were so high that a posting to these outposts fell not far short of a death sentence. Pardoning a man who agreed to serve was a common practice in the eighteenth century, and insolvent debtors and convicted criminals were frequently allowed to enlist. A draft of 'British and Irish sent from the jails in England' was sent to reinforce 1/60th, dying like flies in unhealthy Jamaica in 1783. James Boswell, already behaving like the thoughtful young officer he hoped so much to be, took a drink to a footguards sentry who told him that he was a tailor, enlisted to escape imprisonment for debt.[7] The Press Acts, in brief operation at times of national emergency, swept up 'all such able-bodied, idle, and disorderly persons who cannot upon examination prove themselves to exercise and industriously follow some lawful trade or employment'. On 10 September 1777 a Surrey justice of the peace wrote to Lord Barrington, Secretary at war, to say that:

> John Quin an Irish American 29 Years of Age near six feet high very dirty and ragged seemingly of slow understanding was this morning convicted before me of Orchard Robbing. He is willing to serve as a soldier. I have therefore committed him to the House of Correction in Guildford to await your Orders . . .[8]

A year later the under-sheriff of Berkshire told Barrington's successor that he had a number of convicts in jail who had been sentenced to death for highway robbery and horse stealing but were 'exceedingly proper Fellows either for the Land or the Sea Service . . .'[9] The recruitment of such folk undoubtedly helped make up numbers but it had a damaging effect on the status of the soldier, for it ensured that the honest volunteer with real interest in the army – by no means a rare creature – suffered by association with men who were criminals in civilian life and often continued in scarlet as they had begun in fustian.

The majority of recruits were enticed by the entrancing rattle of the drum and the power of the spoken word, lavishly supported with drink. Colonels of regiments were given 'beating orders' which authorised them: 'By Beat of Drum or otherwise to raise so many men as are to be found wanting.' A potential recruit would be given 'the king's shilling' as a mark of his commitment, and would then be medically inspected – about one-third of recruits failed even this perfunctory examination – before being attested by a magistrate. A recruiting party, usually consisting of an officer, two sergeants and a drummer, went to the regiment's recruiting area and set up in a selection of prominent spots where the drummer beat 'the points of war' (his full repertoire of flams and paradiddles, with some fancy

A recruiting poster for the 7th Light Dragoons, 1809. The regiment's colonel, Lord Paget, was one of the most distinguished cavalry officers of his generation but ran off with Wellington's sister-in-law and was not employed in Spain after 1809. By then the Earl of Uxbridge, he lost a leg at Waterloo.

stick-clicking thrown in for good measure) and the officer and ser-geants declaimed upon the unrivalled opportunities to be had by volunteering for their regiment.

Posters described the attractions that awaited. In 1814 the 7th Light Dragoons announced that:

> Young fellows whose hearts beat high to tread the paths of Glory could not have a better opportunity than now offers. Come forward, then, and Enrol Yourselves in a Regiment that stands unrivalled, and where the kind

treatment the men experience is known throughout the whole Kingdom . . .

NB – This Regiment is mounted on blood Horses, and being lately returned from Spain and the horses young, the men will not be allowed to hunt during the next Season, more than once a week.[10]

Three years before a poster for the 69th Foot – 'commanded by General Cuyler, an officer to whose distinguished merit no language can do justice' announced vacancies for:

A few dashing, high spirited young men, whose hearts beat high to tread the patch of glory. Young men of this description know the opportunity offered to them, which may never occur again, of enlisting into one of the finest Regiments in the Service . . .[11]

Should there still be 'a few young men of high character' who had somehow remained civilians, then the 14th Light Dragoons would consider them.

You have the exclusive right of wearing the black or Imperial Eagle of Prussia; your horses are of matchless beauty; your Cloathing and accoutrements highly attractive, and smart young Britons inspired with military ardour, whose noble and warlike minds are repugnant to the control of unfeeling relatives and friends, have now the glorious prospect of speedy preferment, and two additional troops are to be raised.

And just in case of misunderstanding, it added: 'NB – Smart young Irishmen taken.'[12]

The process was described, without excessive caricature, in The Recruiting Officer (1706), written by George Farquhar, himself a former infantry officer. While Captain Plume is more concerned with finding a pretty girl and so raising recruits 'in the matrimonial way', his sergeant makes a more familiar pitch.

If any gentleman soldiers, or others, have a mind to serve Her majesty, and pull down the French king; if any prentices have severe masters, any children have unnatural parents; if any servants have too little wages, or any

> husband too much wife; let them repair to the noble Ser-
> geant Kite, at the Sign of the Raven, in this good town
> of Shrewsbury, and they shall receive present relief and
> entertainment.

John Shipp was determined to join the army the minute he saw his
first recruiting party: 'It was all about Gentleman soldiers, merry
life, muskets rattling, cannon roaring, drums beating, colours flying,
regiments charging and shouts of victory! Victory!'

In 1812 a recruiting sergeant, Thomas Jackson of the Coldstream
Guards, found that recruits' martial ardour soon faded: 'Some of
them, after sober reflection, repented and said by the way, "Sergeant,
you are leading us to the slaughter-house." I laughed them out of
it, but perhaps they were about right.' Although he complained that
he disliked recruiting, he was then detailed:

> to take a drum and fife, and attend all the wakes, races
> and revels, within twenty miles of London. There we had
> to strut about in best coats, and swaggering, sword in hand,
> drumming our way through the masses, commingled with
> gazing clodpolls, gingerbread mechanics, and thimbleprig
> sharpers.[13]

Appealing to potential recruits as 'gentlemen soldiers' was once
common. Many private soldiers certainly regarded themselves and
their adversaries as gentlemen at the time of Marlborough's Wars.
James Marshall Deane, a literate and perceptive 'private sentinel' in
1st Foot Guards described the assault on the dominant Schellenberg
at Donauwörth during the Blenheim campaign of 1704.

> But no sooner did our Forlorn Hope appear but the
> enemy did throw in their volleys of cannon balls and small
> shot among them and made a brave defence and a bold
> resistance against us as brave loyal-hearted gentleman sol-
> diers ought to for their prince and country . . .[14]

Privates were expected to settle their differences with cold steel, just
like their officers. In 1687 Donald McBane was an apprentice
tobacco spinner in Inverness, but tells us that 'my Mistress began to
lessen my dish, which I could not endure, I being a raw young fellow
who would have eaten two meats in one day. So I went and listed

myself a soldier . . .' The following year he found that the old soldier
who supervised him pocketed all his pay, and his officers would take
no action: 'for at that time if any difference fell out between two
soldiers, they were obliged to decide it with their swords.' He secretly
took lessons in 'the Art of the Small Sword' from a sergeant, and
eventually beat his oppressor, who took six months to recover from
his wounds. McBane enjoyed a long and somewhat chequered career.
He was badly burnt when a grenade went off in his hands in an
attack on a French fortress:

> Killing several men about me, and blew me over the
> Pallasods [palisades]; burnt my clothes so that the skin
> came off me. I . . . fell among Murray's Company of Grena-
> diers, flayed like an old dead horse from head to foot.
> They cast me into water to put out the fire about me.

At Blenheim he was 'four times shot with ball . . . and five times
stabbed with a bayonet and left among the dead.' In 1712 McBane
put his skills with the sword on the market by opening an ale house
and fencing school in London, and fought in prize-fights, whose
contestants used swords with sharp edges but no points, so that the
audience would see plenty of blood but there would be little chance
of the gladiators being killed. After two more spells of service in the
army, in 1726, at the age of 62, he beat Andrew O'Bryan, an Irishman
who had challenged any Scot to take him on, on a stage erected
in the abbey of Holyrood House. His manual of arms, *The Expert
Sword-Man's Companion*, showed the gentleman soldier how to deal
with adversaries armed with a variety of weapons. There were
moments, though, when the respectable 'Beat up his sword, and
sink your body with an Appeal and push quart' was replaced with
altogether less reputable advice.

> If you meet with any Gamekeeper . . . dart your staff at his
> face with your left hand, which he endeavouring to stop,
> slide your right hand to your left, and at full length, hit
> him on the left side of his head . . .

It was small wonder that the notion of the gentleman soldier was
not universally popular.[15]

In 1700 the London *Spy* proclaimed that:

> A Foot Soldier is commonly a Man, who for the sake of
> wearing a Sword and the Honour of being term'd a Gentle-
> man, is coaxed from a Handicraft Trade, whereby he
> might live Comfortably, to bear Arms, for his King and
> Country . . .

The journal, in terminology typical of the tone of the age, went on
to lambast the depraved life followed by the soldier, concluding that:
'He is generally beloved by two sorts of Companion, in whores and
lice; for both these Vermin are great admirers of a Scarlet Coat . . .'[16]
In April 1795 there was a riot in Westminster when a recruiting
sergeant gave a youth a shilling and told him to buy some tobacco
in a nearby shop. The gullible lad did so, and when he returned
'the fellow instantly seized him, and told him he had taken the king's
money and must go for a gentleman soldier.' The boy's yells brought
a crowd, which took the sergeant to the parish pump 'and attempted
to purify him with water.'[17] His victim escaped.

The anti-military prejudice displayed in both these contemporary
accounts reflects a wider animus against soldiers, especially in peacetime. Frank McLynn observes that the verdicts of juries were often
'unreliable and eccentric' where soldiers were concerned. In 1723
Private William Hawksworth was marching through St James's Park
with his footguards battalion when he heard a woman shout an insult
to his regiment. He left the ranks and punched her male companion,
who fell over, fractured his skull and died. Although Hawksworth
obviously had no intention of killing the man, he was found guilty
of murder rather than manslaughter, and hanged. We may have
less sympathy with Lieutenant Lander, who killed a postboy on the
Chatham to London run for failing to make his horses gallop up
Shooter's Hill in Woolwich, and swung for it.

Whether he was induced to believe that he was becoming a gentle-
man-soldier or not, an inquisitive young man was vulnerable the
minute he stopped to talk to a recruiting sergeant. One of these
admitted that if honest means failed:

> your last recourse was to get him drunk, and then slip a
> shilling into his pocket, get him home to your billet, and
> next morning swear he enlisted, bring all your party to

prove it, get him persuaded to pass the doctor. Should he pass, you must use every means in your power to get him to drink, blow him up with a fine story, get him inveigled by the magistrates, in some shape or other, and get him attested, but by no means let him out of your hands.[18]

Drink generally played a key role in the process. Benjamin Harris had already served a short term with the 66th Foot when he met a recruiting party of the 95th Rifles in Ireland: they looked so dashing that he signed on at once, and the group, recruiters and recruits alike, then set off for England.

> We started on our journey in tip-top spirits from the Royal Oak at Cashel; the whole lot of us (early as it was) being three sheets to the wind. When we paraded before the door of the Royal Oak, the landlord and landlady of the inn, who were quite as lively, came reeling forth with two decanters of whisky which they thrust into the hands of the sergeants, making them a present of the decanters and all to carry along with them, and refresh themselves on the march. The piper then struck up, the sergeants flourished the decanters, and the whole commenced a terrific yell.[19]

In 1703 the pious Captain John Blackadder wrote that he was ill-suited for 'this vexing trade' precisely because he did not drink. 'Sobriety itself is a bar to success,' he wrote with evident disdain. 'I see the greatest rakes are the best recruiters.' He went on to lament that:

> This is a sad corps I am engaged in; vice raging openly and impudently. They speak just such a language as devils would do. I find this ill in our trade, that there is now so much tyranny and knavery in the army, that it is a wonder how a many of straight, generous, honest souls can live in it . . . Armies which used to be full of great and noble souls are now turned to a parcel of mercenary, fawning, lewd, dissipated creatures; the dregs and scum of mankind . . .

The fount and origin of so much of this was, of course, the demon drink.[20]

Young men were offered a bounty, whose size reflected the demand for recruits, to persuade them to enlist: in 1803 it was £7 12s 6d, and had risen to 12 guineas by 1805. The sum payable to the recruit was only part of the bargain, for the recruiting officer received another 16s, his recruiting party 15s, and the 'bringer,' often a landlord who had got the man drunk in the first place, £2 12s 6d. Harris admitted that after three days 'drunken riot' the bounty was spent 'in every sort of excess till all was gone.'[21] Sometimes a soldier deserted as soon as he got his bounty, and by the 1840s there was what one author has called 'a vicious circle of ignorance and cruelty and double dealing from which even the well-meaning – officers or soldiers – could not escape.'[22] Recruiting sergeants worked closely with bringers and young men who fled after being cozened into taking the shilling were then pursued by men who were rewarded for recapturing them.

Not all recuits who deserted were innocent men: some soldiers made a career of making off with their bounty. During his first enlistment Harris encountered:

> A private of the 70th Regiment who had deserted from that Corps, and afterwards enlisted into several other regiments; indeed, I was told at the time . . . that sixteen different times he had received the bounty and then stolen off. Being, however, caught at last, he was brought to trial at Portsmouth, and sentenced by general court-martial to be shot.

It was thought that the execution would be 'a good hint to us young 'uns,' and Harris formed part of the sixteen-man firing party, composed of four soldiers from four regiments, which shot him.[23]

Edward Costello joined the 95th from the Dublin Militia in 1807. He received the eighteen guineas paid to those who joined from the militia, only to discover that £4 was immediately taken off him for his kit. He was luckier than most recruits, who found that by the time they had provided drinks for the recruiting party, given the drummer his fee for beating the points of war, and bought the traditional ribbons for the sergeant's wife, there was little left. Costello was a quick learner. He accompanied the recruiting party, clad in an old green coat of the sergeant's, before joining his regiment. The coat attracted the interest of a man who asked what bounty was given and then announced that he would join if he was given the shilling. Costello did not have one to hand.

> However, knowing that we received two pounds for every recruit, I hurried into a public house near at hand, and requested of the landlord to lend me a shilling, telling him the use for which I wanted it. This he very kindly did, and I handed it over to the recruit, who, chucking it instantly on the counter, called for the worth of it in whiskey. While we remained drinking, the sergeant, who I had sent for, arrived, and supplying me with money, the recruit passed the doctor and was sworn in for our corps.
>
> His name was Wilkie, he was an Englishman.[24]

Some recruits did indeed need little persuasion. In April 1842 Robert Waterfield saw the 32nd Foot on its weekly trudge round Portsmouth in full marching order.

> I quickened my pace and came up to the left wing of the Regiment, where I stood till the whole had passed me by, except for the recruits who marched in the rear of all. Amongst the latter my gaze fell upon an old schoolmate; I instantly rushed up to him and caught him by the hand, and was in the act of putting a multiplicity of questions to him when a sergeant tapped me on the shoulder, saying: 'Come, my lad! This is no place to be talking to a friend if you have met one, but come to the barracks on our return and I dare say you can stay with him altogether if you wish!'[25]

Waterfield went up to the barracks and

> a smart young sergeant called Creech, a Dublin man, came to the room I was in, and after a little conversation, in which he painted the army in such glowing colours, that after a little persuasion I took from him half a crown in the Queen's name, and became a soldier . . .[26]

William Cobbett was working as an 'understrapping quill driver' in Gray's Inn. One Sunday he saw a recruiting poster for the marines and although 'I was not ignorant enough to be the dupe of this morsel of military bombast' he felt that he needed a change and determined to join. He duly went down to Chatham and enlisted, as he thought, into the marines, his chosen corps:

> But the next morning I found myself before the captain of a marching regiment. There was no retreating: I had taken a shilling to drink His Majesty's health, and his further bounty was ready for my reception.[27]

For a few artisans who lacked the money or interest to secure a commission but had no wish to join as private soldiers, there was the possibility of joining direct as one of the small number of specialist NCOs. Thomas Bennett, born in Kent as one of 22 children in 1782, was a saddler by trade, and in 1804 he heard that Lieutenant Colonel Bolton of the 13th Light Dragoons needed a master-saddler. He was told that so long as he was steady all would be well, but in case of any misconduct he would be court-martialled and reduced to the ranks. He decided to take the risk, and enlisted on Christmas Eve, receiving a bounty of £13 8s and the rank of sergeant. He did exceptionally well, keeping a library of over a hundred books and owning a violin which he rashly lent to the band-master, for 'the rascal pawned it'. Unfortunately he eventually took to drink, and shortly after Waterloo visited Vauxhall gardens and got: 'pretty well inebriated. On my road home I fell in with some banditti that gave me a complete thrashing which sobered me so that I got home and was put to bed, which I did not leave for some days after.' Things went from bad to worse after the regiment was posted to India in 1818, and, after receiving a disagreeable form of corporal punishment (he was bridled and driven round the riding school) but being allowed to retain his rank, he was invalided out.[28]

Wellington had a mean opinion of the raw material of his army. In 1813 he wrote: 'We have in service the scum of the earth as common soldiers.' In 1831, during the long-running debate about flogging, he was just as forthright.

People talk of their enlisting from their fine military feeling – all stuff – no such thing. Some of our men enlist from
having got bastard children – some for minor offences –
and many more for drink; but you can hardly conceive of
such a set brought together, and it is really wonderful that
we should have made them the fine fellows that they are.[29]

Surgeon Henry Parkin would have agreed with the Duke's first obser-
vation. He spoke of: 'The man who is picked up drunk from the
kennel and brought home, insensible to barracks or hospital, or who
has been one of six, two of his comrades and three prostitutes,
wallowing in the same bed together for a night . . .'[30]

Although there were always many enthusiasts whose hearts did
indeed beat high to tread the paths of glory, most of those who
enlisted were unemployed, driven into the army by what one senior
officer called 'the compulsion of destitution.' Sergeant J MacMullen
thought that this amounted to two-thirds of recruits in 1846, and
the Heath Report of 1909 found that 'well over 90 per cent' had
no jobs.[31] In 1914 only half recruits even laid claim to a trade, and
the army was 6 per cent short of its establishment strength. The
soldier's poor pay, hard life and low status in society all conspired
to make service in the ranks a last resort for many men who took
the king's shilling.

But it is important that we do not follow so many nineteenth
century commentators – for Charles Clode, writing over a century
ago, the working classes were the criminal classes – and assume that
these men were all potential criminals devoid of any sense of
decency. As early as 1726 Daniel Defoe argued that though there
was indeed 'a kind of Poverty and Distress necessary to bring a poor
man to take Arms,' these 'poorest of men may have Principles of
Honour and Justice in them . . .'[32] The honest folk to which he refers
suffered, however, from appalling living conditions, association with
criminals who had been pressed into the army, and a brutal code
of discipline intended to deal with the army's worst elements.

Many experienced officers had no doubt that a harsh disciplinary
code was necessary. Wellington did not simply condemn his soldiers
as scum. He emphasised that they had been turned into fine fellows,
and said of his Peninsular army that: 'I could have done anything

with that army. It was in such perfect order.'[33] He saw discipline as a means to this end, and argued that it had to be coercive and deterrent precisely because of the type of recruits the army received. Conscription 'calls out a share of every class – no matter whether your son or my son – all must march' but voluntary recruiting was bound to attract 'the very worst members of society.'

Most of the non-commissioned soldiers of the age who have left memoirs embarked on their military careers with enthusiasm, and some, like Timothy Gowing, who served with 7th Royal Fusiliers in the Crimea, chose their regiment with care.

> I entered into one of the smartest regiments of our army,
> the Royal Fusiliers . . . I selected this regiment for its noble
> deeds of valour under Lord Wellington in the Peninsula.
> They, the old fusiliers, had made our enemies the French
> shake on many a hard fought field.[34]

It is understandable that most of those for whom enlistment was a last resort or drunken blunder should have left little trace. One exception is Thomas Pococke of the 71st Foot, who enlisted in 1806 in a fit of pique and humiliation after experiencing stage-fright and ruining his acting career. When discharged he left his 'comrades with regret, but the service with joy.'[35] The fact remains that there is a solid corpus of memoirs, letters and diaries left by soldiers of the period who neither fitted Wellington's description nor had much time for those who did.

Private Frederick White of the 7th Hussars, whose death after flogging in 1846 was a turning-point in the history of corporal punishment in the army, seems, superficially, to be yet another example of Wellington's 'scum': he was flogged after threatening an NCO with a poker while drunk. And yet the letter he wrote the District Court Martial which tried him at Hounslow on 10 June is not the work of an illiterate reprobate.

> I am sure it cannot be said that the unfortunate affair was
> premeditated . . . I most deeply regret that the drink I had
> taken had deprived me of all control over myself, and
> obliterated from my mind all those feelings of respect
> which had, up to that time, influenced my conduct. I am

well aware that any crime committed under the influence
of drink obtains but little consideration under that head
– yet from absence of all vindictive feelings on my part,
added to the unconscious state I was in at the committal
of the crime, I hope you will deal leniently with my case . . .

    I am, gentlemen, your Obedient Servant,
    Frederick White[36]

There is abundant evidence that Wellington's strictures applied to
only a proportion of the army. During the flogging debate Lieutenant General Lord Edward Somerset maintained that: 'There are men
of a good station in life who sometimes enlist . . . there are also many
men from the agricultural districts who enlist whose young families
are in a good situation in the labouring classes.[37] Dr William Fergusson was even more forthcoming.

> While a regimental surgeon I have been much among
> common soldiers, and I can vouch that I have never in
> any walk of life fallen in with better men; they certainly
> could not be sober men, but they were usually of excellent
> temper, cheerful, patient, always ready to assist, and bear-
> ing the severest hardship with an equanimity that could
> not be surpassed.[38]

Florence Nightingale was of the same opinion.

> I have never seen so teachable and helpful a class as the
> army generally. Give them opportunity promptly and
> securely to send money home and they will use it. Give
> them schools and lectures and they will come to them.
> Give them books and games and amusements and they
> will leave off drinking. Give them suffering and they will
> bear it. Give them work and they will do it. I had rather
> have to do with the army generally than with any other
> class I have ever attempted to serve.[39]

There are several reasons for the apparent contradiction. The first,
firmly underlined by diarists like Harris and Surtees, is that 'black-
guardism' was confined to a minority of the average regiment. This
was estimated at 10–20 men at the time of the Royal Commission
on Corporal Punishment in 1853, but was probably closer to 10 per

cent in the Napoleonic period. This minority was wholly incorrigible, and its behaviour affronted officers and comrades alike.

The second is that drink was a persistent threat to discipline, and that while it affected the hardened reprobates on a regular basis, relatively few soldiers remained immune from its appeal. Lieutenant George Gleig of the 85th, who was to take holy orders after the Napoleonic wars and serve as chaplain-general in 1844–75, described finding a good store of bread and several casks of brandy in a Spanish village. Even the presence of the enemy would not have prevented a drunken outburst, and so the casks 'were instantly knocked on the head, and the spirits poured out into the streets, as the only means of hindering our men from getting drunk, and saving ourselves from defeat . . .[40] Captain William Webber, Royal Artillery, tells of a case where such precautions were impossible, and:

> The 4th Division in retreating from Valdemoro to Pinto lost 500 or 600 men in a disgraceful manner. Almost 800 broke into a wine cellar and intoxicated themselves to such a degree that very few were able to follow [the retreat]. Many were lying on the ground as if lifeless and became easy victims to the enemy's cavalry. Our light troops retook several, but I hear 350 remain prisoners.[41]

Quartermaster Surtees, normally a sober and well-conducted man, admitted that he 'was led to indulge in the most vile and abominable of all vices, drunkenness, to an extent almost incredible.' He drank a dozen bottle of port with four other officers, was seized with a 'constipation in the bowels' that nearly killed him, and as a result gave up drink and took to religion.[42]

Private Docherty of the 51st ('from the land of Saints') was a good soldier but 'The Devil of a boy for a drop of the crature.' His habits were too much for even the benevolent Lieutenant Colonel Mainwaring, a steadfast opponent of flogging, who had Docherty thrown into a dyke with a rope round his waist and dragged from side to side till he had sobered up, emerging from the mud repentant and 'as black as His Satanic Majesty'.[43]

Drunkenness was a sinister counterpoint to the courage and courtesy of many soldiers: Thomas Pococke of the 71st reckoned that 'the great fault of our soldiers . . . was an inordinate desire for spirits of any kind. They sacrificed their life and safety for drink . . .'[44] Costello pays a handsome tribute to his company commander, Captain Uniacke, who was killed at Cuidad Rodrigo: 'his affability and personal courage had rendered him the idol of the men of his company.'[45] This extraordinary personal regard did not prevent his burial party from being so drunk that they dropped his coffin and broke it. Sergeant Tom Plunket of the 95th was a brave soldier and an excellent shot, but got drunk, tried to shoot his captain, and was reduced to the ranks and sentenced to 300 lashes. His flogging was a shocking affair because of the high regard in which Plunket had been held before his fall. When he pleaded 'Colonel, you won't will you? You cannot mean to flog me' he touched the hearts of all present, and was released after 35 strokes.[46] Most of the memoirs I use here are littered with similar stories. The good man brought down by drink is a feature of the age.

Military crime, most of it caused by drink, peaked in 1868, when 13.7 per cent of the army was court-martialled, with 25,612 convictions among a force of 186,508 men. There was a steady improvement thereafter, as the Army Temperance Society (its members cruelly termed 'tea busters' or 'bun wallahs' by their beery chums) made inroads into drunkenness, and Garrison Institute Coffee Shops offered heat, light and newspapers at trivial cost. Drink remained a problem: when Second Lieutenant George Barrow joined the Connaught Rangers in India in 1884 he wrote that 'drink was the besetting sin of the Connaught men.'[47] Yet there was a steady reduction in drunkenness, and although 9,230 men were fined for it in 1912–13, this represented only some 5 per cent of the regular army: Wellington would have been as delighted and surprised had his army behaved as well.

The contradictions inherent in the British soldier were clearly visible to outsiders. An early seventeenth century comparative assessment of military Europe reckoned that amongst the good points of the British were the fact that:

> They stand by one another, and are often seen to die together.

> They are spirited enough, and have plenty of boldness in warlike exploits, though not very amenable to military customs . . .

But on the other hand:

> Many are given to drink and drunkenness like the Germans. Foreign wines on account of their being accustomed to beer, does not agree with them, and in hot countries over-seas brings on burning fevers . . .[48]

Christopher Duffy suggests of the eighteenth century that: 'The most pronounced moral traits of the English were violence and patriotism.'[49] Samuel Johnson wrote of 'a peasantry of heroes,' and thought that British bravery sprang from a 'want of subordination,' rather than from fixed principles like the love of liberty, and had nothing to do with the mechanical discipline of the Prussians. The Englishman had a high opinion of his individual worth and, thought Johnson, 'they who complain, in peace, of the insolence of the population, must remember, that their insolence in peace is bravery in war.'[50]

Johnson's argument strikes a chord, for the British army's performance often had a narrow focus, and was rooted in the regiment, whose brave performance in one battle stood surety for the next. 'Courage goes much by opinion,' thought Major General Sir Henry Lawrence, killed at Lucknow in 1857, 'and many a man behaves as a hero or coward according as to how he is expected to behave.' A more generalised confidence in national superiority provided a broader framework. A German who served in North America found his allies 'amazingly proud and haughty, and imbued with a scorn for all other nations.'[51] This seems an enduring characteristic, and a British officer who went to war in 1914 surmised that even if the Germans won and invaded England, they would still be laughed at in the villages as ridiculous foreigners.

Lastly, soldiers were profoundly influenced by the example set by their officers. The latter were almost unfailingly courageous in battle, often to the point of self-sacrifice. But they sometimes set a far worse example where drink, women and violence were concerned. Ensign William Thornton Keep of the 77th watched two fellow ensigns indulge in a furious fight 'in sight, unfortunately for them, of the private soldiers and townspeople' until both were arrested.[52] Fist fights between British officers and French civilians were so common in occupied France in 1815 that Wellington had to remind his officers that the practice of 'striking individuals with their fists' 'is quite inconsistent with their duty, and with their character as British officers.'[53]

Officers frequently eloped with local girls and sometimes with soldiers' wives. In the Peninsula, Mrs Bishop, wife of a sergeant in 2/7th, was 'flogged on the breech' by the provost marshal for stealing. The spectacle proved too much for an officer – coyly described as 'Colonel E, of the – regiment,' who ran off with the lady.[54] Lieutenant Kelly of the grenadier company of the 40th eloped with the daughter of a Portuguese general after a running battle in which the lieuten-ant's grenadiers, who had turned up to assist their officer in his hour of need, saw off their pursuers. The couple were married by the chaplain of a Portuguese *caçadore* battalion – Kelly was presumably a Roman Catholic – and although there was an enormous row which involved both Wellington and his judge-advocate general, they were soon forgiven. Captain the Hon Sanders Gore of the 94th set up house with a girl and was killed when Spanish police attacked his quarters in an attempt to recover her. Another Lieutenant Kelly decamped with the wife of Private Noah Cooper, and then struck Cooper when he asked for her return. A court-martial ordered him to be cashiered, but the Prince Regent reduced the sentence to a reprimand, allowing Kelly, an ex-ranker, to sell his commission.

Cobbett was one of the many critics who complained that the drunken behaviour of officers was rarely punished while severe pen-alties were meted out to soldiers for similar conduct. Robert Waterfield wrote that the behaviour of some young officers of the 32nd and 67th Regiments, in garrison at Portsmouth, brought com-plaints from cabmen: 'He has just knocked my hat over my eyes, sent me sprawling in the gutter, and drove away with my cab.' A young civilian had had his sweetheart 'grossly insulted' by subalterns of the 32nd. These 'pranks' were carried out with impunity, while, thought Waterfield, 'a poor private for staying out till 10 or 11 o'clock at night would be punished more severe than what a common thief would be in any gaol in the United Kingdom.'[55] In the 1830s Captain Clark of the 9th Lancers horse-whipped the collector at the Hammersmith toll-gate for having the impertinence to demand his toll, and a young officer who had difficulties with his aitches was so badly bullied that he left the 4th Hussars. Officers led by example, and there were times when they did too little to prevent patriotism from degenerating into chauvinism, enthusiasm into excess, and courage into cruelty.

EPAULETTE GENTRY

THE COMMISSION LIES in front of me in a puddle of light from my desk lamp, a little over 12 inches long and 9 deep, its parchment still creamy despite the passage of time, and is folded in quarters to slip easily into an inside pocket. It is 160 years, almost to the day, since 29 December 1840, when Queen Victoria signed it and appointed her trusty and well beloved Robert William Lowry, Gentleman, to be an ensign in her 47th Regiment of Foot. A commission: proof of gentlemanly status and military authority, a buyable commodity to some (it would have cost Ensign Lowry's parents at least the regulation price of £450) but impossible aspiration to others. Lowry's first commission was followed, over the years, by new ones for successive ranks: he was to die in his bed, fifty years later, as a lieutenant general and Companion of the Bath.

About two-thirds of the commissions in the period 1660–1871 were obtained by purchase, the remainder being gained by seniority, through patronage or as a reward for long, gallant or distinguished service. However, the pattern was uneven. In wartime the demand for officers outstripped the supply of would-be officers who could afford commissions, and in the large army of 1810 as many as four-fifths of all commissions had been obtained by means other than purchase. A similar process occurred during the Crimea, when non-purchase commissions shot up from 319 out of a total 862 in 1854 to 1,271 of 1,736 in 1855.

The purchase of commissions was firmly established before George I came to the throne, although the Mutiny Act of 1695 contained a clause obliging officers to swear, before their commission could be registered, that they had not paid anyone for it. The first Hanoverians did not much like purchase, but it had created such a vested interest that they could scarcely oppose it without alienating precisely those elements of the body politic upon whose support they relied. They did, however, establish a firm control over the way the system worked, with a Royal Warrant of 1720, occasionally revised thereafter, establishing the tariff for commissions, obliging an officer to sell only to another with a rank immediately below his own, and enshrining the Crown's right to approve the transaction. They also succeeded in altogether stamping out the purchase of regimental colonelcies, which was not uncommon before 1715.

Other rampant abuses were also dealt with. The commissioning of children had begun in the reign of Charles II, and in William's reign one of his godchildren, Theresa Douglas, daughter of Lieutenant Colonel John Douglas of Hamilton's Regiment, was not only given the king's name but a captaincy in the regiment. She went on half pay in 1714 and was struck off in 1717. In 1711 it was ordered that commissions were not to be given to persons under 16, although there were frequent breaches of the rule. Lord George Lennox, second son of the Duke of Richmond, became an ensign in 1751 at the age of thirteen and was lieutenant colonel commanding the 33rd Foot only seven years later at the age of twenty. The Duke of York, as commander-in-chief, tightened things up further, insisting on the minimum age of 16, and decreeing that an officer must serve two years as a subaltern before attaining a captaincy and required at least six years' service before becoming a major. In 1809 these time limits were increased to three and eleven years respectively, and a major required a minimum of nine years' service before he could become a lieutenant colonel.

The notion that an individual could purchase military rank, up to and including that of lieutenant colonel, which could involve the command of a regiment in wartime, seems wholly bizarre in modern eyes, and was, indeed, increasingly perceived to be unsatisfactory by contemporaries. However, the arguments in its favour were by no means derisory. Charles Clode, writing shortly before the abolition of purchase in 1871, suggested that an officer's pay was simply an honorarium, and purchase indicated the importance of attracting 'men of independent means – not merely professional officers' to the service. He pointed out that Wellington had admired purchase because 'it brings into the service men of fortune and character – men who have some connection with the interests and fortunes of the country . . .'[56] Sir John Fortescue, looking back at the era with affection, argued that it was economical, for an officer's pay scarcely exceeded the interest on the price of his commission; secure, for officers were bound over on good behaviour in the price of their commissions, forfeit if they were cashiered; and convenient, because it ensured a steady flow of promotion.

And at least some of the counter-arguments were based on serious misunderstandings. J. C. Hudson's book of 1842 on career guidance warned parents that the army 'is no place for the son of a poor man to enter as an officer . . . The ordinary mode of obtaining a commission is by purchase, and the applications for purchasing are said to be so numerous that a large proportion are necessarily refused.'[57] Byerley Thompson went further, telling his readers that it was not simply the case that most commissions were only to be had for purchase, but in consequence NCOs were 'compelled not only to obey the orders, but to instruct in the way of giving orders, a young gentleman who in the division of battle knows no more than a spinster.'[58] Commentators like W. H. Russell were not slow to poke fun at officers whose breeding did not match their brains. He wrote of an incident in the Crimea when:

> Lord Dunkellin, Captain Coldstream Guards, was taken prisoner on the 22nd. He was out with a working party of his regiment which had got a little out of their way, when a number of men were observed in the dawning light in front of them. 'There are the Russians' exclaimed one of the men. 'Nonsense, they're our fellows,' said his lordship, and off he went towards them, asking in a high tone as he got near, 'Who is in command of this party?' His men

saw him no more, but he was afterwards exchanged for
. . . [a captured] Russian artillery officer.[59]

The apparent link between purchase and incompetence was always
emphasised by the system's critics, who were less swift to acknowledge
that, unfair and illogical though purchase unquestionably was, it did
permit the rich and competent to rise quickly. The future Duke of
Wellington became lieutenant colonel of the 33rd Foot at the age of
twenty-five, at least ten years younger than a very capable officer
might expect in 2001.

Finally, dissatisfaction with purchase underlay William Napier's
much-quoted complaint that the army of his day wilted under 'the
cold shade of the aristocracy.' This assertion has been comprehen-
sively demolished by Michael Glover in *Wellington's Army*, but long
before that, in 1855, the Earl of Malmesbury effectively rebutted the
accusation in the House of Lords. After a detailed study of the Army
List, he observed that only one-sixth of the officers in the Grenadier
Guards – 'a regiment particularly charged with guarding the throne
of an ancient monarchy' had a blood connection to the peerage. In
the first ten regiments of line infantry there were only seven sons
and brothers of peers. 'In the first seven regiments of heavy dragoons
there were only three such officers; and in the last ten regiments of
infantry there were fewer still . . .'[60]

In outline the purchase system was simple enough. A young man
bought his first step, as ensign in the infantry or cornet in the cavalry,
and then bought successive promotions as vacancies appeared
because officers retired, sold their commissions or transferred to
another regiment. Commissions were bought from, and sold back
to, the government. But they were often deemed more valuable than
the price laid down in the warrant, and so the purchaser had to add
a privately agreed non-regulation premium, which went directly to
the seller. The transaction was usually handled by the regimental
agent, a useful intermediary, since it was in theory illegal to pay
more than the regulation price for a commission.

The investment involved was considerable. In November 1854
Edward Cooper Hodge, who commanded the 4th Dragoon Guards
throughout the Crimean War, reflected on the cost of his own com-

missions. His cornetcy had cost him nothing, having been given him through the Duke of York's patronage: had he had to pay for it, it would have cost £840. To the regulation price of his lieutenancy (£350 on top of the value of his cornetcy) he had added a non-regulation £250. His captaincy was £2,035 on top of his lieutenancy, with £1,200 extra; his majority £1,350 more than the value of his captaincy, with £1,435 extra, and his lieutenant colonelcy £1,600 more than the majority with an added non-regulation £1,400. He estimated that he had actually paid £9,620, £4,285 of that in non-regulation payments.

Until a War Office warrant of 23 October 1855 an officer lost the value of his commission if he was killed, although exceptions were often made for particularly gallant service, when an officer's dependants might be allowed to sell the commission. Thereafter, as Hodge observed, 'if I am killed or die of wounds within six months of receiving them, my mother and sisters will receive £6,175' – the full regulation price of his lieutenant colonelcy.[61] He would, however, lose all the non-regulation payments and the value of his free cornetcy, and calculated (though his arithmetic seems wobbly) his potential loss at £4,445 'which I shall have paid the country for graciously allowing me to serve her'.

An officer selling his commission was generally obliged to offer it to the most senior officer in his regiment of the rank immediately below his own. If this officer were unable or unwilling to purchase, then it would be offered to the next in seniority. A vacancy in anything but the most junior rank created 'a chain reaction within a regiment, since nobody could move up the ladder without at the same time selling, thus requiring a chain of purchasers.'[62] A vacant lieutenant colonelcy meant five other vacancies (four after the rank of captain-lieutenant disappeared) as everyone stepped up a rank. Moreover, with each move all officers moved up one place in regimental seniority: the promotion of the senior captain to major saw a new senior captain, and as the senior lieutenant advanced to captain, so all the subalterns moved forward a pace in seniority.

The appearance of a likely vacancy signalled a burst of activity amongst junior officers, who often clubbed together to find sufficient money to persuade their senior to sell out and start a chain reaction

from which all would profit. In May 1777 John Peebles, senior lieutenant of the 42nd, spoke to his commanding officer, who wanted
him to give a non-regulation £50 to the ailing Captain Lieutenant
Valentine Chisholm if he agreed to sell out.

> I thought it was too much, and am of opinion that Mr
> Chisholm should either sell or serve, that as he was no
> longer able to serve he should not expect promotion, if
> he sold the regulation price was as much as he could
> expect in the current state of affairs, however to facilitate
> the matter & make it as well for poor Chisholm as we
> could, I agreed to give the £50, 20 of which Lts [John]
> Rutherford and [Robert] Potts agreed to make up equally
> betwixt them on the above conditions & Ensign [Gavin]
> Drummond gives £30, which with the regulation price
> from Ens. Campbell makes up the 600 guineas to Chis-
> holm if I succeed to this captaincy.[63]

The scheme duly bore fruit, and on 31 October Peebles was duly
promoted captain lieutenant, with Rutherford stepping up to senior
lieutenant, Campbell purchasing the vacant lieutenancy and Drum-
mond moving up in the ensign's list, ready for a lieutenancy. Sir
William Howe's order book is punctuated by promotion lists which
testify to the inexorable operation of the system. Thus on 13 August
1776, from his headquarters on Staten Island, Howe announced:

> 17th Regt
> Ensign Isaac Cary to be Lieut
> Vice Lord Borriedale by Purchase
> Robert Ludlow Gent to be Ensign
> Vice Cary by Purchase[64]

An officer who wished to quit active service could either sell out
altogether, receiving the price of his commission, as, in effect, a
pension fund. As he would often have gained at least one promotion
without purchase, he would make a small capital gain into the bargain. If he wanted to receive a regular income and to retain the
value of his commission without selling it, he could go onto half-pay.
The half-pay list contained officers who were content to give up
active service – indeed, some young gentlemen bought half-pay com-

missions without any apparent intention of serving – and others who had no active employment because their regiments had been disbanded, but who wished to serve on if they could. Some of the latter bought full-pay commissions and resumed their careers, and others might be provided with non-purchase vacancies as they arose in established units, or appointed to newly raised ones.

Non-purchase vacancies occurred when an officer died or was cashiered, or in wartime when new units were raised or existing ones augmented, although the commissions thus granted could not generally be sold. In the case of death vacancies the iron rule of seniority applied, and the senior officer of each rank stepped up to fill the slot. It was possible for an officer to work steadily up his regiment by attaining non-purchase vacancies, by seniority, as they came up, and the process was easier if his regiment was repeatedly knocked about on the battlefield. Jacob Brunt enlisted in 1770, and was commissioned as ensign and adjutant of the 55th in 1793. Four months later he transferred to the newly-raised 83rd as a lieutenant, and spent the rest of his career in that regiment, reaching each new rank without purchase to become a lieutenant colonel on 13 July 1811, just 41 years after he first joined as a private soldier.

Promotion by seniority was always slow and was not sure. If an officer was taken prisoner his rank and seniority were frozen, but, all being well, on his emergence from captivity he would be promoted to the rank he would have reached had he not been captured. Being 'noted on the invalid list' also delayed promotion, though it did not prevent Matthew Sutton of the 97th from being promoted to major in 1813 although he was totally blind. A court-martial might suspend an officer from rank and pay, and while in limbo he would miss any promotions due him.

Each of Brunt's promotions beyond ensign, of course, meant advancement for at least one other officer. Howe's order book sets out the process for a promotion in August 1775:

> 49th Regt
> Captn Lieut James Grant to be Captain
> Vice Heptune Dead
> Lieut Robert Wilson to be Captn Lieut
> Vice Grant Preferred

> Ensign Willm Roberts to be Lt
> Vice Wilson Preferred
> Joseph Wrigglesworth Volunteer to be Ensign
> Vice Roberts preferred[65]

Here the fortunate Mr Wrigglesworth has profited from a non-purchase ensigncy. He had been a gentleman volunteer, doing duty as a private soldier but messing with the officers, learning his trade and awaiting a recommendation for a commission. Light dragoon officer Thomas Brotherton wrote of the Peninsula that:

> The *volunteers* we had with the army ... always recklessly exposed themselves in order to render themselves conspicuous, as their object was to get commissions given to them without purchase. The largest proportion of these volunteers were killed, but those who escaped were well rewarded for their adventurous spirit.[66]

In 1812 George Hennell, son of a Coventry ribbon manufacturer in a moderate way of business, went out to Spain with a letter of introduction to Sir Thomas Picton. Picton attached him to the 94th Foot as a volunteer, and two days later he took part in the storming of Badajoz. It is hard to think of a more trying baptism of fire, but when Hennell reached the wall of the fortress he showed insight and courage.

> The dead and wounded lay so thick that we were continually treading on them (I must tell the facts). The men were not so eager to go up the ladders as I expected they would be. They were as thick as possible in the ditch and, the officers desiring them to go up, I stopped about two minutes likewise. The men were asking 'Where is the 74th?' 'Where is the 95th?' I perceived they were looking for their regiments rather than the ladders, I went up the ladder, and when about half way up I called out 'Here is the 94th!' and was glad to see the men begin to mount.[67]

This gallant action was the making of him, for he was speedily commissioned into the 43rd Foot.

'You are a fortunate fellow indeed,' said a brother officer. 'Why, many have been 6, 8 and 12 months volunteers in this country before they get their commissions . . .' Like most other regiments, however, the 43rd required all newly-joined officers, whatever the source of their commissions, to carry out basic training, sending them, as Lieutenant John Cooke wrote:

> to drill with a squad composed of peasants from the plough and other raw recruits, first learning the facings, marchings and the companies' evolutions. That being completed, the officer put on cross-belts and pouches and learnt the firelock exercises; then again he marched with the same; and when it was considered that the whole was perfect, with and without arms, they began to skirmish in extended file, and last of all learned the duties of a sentry, and to fire ball cartridge at a target.[68]

It was not until the adjutant was satisfied that he could put a company through its evolutions that he was considered trained: the process took about six months of four one-hour drills each day.

A more formal version of officer training was available from 1801. Attendance at the Royal Military College at Sandhurst, where it had migrated in 1812 following brief sojourns at High Wycombe and Great Marlowe, was neither obligatory for potential officers nor certain to produce a free commission. Indeed, Sandhurst never filled its quota of 400 cadets, reaching a maximum strength of 330 in 1818 and sinking below 200 in 1824. Part of the establishment's lack of attraction stemmed from the fact that it offered only a limited number of free places: a family which could afford to send a boy there for two years would often opt to buy him a commission instead. In the period 1838–48 650 cadets entered the college: 350 were given free commissions and another 200 failed to pass out and bought commissions.

'Raising for rank' enabled militia officers to gain regular commissions by persuading set numbers of their militiamen to volunteer for the Regular army. George Siddons, assistant surgeon of the Royal South Lincolnshire Militia, must have had remarkable powers of persuasion, for despite his commanding officer's opposition he took a hundred militiamen into the army and was rewarded with a 2nd lieutenant's commission in the crack 95th.

Over the past twenty years a growing volume of research has revealed the existence of a much larger body of 'subaltern officers of advanced age and experience promoted from amongst the non-commissioned officers' than had previously been recognised.[69] Vacancies for free commissions might be filled from the half-pay list, or increasingly by the commissioning of deserving sergeant-majors or sergeants: in 1756 alone four NCOs were commissioned into the 56th Foot and three into the 33rd. When the 3rd Foot gained a second battalion in 1756 it gained its officers from a variety of sources, including the quartermaster and four lieutenants from the ranks of the 1st Battalion. Thomas Barrow, father of George, the author of *Lavengro*, enlisted in 1783, became a sergeant nine years later and retired as a captain.

Joseph Barra, born in Sussex in 1780, enlisted first in the Warwick Militia and then in the 11th Light Dragoons. He was a sergeant by 1804, and in 1807 he was commissioned without purchase into the 16th Light Dragoons, gaining a non-purchase lieutenancy in 1808 and a captaincy in 1815. His brother officers presented him with a handsome engraved sword, and when he was placed on half-pay in 1816 took pains to secure him the appointment as adjutant of the Earl of Chester's Yeomanry. There too he was an outstanding success, and his calming behaviour in the Macclesfield riots of 1824 brought him the thanks not only of the mayor and corporation, but also of Sir Robert Peel, the Home Secretary. He was buried at Knutsford in 1839 with full military honours, with his presentation sword on his coffin.

The career of John Shipp was more varied. He was raised an orphan, by his parish, but his heart kindled with excitement when he heard a band play 'Over the Hills and Far Away', and he enlisted in the 22nd Foot in 1797. Although repeatedly in trouble – he once escaped flogging by his commanding officer's personal intervention – he became a sergeant and went to India, admitting that 'my ambition was to make a name for myself in the field.'[70] During Lord Lake's fruitless and costly siege of Bhurtpore in 1805, he volunteered for repeated storming parties and was commissioned without purchase into the 65th, where he was greeted cordially in the officers' mess. 'All the officers of the corps flocked round me, and greeted me in the most handsome and friendly manner . . . Had I been the son of a duke my reception could not have been more flattering or friendly.'[71] He moved as a lieutenant to the 76th only three weeks later, and after his return to England he was, in consideration of his distinguished services in the field, allowed to sell his commission to pay off his debts, for non-purchase commissions could not normally be sold.

Shipp re-enlisted, this time into the 24th Dragoons, and had reached the rank of sergeant-major before he was again commissioned, into the 87th Foot. In 1823 a dispute with his major saw him court-martialled and sent on half pay. He had received six wounds from musket-balls, and sixteen pieces of bone had been removed from two injuries to his skull. Despite his own misfortunes, Shipp remained proud of his military career. He comments on the popularity of Lake – 'truly my friend, as he was of every soldier in the army' – and gives an instance of the way in which the close personal attention of senior officers could turn even the purchase system to men's advantage.

> A very old Lieutenant had given up all hope of getting a company that was vacant, knowing full well that he could not afford to buy it. I was standing by him when the orderly book, showing his promotion by purchase, was put in his hands. He looked at it and said 'There must be some mistake. I have not a rupee to call my own.' Just then Colonel Lake, his Lordship's son, came up and wished him joy of his promotion. 'There must be some mistake,' the man answered, 'I cannot purchase.' 'My father knows you cannot,' said the Colonel, 'so he has lent you the money which he never intends to take back.'[72]

Gallantry decorations were not available until the end of the period, and a commission was sometimes awarded for an act that would later have earned an award. In 1745 Sergeant Terence Molloy of the 55th Foot held Ruthven Barracks near Kingussie with twelve men. When a substantial Jacobite force appeared and ordered him to surrender, he replied: 'I was too old a Soldier to surrender a Garrison of such strength without bloody noses,' and when told that he faced hanging for his refusal, 'told them I would take my Chance.'

General Sir John Cope recommended the Secretary of State for Scotland that Molloy 'be made an officer for his gallant behaviour', and he was promoted direct to lieutenant. Although Molloy was compelled to surrender when the Jacobites attacked again, this time with artillery, he did so on terms that allowed him to march his men off to the nearest royal garrison.

Sergeant Bernard McCabe of the 31st Foot was commissioned after his exploits at Sobraon in 1846, when he took the regimental colour from its fallen ensign and planted it on the Sikh parapet. He became something of a martinet, and during the siege of Lucknow, where he was killed under predictably gallant circumstances, he roundly abused a sentry who had not shot at him because he recognised him doing his rounds.

> Officer, very severely: 'You should have fired, sir. You are not supposed to know anyone outside your post, especially at night, sir.'
> Sentry: Then by J . . . C . . . the next time you will come the same way at night I will accommodate you. I will shoot you right enough.[73]

Molloy, Barra and McCabe were 'genuine' rankers – although Barra's commanding officer observed that 'his manners [are] very quiet and perfectly like a gentleman' – rather than men like George Hennell, who felt perfectly comfortable on fishing trips with the officers and at 'a masquerade at Col Campbell's' while still only a volunteer.[74] There are occasional examples of 'gentlemen rankers' who served as private soldiers rather than volunteers, but who came, broadly, from the same background as most of their officers. Some were fortunate and obtained commissions, but for others the motives that had led to their enlistment in the first place – drink or financial impropriety – continued to dog them.

William Surtees knew several former officers who served with him in the ranks of the 95th in the hope of making their way again. Conway Welch, former adjutant of a militia unit, the Surrey Rangers, 'got on to the rank of corporal, but, being excessively wild, I believe he never attained a higher rank.' A former officer in the Caithness Legion, reduced at the Peace of Amiens, rose to pay sergeant but had a problem with his accounts, and shot himself. James McLaughlan had been an officer in the light company of the 35th but had sold his commission to pay gambling debts. He went to the Helder as a gentleman volunteer and regained his commission, but lost it again and signed on as a private. He tried to desert to the French, but was captured, court-martialled and sentenced to transportation for life. Surtees was shocked at his downfall: 'I understand a sister of his was at Shorncliffe at the time of his trial, etc, the wife of a brevet lieutenant colonel in the 4th Regiment. What she must have felt.'[75]

Very different was the case of Charles Robert Cureton, who was gazetted a lieutenant in the Shropshire Militia in 1806. He got into financial difficulties and faked suicide by leaving his clothes on a beach while he took ship for London and enlisted into the 16th Light Dragoons under the name of Robert Taylor. He was a corporal and then sergeant in Thomas Brotherton's troop, until Lord FitzRoy Somerset, Wellington's Military Secretary – who had known him in his previous existence – took him off to be a confidential clerk and galloper at headquarters. He was commissioned into the 40th Foot in 1814, exchanged into the 20th Light Dragoons in October that year, was lieutenant and adjutant in 1816 and transferred to the 16th Lancers in 1819, being promoted captain in 1825, major in 1833, lieutenant colonel in 1839 and colonel in 1846.

Cureton served in Afghanistan in 1839–40, and commanded first a cavalry brigade and then the cavalry division in the first Sikh War. He was killed as a brigadier-general at Ramnagar in the second Sikh War, unsuccessfully trying to prevent Lieutenant Colonel Thomas Havelock (brother of Sir Henry, one of the heroes of Lucknow) from leading his regiment, the 14th Light Dragoons, into a gully full of Sikh infantry. Sergeant Thomas Pearman saw how:

> General Cureton came down with the staff, and went to find Colonel Havelock, when a shot struck him. He threw up his arms and life was gone. Also, the colonel of the 1st Native Cavalry on the staff was shot at the same time. We buried them like soldiers with their cloaks round them, all in one grave at the village of Ramnagar.'[76]

Brotherton had the highest regard for him. He was invited to meet him at dinner at FitzRoy Somerset's house:

> Although he had perfectly the manners of a gentleman, though he had risen from the ranks, he never presumed, and showed me the same respect and deference as when he was a corporal in my troop. When the clasps for the battles of the Peninsula were issued, instead of sending his application for his share of them (which was every battle that had been fought, as he had been present at all of them) through the regular channel to Horse Guards, by way of paying me a compliment he sent it through me, saying 'I knew his services better than anyone.'[77]

Sometimes the 'interest' which gained a man his commission could be very loosely defined. When Thomas Morris joined the light company of the 73rd in 1812, 'the finest set of men I ever saw, being a mixture of English, Irish and Scotch,' its commander had been commissioned from the ranks.

> Report said that he was indebted for his promotion, to his beautiful black eyes and whiskers, which had attracted the notice of his colonel's lady; who had sufficient influence to obtain for him a commission as ensign.

The captain's brusque and eccentric manner made him difficult to deal with. His ensign, 'a fine manly fellow named Loyd (sic)' would not be bullied by the captain. 'One day the latter said to him 'Damn you, Sir, I'll let you know that I am your captain!' The ensign replied. 'And, Sir, you will please to recollect, at the same time, that I am Ensign Loyd, and a gentleman.'[78]

It was partly because of episodes like this that many senior officers retained grave doubts about commissioning from the ranks. Wellington told the 1836 Royal Commission on Military Punishment that they:

> do not make good officers; it does not answer. They are brought into a society to the manners of which they are not accustomed; they cannot bear at all being heated in wine or liquor . . . they are quarrelsome, they are addicted to quarrel a little in their cups. And they are not persons

that can be borne in the society of the officers of the
Army; they are different men altogether.[79]

In 1862 General Sir Hugh Rose argued that:

> Neither the officer so raised, nor the officer of a superior
> class in life with whom he associates, nor the soldiers he
> has to govern, are benefited by what is a very disadvan-
> tageous anomaly, the transfer of a man of a very different,
> inferior and educated class in life, to one superior in all
> these respects.[80]

There is some evidence that soldiers, too, preferred officers of the
traditional stamp. Rifleman Benjamin Harris of the 95th claimed
that:

> I know from experience that in our army the men like
> best to be officered by gentlemen, men whose education
> has rendered them more kind in manners than your
> coarse officer, sprung from obscure origin, and whose
> style is brutal and overbearing.

He added that:

> those whose birth and station might reasonably have made
> them fastidious ... have generally borne their miseries
> without a murmur; whilst those whose previous life, one
> would have thought, might have better prepared them for
> the toils of war have been the first to cry out and complain
> of their hard fate.[81]

Sometimes, he believed, soldiers were driven to insubordination 'by
being worried by these little-minded men for the veriest trifles, about
which the gentleman never thinks of tormenting him.'[82]

Sergeant Thomas Morris of the 73rd disagreed vehemently. He
had hoped 'that by good steady conduct, or by some daring act of
bravery, I should be fortunate enough to gain a commission' and
was disappointed that he did not do so. He thought that rankers
could make good officers, but 'the man who obtains a commission
by merit in the British army is placed in a most unpleasant and
unenviable position' because other officers did not treat him properly. He described how a commissioned ranker in the Guards,

promoted by patronage from the Duke of York, asked the Duke to be unmade because his brother officers 'positively refused to associate with him.' The Duke solved the problem by walking arm-in-arm with the new officer while the regiment was on parade, after which the officers were 'very anxious to cultivate the acquaintance of an officer, who appeared to be such an especial favourite with the Duke.'[83] The issue was often one of regimental culture, and the behaviour of officers in a battalion's mess varied enormously.

In 1836 Lieutenant Thomas Blood, a commissioned ranker, suggested that one-third of first commissions should be granted to NCOs: this was in fact the policy laid down by the French military service law of 1832, the Loi Soult. He believed that such individuals knew the habits of private soldiers so well that they were unlikely to be deceived by malingering – which is, no doubt, one reason why they were not always popular with soldiers.

Strictly speaking only the vacancies caused when officers were killed, or died of wounds received in battle were filled, without purchase, by regimental seniority. The commander-in-chief had the right to nominate officers to other vacancies, such as those arising when an officer died (as so many did) in shipwreck, was cashiered or was promoted to major general and so left a regimental vacancy. However, the Duke of York, General Sir David Dundas, and the Duke of Wellington, commanders-in-chief for so much of the period, were well aware that the exercise of their patronage to move deserving officers into other regiments was likely to cause great resentment amongst those superseded, and Wellington claimed, not wholly accurately, that he had only promoted two or three officers this way. Officers sometimes found the promotion of contemporaries by interest intensely frustrating. In January 1812 William Tomkinson wrote: 'Major Stanhope was gazetted out of the 16th to the 17th Light Dragoons as Lieutenant Colonel, in regard for the long campaign he has had in Bond Street since the time he left the 16th in July 1810.'[84]

When commander-in-chief, Wellington complained that he was 'beset by applications from members of the higher classes for vacant appointments within his gift,' and though he resisted them initially, Joachim Stocqueler suggested that eventually 'he made the partial sacrifice of the claims of merit to those of political or party interest one of the cardinal rules of his official conduct, thereby ignoring all the old professions of 1827.'[85] His successor at Horse Guards, the kindly Viscount 'Daddy' Hill, was easily influenced by old comrades and deserving widows: when the future General Sir Daniel Lysons was approaching the age of eighteen and eager for a commission, his brother in law, a baronet, approached Hill, and young Lysons immediately found himself gazetted an ensign in the 1st Royal Regiment.

Many promotions for gallant or distinguished service took an officer away from his own regiment and into one where commissions were less sought after. Lieutenant Matthew Latham of The Buffs (3rd Foot) was terribly wounded at Albuera, with his face split by a sabre-cut and an arm lopped off as he defended the king's colour from French hussars and Polish lancers. He eventually ripped it from its staff, stuffed it into his tunic, and fell, unconscious, upon it. His brother officers gave him a special award, the Prince Regent paid for his medical treatment, and he was given a captaincy – in a West India regiment. John Gurwood led the Light Division's Forlorn Hope at Cuidad Rodrigo, but, as thirty-third lieutenant in the 52nd he was too junior to be promoted in his own regiment, and was given a captaincy in the Royal Africa Corps.

A notable exception to the Duke of York's reluctance to use his prerogative to promote officers came when vacancies were caused by disciplinary action. The 85th was already in trouble before it went to Portugal in 1811: the commanding officer was sluggish, one captain was cashiered and another killed in a duel. Wellington sent it home after eight months, and things then went from bad to worse. The senior major was twice court-martialled on charges brought by the paymaster, who failed to produce evidence to prove them and was himself dismissed. A captain and lieutenant were cashiered after an affray in which the adjutant 'had his nose pulled and his posterior kicked.' A lieutenant was tried for indulging in a horse-whipping competition with an ensign in a public house, but escaped on a plea of self-defence. Finally, after a flurry of other courts-martial, the Duke of York publicly urged the commanding officer to retire and removed every single officer in the regiment, replacing them with officers who had distinguished themselves in other units. This radical surgery cured the disease, and the 85th performed very creditably in the Peninsula and North America.

The importance of seniority as far as regimental promotion was concerned was critical. But while seniority could only be earned, it was possible for long or distinguished service to bring an officer a promotion by brevet, which did not alter his regimental rank or seniority date, but gave him a new rank and seniority in the army as a whole. Brevet promotion was available only to an officer who was already a captain, and could not take him beyond lieutenant colonel. An officer with brevet rank did duty in his regimental rank unless circumstances arose when the senior officer by army rank was required, say, to take command of a brigade. This could make an officer with brevet rank briefly the superior of his own regimental commanding officer. On one occasion a major of a cavalry regiment, senior, by his brevet as a lieutenant colonel, to his own commanding officer, assumed command on a field day when the brigade commander was absent. He looked the man up and down, and then ordered, dismissively: 'Take your wegiment home, sir.'

Brevet rank gave only a little extra pay – and then not in all arms – but it did put an officer in a strong position to claim promotion by patronage in a regiment other than his own. Most brevets were given for long service, and there were successive victory brevets from May 1811 to Waterloo, when the brevet promoted fifty-two majors and thirty-seven captains. Tradition prescribed that the aide de camp bearing a victory dispatch received a brevet, although only if this would not breach promotion regulations. Captain Ulysses Burgh brought the Busaco dispatch to London in 1810 and was gazetted to a brevet majority, only to have it cancelled when it was realised that he lacked the seven years service required. He got his promotion the following year, when he had put in sufficient time.

Officers were able to exchange with comrades of the same rank in different regiments, and did so for a variety of reasons. Sometimes it was to avoid an unpopular posting. Light cavalry regiments were regularly sent to India in the nineteenth century, and, as we have seen in the case of Captain Anstruther Thompson, officers who did not wish to serve abroad often exchanged with those were prepared to go. Similarly, an officer whose prospects of promotion in his own regiment seemed poor could exchange with a less ambitious individual into one where his chances were better. It was even possible to use exchange to gain promotion in one's chosen regiment. In March 1813 Lieutenant Charles Kinloch of the crack 52nd Light Infantry was six steps from a captaincy and there had been no sales for over four years. He bought a captaincy in the less sought-after 99th, and immediately exchanged with an elderly captain in the 52nd who was on the point of leaving the army. He was back in his old regiment as a captain without ever actually leaving it.

William Tomkinson gained his captaincy by similar sleight of hand. In March 1812, while he was serving as a lieutenant with the 16th Light Dragoons in the Peninsula, too junior to hope for a promotion by seniority, his father Henry bought him a captaincy in the 60th Foot, a large regiment with plenty of vacancies. He then exchanged with a captain in the 16th Light Dragoons, though he had to pay a hefty non-regulation premium to do so, for captaincies in the 16th were a good deal more desirable than those in the 60th. The colonel of the 16th, General Sir George Anson, was privy to the deal, for he told Henry Tomkinson that he looked forward to receiving the £1,650 which it would cost William to exchange back to the cavalry as a captain. However, £997 10s, the value of his cavalry lieutenancy, which he was selling, would eventually be offset against this. He concluded: 'I confess myself very anxious to secure your son's return to the 16th Light Dragoons.' Young William continued to serve with the 16th while all this was going on.[86]

Officers who conducted exchanges, which required the approval of the commander-in-chief and their regimental colonels, had to sign a certificate saying that no financial 'consideration' was involved, but money did indeed change hands, and an inducement proved especially attractive to an officer who was thinking of leaving the service in any event and could be persuaded by money. Field-Marshal Sir Evelyn Wood frankly admitted that he had manipulated the system to his advantage. He exchanged into the 73rd Foot as a captain from the 7th Lancers, but when his new regiment was ordered to Hong Kong in 1865, commanded, moreover, not by 'the pleasant Colonel, who commanded it when I joined . . . [but] by a man I disliked . . . I paid £500 for an exchange to the 17th Regiment.' In 1866, when the

17th too was warned for duty abroad, Major Wood considered a return to the cavalry, but although his prospective commanding officer was prepared to lend him the money to pay off the incumbent major, Wood decided against it. Instead, he went onto half pay and negotiated possible exchanges with three infantry majors. He had settled on one, but 'a Captain who had been a Colour Sergeant at the Alma wrote me a manly letter, appealing to my feelings as a soldier not to stop his advancement by coming into the regiment.' He accordingly paid £2,000 to exchange into the 90th Light Infantry.[87]

The gentlemen of the Ordnance, officers of the artillery and engineers, had mixed feelings about purchase. It never applied to their own corps, and their promotion prospects were dominated by the order in which they passed out from the Royal Military Academy at Woolwich, established in 1741 to train the officers of both arms. Promotion was almost entirely by seniority, and advancement was glacial. Jacob Brunt's ascent of the 83rd Foot was lightning fast by comparison with Thomas Downman's progress through the Royal Horse Artillery. Both were commissioned in the same year, 1793, and while Brunt became a lieutenant colonel in 1811 Downman did not reach the rank regimentally (though he gained it by brevet in 1812) until 1825.

Cavalié Mercer was one of the most capable gunner officers of his generation, and at Waterloo his troop played a crucial role in the defence of Wellington's centre right. But Mercer, although commissioned in 1799, was still only a 2nd Captain (a species of junior captain existing only in the Ordnance and not even eligible for brevet promotion till 1813) at Waterloo, and in 1825 he went off to Canada as a brevet major. After the Napoleonic Wars promotion in the artillery was appallingly slow. In 1832 the junior of each rank averaged thirty years service for a 1st captain and over 34 years for a lieutenant colonel: Sir George Wood, who commanded the artillery at Waterloo, was still only a major twenty-one years later.

Unlike the officer corps in most other European armies, the British army was never dominated by noblemen, in part because there were relatively few. There were only 167 male peers in England in 1710, rising to 220 in 1790, in contrast (though we are not comparing like with like) to the perhaps 110–120,000 French nobles in about 25,000 noble families in France in 1789. In the 1720s, 62 per cent of Russian officers were noble and thereafter it became more difficult for non-nobles to gain commissioned rank. In 1767, Poland restricted first commissions, except in the artillery, to nobles, while a French ordinance of 1781 required the possession of four degrees of nobility for promotion above the rank of captain.

Such restrictions, which were swept away in France by the Revolution, and substantially weakened elsewhere by the Napoleonic wars, were always impossible in Britain, although at the top of the social scale perhaps a quarter of officers came from the nobility and landed gentry. There was a sound sprinkling of wealthy men, even in apparently 'unsmart' regiments: Sir Charles des Voeux did not accrue the £300,000 he left in 1858 from his half-pay captaincy in the 63rd Foot. But far more important was 'that class of poor and honourable gentlemen' described by the Prince de Ligne.

> They grew up the sons of valiant squires, who were themselves accustomed to country life and the hunt. From the age of twelve they conditioned themselves to hardship, sleeping in the woods with their dogs, arresting poachers, ands fighting every now and then with some neighbour's son over the possession of a hare.[88]

They were well summed up by one eighteenth century officer, who described himself as 'a private Gentleman without the advantage of Birth or Friends.' These minor gentry formed the great majority of regimental officers, although their lack of money and patronage tended to prevent them from rising as high as men with connections to match their cash.

Scotland and Ireland, whose disproportionate impact on the army we have already recorded, produced prolific but impecunious minor gentry whose sons often became officers. Sir Walter Scott told the Duke of Wellington that:

> Your Grace knows that Scotland is a breeding, not a feeding country, and we must send our sons abroad, as we sent our black cattle to England; and, as old Lady Charlotte, of Ardkinglass, proposed to dispose of her nine sons, we have a strong tendency to put our young folks 'a' to the sword.[89]

It was said that if you went into the mess of the 38th Foot and shouted 'Campbell' a quarter of those present would turn round, while the 22nd Foot, despite its affiliation to Cheshire, was so notable for its Irish officers that it even had an agent in Dublin. At the beginning of the period Huguenots, expelled from France after the Revocation of the Edict of Nantes in 1685, also formed a recognisable group, with Field Marshal Jean, Viscount Ligonier (1680–1770) at their head.

Family tradition was important, from Scots families like the Tullochs and Irish like the Goughs, in the Army List generation after generation, to the Adyes, so well represented in the Royal Artillery from 1757 to the Second World War. Field Marshal Lord Wavell was later to write that while he felt no special inclination to a military career, it would have taken more independence and character than he possessed to have avoided one simply because all his male relatives were serving soldiers: he took the line of least resistance. J.A. Houlding, historian of the eighteenth century army, traces the development of 'army families' back to the period 1715–1730, when their new professionalism, the product of the institutionalised standing army, was quite different to earlier mercenary professionalism of families like the Kirkes and the Douglases.

Clergymen's sons often became officers, with Major General Sir John Inglis, a hero of Lucknow, as perhaps the most striking example. One survey has identified 10 per cent of serving colonels in 1854 having fathers who were clergymen, and by 1899 'clergy' and 'peerage and baronetage' each accounted for 12 per cent of colonels' backgrounds. Finally, as the nineteenth century wore on, there was an increasing flow of young men from the new public schools. Much as the late 20th Century mocked the 'country squire as muscular clergyman,' these gallant and determined gentlemen were to form the backbone of the late Victorian army.

When the 32nd Foot embarked for India in May 1846 it was a microcosm of the line infantry of the age. Its officers included three sons of landowners, eight of officers or former officers, and fourteen of varied middle-class occupations, including sons of a bishop, two clergyman, an Indian judge, a East India Company civil servant, a colonial administrator, a Canadian businessman, a city merchant, a

West India merchant and a bank manager. When the regiment earned its place in the military pantheon by defending Lucknow, it included three ranker officers: William Rudman, the adjutant, John Langran Giddings, the paymaster, and Bernard McCabe of Sobraon fame, captain by regimental rank but lieutenant colonel by brevet for brave and distinguished service. McCabe was mortally wounded on 29 September 1858. His mother, who lived in Dublin, was granted a pension, and his chief executor was his brother Terence, a fish salesman of Ashton-under-Lyme.

Throughout the period the social origins of those who finished up in officers' messes or soldiers' barrack rooms were far less stereotyped than might be supposed. The experienced Sergeant Roger Lamb argued that officers and men were often far closer than the difference in rank implied. 'Attachments of persons in the army to each other terminate but with life,' he wrote:

> The fondness of the officer continues with the man who fought under his command, to the remotest period of declining years, and the old soldier venerates his aged officer far more than perhaps he did in his youthful days: it is like friendship between school-boys, which increases in manhood, and ripens in old age.[90]

Lieutenant Calvert of the 23rd had promised in 1784 that he would always help Lamb if he could, and the two were happily corresponding twenty-five years later.

IV

HORSE, FOOT, GUNS
— AND WOUNDS

MARCHING
REGIMENTS

THE REDCOATED, pipeclayed infantry of the line made up not simply the bulk of the army as a whole, always at least three times the size of the cavalry, but formed the largest single element of all overseas expeditions. In 1748 there were the equivalent of two regiments of Household and 21 of line cavalry to three regiments of foot guards and 66 of line infantry. At full wartime strength in 1815 the army included three regiments of Household and 37 of line cavalry, to three regiments of foot guards and 104 regiments of line infantry, most with more than one battalion. The British, KGL and Hanoverian element of Wellington's army at Waterloo consisted of 35,388 rank and file of infantry, 10,155 cavalry and 120 pieces of artillery with 5,621 gunners and drivers. The force initially sent to the Crimea in 1854 totalled 26,000 officers and men, forming 28 infantry battalions, ten cavalry regiments and 66 guns.

In the eighteenth century the infantryman's red coat earned him the nickname 'Thomas Lobster': on 12 April 1740 *The Craftsman* magazine contained an apocryphal 'Conversation between Thomas Lobster, soldier, and John Tar, sailor.' The name 'Thomas Atkins' did not appear till much later, originating in 1815 as the example of how to compile the Soldier's Pocket Book, and becoming the soldier's nickname by the 1880s. The red coat was definitively British.

In 1812, when Lieutenant Macpherson of the 45th Regiment (breathing with some difficulty because a musket-ball, providentially deflected by a Spanish silver dollar, had broken two ribs) could not find a British flag for the flagpole above the castle in Badajoz, he ran up his own red jacket.

Although the raising of rifle regiments was to see some footsoldiers turn out in less conspicuous dark green, they remained in the minority: the infantryman remained the redcoat par excellence. The style of his uniform varied with the trends of fashion and the demands of the service. At the beginning of the period he wore a substantial white waistcoat under a knee-length red coat with skirts that might be hooked back to free his legs for marching, deep turned-up cuffs, and broad lapels that could be buttoned across his chest or turned back to show a kaleidoscope of facing colours, blue for the 1st Royal, sea green for the 2nd Queens, buff for the 3rd, known for that very reason as The Buffs, and on to the green of the 66th. White lace framed his buttonholes and edged cuffs and lapels. Breeches were generally white, with long buttoned gaiters over them, white for peacetime and grey, black or brown for active service.

Most infantrymen wore a black felt tricorne hat laced with white, but fusiliers, grenadiers, drummers and pioneers sported an embroidered mitre cap, with bearskin caps appearing from the early 1760s and becoming regulation from 1768. Soldiers of picket companies, and the light companies which replaced them on a permanent basis from 1771, wore a variety of caps, usually a leather skullcap with a crest, peak, and decorated front plate. Corporals showed their rank by a loose white worsted knot hanging from the right shoulder, which may have originated, in the days of the matchlock musket, in the extra skein of slow-match carried by corporals: sergeants added a red sash striped with the facing colour. The officers of battalion companies wore a single epaulette on the right shoulder, with field officers and flank company officers sporting one on each shoulder.

Officers had a broad crimson sash, knotted at the left hip in the infantry and worn over the shoulder by highland officers. This originated in the large netted silk sash worn by officers on both sides in the English Civil War, when it was often big enough, when unfolded, to make an impromptu stretcher for its owner. Highland officers wisely continued the practice: William Gordon-Alexander observed that his comrades of the 93rd in the Indian Mutiny wore a sash which was 'about four or even five times the width of the English one, and could always be utilised to carry its wearer, if wounded, off the field.'[1] Even the English version was not without its use. When Colonel Thomas Graham's horse fell over a precipice on a night march in Spain, Graham managed to hang onto some bushes. There was a cry of 'Put down a pike and sash to him,' and he was hauled to safety. And when Lieutenant General Sir John Moore was buried on the ramparts of Corunna in 1809, his staff officers used their sashes to lower him into his grave.

The demands of campaigning in North America during the Seven Years' War led to coats being cut short, for long tails easily became tangled in the undergrowth. The fashion migrated to units at home – an inspection report on the 62nd Foot in Ireland in 1775 complained of 'coats cut so short I must call them jackets'. It was revived in the American war (though Hollywood gives us little hint of it) when severe modifications to dress often included the removal of lace, lapels and epaulettes. Short-skirted coats were officially introduced for the rank and file in 1797, but officers' coats remained long, with minor alterations to cut. There was, however, a major change in appearance in 1801–2 when the stove-pipe felt shako with its brass plate replaced the tricorne, although officers favoured a bicorne cocked hat.

In 1812 officers were given short-skirted jackets like their men, and all ranks switched to the attractive 'Belgic' shako with a high false front, although light infantry clung to the old stove-pipe version. The 28th Foot also retained the old shako, and wore it at Waterloo, complete with the regiment's unique distinction of a 'back badge,' a small sphinx worn at the rear of the shako to commemorate the regiment's courage at Alexandria in 1801, when its rear rank had faced about to beat off a French attack. William Keep, now serving in the 28th, after being invalided out of the 77th with Walcheren fever, was not pleased about the change, and told his mother that:

> The Prince Regent I think is very inconsiderate in ordering
> such constant deviations in our uniform. Long coats,

fringe epaulettes and cocked hats are now to be abolished. A new cap came down yesterday for me from Bicknells in Bond Street, the price of which is £3 16s. Tailors have just arrived from Plymouth to take our measure for the new jacket, the cost of which is £5 16s and the new bullion epaulettes will cost £2 4s. Next a sabre instead of the present sword will cost 3 or £4 more and the Colonel has put it in orders that we are to provide ourselves with grey overalls instead of the present trousers, with patent leather ends and chains [beneath the instep] which will cost £3 10s a pair. This is a sad interruption to schemes of economy.[2]

Not all objections were financial. There were fears that the new uniform would not show off portly officers to their advantage. 'We are all in consternation at the idea of the dress of the army being altered from cocked hats and coats to caps and jackets,' wrote Lieutenant John Mills of the Coldstream Guards. 'Ye heavens, what will become of crooked legs, large heads and still larger hinder parts?'[3]

The first permanent light infantry regiment – there had been short-lived units in the Seven Years' War – the 90th (Perthshire Volunteers) was raised in 1794 and six other line regiments – the 43rd, 51st, 52nd, 68th, 71st and 85th – were converted to light infantry subsequently. They had red coats, but all ranks wore short jackets from the start, badges featured the bugle-horn used by light troops to transmit orders, and musket-barrels were browned to minimise reflection. The Experimental Corps of Riflemen was formed in 1800 by Colonel Coote Manningham and Lieutenant Colonel the Hon William Stewart by drawing in drafts from thirteen line and 33 Fencible regiments. It was brought into the line as the 95th (Rifle) Regiment in 1802, and a second battalion was raised in 1805. The 95th wore dark green uniforms from the start, with officers sporting light cavalry style sabres and pelisses.

The 60th (Royal American) Regiment had been raised as line infantry, albeit with an emphasis on light infantry tactics, but in 1797 it gained a third battalion, recruited from a variety of foreign regiments, four hundred of its recruits coming from Hompesch's Mounted Rifles. This battalion wore green uniforms and had 'rifle bags' of brown leather instead of the usual knapsacks. Two more green-clad battalions of the 60th were raised in 1799 from German and other prisoners of war, with another following in 1813. The enlistment of foreigners often produced difficulties. Rifleman Harris saw French prisoners who had volunteered to serve in the British army: 'smart looking fellows [who] wore a green uniform something like the Rifles.' One deserted, aggravated his crime by gross insubordination when caught, and was sentenced to flogging. 'When the culprit heard the sentence read out to him,' recalled Harris, 'he was a good deal annoyed, and begged that he might be shot as would have happened to him in his own country.' It was explained to him that this could not be done, and he was duly flogged, although, said Harris: 'all of us would have been glad to see him forgiven.'[4] The 60th was pruned to two battalions after Waterloo, but did not become entirely British till 1824.

Infantry uniforms became more elaborate after Waterloo, with the broad-topped 'Regency' shako and long-tailed coats. A bell-topped shako was introduced in 1829, and all three regiments of foot guards took to the bearskin cap in 1831. Officers, all ranks of the guards and, from 1836, sergeants of the line, adopted a double-breasted coatee, with long tails and no lapels. The cylindrical 'Albert' shako, with peaks fore and aft, was introduced in 1843, but in 1855 it was replaced by a lower and lighter version. In the same year a tunic, initially double-breasted, replaced the coatee, and officers lost their epaulettes, retaining only a twisted gold cord to retain the sash, now worn across the left shoulder, and showing their rank by a complex system of collar and cuff badges. But although the soldier's silhouette was now quite different to that of a century before, the familiar facing colours still glowed on collar and cuffs.

The senior Highland regiment was the 42nd Foot, which from its first raising wore a kilt in dark 'government tartan' which gave it the name 'The Black Watch'. As John Peebles confessed, it took to 'trowsers' in North America, and there were other times when the kilt had its limitations. When Wellington's army was in the Pyrenees in the winter of 1813–14 the nights were freezing – one soldier was awakened by the sobs of youngsters:

who had not been long from their mothers' fire-sides . . .
The weather was so dreadful, the 92nd Regiment got grey
trousers served out to them. They could not live with their
kilts; the cold would have killed them.[5]

Not all the other Highland regiments (the 72nd, 73rd, 78th, 79th, 91st
92th, and 93rd) retained Highland dress, with the 73rd and 93rd being
ordered to discontinue it in 1809 because it was considered 'an
impediment to recruitment.' Lieutenant Innes Munro of the 73rd
certainly found it impractical on campaign in south India 1780:

> Our regiment has found it impossible to wear the High-
> land dress in this country; we are therefore now clothed
> in white hats and trousers, which are better suited to a
> hot climate. Notwithstanding this, I believe that some of
> our soldiers would have braved the utmost rage of the
> mosquitos rather than quit their native dress.[6]

The 42nd, 79th and 92nd all wore the kilt in the Peninsula and at
Waterloo, and in the Crimea the 42nd, 79th and 93rd formed a kilted
Highland Brigade under the formidable command of Major-General
Sir Colin Campbell. Kilts wore out in the Peninsula and were often
refashioned into trews. The kilt caused a considerable stir when the
British army entered Paris in 1815, and artists made much of its
effect on French ladies when braw Highlanders stooped to ground
arms.

Regiments in Highland dress wore a blue knitted bonnet with a
diced border, covered with black ostrich feathers fastened to a wire
cage. William Gordon-Alexander found it very practical, for it was:

> Not only the most sensible head-dress in the British army
> as a protection against sword-cuts but also being, *when
> properly made up*, the most perfectly ventilated and coolest
> one for hot climates hitherto invented.[7]

It was also, he noted with Caledonian approval, economical, 'owing
to the extraordinary time the feathers will last.'

Dress regulations were widely breached, as the reports of
inspecting officers testify. Old items remained in use long after they
should have disappeared, and some regiments, or independently-
minded officers in them, sported non-regulation items. William

Bragge of the 3rd Light Dragoons saw one officer who had allegedly brought fifty luggage-boxes to Spain. 'He is a pretty Man, remarkably neat and wears a Blue Velvet Foraging Cap, gold Tassel and band of the same edged with white Ermine,' wrote Bragge. 'How nice.'[8] Lieutenant Colonel Charles Donellan of the 48th was mortally wounded at Talavera in 1809 dressed like an eighteenth-century officer in white buckskin breeches with a tricorne hat over powdered hair. He completed the picture by behaving with old-fashioned courtesy when hit, handing over command by saying: 'Major Middlemore, you will have the honour of leading the 48th to the charge.'

Senior officers often set a bad example. Wellington wore a trim blue civilian frock coat, while Picton usually affected a black coat and top hat and tolerated casual dress amongst his staff officers. A combination of Picton's bad temper with the scruffy uniform of his entourage led swells to quip about 'the bear and ragged staff.' At Albuera Major General Daniel Houghton led his brigade onto the field dressed in a green frock coat, but his servant brought him his regulation jacket. An officer of the 29th wrote that: 'He immediately, without dismounting, stripped off the green and put on the red one; it may be said that this public display of our national colour and British coolness actually was done under a salute of French artillery, as they were cannonading at the time.'[9] Houghton was killed almost immediately.

For all his insistence on the punctilious obedience to orders, Wellington regarded dress regulations with indifference. Grattan wrote that:

> Provided we brought our men into the field well appointed, with sixty rounds of good ammunition each, he never looked to see whether their trousers were blue, black or grey . . . we might be rigged out in all the colours of the rainbow if we fancied . . . scarcely any two officers were dressed alike. Some with grey braided coats, others with brown, some again liked blue: while many others, perhaps from choice, perhaps from necessity, stuck to the 'old red rag.'[10]

Wellington declined to involve himself in the Prince Regent's tasteful redesigning of uniforms, begging only that they should be 'as different as possible from the French in everything.' Here he was unsuccessful, for military uniforms tend to ape the dominant military nation of the age, and if the infantry's red coat remained distinctive, British cavalry changed, in the very middle of the war, to a French-style uniform which led to frequent misunderstandings. 'Although I had the family eye of a hawk,' he declared, 'I have frequently been within an ace of being taken . . .'[11]

For much of the period soldiers fought in what was often a simpli-fied version of full dress. The process of toning down the flashier embellishments for active service could be overdone. John Shipp saw that:

> A young officer had taken off his epaulettes, and the plate and feather from his cap, and looked for all the world like a discharged pensioner . . . in order to look as much like a private soldier as possible, and avoid being singled out by the enemy.

Although 'his intentions were right enough,' the business left him open to 'ridicule and criticism,' and he left the regiment soon after-wards.[12] There were also times when the difficulty of obtaining replacement items led to officers and men dressing peculiarly, as the war correspondent W. H. Russell saw in the Crimea.

> It was inexpressibly odd to see Captain Smith of the — Foot, with a pair of red Russian leather boots up to his middle, a cap probably made of the tops of his holsters, and a white skin coat tastefully embroidered down the back with flowers of many-coloured silk, topped by a head-dress à la dustman of London, stalking gravely through the mud of Balaclava, intent on the capture of a pot of jam or marmalade. This would be rather facetious and laughable were not poor Captain Smith a famished wretch with bad chilblains, approximating to frost-bites, a touch of scurvy, and of severe rheumatism.[13]

Just as the fighting in North America had its impact on British uni-form, so too campaigns in India and South Africa led to further change. Lieutenant Webber-Smith of the 48th, fighting the Coorgs in the jungles of south India, lamented: 'Our beautiful red coats –

our shakoes – our white belts and glittering breastplates were the bull's eye of the target [the enemy] could see a mile off. No men have a chance in jungle warfare in such dress.'[14] After Waterloo officers often wore blue frock coats, and the short red shell jacket was widely used for campaigning in India. Shakoes had black oilskin covers, and were often abandoned entirely for a low, peaked forage cap, worn with a white cover which might extend to cover the back of the neck, a style known as a Havelock.

The Mutiny saw the large-scale adoption of practical uniform. Richard Barter tells us that when the 75th set off for Delhi in 1857 'two white jackets and trousers constituted the uniform and in fact the whole outward clothing of every officer and man.'[15] Arthur Moffat Lang volunteered for Delhi and found himself 'very nearly in the fashionable suicide condition . . . I wait in suspense, [and] make up khaki trowsers, tunics and turbans in the most hasty manner . . .'[16] The 93rd obtained some 'very ugly loose brown coats of some stout cotton material with red collars and cuffs' ands wore these, with kilts and feather bonnets, throughout the Mutiny.[17]

The army's attachment to the red coat proved remarkably durable. Part of this was because of its undoubted success in what has been termed 'the seduction principle' bound up in the design of uniform. Henry Mayhew, in his interview-based study of London labour and the London poor, thought that it was a major ingredient in soldiers' success with 'dollymops': servant girls, nursemaids and shop girls, neither professional prostitutes nor of adamantine virtue. Nursemaids, in particular, were always ready to succumb to what he called 'scarlet fever'. Sir Garnet Wolseley echoed the point in *The Soldier's Pocket Book*. 'The better you dress a soldier,' he wrote, 'the more highly he will be thought of by women, and consequently by himself.'

Khaki (from the Persian for dust-coloured) made its appearance in the Mutiny, when white uniforms were dyed locally with materials that included coffee, curry powder and mulberry juice: the 32nd, cooped up in Lucknow, even used the office ink. Lieutenant Colonel Campbell of the 52nd Light Infantry tells how:

> I had a suit per man of white clothing dyed at Sealcote immediately I arrived there from Lucknow, and we

marched out of that place to join the Punjab movable Column in it. My reason at the time for adopting it was the ulterior view of diminishing the Indian kit, on account of the difficulty of getting the white trousers and jackets washed quickly. The men were obliged to have five pairs of trousers, whereas with the *khaka* two were sufficient. Moreover, I thought it would be a good colour for service.[18]

However, khaki was never really popular with soldiers, who preferred to cut a more flamboyant figure. It did not become standard campaign dress even in India till the Second Afghan War of 1878. Elsewhere there were concessions to local conditions – Wolseley put his men into grey serge smocks and trousers for the 1873 Ashanti expedition – but in the Zulu War of 1879 and the First Boer War of 1881 British regulars still fought in red coats. The 'old red rag' had one of its last outings in a style that the men who attacked Bunker Hill in 1775 might have sympathised with. In 1881 1/58th lost 171 officers and men at Laing's Nek in South Africa, attacking in close order bayonets fixed and colours flying, in the expectation that its Boer opponents would be terrified by the spectacle. The Egyptian campaign of 1882 was the last time that British soldiers wore red coats in action, though it remained standard peacetime walking-out dress till 1914.

The infantryman lived like some huge red hermit crab, with most of his possessions girt about his person. In the eighteenth century buff leather cross-belts, with a brass shoulder-belt plate ('breast-plate') at their intersection, whitened with pipe-clay supported ammunition pouch and bayonet, a white linen haversack hung at his side, and a large canvas knapsack, painted brown or yellow, sat squarely on his back. From 1805 a wood-framed canvas knapsack designed by the army contractor John Trotter came into service. It was 18ins broad, 13ins high and 4ins deep, and was painted first brown and then black. The Trotter was succeeded in 1824 by a knapsack with wooden boards at top and sides, whose dimensions were steadily reduced until the 1857 pattern, which remained in service till replaced by a wholly new species of valise equipment in 1871. The soldier's grey greatcoat, and tent if he had one, were often worn rolled and strapped to the top of the knapsack.

The whole ensemble was anything but comfortable, as Rifleman Benjamin Harris discovered when he disembarked in Portugal in 1808.

> The weight I myself toiled under was tremendous, and I often wonder at the strength I possessed at this period, which enabled me to endure it; for indeed, I am convinced that many of our infantry sank and died under the weight of their knapsacks alone. For my own part, being a handicraft I marched under a weight sufficient to impede the free motions of a donkey; for beside my well-filled kit, there was the great-coat rolled on its top, my blanket and camp kettle, my haversack, stuffed full of leather for repairing the men's shoes, together with a hammer and other tools ... ship-biscuit and beef for three days. I also carried my canteen filled with water, my hatchet and rifle, and eighty rounds of ball cartridge in my pouch; this last, except the beef and biscuit, being the best thing I owned, and which I always gave the enemy the benefit of when proximity offered.[19]

The inexperienced made a rod for their own backs by carrying non-essentials. When William Surtees set off for the Helder he had to abandon several shirts 'fine enough for an officer' provided by his mother. Eventually he threw away his haversack and stuffed its contents into his knapsack, but the extra weight and his unfamiliarity with its straps and buckles made it hang so low that it hindered his stride: he was nearly captured as a result.

Officers were not generally expected to carry their own kit, which travelled with the regimental baggage or, as was frequently the case, on privately-purchased horses or mules escorted by a soldier-servant. There were exceptions. When Sir John Moore took his army to the Peninsula in 1808 he ordered officers' servants to rejoin the ranks. Ensign John Aitchison of the 3rd Guards found this 'a most commendable regulation ... which besides lessening the baggage of the British army, that has been so enormous hitherto, will add forty effective men to each battalion.' He thought that although it would make officers less comfortable, 'whatever is conducive to the general good, it requires but example and a little persuasion to make them adept.

I have weighed what I have to carry and find it amounts to 27 pounds.'[20] He was speedily disabused, and found that many officers were far more lavishly equipped.

Even when stripped down to basics an officer's kit could still be substantial. William Keep pruned his portmanteau to contain:

> half a dozen shirts only, 1 pair of boots, pantaloons and great coat, 4 pairs of cotton stockings and 3 of worsted. I bought these by the advice of old soldiers who vouch for the benefit I shall derive from them with wet feet . . . most of the officers have what are called boat cloaks, made of a kind of plaid and lined with green baize.[21]

Lieutenant George Gleig of the 85th settled for two portmanteaux, which could be slung on each side of a mule's back.

> In one portmanteau then, I deposited a regimental jacket with all its appendages of wings, lace etc; two pairs of grey trowsers; sundry waistcoats, white, coloured and flannel; a few changes of flannel drawers; half a dozen pairs of worsted stockings and as many of cotton. In the other were placed six shirts, two or three cravats, a dressing case completely filled, one undress pelisse. Three pairs of boots, two pairs of shoes, with night-caps, pocket-handkerchieves etc in proportion . . .[22]

Even a desperate affair like the Indian Mutiny made only limited inroads into officers' baggage. Lieutenant Gordon-Alexander's comrades 'started out with the smallest kit they could arrange for a campaign of unknown duration: my own baggage, for instance, consisted of two small bullock-trunks and a feather-bonnet case.' This was indeed short commons, and later he expanded into 'two of the largest and best built four-bullock country carts, one small two-bullock cart for my servants, six camels and my pony.[23]

The infantryman's personal weapon was the .75in muzzle-loading flintlock musket known to history as Brown Bess –perhaps a derivative of the German *Büsche*, gun, or perhaps because its stock or barrel was brown – but more plainly termed a firelock in most contemporary accounts. It evolved in the early eighteenth century and was to have numerous variants, notably a Long Land pattern with a 46in barrel, a Short Land pattern with a 42in barrel, and the wartime economy version, the India pattern with a 39in barrel. Barrel, lock, ramrod and sling-swivels were steel, and furniture like butt-plate, trigger-guard and ramrod pipes were brass. During her heyday Bess was the best military musket in Europe, sturdier than her more elegant French dancing-partner, and, her lead ball impelled by good-quality black powder (an area where Britain had a clear advantage) was indeed the 'out-spoken, flinty-lipped brazen-faced jade' that Kipling was to call her.

A musket had a life expectancy of eight to ten years. Its barrel was often worn out early by frequent rubbing with wet brick-dust that produced a pleasing shine but removed the metal, rendering it liable to burst. Worse, the sear against which the cock engaged became dangerously worn, so that muskets went off at half-cock, when they were in theory safe, or fired immediately the cock was drawn fully back. In 1774 the 11th Foot carried out a review where the inspecting officer reported 'some Firelocks going off when loading – some upon the Mens' Shoulders.'[24] At Waterloo Lieutenant Strachan of the 73rd, who had just joined the regiment and was anxious to see action, was marching in front of a line of men with their muskets at the trail, carried horizontally, muzzle forwards. A corn-stalk got entangled with the trigger of a half-cock musket, which went off, hitting Strachan in the back and killing him instantly. And, like other small arms across the ages, the musket was susceptible to accidents caused by tired or careless men. While the soldiers of the 43rd Regiment were cleaning their muskets after the bloody storm of Badajoz a soldier accidentally fired his, killing a corporal on the spot.

Even when at its best the musket was not wholly reliable. To load it the soldier bit open a cartridge made of paper, twisted and tied shut, that contained powder and ball. This in itself was disagreeable: in his first action Surtees fired over 150 rounds, 'the powder of which, in biting off the ends of the cartridges, had nearly choked me.'[25] With the musket at half-cock, he dribbled some of the powder into the weapon's flash-pan, which he then closed off by moving the steel backwards. The remainder of the powder, with the ball on top of it, went into the muzzle, and the paper cartridge was rammed home on top as wadding. To fire, the soldier brought his weapon to full cock and pressed the trigger. The cock flew forward, its flint striking the steel, which also moved forwards, allowing the sparks produced by the impact to ignite the powder in the pan. This set off the main charge, and, with a comforting roar – much more like the flat boom of a modern shotgun than the sharp crack of a rifle – the musket fired.

And then again, it might not. Flints, most of which came from the Suffolk town of Brandon – though American flints were popular, and for some years the expression 'A Yankee flint is as good as a glass of grog' was in wide currency – had a useful life of twenty to thirty shots, but gave no warning of imminent failure. To change the flint the soldier unscrewed the jaws of the cock, perhaps by slotting a turnscrew, stowed inside the lid of his ammunition pouch, into the hole in the screw which held the jaws together, and inserted the new flint, cushioned against the jaws' grip by a piece of leather or stout cloth. Even if the flint duly sparked, with its characteristic throat-catching smell and wisp of smoke, the powder it ignited might not set off the main charge: the weapon would have 'flashed in the pan.' This was a common occurrence. One officer tried to pistol a drunken sergeant in the chaos of Badajoz after its capture, but was afterwards relieved that a flash in the pan prevented him from doing so. The future Field Marshal Lord Roberts owed his long and distinguished career to the fact that when he won his Victoria Cross in the Mutiny, capturing an enemy colour and cutting down its escort, one of his opponents aimed a musket at him at point-blank range only to have a flash in the pan.

Wind and rain made the whole business of loading more difficult. In heavy rain muskets could become altogether useless. In the eighteenth century soldiers tucked their muskets under their wide lapels to give them some protection: Private Edward Linn of Campbell's Regiment tried to keep his powder dry like this at Culloden. In the nineteenth century they had no such shelter. A sudden rainstorm might simply close down the infantry battle – there were occasions when both sides simply gave up – or give a decisive advantage to attacking cavalry. At Albuera in 1811 Colborne's brigade was already in trouble, with the French coming in on its right flank, when a rainstorm swept the field. Muskets could not be reloaded, and enemy horsemen, many of them lancers, whose weapons outreached the musket and bayonet, did dreadful damage: the brigade lost 1,413 of its 2,066 men. The Polish lancers gave little quarter: Major William Brooke of 2/48th believed 'many of them to have been intoxicated, as they rode over the wounded, barbarously darting their lances into them.' The Buffs, Colborne's right-hand (and therefore most vulnerable) battalion lost 643 of its 755 officers and men, with the unusually high proportion 216 killed to 248 wounded, with another 179 missing.

The French Colonel Marcellin Marbot saw things from the cavalryman's viewpoint when his *chasseur* regiment charged Prussian infantry on the Katzbach in 1813 after rain had made their muskets useless.

> I tried to break the square but our horses could only advance at the walk, and everyone knows that without dash it is impossible for cavalry to break a well-commanded battalion which boldly presents a hedge of bayonets ... The position on both sides was truly ridiculous; we looked each other in the eyes, unable to do any damage, our swords being too short to reach the enemy, and their muskets refusing to go off. Things went on like this for some time till General Maurin sent the 6th Lancers to our aid. Their long weapons, outreaching the enemy's bayonets, soon slew many of the Prussians, enabling the chasseurs to penetrate the square, where they did terrible execution. In this fight the sonorous voice of Colonel Perquit could be heard shouting in a rich Alsatian accent, '*Bointez, lanciers, bointez.*'[26]

Knowing soldiers would fire their damp muskets before battle if the powder could be persuaded to ignite. Private Matthew Clay, 3rd Guards, did so on the morning of Waterloo.

> I discharged its contents at an object, which the ball embedded in the bank where I had purposely placed it as a target. While so employed we kept a sharp lookout on the enemy ... at the same time having well attended to those things usual for a soldier to do ... when not actively engaged, viz examining the amount and state of ammu-

nition remaining after previous engagements, also putting
his musket into fighting trim, well oiled, flinted etc ...
The flint musket then in use was a sad bore on that
occasion, from the effects of the wet, the springs and the
locks became wood-bound and would not act correctly,
and when in action, the clumsy flints also became useless.[27]

Persuading the musket to fire was barely the start. Sometimes soldiers
loaded with 'running ball,' simply dropping the ball in after the
powder and tapping the butt on the ground to seat the charge rather
than ramming it home. This was a standard procedure for a sentry,
who would usually not require a loaded weapon when he came off
duty and would find the extraction of the charge using a threaded
'worm' on his ramrod a tedious task. It was also done by soldiers
who were more interested in the volume than the quality of their
fire, or who wished to avoid the sharp kick which came from a
well-rammed charge: Thomas Pococke of the 71st found his shoulder
'black as coal' after firing 120 rounds. The practice was often looked
upon in British regiments as an unsoldierly, foreign trick. This was
because the ball would have little force when it emerged from the
muzzle: indeed, if the soldier was aiming low, it might trickle out of
its own accord.

Even if a well-rammed charge blew the ball powerfully on its way,
it was far more likely to miss than to hit its target. The Prussians
experimented with a battalion of line infantry firing at a canvas target
100 feet long by 6 feet high. At 225 yards 25 per cent of shots hit
the target; this increased to 40 per cent at 150 yards and 60 per
cent at 75 yards. In 1779 a battalion of Norfolk Militia hit a similar
large target with 20 per cent of two volleys fired at a range of 70
yards, and its colonel was most gratified. A British trial with the
percussion musket in 1846 was more encouraging. Yet although
the target was 11ft 6in high and 6ft wide and the shots were fired
deliberately, not in the stamp, slap and crash of a battalion volley,
all ten rounds missed at 250 yards and only half hit at 150 yards.
The report concluded that 'musketry fire should not be made at
a distance exceeding 150 yards and certainly not exceeding 200
yards ...'[28] Practical experience confirmed this recommendation.
When the 75th advanced on a strongly-held position at Badli-ke-Serai

on its way to Delhi in 1857 it was engaged by infantry 150 yards away – 'rather too far for them to do much execution with the old Brown Bess,' as Richard Barter put it. 'And besides,' he added, 'they were firing high and wildly, which was noted by their officers who kept laying their swords along the barrels of their men's firelocks, and calling out, "Take low aim, take low aim."' [29]

Moreover, these experiments were carried out under ideal conditions with nobody firing back, and such results were never attained on the battlefield. Colonel George Hanger, writing in 1814, reckoned that although a soldier's musket might hit a man at 80 or even 100 yards, a man would be very unfortunate indeed to be hit at 150 yards by the man who aimed at him. The Comte de Guibert though that one hit in 500 rounds fired was a reasonable score. Perhaps the best achievement of musketry in the whole period came at Maida in Calabria 1806, when Kempt's light brigade, 630 strong once officers and sergeants are deducted, fired three volleys, the first at 115 yards and the last at 30. Some brave Frenchmen came to handstrokes and were bayoneted, and the French suffered 430 casualties, to which must be added a few lightly wounded who got away. The statistics can be no more than rough, but Kempt's men seemed to have achieved the remarkable hit rate of one hit for just over four rounds.

An experienced soldier, loading and firing at will, might get off as many as four rounds a minute, but this dropped to a more reasonable rate of two or three if his regiment fired in volleys or his weapon became clogged with the stinking black debris left by every discharge. He carried a steel picker and small bush attached by a chain to a coat-button or cross-belt, and used them to keep the touch-hole clear of fouling. Firing produced abundant grey-white smoke, with a distinct puff bursting from the touch-hole before the smoke-cloud of the main charge. In still or damp weather the smoke lay thick over the battlefield. An officer of an earlier generation described how 'the air was so darkened by the smoke of powder, that . . . there was no light seen, but what the fire of the volleys of shot gave.' [30] Not all the powder burned in the barrel, which helped to give the musket a long muzzle flash, flaring out through the smoke like a lighthouse in fog, and meant that wounds were often complicated by the

presence of unburned powder as well as wadding. A man shot at
very close range might easily have clothing and equipment ignited:
the body of the unlucky Emperor Maximilian of Mexico, shot by
firing-squad in 1867, smouldered after execution.

The Baker Rifle, initially produced by the Whitechapel gunsmith
Ezekiel Baker in 1800 for the Experimental Corps of Riflemen, and
thereafter issued to the 95th and the rifle battalions of the 60th, was
altogether more accurate. Its flintlock ignition was no better than
that of Brown Bess, and its eight deep-cut barrel groves, which
imparted a stabilising spin to its bullet, were so vulnerable to fouling
that bullets had to be hammered home hard with a wooden mallet.
But it was a formidable weapon. When Surtees joined the 95th he
found that his training was quite different from that in the line, with
light infantry drill, and 'shooting at the target' under Major Wade,
who was 'one of the best shots himself that I have ever seen. I have
known him, and a soldier of the name of Smeaton, hold the target
for each other at the distance of 150 yards, while the other fired at
it, so steady and accurate was their shooting.'[31] Although the 95th
could fight like conventional infantry, they were most effectively
employed as skirmishers, in front of the main line, as Bugler William
Green wrote of Corunna:

> Our bugles sounded the advance; away went the kettles;
> the word was given 'Rifles in front extend by files in chain
> order!' The enemy's sharpshooters were double and triple
> our numbers. We soon got within range of their rifles,
> and began to pick them off. We held them in check until
> our light division formed in line, and then the carnage
> commenced.[32]

From the 1830s, the introduction of the percussion lock, based
around a small brass cap filled with fulminate of mercury which,
when struck by the weapon's hammer produced a spark to fire the
charge, made muskets more reliable. But it was not until 1851 that
the first muzzle-loading percussion rifle came into general service,
and even then it did not entirely replace Brown Bess until after the
Indian Mutiny.

The musket was fitted with a 16in bayonet of fluted steel, attached to its muzzle by a collar which fitted over a lug on the barrel to which it was secured by the push-and-twist action that has given the name bayonet-fitting to the familiar light-bulb. Bayonets frequently worked loose or, more rarely, were unfixed by desperate opponents in the press of hand-to-hand fighting. Some East India Company Brown Bess bayonets were fitted with a spring which gripped the lug, and bayonets for the percussion rifle had a locking-ring which was twisted to secure them. The Baker was fitted for a handsome brass-hilted sword-bayonet, and for that reason the Royal Green Jackets still order 'fix swords' rather than 'fix bayonets'. The logic for the sword bayonet was that a trained marksman would not generally wish to fire with his bayonet fixed, thereby unbalancing the weapon, but still needed cold steel to hand.

The sword bayonet was used far more often in bivouacs than on the battlefield, for it was a handy tool for lopping off branches to make shelters, or chopping up firewood. It was the cause of at least one bizarre accident. At Waterloo two soldiers, apparently in Lieutenant John Kincaid's company of the 95th were killed when their bayonets struck sparks from an ammunition wagon (they were cutting it up for firewood) and caused an explosion. Even the standard Brown Bess bayonet had its alternative uses. It was regularly poked into earth floors in the Peninsula and India to discover whether the inhabitants had buried anything worth looting. Kipling later described the process:

> . . . pour some water on the floor
> where you 'ear it answer 'ollow to the boot
> when the ground begins to sink, shove your baynick down the
>   chink
> An' you're sure to touch the Loo! loo! Lulu! loot! loot! loot!

It also made a handy candlestick. Officers sometimes dined in the field on a rectangle of turf between two narrow trenches in which their legs dangled, with bayonets stuck in the ground to hold candles.

Bayonets were often fixed but more rarely used. General Louis Trochu, an experienced nineteenth-century French infantry officer, knew of only three bayonet-fights during his entire career, one of them the result of an accidental collision in the fog at Inkerman in the Crimea. In the majority of infantry battles there was an exchange of fire after which the most confident party advanced with cold steel, persuading its opponents to seek an urgent appointment elsewhere. This was the hard logic of Bunker Hill at the beginning of our period and at Laing's Nek at its end. British tactics in each case were based on the false assumption that the defenders, not being 'proper' soldiers, simply would not face redcoats coming on with measured tread and utter confidence. This confidence, embodied in the fixed bayonet, was at the very heart of battlefield performance. Sergeant Roger Lamb charged with Colonel Webster's brigade at Guilford Court House in 1781.

> After the brigade formed across the open ground, the colonel rode to the front, and gave the word, 'Charge'. Initially the movement was made, in excellent order, in a smart run, with arms charged; when arrived within forty yards of the enemy's line, it was perceived that the whole of their line had their arms presented, and resting on a rail fence ... At this awful vision a general pause took place; both parties surveyed each other for the moment with the most anxious suspense. Nothing speaks *the general* more than seizing on decisive moments; Colonel Webster rode in front of the 23rd Regiment, and said with more than even his usual commanding voice ... 'Come on, my brave Fuziliers.' This operated like an inspiring voice, they rushed forward amidst the enemy's fire; dreadful was the havoc on both sides.[33]

There were, however, occasions when formations of determined and bravely led infantry might sustain long and bitter firefights, especially if they were attacking or defending a post of visible importance. During the Seven Years' War Private Samuel Hutton of the 12th Foot wrote that:

> The severest action I was ever in was that of Brucker's mill, on the twenty-first of September 1762. We were in a redoubt, the enemy were in the mill; we were determined to have their mill, and they were resolved to have our redoubt ... The oldest soldiers never saw such a cannonade. There were nearly fifty pieces of cannon employed on both sides, and their execution was confined to a space

of about four hundred paces; and neither the fire of the
artillery, nor of the musketry, or the two opposite posts,
were intermitted for a single instant, firing nearly fifteen
hours ... The result was that we kept the redoubt, and
the French retained the mill.[34]

The firefight at Albuera in 1811 was also remarkable. Captain Moyle
Sherer of the 34th Regiment admitted that:

> To describe my feelings throughout this wild scene with
> fidelity, would be impossible; at intervals, a shriek or a
> groan told me that men were falling around me; but it
> was not always that the tumult of the contest suffered me
> to catch these sounds. A constant feeling to the centre of
> our line, and the gradual diminution of our front, more
> truly bespoke the havoc of death. As we moved, though
> slowly, yet ever a little in advance, our own killed and
> wounded lay behind us; but we arrived among those of
> the enemy, and those of the Spaniards who had fallen in
> the first onset: we trod among the dead and dying, all
> reckless of them.[35]

Waterloo stands out amongst the battles fought by the British army
for its intensity and duration. The sergeant major of the 73rd Foot,
'a brave soldier who had been through the whole of the engagements
in the Peninsula' turned, deadly pale, to his colonel and said: 'We
had nothing like this in Spain, Sir!' However, actions between individual infantry units followed the traditional pattern, with the loser
turning after a brief exchange of fire. Captain Harry Powell of 1st
Foot Guards watched the decisive repulse of the Grenadiers of the
Imperial Guard towards the close of the day. He saw them:

> ascending the rise *au pas de charge* shouting '*Vive l'Emper-
> eur*'. They continued to advance until within fifty or sixty
> paces of our front, when the Brigade was ordered to stand
> up. Whether it was from the sudden and unexpected
> appearance of a Corps so near to them, which must have
> seemed as if starting out of the ground, or the tremen-
> dously heavy fire we threw into them, *La garde*, who had
> never before failed in an attack, *suddenly* stopped. Those
> who from a distance and more on our flank could see the

affair, tell us that the effect of our fire seemed to force
the head of the Column bodily back![36]

In North America attacks on enemy bivouacs were sometimes
launched at night, and in Spain attempts to storm fortresses also
took place under cover of darkness, with the attackers either rushing
breaches made by artillery or mines, or attempting to ascend the
walls on ladders. Under these circumstances a firefight deprived the
attackers of the momentum they needed to cross the dangerous
space as quickly as they could, and musketry was often as likely to
harm friend as foe. These attacks were often made with muskets
that were unloaded or even deprived of their flints: in America
Major-General Grey earned the nickname 'no flint' for his fondness
for such raids. At Brandywine in 1777 numerous Americans were
bayoneted in their camp under controversial circumstances: one
man's surprise of a sleeping enemy is another man's massacre. The
patriots swore to get revenge, and the 66th Regiment, which had
carried out the attack, proudly dyed its white plumes red so that
they would know whom to blame.

In night assaults on Peninsula fortresses men still stopped, as if
by reflex, to snap off their unloaded muskets, with officers yelling:
'Recollect you are not loaded! Push with the bayonet!' Grattan
describes the scene as Sergeant Pat Brazil, with Privates Swan and
Kelly of the 88th topped the ramparts of Ciudad Rodrigo in 1812,
jumped into a French gun-pit:

> and engaged the French cannoniers hand to hand, a ter-
> rific but short combat was the consequence. Swan was the
> first, and was met by the two gunners on the right of the
> gun but, no way daunted, he engaged them, and plunged
> his bayonet in the breast of one; he was about to repeat
> the blow upon the other, but before he could disentangle
> his weapon from his bleeding adversary, the second
> Frenchman closed up on him and by a *coup de sabre* severed
> his left arm from his body, a little above the elbow; he fell
> from the shock, and was on the eve of being massacred,
> when Kelly, after having scrambled under the gun, rushed
> onward to succour his comrade. He bayoneted two French-
> men on the spot, and at this instant Brazil came up; three

of the five gunners lay lifeless, while Swan, resting against an ammunition chest, was bleeding to death . . . Brazil . . . in making a lunge at the man next to him . . . slipped on the bloody platform, and he fell forward against his antagonist, but as both rolled under the gun, Brazil felt the socket of his bayonet against the buttons of the Frenchman's coat.[37]

Cavalrymen and their mounts were bayoneted when they collided with infantry, as William Tomkinson discovered in 1809. He recalled that 'I was in the act of firing my pistol at the head of a French infantry man' when he was hit in both arms, and his horse was bayoneted. 'He went full gallop to the rear,' wrote Tomkinson, 'and coming to the fence of an enclosure he selected a low place in it under a vine tree, knocked my head into it, when I fell off him.'[38] Private Maxwell of the 51st bayoneted a French dragoon with such enthusiasm that he could only withdraw the weapon by placing his foot on the man's chest. In 1813, Corporal William Wheeler of the 51st came upon the scene of a recent clash between French and Spanish infantry, 'and a desperate job it must have been and no mistake about it, for the contending parties lay dead bayonet to bayonet. I saw several pairs with the bayonet in each other.'[39] John Cheshire, a native of Stockwell, served in the British Legion raised to fight in Spain in the Carlist wars of the 1830s and is recorded, on his pension certificate as having '35 bayonet wounds in various parts of his body' though without any hint as to how he came by them.[40]

In the eighteenth century officers of battalion companies carried spontoons or half-pikes, while grenadier and light company officers had light muskets called fusils or fusees, a practice remembered in the words of the song 'The British Grenadiers'

> When we are commanded to storm the palisades
> Our leaders march with fusees, and we with hand-grenades
> We throw them from the glacis about our en'mies' ears
> With a tow-row-row-row-row
> To the British Grenadiers

These firearms were a good deal more practical than spontoons in North America, and most officers of battalion companies seem to have used them. The grenade, a ceramic or cast-iron globe filled with powder and ignited by a slow match, had gone out of British service in the early eighteenth century, but its trappings, like the case on the cross-belt that had held the slow-match with which its fuse was lit, soldiered on a little longer.

The custom of North America seeped back to Britain, and in 1784 an inspection report on the 63rd Foot noted that it had 'just returned from America where the officers never made use of espontoons; saluted with swords.' Inspection returns for the 3rd, 19th and 22nd Foot also noted that spontoons were no longer carried.[41] However, until 1792 battalion company sergeants carried the halberd, an axe-like weapon on a long staff, and from then till 1830 they bore a nine-foot half-pike. This was by no means a useless weapon, not least when plied by the NCOs protecting regimental colours. At Waterloo Lieutenant Belcher of 1/32nd was struggling with a French officer who had seized his colour, when 'the covering Colour-Sergeant, named Switzer, thrust his pike into his breast . . .' And it had other uses. At Corunna Charles Napier used one to push some of his soldiers over a low wall, held by French infantry. As he did so 'my orderly sergeant, Keene, with his pike' shoved up the muskets of four or five Frenchmen who were aiming at him from the other side 'which saved me from being blown to atoms, as it was my face was much burned . . .'[42] At Waterloo 3/1st Guards was under such pressure, as one of its sergeants recalled: 'that files upon files were carried to the rear from the carnage, and the line was held up by the serjeants' pikes against the rear – not from want of courage on the men's parts (for they were desperate), only for the moment the loss so unsteadied our line.'[43]

In 1700 the sword was one of the distinguishing marks of the gentleman: 'dress and equipment were ruled by unwritten but inflexible laws which now ordained that no man with pretensions to gentility could be seen abroad without a small-sword at his side . . .'[44] By the middle of the eighteenth century gentleman no longer slipped them beneath their pillows at night or hung them from the backs of their chairs while dining, but they still wore them whenever they left home. In town the small-sword, a slim thrusting weapon descended from the older rapier, was *de rigeur*, while in the country a man might wear a short hunting sword or hanger. The style of swords and the manner of their wearing varied with fashion, and young men-about-town indulged themselves with the latest and smartest versions, most of which cost between £5 and £15. Swords were useful if their owners fell on hard times, and pawnbrokers were for ever lending money on them to pay off gambling debts: Smollet's character Roderick Random borrowed £7 against a sword with a cut steel hilt inlaid with gold. The wearing of swords by civilians declined in the 1770s – Beau Nash the king of fashionable Bath, had a particular horror of them – and, save for military or court use, ended with the eighteenth century.

In the 1750s infantry officers carried a discreetly militarised version of their everyday swords: usually only the iconography – perhaps trophies of arms embossed on the hilt – identified the weapon as military. In 1786 the adjutant general announced:

> His Majesty having been pleased to announce that the Spontoon be laid aside and that in lieu thereof the Battalion Officers are in future to make use of swords, it is His Majesty's pleasure that the officers of Infantry Corps shall be provided with a strong, substantial, uniform sword, the blade of which is to be straight and made to cut and thrust . . .[45]

The regulation pattern changed in 1796, when infantry officers were ordered to carry sword with a straight cut and thrust blade and a gilt hilt resembling that of the civilian small sword. It was not a great deal of use in battle: Captain Mercer complained that 'it was good neither for cut nor thrust, and was a perfect encumbrance.' However, it could be used for duelling: in 1815 Wellington emphasised that officers should not leave their quarters without their swords, and thought that they should receive fencing lessons for encounters with disgruntled French officers. Flank company officers received a stirrup-hilted sabre in 1803, and this was a more serious weapon altogether. A universal pattern sword for non-Highland line infantry was introduced in 1822: it had a gently curved pipe-backed blade and a gilt basket hilt. The blade was changed to a fullered (grooved) version in 1844, and this pattern remained in service till 1895. Most Highland officers carried basket-hilted broadswords popularly but wrongly called claymores, though many wielded non-regulation patterns.

Officers bought their own swords, and were expected to buy pistols too, although here there was not even a regulation pattern. Flintlock holster pistols were widely used in North America and the Peninsula. William Keep wrote that: 'The pistols are a good thing to be provided with because circumstances may occur to render them particularly useful. However, I dare say I shall be able to get pistols without purchasing them.'[46] Percussion revolvers, often made by Colt or Adams, were popular in the Crimea and the Mutiny.

Lieutenant Henry Clifford's revolver let him down at Inkerman in 1854, where the fog, confusion and close proximity of determined Russian attackers and British defenders led to an unusually vicious and lengthy close-quarter battle. He was aide de camp to Brigadier General George Buller, and, with his commander and the 77th Regiment, he followed the sound of firing to reach the front. Seeing a mass of Russians, he urged Buller: 'In God's name, fix bayonets and charge.' Clifford drew his revolver and set off accompanied by a dozen men of the 77[th.]

> 'Come on,' I said, 'my lads!' And the brave fellows dashed in amongst the astonished Russians, bayoneting them in every direction. One of the bullets in my revolver had partly come out and prevented it revolving and I could not get it off. The Russians fired their pieces within a few yards of my head, but none touched me. I drew my sword and cut off one man's arm who was in the act of bayoneting me and a second seeing it, turned round and was in the act of running out of my way when I hit him over the back of the neck and laid him dead at my feet.[47]

Clifford was passing some wounded prisoners next day when the man whose arm he had severed called out to him: 'he laughed and said "Bono Johnny." I shook his hand and tears came to my eyes. I had not a shilling in my pocket; had I a bag of gold he should have had it.' Clifford thought that 'the excitement was certainly tremendous while it lasted, and it is well perhaps it is so, for I am sure in cold blood I could never strike a man as I did.' His conduct at Inkerman earned him the Victoria Cross.

Hand to hand fighting was comparatively rare in Europe and North America: indeed Benjamin Harris said that he had never seen bayonets crossed, and the sight of a soldier of the 43rd and a French grenadier who had bayoneted one another simultaneously was regarded 'with much curiosity' by the riflemen. However, such fighting was a grimly regular feature of the Mutiny. 'We have been sharpening our swords, kukris and dirks,' wrote Lang from Delhi Ridge, 'and tried cutting silk handkerchiefs after breakfast: my 'favourite' fighting sword, Excaliber, one of Aunt Mary's presents, has now an edge like a razor and a surface like a mirror.' However, he discovered that it was no easy matter to kill a man with it: 'I cut at several, but never gave a death blow.'[48] And Europeans were often at a disadvantage in swordplay: 'Captain Best ... ran a sowar [Indian trooper] through who writhed up the blade and slashed Best's neck nearly through.'[49] One of Lieutenant Gordon-Alexander's comrades was saved by his Highland headdress:

> because the talwar [sword] cut, coming down on top of his feather bonnet, the wires of which bent inwards, glanced off and merely split his ear and cut his cheek, instead of splitting his skull in two, as it would most certainly have done had we been wearing those hideous and inefficient substitutes for the feather bonnet...[50]

Richard Barter 'polished off a gunner with a backstroke of my sword on my way as I passed him' as he burst into Delhi through the Kashmir gate. Once inside, his regiment found itself fighting bitterly against some Indian troopers who were defending a large house.

> Our men quickly made a lodgement on the ground floor, and hunting the sowars from storey to storey at last bayonet met sword on the broad flat roof on which in a moment not a trooper remained alive: all were hurled over the balustrade which ran round the top, and it was a strange sight to see them come tumbling down in their jackboots and plated head pieces...[51]

There was further savage hand-to-hand fighting at Lucknow, where Lieutenant William McBean, who had risen from the ranks to become adjutant of the 93rd rushed into the Begumbagh after its walls had been breached and cut down eleven men with his broad-sword. When the general who presented him with the Victoria Cross congratulated him on a good day's work, McBean replied: 'Tuts, it did'na take me twenty minutes.' In later fighting on the North-West Frontier the hirsute Orcadian George Broadfoot emerged from an action in which he had cut down three opponents musing on 'how *soft* a man's head is'.

The fiercest struggles took place when colours were assailed. An infantry battalion had two colours, known collectively as a 'stand,' the King's or Queen's colour consisting of a Union flag with regimental badges in its centre, and the regimental colour of the facing colour with a Union in the upper canton and the appropriate iconography, usually the regiment's number within a laurel wreath. The addition of battle honours to colours became more common after 1802, but they never attained the profusion seen on modern colours. A stout buff leather shoulder belt supported the colour-pike at appropriate moments, and a brass-capped case of oiled canvas sheathed the colours in camp or on the line of march.

Colours had been intended to help a soldier locate his own unit in the press of battle, and the ritual of trooping them through the ranks of the regiment was intended to ensure that he knew what they looked like. Part of their value was still practical. They provided a visible pivot on which men could take their dressing, and were a rallying point if things went wrong. At Buenos Aires they were hung from windows so that men could see where their regiment was in the chaotic street fighting, and in 1842 when the 13th Light Infantry was vainly hoping to attract survivors from the retreat from Kabul to the safety of Jellalabad, it kept its colours flying over the main gate by day, replacing them with a lantern at night.

They were the subjects of elaborate protocol. If a regiment had the freedom of a town it was entitled to march through with drums beating, bayonets fixed and colours flying, and terms of capitulation would specify whether colours were permitted to fly (an honourable concession) or should be cased (something of a slur). Adding a colour party to an escort or guard enhanced the honour conferred by this detachment. Julius Frederick Wasmus, company surgeon in a Brunswick Regiment in North America, reported that when Burgoyne paid a formal visit to Indians on 19 July 1777 'a detachment from the 9th Regiment, as the oldest [most senior] of the army, went to the savages' camp as guards to Lieut Gen Burgoyne. The detachment consisted of one officer and 50 men with their flag.'[52]

Made of silk and measuring 6ft 6ins long by 6ft deep, on a pike 9ft 10ins high, colours were not easy to cope with. They were carried in action by the junior ensigns, and passed on amongst the subalterns, by reverse seniority, as tiredness, wounds or death overcame their original bearers. Ensigns were often very young: the Hon George Keppel bore the regimental colour of 3/14th at Waterloo just five days after his sixteenth birthday. One ensign admitted to being blown off his feet when the wind caught his colour at a review, and Charles Hamilton-Smith's painting of an ensign of the 9th in the Peninsula shows that he has part-furled his colour for better control. The sixteen year old Thomas Brotherton, an ensign in 2nd Guards before joining the cavalry, carried his colour ashore under fire in Egypt after his boat was sunk crossing a lake. 'The lake was very shallow, so much so that [Ensign] Beckett stalked along walking with his colour in his hand with the water just up to his chin,' he wrote. 'I had to swim and carry my colour, which was no easy job but I would have died, of course, sooner than let it go . . .'[53]

Colours were consecrated before being presented by a member of the royal family or other distinguished individual, and were regarded as the very soul of a regiment's honour. Gordon-Alexander tells us about his own colours before he even begins his story.

> The old colours of the 93rd, which had been presented by the great Duke of Wellington in the year 1834, and had been carried throughout the campaign in the Crimea, were replaced on May 22, 1857, by new colours received at the hands of His Royal Highness the Duke of Cambridge, who had but recently been appointed Commander-in-Chief.[54]

The 'tattered remnants' of the old colours were laid up in Glasgow Cathedral above the memorial to the regiment's Crimean dead. The Sikh War colours of the 31st still hang in Canterbury Cathedral,

The presentation of new colours to the 13th Regiment by Prince Albert in 1845. The ensigns kneel to receive the colours, which have already been blessed by a chaplain, while the regiment presents arms.

and the memorial tablet below them includes the names of Ensigns Tritton and Jones, killed carrying them at Sobraon, where Sergeant Bernard McCabe earned glory and a commission by picking up the regimental colour and planting it on the Sikh breastwork. We should not be surprised that colours became so badly damaged. In the centre of the regimental line, they formed an obvious target and, rising high above the surrounding ranks, were regularly hit by projectiles which would otherwise have passed harmlessly overhead. At Corunna an experienced Scots officer urged Charles Napier to leave the butts of the colour pikes grounded as long as possible, so as to minimise the target the colours offered. Napier followed his wise advice, but immediately lost both his ensigns when the colours were eventually raised to full height. Ensign Edward Furnace was badly wounded carrying the king's colour of the 29th in the firefight at Albuera, but refused to give it up and was shot dead soon afterwards. W. H. Russell saw Russian fire concentrate on colour parties at the Alma, and blamed this for the heavy losses amongst subalterns and sergeants. 'The Colours carried by Ensigns Pym and Row were in tatters,' wrote Richard Barter, 'a shell had burst straight between them and torn the silk to ribbons.'[55]

Officers and sergeants routinely risked their lives in the defence of their colours. When Sergeant William Lawrence was ordered to the colours of the 40th late in the afternoon of Waterloo he knew it was tantamount to the death sentence.

> This . . . was a job I did not like at all; but still I went to work as boldly as I could. There had been before me that day fourteen sergeants already killed and wounded while in charge of these colours, with officers in proportion, and the staff and colours were almost cut in pieces.[56]

At much the same time the 73rd simply ran out of subalterns to carry the colours, 'which had been completely riddled, and almost separated from the staff' so they were 'taken from the staff, and . . . rolled round the body of a trusty sergeant (Weston) with instruction to take them to Brussels for safety, as we no longer had any officer to carry them.'[57]

The 88th was advancing in line Salamanca in 1812 when, as William Grattan relates:

> The Colonel of the 22nd French Regiment stepped out of the ranks and shot Major Murphy dead at the head of his regiment . . ., a number of officers were beside Murphy. It is not easy at such a moment to be certain who is the person singled out . . . Lieutenant Moriaty, carrying the regimental flag, called out, 'That fellow is aiming at me!' – 'I hope so,' replied Lieutenant D'Arcy, who carried the other colour, with great coolness – 'I hope so, for I thought he had *me* covered!' He was not much mistaken; the ball that killed Murphy, after passing through him, struck the staff of the flag carried by D'Arcy, and also carried away the button and part of the strap of his epaulette! . . . I mention it as a strong proof of the great coolness of the British line in their advance against the enemy's column.[58]

Colour-parties were the object of attack by infantry and cavalry as well as targets for musketry, and, as at Albuera, became islands of sheer fury in a sea of slaughter. Ensign Edward Thomas, another sixteen year old, courageously bore the regimental colour of the

Buffs, crying out 'Rally on me men, I will be your pivot' as the cavalry broke his battalion. When French horsemen called on him to give up his colour he replied 'Only with my life' and was at once cut down. He was buried that evening with 'all possible care' by the only two unwounded survivors of his company. Sometimes, when an ensign was *in extremis* with the sergeants of the colour-party dead around him, he would rip the colour from its staff and fall on top of it. Lieutenant Matthew Latham did this with the king's colour of the Buffs at Albuera, and at Waterloo Ensign Christie of 2/44th, with a lance-point jabbed through his eye and on into his jaw, grabbed his colour from the lancer who had seized it and covered it with his body. At Albuera Ensign Richard Vance, sixteen years old and just six weeks in the service, carried the regimental colour of the 29th until there were so few soldiers of the regiment left on their feet that he thought its capture inevitable. He tore it from its staff and hid it in his jacket: it was found on his body that evening.

At Quatre Bras there was a desperate mêlée when 2/69th was mistakenly ordered out of square and into line and then charged by watchful French cavalry. The king's colour was taken, but Volunteer Clarke, doing duty as ensign to the regimental colour, cut down three cavalrymen who attacked him and retained his colour, at the price of 22 sword wounds. When the 44th Regiment made its last stand at Gandamak on the retreat from Kabul in 1842, Captain Souter wrapped a colour round his body. Ironically it might have helped save him, for the Afghans thought that the life of a man with such a richly-embroidered waistcoat must be worth preserving.

Colours were lost from time to time. It was always a matter of grief, though this might be blunted if the loss took place in a wholesale capitulation like Saratoga or Yorktown, for which the regiment would not be held directly responsible. In March 1814 an expeditionary force, composed largely of inexperienced second battalions, was sent to the Netherlands under Sir Thomas Graham and botched an attack on Bergen-op-Zoom, where it was cut off and forced to surrender. Amongst the battalions which lost its colours there was 2/69th, which puts Clarke's action at Quatre Bras into proper perspective, for losing one stand of colours in 1814 and another in 1815 could scarcely have been countenanced. Thomas Morris tells us that the 69th set its tailors to work to make a new colour, but the subterfuge was exposed when the captured item was exhibited in Paris. He thought that 'though it is unfortunate in a regiment to lose its colours, yet if they are taken while they are contending with a vastly superior force, as was the case in this instance, it cannot reflect any disgrace on the men.'[59] Five colours were lost at Albuera, a stand each from the 48th and 66th, and one from the Buffs, all of Colborne's brigade. In his after-action report the divisional commander, Major General Sir William Stewart, emphasised that 'they were not so lost until the officers who bore them were killed.'

British infantry put as much effort into the capture of their enemy's colours – eagles in the case of the Napoleonic French – as the defence of their own. It is a measure of the value accorded these totems, and the valour with which they were defended that they were rarely taken in open field, and regiments which did take French eagles generally embodied them in their own iconography, like a symbolic scalp hung from the regimental tepee. Lieutenant Pearce of the 44th took the eagle of the French 62nd Line at Salamanca: it was jammed onto a sergeant's pike, to the accompaniment of much cheering. At Barossa Ensign Keogh of the 87th made for the eagle of the French 8th of the Line 'but was run through by several of those who supported it, and fell lifeless on the ground.' His comrade Sergeant Patrick Masterson piked Sous-Lieutenant Edmé Guillemin, its bearer, and took the eagle, celebrating his achievement with the deathless shout: 'Bejabers, boys, I have the cuckoo.'

The infantryman's life in barracks and performance on the battlefield were alike dominated by drill. This was not, as it has now become, an activity designed to impart military spirit and convey an impression of soldierly bearing on parade, but an absolute prerequisite of battlefield performance. Even Paddy Griffith, who rightly observes that drills were 'really no more than an ideal to be aimed at,' and which rarely survived first contact with broken or uneven terrain, acknowledges that 'battlefield manoeuvres could normally be achieved rather faster with drill than without it.'[60] The increasing importance of light troops changed the character of some drill. The Experimental Rifle Corps and the 95th which sprang from it emphasised 'the thinking fighting man' with a 'battle drill' which fostered individual initiative and responsibility – but did not diminish its importance.

Drill took the soldier from individual 'manual exercise' through collective 'platoon exercise' to larger-scale 'evolutions,' 'firings' and 'manoeuvres'. It was prescribed by official regulations, modified by the work of individual theorists (unkindly termed 'fertile geniuses' by the Duke of Cumberland) and regimental practice, which produced what modern soldiers would term standard operating procedures. Numerous publications were concerned with it, ranging from official drillbooks to practical handbooks like Captain Bennett Cuthbertson's *System for the Complete Interior management and Oeconomy of a Battalion of Infantry* published in Dublin in 1768, and financed by the subscription of almost a thousand regular officers.

There is no space in these pages for a discussion of the tactical debate of the late eighteenth century, when theorists and practical soldiers alike debated the relative merits of line and column. The line optimised the delivery of fire, but was difficult to move across anything but the most even country and was vulnerable to attack in flanks or rear: hence the merit of the 28th's front and rear rank battle at Alexandria in 1801. The column was infinitely superior for movement, by road or cross-country, and, especially when combined with the preparatory fire of artillery or skirmishers, was a formidable instrument for delivering an assault.

All armies strove, by and large, to move in column and fight in line: the French cocked hat, when worn across the wearer's head, was described as being '*en bataille*,' as opposed to '*en colonne*' when worn fore and aft. Revolutionary French armies did indeed make good use of assaulting columns screened by skirmishers, but by the Napoleonic period the *ordre mixte* of a battalion in line supported by two battalions in column was popular and practical. Sometimes French columns in the Peninsula collided with British lines because the latter were covered by a crest, safe from fire and view, and sometimes the French simply underestimated the cohesion of a line when assailed by a column. Thomas Bugeaud, French infantry officer in the Peninsula and pacifier of Algeria in the 1840s, gives us the classic description of column versus line.

Fig. 1. The Colonel. 2. The Major. 3. The Adjutant. 4. The Captains of Companies. 5. The Covering Sergeants. 6. The Battalion Aides. 7. The Original Formation of the Column. 8. The Pickett Line.
A BATTALION IN QUARTER-DISTANCE COLUMN RIGHT IN FRONT DEPLOYING ON THE LEADING COMPANY.

A battalion in quarter-distance column, its companies echeloned forward on the right company. It has begun to deploy into line on the leading company: markers show the positions to be taken up by the following three companies, and other markers can be seen breaking away from the column to the rear to take up their positions under the watchful eye of the mounted adjutant.

Fig. 1. The Lieutenant-Colonel. 2. The Major. 3. The Adjutant. 4. Captains of Companies. 5. Covering Sergeants. 6. Threes-rear. 7. The Band.
A BATTALION WHEELING FROM LINE INTO OPEN COLUMN, RIGHT IN FRONT

A battalion wheeling from line into open column, in which its companies have sufficient distance between them to wheel back into line. In close column, like the quarter-distance column above, the distance between the companies was reduced. Though these illustrations come from a tactical manual of the 1860s, this drill would have intelligible to a Napoleonic infrantryman.

The English generally occupied well-chosen defensive positions having a certain command, and they showed only a portion of their forces. The usual artillery action first took place. Soon, in great haste, without studying the position ... we marched straight in, taking the bull by the horns. About 1,000 yards from the English line the men became excited, called out to one another, and hastened their march; the column began to get a little confused. The English remained quite silent with shouldered arms, and from their steadiness appeared to be a long red wall ... The contrast was striking; in our innermost thoughts we all felt that the enemy was a long time in firing, and that this fire, reserved for so long, would be very unpleasant when it came. Our ardour cooled. The moral

217

appearance of steadiness, which nothing can shake (even if it be only appearance), over disorder which stupefies itself with noise, overcame our minds. At this moment of intense excitement, the English wall shouldered arms; an indescribable feeling would root many of our men to the spot; they began to fire. The enemy's steady, concentrated volleys swept our ranks; decimated, we turned round seeking to recover our equilibrium; then three deafening cheers broke the silence of our opponents; at the third they were on us, pushing our disorganised flight.[61]

For the reverse of the medal we have the account of Thomas Pococke of the 71st, who was preparing for a church service at Vimeiro in 1808 when he heard the drums beat up the long roll of the general call to arms.

> We marched out two miles to meet the enemy, formed line and lay under cover of a hill for about an hour, until they came to us. We gave them one volley and three cheers – three distinct cheers. Then all was as still as death. They came upon us, crying and shouting, to the very point of our bayonets. Our awful silence and determined advance they could not stand. They put about and fled without much resistance.[62]

The line was three ranks deep in the eighteenth century, and Sir David Dundas, whose preoccupation with drill earned him the nickname 'Old Pivot', always argued that the third rank was needed to fill gaps in the other two. However, in 1801 it was officially accepted that two ranks would suffice, and regiments had often formed two deep before that. Men stood together so closely that each could feel the touch of his neighbour's elbows. Lieutenant Colonel Alexander Wallace of the 88th urged his men to 'mind the tellings off, and don't give the *false touch* to your right or left hand man; for by God, if you are once broken you'll be running here and there like a parcel of *frightened pullets*.'[63]

In the eighteenth century a battalion, formed up in line by companies, would be 'told off' into 14 ad hoc platoons. These were then designated platoons of the first, second and third firing, so that the battalion could fire successive volleys, with some muskets always loaded and the fire rippling out from its front in a regular pattern. It was difficult to maintain this cohesion under the stress of battle, and a veteran of Dettingen in 1743 wrote of the British infantry that:

> They were under no command by way of Hyde Park firing, but the whole three ranks made a running fire of their own accord, at the same time with great judgement and skill, stooping all as low as they could, making almost every ball take place . . . The French fired in the same manner, I mean without waiting for words of command, and Lord Stair did often say that he had seen many a battle, and never saw the infantry engage in any other manner.[64]

Although telling off into platoons continued into the nineteenth century, it gave a soldier something extra to remember at a moment of gripping crisis, and it was more common to use the company or half-company as a sub-unit for volley-firing. Battalions might, at least at the start of an action, produce a simultaneous volley, or fire by ranks, with company commanders taking control if confusion grew, as it so often did, and eventually individuals simply loading and firing as fast as they could – a 'running fire' – and closing to the centre as the ranks were thinned by casualties.

For the attack, a battalion would move off into column and then deploy into line, as John Spencer Cooper of 7th Fusiliers tells us by recalling the orders he received for a battle in Spain:

> 'Form close column;' 'prime and load;' 'fix bayonets;' 'shoulder;' 'slope;' 'silence;' 'steady;' 'deploy into line;' 'forward.' We moved across the plain in three or four parallel lines towards the French batteries which now opened upon us briskly.[65]

The advance in line grew increasingly harrowing as shot reached the attackers. 'As soon as the enemy's roundshot came hopping along,' remembered Gowing of the advance at the Alma, 'we simply did the polite – opened out and allowed them to pass on.' As the range closed, first canister from field guns and then musketry from massed infantry hit the attackers. 'Gaps were made in the different companies only to be filled up next moment,' writes Richard Barter.

And still the line advanced . . . not a sound to be heard
save now and then a suppressed shriek of pain as someone
was freshly wounded followed by a sharp word of command, 'Close up men,' Close up' and 'Mind your dressing.'
I saw a shrapnel shell burst right in the face of one of the
Companies of the right wing. It tore a wide gap and the
men near it involuntarily turned away from the fire and
smoke. I called out, 'Don't turn, men, don't turn,' and was
at once answered, 'never fear Mister Barter, sir, we ain't
agoing to turn.'[66]

At this moment the battle hung in the balance, for the attackers
might indeed turn, which is what happened when Pakenham
launched a frontal assault on American breastworks at New Orleans
in January 1815. There, 2/44th who preceded the main attack, carrying ladders and fascines, lacked the staunch cohesion of the 75th
before Delhi. The battalion moved up in scattered parties which
did little for its cohesion, and when it came under fire some
soldiers dropped their burdens to shoot back ('No-Flint' Grey
must have turned in his grave) and others scampered to the rear.
Pakenham was shot as he tried to stop them, shouting: 'For shame!
Recollect you are British soldiers.' Without effective means of crossing the obstacles before them the remaining attackers showed
no marked enthusiasm, and although Lieutenant Colonel Robert
Renny of the 21st and a few other gallant souls fought their way
into the American position, and were killed there, the attack was a
fiasco.

But if the attackers did not quail, the defenders might well flee
and the balance was a fine one, with courageous leadership so often
tilting it. If both remained steadfast there would then be a firefight,
as George Gleig recalls:

the French fired a volley. It was well directed, and did
considerable execution, but it checked not our approach
for a moment . . . after having exhausted several discharges
of musketry, we succeeded in getting within charging distance. Then, indeed, another cheer was given, and the
French, without waiting for the rush, once more broke
their ranks and fled.[67]

Barter saw the same thing in the Mutiny. As the 75th charged:

> The Enemy followed our movements, their bayonets were
> also lowered and their advance was steady as they came
> on to meet us, but when that exultant shout arose they
> could not stand it, their line wavered and undulated, many
> began firing with their firelocks at their hips and at last
> as we were closing on them the whole turned and ran for
> dear life . . .[68]

If threatened by cavalry, a battalion would form square unless its
flanks were so secure that it had no risk of being encircled, or was
caught so flat-footed that it had no time to react. There were several
ways of forming square. It was often easiest for three centre companies to stand fast while the others folded back to form a square
or an oblong, with the flank companies closing up its rear. At Quatre
Bras the ever-reliable 1/42nd, caught before its square was properly
formed, nonetheless closed it up by main force, killing the
cavalrymen inside the square and beating off their comrades outside.
However, a few men carrying to the rear their wounded commanding
officer, Lieutenant Colonel Sir Robert Macara, were caught in the
open and speared by lancers.

More fortunate commanding officers would take station with the
colours, musicians and drummers in the centre of the square.
Although a well-conducted square was almost impossible to break,
it offered an easy target for artillery, and at Waterloo the squares
formed up to face the successive waves of French cavalry suffered
severely. Indeed, had the attacks been better co-ordinated with artillery the day might have had a different outcome. Ensign Gronow
thought that:

> our squares presented a shocking sight. Inside we were
> nearly suffocated by smoke. It was impossible to move a
> yard without treading upon a wounded comrade, or upon
> the bodies of the dead; and the loud groans of the
> wounded and dying were most appalling.
>
> At four o'clock our square was a perfect hospital, being
> full of dead, dying and mutilated soldiers . . .
>
> When we received cavalry, the order was to fire low,
> so that on the first discharge of musketry the ground was

strewed with the fallen horses and their riders, which impeded the advance of those behind them and broke the shock of the charge . . .[69]

It was the apotheosis of the British footsoldier. Small wonder that Wellington, too often grudging in his praise, admitted: 'I never saw infantry behave better.'

GALLOPING
AT EVERYTHING

I F WELLINGTON was sometimes hard on his infantry, he was
even more critical of his cavalry. He accused them of 'galloping
at everything', a judgement repeated by many historians.[70]

We have already seen how the horse and dragoons of the early
eighteenth century became homogenised into heavy cavalry, while the
light dragoons, raised as part of the trend towards light troops in the
second half of the century, were themselves gradually transformed
into hussars and lancers, with the last of the light dragoons dis-
appearing after the Crimea. The functions of heavy and light cavalry
were, at least in theory, distinct. Heavy cavalry existed primarily to
break the enemy's horse or foot by charging it on the battlefield, while
light cavalry was expected to excel at 'piquet and patrol work,' on the
one hand forming the eyes of the army, and on the other preventing
the enemy's light cavalry from gaining useful information.

Yet the *Queen's Regulations* of 1844 argued that Britain had too
little cavalry to preserve the old functional distinctions and decreed
that 'both the *Heavy* and *Light Cavalry* should be equal to the *Charge
in Line*, as well as to *the Duties on Out-Posts,*' it was simply recognising
an accomplished fact.[71] The 1796 cavalry drillbook drew no distinction between heavy and light cavalry, and in 1858 Captain Valentine
Baker declared: 'We have no real light cavalry in the British service.'[72]

This reflected the fact that hussars and light dragoons rode scarcely lighter than their cousins the heavies, and that, from the very first days of British light cavalry the charge on the battlefield had drawn them on like a martial magnet.

At Emsdorf in 1760 the 15th Light Dragoons carried out a charge which broke five battalions of foot and took their colours. The same regiment, charging alongside Austrian hussars at Villers-en-Cauchies in 1794, crashed squarely into a great mass of Revolutionary infantry. Although they lost their commander, Captain Aylett, on the bayonets of the front rank, the 15th broke the infantry and then carried out a vigorous pursuit marred by the fact that no prisoners were taken, although Sir John Fortescue suggested that 'three hundred men need no excuse for taking no prisoners when attacking five thousand.'[73]

The 3rd Light Dragoons distinguished themselves at Mudki in the Sikh Wars, earning the nickname 'Mudkiwallahs', and the 16th Lancers made their reputation in desperate charges at Sobraon and Aliwal. Finally, the charge of the Light Brigade in the Crimea is abiding testimony of the preparedness of British light cavalry to charge home. As was so often the case with the misfortunes of British cavalry, poor command was chiefly to blame for the affair, but thundering in against the front of an enemy battery was scarcely the function for which light cavalry had been intended. Already heavy in equipment, it had become heavy in attitude too.

But this, of course, is part of the indictment against the cavalry, embodied in what Wellington called:

> a trick our officers have acquired of galloping at everything and then galloping back as fast as they galloped on the enemy. They never consider their situation, never think of manoeuvring before an enemy – so little that one would think they cannot manoeuvre except on Wimbledon Common; and when they use their arm as it ought to be used, viz. offensively, they never keep nor provide for a reserve.[74]

There were indeed cavalry calamities. The best known of them was 'Slade's Affair', the action at Maguilla in June 1812, described by Sir Charles Oman as 'the unluckiest combat that was ever fought by the British cavalry in the Peninsular War.'[75] Part of a brigade under Major General John Slade charged and broke an inferior French force, but drove it back onto the French main body which promptly counter-attacked, capturing two officers and 116 men. Bad luck and poor tactical handling by Slade had much to answer for, but it was scarcely a major reverse. In 1848 William Havelock rashly led his 14th Light Dragoons into a nullah packed with Sikh infantry at Ramnagar, and lost 42 men killed and wounded. His better-known brother Henry put it down to the hunting spirit. 'Old Will was a foxhunter,' he reflected, 'before he became a cavalryman.'

The most serious cavalry setback of all was the episode at Chilianwalla in 1849, when Brigadier Alexander Pope's brigade (9th Lancers, 14th Light Dragoons and 1st and 6th Bengal Native Cavalry) went 'threes about', a manoeuvre in which each group of three soldiers wheeled to face the rear, when assailed by Sikh horsemen. Then, in the words of Major James Hope Grant, commanding a squadron of the 9th, they 'appeared, having gone about, to have got panic-struck.'[76] Pope himself was mortally wounded, and his brigade lost 17 killed and 39 wounded. The failure of the cavalry that day may well have prevented the British from winning a conclusive victory, but the wider consternation caused by the affair said much about their disregard for a 'native' opponent. The Sikhs were formidable soldiers, and inexperienced commanders who took needless risks when dealing with them were likely to have their rashness punished.

Alongside these setbacks must be set the triumphs of the 14th Light Dragoons at Emsdorf and Villers-en-Cauchies, light cavalry triumphs at Sahagun and Benavente, the decisive charge of Major General John Gaspard le Marchant's heavy cavalry at Salamanca, the penetration – against all the evidence of the age – of Sikh squares by the 16th Lancers at Aliwal, and the wholly successful charge of the Heavy Brigade at Balaclava.

Heavy cavalry, with the exception of 'The Horse Guards Blue', wore scarlet. It exchanged tricornes for bicorne cocked hats in the mid-eighteenth century, and from 1800 took to a low shako for wear in the field. In 1811 metal helmets which bore a deceptive similarity to those worn by French heavy cavalry came into service, and, with several changes of pattern, were worn for the remainder of the period. At the same time white buckskin breeches and tall jackboots were replaced for field service by blue-grey overalls reinforced by leather at foot and inside leg. The 2nd Royal North British Dragoons, better known as the Royal Scots Greys, wore a fur cap, more like an infantry grenadier cap than a hussar busby, as a regimental distinction. Like their cousins in the infantry, heavy cavalry officers wore sashes, knotted, in their case, over the right hip.

Light dragoons started in red jackets but changed to blue in 1785, and wore a low helmet not unlike the crested skullcap worn by light infantry, with cocked hats for peaceable occasions. From about 1789 they sported the elegant Tarleton helmet – named after Sir Banastre Tarleton, absurdly caricatured as the villain in *The Patriot* – with a leather and metal skull and bearskin crest. The fronts of their tight-fitting jackets were heavily braided, and their blue or white breeches tucked into boots. In 1811, influenced by the same imitation of French fashion which saw the heavy cavalry adopt the helmet, light dragoons began to wear a wide-topped shako, a short-tailed blue jacket with broad lapels of the regiment's facing colour, and overalls similar to those of heavy cavalry.

Regiments which converted to hussars turned out in full hussar rig, with tight, braided dolmans, furred pelisses slung from the left shoulder, barrelled sashes in place of the scarlet sash, fur busbies and tight breeches. Lancers, formed after the Napoleonic wars, again in imitation of continental preferences, wore a flat-topped lance-cap based on the Polish czapka. We have seen how William IV briefly put light cavalry into scarlet, but, with the exception of the 16th lancers, they soon reverted to the familiar blue.

Heavy cavalry had traditionally ridden large horses, the so-called 'Great' or 'Black' horse, standing at over sixteen hands, with dragoons on lighter and cheaper nags. Ann Hyland's pioneering work on the medieval warhorse suggests that the Great horse was rarer than we think, and it was certainly rarely seen during and after the Napoleonic period. We know that the dragoons of Napoleon's Imperial Guard were mounted on horses averaging 15 hands, and Commanche, the charger of Captain Miles Keogh who was killed at the Little Big Horn in 1876, and stands stuffed and rather moth-eaten in the University of Kansas, is 15.2 hands. The Marquis of

Granby's Royal Foresters, raised during the Seven Years' War, had bigger men and bigger horses than most other light dragoon regiments: it was reported to have 'not a man under 5ft 5 and 3/4ins; near 300 horses, none under 14 hands, and the greater part above 15 hands.'[77]

In 1796 a Board of General Officers tasked with enquiring into the state of the cavalry reported that suitable horses were hard to come by, and officers were consequently allowed to ride horses that stood not under 15 hands. In 1813, of the 2nd Dragoons' 708 horses, 57 were 16 hands (the same height as many modern hunters) 256 15.2 hands, 340 14.2 hands and 55 14 hands. In 1909 the Board of Trade publication *Types of Horses Suitable for Army Remounts* reckoned that line cavalry – still, at that time, expected to charge with sword or lance – required a horse 'of hunter stamp. Height 15.2 hands, cost £40 in Ireland, a black gelding.'

Officers were responsible for buying their own steeds, and an officer who failed to procure a suitable mount risked having his colonel buy one on his behalf for a sum not exceeding £50 and stop the money from his pay. Charles Parquin, a French light cavalry officer who fought in the Peninsula, comments on the splendid quality of British officers' chargers. One of his comrades, in hot pursuit of an Englishman, was exasperated to hear his adversary, comfortably ahead in the race, turn and shout: 'I presume that is a Norman horse you are riding, sir.'[78]

Officers' chargers and the troop horses ridden by NCOs and men were often exported from England, although indigenous breeds generally stood local conditions better. Getting mettlesome horses onto transports was no easy task, as William Tomkinson saw when his charger Bob was swung aboard a transport at Falmouth in canvas slings. Bob:

> twice kicked himself out and was near being lost. He stood on the deck of the vessel for some time while they were putting a fresh pair of slings on him, and nearly killed the second mate of the vessel by kicking him overboard. The man fell the whole height the vessel, there being no water near the quay at which we embarked. He was left behind sick at Falmouth.[79]

Bob carried his master in many a desperate venture, and eventually returned safe to England after five campaigns, 'the servant reporting that he knew his way back to the stable at Dorfold perfectly. He lived for many years to carry his master with the pack of harriers kept by him.'[80] His successor was the one-eyed Cyclops, who bore Tomkinson at Waterloo, where, after the 16th Light Dragoons had broken some French infantry in a charge, he literally rode down some of his adversaries, and 'trod the heavier for not seeing them.'[81] Thomas Brotherton was less lucky. At Fuentes d'Onŏro:

> I had my charger shot under me, and got a troop horse
> which was also shot under me, through the head by the
> pistol of a French officer, so closely that my own face was
> singed. The animal fell . . . but on rejoining the main body
> of the regiment I found that the poor animal had risen
> by an effort, gone back to where the regiment was formed,
> placed himself in the ranks in his own squadron, and then
> fell dead![82]

As a rule more horses were killed by privation or climate than by the enemy. Wellington called the Peninsula 'the grave of horses', and the diaries of cavalry officers who served there testify to constant problems caused by lack of forage. The Marquess of Anglesey, historian of the British cavalry, tells us that a horse's daily ration in barracks consisted of 12lbs of hay, 10lb of corn and 8lb of straw, shifting to 18lb of hay and 8lb of corn on campaign. A horse drinks about five gallons of water a day in cool weather, and much more if the weather is hot. This individual ration multiplied into a staggering logistic burden. Sir John Bisset, for a time commissary-general in the Peninsula, reckoned that the army had a grand total of just under 25,000 draught and horses and baggage mules. A three-regiment brigade of cavalry, with 1,658 horses and mules, needed almost 20,000 lbs of fodder each day. The feat of supplying the army with fodder was prodigious, and was complicated by the fact that horses often respond to a sudden change of diet by contracting colic, a potentially fatal form of equine indigestion. Commissary August Schaumann believed that the British cavalryman made matters worse because he: 'looks upon his horse as a machine, an incubus, which is the source of all his exertions and punishments. He ill-treats it.

And even when forage lies within his reach he will not, of his own accord, lift a finger to get it.'[83] He believed that the KGL cavalry had a much better understanding of their horses, although he acknowledged that the 14th and 16th Light Dragoons were exceptions to this rule. It is small wonder that horses died like flies.

Losses were even heavier in the Crimea, and in the six months from October 1854 to March 1855, 932 of the cavalry division's 2,216 horses died of sickness. Even those that survived the winter were scarcely recognisable. When George Loy Smith rebuked a man for not knowing his own horse, the soldier replied: '"Really, sergeant-major, I do not know him." The fact was they had eaten one another's manes off, and their eyes had become so small, through starvation and cold.'[84] Richard Temple Godman of the 5th Dragoon Guards reported that he had found stabling for one of his three horses, but the creature 'has conducted himself so badly by eating all the boards and rafters within his reach' that he would have to find new accommodation.[85] The steady decline of the cavalry's horses affected Lieutenant Colonel Hodge, who wrote: 'This then is to be the end . . . When all our men's things are destroyed, saddles gone and horses killed they will tell us that we have neglected our regiments. It is too dreadful to think about.'[86]

In addition to the soldier himself, the charger or troop horse carried saddle, bridle, equipment and weapons which might double the soldier's weight. A Napoleonic light cavalryman rode at 20 stone (280 lbs) and a heavy cavalryman even more. There was saddle and bridle, the latter with both curb and snaffle bits, and double reins. A blanket went beneath the saddle and a cloth shabraque over it, and light cavalry wore a sheepskin over that. A pair of holsters, replaced by wallets from the 1840s, hung in front of the saddle, covered by decorative holster caps in peacetime and perhaps a rolled cloak in war. A cylindrical valise, made of canvas and leather with regimental devices on its end, was strapped behind the saddle.

If the sword was losing its importance in the infantry, it remained the cavalryman's chief weapon. At the start of the period heavy cavalry carried a straight sword with a steel basket guard, and light dragoons, from their formation, had a straight-bladed stirrup-hilted sabre which could be used to cut or thrust. In 1796 the swords for

heavy and light cavalry polarised distinctly. The heavy cavalry sword
had a straight blade with a hatchet point (later modified, by having
its back ground down, to a spear point) and a flat disc guard with
a single knuckle-bow. The light cavalry sabre had a heavy, curved
blade and a steel stirrup-shaped guard.

The 1796 pattern heavy cavalry sword has a poor reputation[87]
and it certainly lacks the natural killing swing of the light cavalry
version. Yet well sharpened, and plied with determination, it was no
mean weapon. At Waterloo, Sergeant Charles Ewart of the Greys
crashed into a French brigade to capture the eagle of the 45th Line-
and tells us just what the sword could do in the right hands.

> It was in the charge that I took an eagle from the enemy.
> He and I had a hard contest for it; he made a thrust at
> my groin, I parried it and cut him down through the head.
> After this a lancer came at me; I threw his lance off by my
> right side, and cut him through the chin upwards through
> the teeth. Next, a footsoldier fired at me, and then charged
> me with his bayonet, which I also had the good luck to
> parry, and then I cut him down through the head; thus
> ended the contest.[88]

The light cavalry pattern was even more formidable. In the action
at Campo Mayor on 25 March 1811 Corporal Logan of the 13th
Light Dragoons cut down a trooper of the French 26th Dragoons
and was then set upon by the regiment's commanding officer, the
brave and respected Colonel Chamorin. Logan first cut him about
the face, severing his chinstrap so that his brass helmet fell off, and
then split his skull. An officer of the 13th saw the wound the following
day when the French sent a burial party under a flag of truce. The
blow 'nearly cleft his skull asunder, it cut in as deep as the nose
through the brain.'[89] Charles Parquin of the French light cavalry
wrote that:

> We always thrust with the point of our sabres, whereas
> they always cut with their blade which was three inches
> wide. Consequently, out of every twenty blows aimed by
> them, nineteen missed. If, however, the edge of the blade
> found its mark only once, it was a terrible blow, and it was
> not unusual to see an arm cut clean from the body.[90]

Marcellin Marbot found himself set upon by two British hussars, and 'in a few seconds my shako, my wallet and my pelisse were all in strips.' But the blows were all inaccurate, and although he soon received a thrust in the ribs, he replied with 'a vigorous backhander: my blade struck his teeth and passed between his jaws, as he was in the act of shouting, slitting his mouth to the ears.'[91] Cornet Francis Hall of the 14th Light Dragoons saw his men hacking away at French horsemen at Fuentes d'Onoro, and their blows:

> Obliged them to cower in their saddlebows. The alarm, indeed, was greater than the hurt, for their cloaks were so well rolled across their left shoulders that it was no easy matter to give a mortal blow with the broad edge of a sabre whereas their swords, which were straight and pointed, though their effect on the eyes was less formid- able, were capable of inflicting a much severer wound.[92]

There was a continuing debate as to whether swords were best used for cutting or thrusting, and nineteenth century cavalry swords sought to compromise. However, the Scottish swordsman Donald McBain had always argued that 'The Small Sword hath great odds of the Broad, for the Small Sword kills, and you may receive forty cuts and not be disabled,' and by the end of the century he seemed to be proved right.[93] In 1821 cavalrymen received a new pattern sword with a lightly curved blade, a steel three-bar guard for light cavalry and a bowl guard for heavy cavalry. This was replaced in 1853 by a universal pattern sword, issued to heavy and light cavalry alike, with a three-bar hilt and a curved cut and thrust blade. The weapon was not well regarded, as Lieutenant Colonel Henry Darby Griffith of the Greys, who charged with the Heavy Brigade at Balaclava, told the War Office in 1854:

> Our swords are very defective – as in our engagement when our men made a thrust with the sword they all bent and would not go into a man's body and many of our poor fellows got sadly wounded and some lost their lives entirely from the unserviceable state of their arms. They were quite good enough for home service but quite unfit for active service.[94]

But Evelyn Wood, who talked to Naval Brigade doctors who treated the wounded, was told that the sword-cuts inflicted by the heavies were 'appalling, in some cases the head-dress and skull being divided to the teeth.' It was the thick Russian greatcoats that had kept out the thrusts.[95] It was not until 1908 that the cavalry sword was at last optimised for thrusting, and the pattern of that year, with its thin blade, large bowl guard and pistol-grip hilt which enabled the user to align the blade perfectly, was perhaps the best sword issued to the British army. It was, though, just a little late.

In any event the thrust was not without risk. Captain William Morris, who commanded the 17th Lancers at Balaclava, had always championed the use of the point. After he rode round the flank of the Russian battery charged by the Light Brigade he headed for a hussar officer, sword in his outstretched arm, edge outwards. He dipped the point under the Russian's guard and suddenly found his hilt against the man's chest as his horse's momentum drove the blade home. He could neither extract it, nor disentangle his hand from the sword-knot that attached it to the weapon's hilt, and was helpless as Cossacks closed in and cut him about the head, knocking him from his horse. The timely arrival of a Russian officer saved his life, for the Cossacks would have killed him where he lay, rather than taking him prisoner.

In a cavalry mêlée, men found that they needed to use point and edge: the former when the speed of impact was with them, and the latter when closed up in the press. A trooper of the 8th Hussars described the brawl behind the Russian battery at Balaclava.

> I had three Russians to deal with at once ... An Hussar made a desperate slap at my head which I parried, and with cut 'number two' gave him such a tremendous slash in the neck that it sickened me to look on. . . . I now had to wheel to meet a Polish lancer who was just charging me full tilt. I saw that the butt of his lance was fixed against his thigh, and that he gave his lance a slight quiver, and that he seemed to know how to use it too. I bent down slightly on my saddle, received his lance on the back of my sword which passed over my shoulder, at the same instant that the point of my weapon, through the mere

rush of the horses passing each other, entered his breast, and went clean through him, coming out at his back, so that I was forced to draw it out with a wrench as he rolled over the crupper.

A Cossack was now upon me, but as I reined back in time his aim failed, and he shot by my horse's head, and I then rode after him, and knocking over man and horse with my own, so that I was all but unseated.[96]

In the Sikh Wars and the Mutiny British cavalry felt the effect of blades which were carefully sharpened and then kept in leather-covered wooden scabbards which did not dull their edge. One light dragoon sergeant, ordered to mount just after unearthing a turnip, slipped it into his shako, where it saved his life by absorbing sword-cuts, and his comrades resorted to more decorous expedients like wrapping cloth round their shakos. The Scinde Irregular Horse had steel chain sewn along the outside of their coat-arms and breeches. The practice of sewing curb-chains, properly part of the bridle, along the epaulette to ward off sword-cuts was to evolve into the shoulder-chains worn today in dress blues by British cavalry officers.

The fact remained that the tulwar, the curved Indian sword, had, all too literally, the edge on its European opponent. In 1849, Gough authorised his men to carry tulwars instead of their regulation swords. An infantry officer who visited the field of Ferozeshah the day after the battle saw a characteristic sight: the bodies of a light dragoon sergeant with a mighty cut in the back of his neck, and his sergeant-major with his right arm lopped off and a deep cut across his face. It was some consolation that they lay in a ring of Sikh corpses. In the Indian Mutiny a cavalry surgeon complained that British swords seemed to do little damage, but he had treated a sergeant with his bridle-arm severed above the elbow. He saw another cut sever not only the crupper of a trooper's saddle but also the spine of his horse.

The lance appeared in the British army after the Waterloo. It was at first intended to attach a lance troop to each cavalry regiment, but in 1816 the 9th, 12th, 16th and 23rd Light Dragoons were converted to lancers. The first lances were an unwieldy 15 or 16ft, but soon settled down to a weapon about 9ft long, made of ash till 1877 and bamboo thereafter. Captain Lewis Edward Nolan, who was to bear the order which launched the Light Brigade on its charge, favoured the lance because of 'the morale effect produced (particularly on young soldiers), not only by its longer reach, but by the deadly effect of the home thrusts.'[97] A corporal who charged with the 16th Lancers at Aliwal agreed that 'our lances seemed to paralyse them altogether', although it seems likely that for close combat many troopers jetti-soned their lances and drew their swords. Lancers were at a disadvan-tage against a swordsman who got inside their reach, and in one of history's last sword versus lance contests, which took place between British and German cavalrymen outside the Belgian town of Mons on 21 August 1914, the German lancers dropped their weapons at close quarters. On balance the lance did have its uses in a charge, particularly against infantry, who might lie down to avoid a sword-thrust, but required a high level of training and was an encumbrance on outpost work.

The regiments of light dragoons converted to lancers in 1816 gave up their carbines when they received the lance. In the eigh-teenth century dragoons had carried a musket with a 42 inch barrel and a bore of .65in. The light dragoon version had a 36 inch barrel, and in 1796 this shrunk to only 26 inches and was now a true carbine, with its ramrod slipping through a swivel at the muzzle so that it could not be dropped, compelling the trooper to dismount to retrieve it. The two carbines most commonly used in the Napoleonic period were Elliot's pattern with a 28 inch barrel and Paget's with a barrel only 16 inches long. The former was named after General George Augustus Elliot, Colonel of the 15th Light Dragoons, and the latter after General Henry, Lord Paget (later Marquess of Anglesey), Colonel of the 7th Light Dragoons. They were replaced by the per-cussion Victoria carbine in 1836.

Dragoon muskets had been slung across their owners' backs, but from the mid-eighteenth century carbines were hung from broad belts which crossed the left shoulder. A loose ring slid along a bar opposite the carbine's lock, and was attached to the belt by a stout spring clip. The arrangement ensured that the carbine was always to hand, and enabled a trooper to load and fire it on horseback or on foot. When not in use it hung, muzzle down, at his right thigh.

Thus suspended the weapon was often an encumbrance, especially at the gallop, and from the 1860s the carbine was carried in a slim leather bucket attached to the saddle. This was a great deal more comfortable, but meant that if the soldier lost his horse he lost his carbine too. Cavalrymen also carried a pair of pistols, of different patterns for heavy and light cavalry until the introduction of a universal New Land Pattern in 1814. In 1837 the Master-General of the Ordnance, himself a cavalry officer, commented on the 'worse than uselessness of the pistol'. Athough lancers, who had no carbines, received a percussion pistol in 1842, the weapon passed out of use by regular cavalry, save for officers, senior NCOs, and trumpeters.

Cavalry firearms seldom get much credit. In the seventeenth century commanders like Gustavus Adolphus and Prince Rupert had emphasised that cavalry's business was to charge home with the sword, not pop off its pistols at a distance, and Marlborough deliberately issued his troopers with just a couple of rounds of pistol ammunition so that they could defend themselves when foraging. It was axiomatic that a cavalry unit that received a charge with carbine fire would be broken: Frederick the Great declared that he would cashier any cavalry officer who remained stationary to await a charge. Quartermaster Surtees joined a party of spectators watching Captain Hancox's squadron of the 15th Light Dragoons charge a squadron of the French 13th Hussars at Tarsac in southern France. The French stood to receive the charge and were beaten with the loss of 25 prisoners. Their wounded captain kept informing his captors 'I'm as brave as a lion' and 'I'm as brave as the devil' and 'could scarcely be got to hold his piece while the surgeon was tending him.'[98] But he had not been wise to stand still to await the charge.

Cavalry outposts consisted of outlying pickets or vedettes, of a couple of mounted troopers each, with a larger in-lying picket, under an officer, closer to the main position. If the enemy made a serious approach the vedettes fired their carbines, less in the hope of causing casualties than of alerting their comrades, and then circled their horses to the left to signify approaching infantry or to the right for cavalry. William Tomkinson declared that:

> I defy anyone to name a more exhilarating sound (which can alone be compared to a tally ho! on unkennelling a fox) than of a shot falling on the ear from the direction of the outlying picket. [Further shots put] the whole camp or quarters in motion; while cries of 'Get my horse!' 'Where is the trumpeter?' 'Mount the in-lying picket' or 'Pack my baggage' reverberated to its utmost limits . . . [99]

Unlucky souls were occasionally hit by carbine fire: Private Levi Grisdale of the 10th Hussars creased General Lefebvre-Desnouëttes across the cheek before capturing him at Benavente in 1808. But at Delhi Richard Barter's comrades scarcely paused in the stride while receiving 'a salute from their carbines' from some Indian cavalry.

Flintlock and percussion pistols were useful for giving the alarm, and might kill men and horses in mêlées, but were far less effective than swords. However, the cap and ball revolver, widely used by officers in the Crimea and the Mutiny, was a different matter altogether. It was very much more reliable, and gave its user five of six shots before he needed to reload. Barter was very pleased with his revolver 'a small Colt which formerly belonged to poor Harrison, from whose body I got it after he was killed and I afterwards purchased it at his auction for 167/- . . .'[100] In February 1859 Lieutenant Stourton of the 8th Hussars found that he could not get within cutting distance of a camel-mounted adversary as his horse kept swerving (horses hated the smell of camels), when a helpful sergeant reminded him of his revolver: he brought down camel and rider with a single lucky shot.

Important though outpost work was, British cavalry, heavy and light, saw the charge as the hallmark of its profession. It was normally delivered with a regiment's soldiers formed up in line, knee to knee in two ranks. In an ideal world a cavalry commander would keep a second similar line 4–500 yards from the first, and would hold a reserve, in column for ease of control, as far back again. Wellington prescribed this sequencing of attacking lines as a result of his experience in the Peninsula and at Waterloo, and part of his criticism of British cavalry commanders centred upon their failure to preserve support lines and reserves, so that the fruits of early success were

often lost – as, indeed, had been the case in 'Slade's affair' at Maguilla in 1812.

We see a similar process at Waterloo. The Union Brigade,
launched, at just the right moment, smashed right through a corps
of infantry advancing against Wellington's centre and galloped on
to cut up its gun-line. Major George De Lacy Evans, aide de camp
to Sir William Ponsonby, the brigade commander, tells how:

> The remainder of the enemy fled as a flock of sheep across
> the valley – quite at the mercy of our Dragoons. In fact
> they went so far our men got out of control. The General
> of the Brigade, his Staff and every Officer within hearing
> exhorted themselves to the utmost to re-form the men;
> but the helplessness of the Enemy suffered too great a
> temptation to the Dragoons and all efforts were abortive
> ... the French lancers continued to advance on our left
> in good order. If only we could have formed a hundred
> men we could have made a respectable retreat and saved
> many; but we could effect no formation and were as help-
> less against their attack as their infantry must have been
> against ours ...[101]

Major General the Earl of Cardigan who commanded the Light
Brigade at Balaclava, was no military genius, but he drew up his
brigade in two lines, wisely putting his single lancer regiment, the
17th, in the centre of the first line where it might be expected to do
most damage. He told Colonel Lord George Paget to 'take command
of the second line, and I expect your best support, mind, your best
support.' 'Of course, my Lord, you shall have my best support,'
replied Paget. At the last moment the divisional commander, Lieutenant General the Earl of Lucan, intervened and created a reserve
by ordering the 11th Hussars, one of the second line regiments, to
drop back. The second line started off too close to the first, and
Paget first tried to slow down to leave a 200 yard gap, but soon
found that the first line was getting away from him and tried to
speed up. Eventually one of Paget's regiments missed the Russian
guns altogether, and the 11th Hussars struck it only in part. Even
with brave, well-trained horsemen the preservation of distinct first,
second and reserve lines was no easy matter.

Cavalry would begin its charge at the walk, and then break into a trot, covering the ground at 8mph until it was within 300 yards of its objective, when it would break into a gallop, moving at 12mph. At about 50 yards from the target the ten-note ripple of the charge would be sounded. In the late nineteenth century soldiers were taught to remember trumpet and bugle sounds by words, and the words for the charge were 'Let em go – at em boys – now for a charge!' The whole body then thundered on 'at the utmost speed of the slowest horses' until impact. Frederick the Great's cavalry general Friedrich Wilhelm von Seidlitz maintained that in the charge a soldier's weapon was a matter of indifference: he must be well mounted, and 'should bear in mind the unshakeable resolution to ride the enemy down with his horse's breast.'

If charged with this sort of confidence opposing cavalry or infantry might break before or at the moment of contact. At Waterloo Vandeleur's light cavalry brigade charged a strong body of French infantry late in the day.

> The enemy's infantry gave us a volley, and being close at them . . . we made a rush and went into their column with the companies which were stationed in front, they running into the square for shelter. We completely succeeded, many of their infantry immediately throwing down their arms and crowding together for safety. Many, too, ran away up the next rising ground.[102]

When cavalry charged cavalry, one side almost always hesitated before contact: William Tomkinson saw only one charge that resulted in a static sword-fight. A man's spirits often quailed in the terror and excitement as the two sides approached at high speed. One of Thomas Brotherton's men deliberately cut his own horse across the head in the latter stages of a charge, and was only discovered because the enemy 'turned back just before we reached him, thus exposing the man's trick.'[103] In the Mutiny, Assistant Surgeon John Henry Sylvester saw a squadron of 17th Lancers charge a body of Indian cavalry. Both sides started off with great determination but then the Indians, 'dreading the crash, hesitated, slackened their pace, halted, opened out, and fled. Some fell speared at once, the remainder were pursued seven miles . . .'[104]

But infantry that stood its ground, undeterred by the oncoming mass, was likely to succeed. In July 1810 a French detachment, bravely charged by the 14th Light Dragoons, formed square and fired on order: 'the dragoons rode up to the enemy's bayonets, and [Lieutenant Colonel] Talbot fell in the enemy's ranks, shot through the body.' In March the following year Captain Thomas Browne of the 23rd Foot watched British light dragoons attack a French rear-guard of 150 infantry:

> under the command of a French Officer, mounted on a miserable little-bit-of-a-Pony, who immediately formed his Detachment up into two Squares. Whilst one of these Squares retreated, the other kept up a constant fire, on our Squadron of Cavalry attempting to charge it. The horses would not face it and many of them were killed. When the retreating Square was pursued, it halted, and began the same sort of unapproachable fire; the other then commenced its retreat, & passing by the Square that was engaged, which in its turn moved off, when its partner in the conflict had stopped and faced our Cavalry.

The French made good their retreat into a wood where the cavalry could not follow. Their officer was the last man to enter cover, and waved his hat to his opponents as he did so. Although British eyewitnesses naturally hoped to see the detachment taken, 'it was not possible to withhold from the gallantry and skill of its Commander, a sort of reluctant congratulation on his escape . . .'[105]

Even if an infantry formation was briefly broken, for instance by a dead horse making a gap, steady infantrymen could still do terrible damage to cavalry who entered, as Sergeant William Gould recalled of Aliwal:

> We had to charge a square of infantry. At them we went, the bullets flying around like a hailstorm. Right in front was a big sergeant, Harry Newsome. He was mounted on a grey charger, and with a shout of 'Hullo, boys, here goes for death or a commission,' forced his horse right over the front rank of kneeling men, bristling with bayonets. As Newsome dashed forward he lent over and grasped one

of the enemy's standards, but fell from his horse pierced by 19 bayonet wounds.

Into the gap made by Newsome we dashed, but they made fearful havoc among us. When we got out on the other side of the square our troop had lost both lieutenants, the cornet, troop-sergeant-major, and two sergeants. I was the only sergeant left. Some of the men shouted, 'Bill, you've got command, they're all down.'[106]

Confident, well drilled infantry often had a low regard for cavalry – their own and the enemy's. At Waterloo, as two soldiers of the 14th Regiment stood in square, one was dismayed to see their own cavalry streaming back in disorder through the gaps between adjacent squares. His mate told him not to worry, 'for we must blow the froth off before we come to the porter.'

THE NIMBLE GUNNER

I T WAS NOT UNTIL the early twentieth century, when artillery was able to produce effective indirect fire, engaging targets which were invisible to the guns but were engaged by fire directed by an observer, that it came to dominate the battlefield. Indeed, the defining characteristic of land warfare that century was that most casualties were inflicted by men their victims never even glimpsed. 'The advantage is all with the shell,' claimed one, 'and you have no comeback.' Yet even in the nineteenth century the power of the gun should not be underestimated. A battery firing canister at 600 yards had the same effect on its target as a battalion firing volleys at 100 yards. Although the variable quality of powder and metal meant that exploding shells were notoriously erratic, solid roundshot were deadly against packed formations. A single ball killed or disabled an officer and 25 men of the 40th Foot at Waterloo, and at the Alma in 1854 Captain Arthur Tremayne 'never saw a more ghastly sight than rows of Russians with their skulls blown off' where the retreating Sousdal Regiment had been raked by British guns.

When the Light Brigade charged Colonel Prince Obolensky's No 3 Battery of the Don Cossacks in the North Valley at Balaclava it received concentrated fire which typified the performance of artillery in the age of horse and musket. Its first casualty, Captain Nolan, was hit when a Russian shell burst in front of him. This was what the

British termed 'common shell,' a cast-iron globe filled with black powder and initiated by a fuse which was ignited by the flash of powder as the cannon was fired. A similar projectile, invented by Lieutenant Henry Shrapnel, Royal Artillery, and known in the British service as spherical case, had musket balls mixed with the bursting charge, and exploded to scatter them widely.

The shells were fired by the four 9 pdr howitzers in the Russian battery. Howitzers, which had shorter barrels than field guns, and a distinct chamber at the base of the barrel, were intended to fire shell, and were always in a minority. Hollywood misleads us into imagining that most projectiles fired in the era were shells: they were not. Far more common was the solid iron roundshot, fired from weapons such as Colonel Obolensky's four 6 pdr guns. Roundshot were ideally pitched low so as to hit the ground just in front of the enemy's front rank, and ricochet through the depth of the enemy's formation, causing havoc at every bound. These missiles were clearly visible as they bounded on. At Inkerman Henry Clifford had just fetched his brigade commander a fresh horse, for the previous one had been killed by a roundshot, when:

> I saw a cannon ball strike some yards in front of him. I called out, but he could not see it and fortunately did not move, for the cannon ball struck his horse in the chest, a little higher up than the first, and remained in the poor animal's side, giving the General a severe contusion upon the left knee.[107]

Roundshot, too, were soon hitting the Light Brigade, as Private James Wightman observed:

> Sergeant Talbot had his head carried clean off by a round shot, yet about thirty yards further the headless body kept the saddle, the lance at the charge firmly gripped under the right arm.[108]

Talbot was luckier than others. At Badli-ke-Serai Richard Barter saw Colonel Chester, adjutant general of the Bengal army, after:

> a shot had evidently alighted on the holster pipes, smash-ing the horse's back and cutting it open, and at the same time disembowelling the rider. The horse was rolling in

TOP LEFT The weedy and tubercular Major General James Wolfe was killed at the moment of victory at Quebec in 1759.

CENTRE William, Viscount Howe, was one of three martial brothers. He fought at Quebec, and was a promising leader of light troops. Leading the attack at Bunker Hill with characteristic courage, he enjoyed considerable tactical success as commander in chief in North America, but had a poor strategic grasp and resigned his command in 1778.

LEFT Major General Robert 'Black Bob' Craufurd was an iron disciplinarian who led the Light Brigade and then the Light Division in the Peninsula. He was mortally wounded at the storming of Ciudad Rodrigo in 1812.

INSCRIPTION FOR THE TOMB TO BE ERECTED

TO THE MEMORY

OF THE

MARQUIS OF ANGLESEA'S LEG.

Here rests, and let no saucy knave
  Presume to sneer or laugh—
To learn that mould'ring in this grave
  Is laid—*a British Calf.*

For he who writes these lines is sure,
  That those who read the whole,
Will find such laugh were premature,
  For here, too, lies—*a Sole.*

And here five little ones repose,
  Twin-born with other five ;
Unheeded by their brother toes,
  Who all are now alive.

A leg and foot, to speak more plain,
  Rest here of one commanding ;
Who, tho' his wits he might retain,
  Lost *half his understanding.*

And when the guns, with murder fraught,
  Pour'd bullets thick as hail—
Could only, in this way, be brought
  To give the foe—Leg Bail.

Who now in England just as gay,
  As in the battle brave,
Goes to the rout, review, or play
  With—One Foot in the Grave.

Fortune in vain here showed her spite,
  For he will still be found—
Should England's sons engage in fight,
  Resolv'd to stand his ground.

But Fortune's pardon I must beg,
  She wish'd not to disarm ;
And when she lopp'd the Hero's leg
  She did not seek his ᴴ—ᴬᴿᴹ.

And but indulg'd a harmless whim,
  Since he could walk with One ;
She saw two Legs were lost on him
  Who never deigned to ʀᴜɴ.

Harrild, Printer, 20, Great Eastcheap.

Lord Uxbridge, later Marquess of Anglesey, had his leg amputated at Waterloo.
His leg was buried properly, and this inscription was penned for its tomb.

Richard Barter features prominently in these pages. Adjutant of the 75th Regiment in the Indian Mutiny, he wrote penetrating accounts of the action at Badli-ke-Serai and the Siege of Delhi, later becoming a general.

Florence Nightingale, who entered the popular pantheon as 'The Lady with the Lamp' at Scutari.

Hugh, Viscount Gough, had a fine fighting record in the 87th Foot before commanding the army in the Sikh Wars. Known as 'Old White Coat' because of his distinctive battle dress, his tactics were direct and unsubtle. Though replaced by Charles Napier after Chilianwallah, he won a conclusive victory at Gujerat before Napier arrived.

Lord Raglan served as Wellington's military secretary and lost an arm at Waterloo. Recent studies have done much to rehabilitate his battered reputation as commander-in-chief in the Crimean War.

ABOVE LEFT This photograph of Harry Smith as a general in old age, *c.*1860, still radiates something of the quality that made him one of the stars of 'the bloody, fighting 95th', in the Peninsula.

ABOVE Footguards officer, man- about- town and diarist, Captain Howell Rees Gronow.

LEFT Mutiny trio: Sir Colin Campbell (left) Sir James Hope Grant and Sir William Mansfield.

French and British Guards officers enjoy a gentlemanly exchange before settling to the business of killing, Fontenoy 1745.

The 42nd Regiment (Black Watch) lost 314 and had 333 wounded from their dogged attack on Fort Ticonderoga in 1758. Here the artist, who has taken some liberties with their uniform, shows them doggedly trying to negotiate the *abatis* of felled trees in front of the French ramparts.

Major General Edward Braddock's defeat on the Monongahala, 1755.

The storming of Seringapatam, 1799. Establishing a practicable breach with heavy guns was the usual prerequisite to a successful storm, although, as this illustration shows, the breach itself was generally stoutly defended.

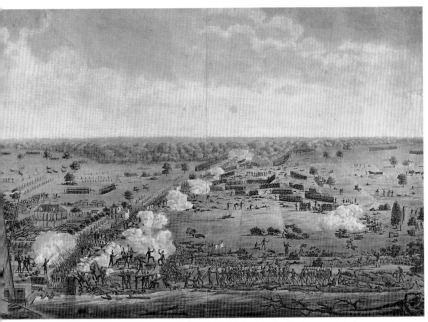

In January 1815, Wellington's brother-in-law Sir Edward Pakenham attacked well-prepared American defences outside New Orleans and was beaten off with 1,500 casualties. He was among the dead.

This illustration, based on a sketch by an officer of the 31st (Huntingdonshire) Regiment, shows the regiment advancing against the Sikhs at Mudki in 1845.

Into the jaws of death: the charge of the Light Brigade at Balaclava, as seen from the Fedioukine heights. To the left, the Russian guns, backed by cavalry, await the charge. Lord Cardigan leads his first line (13th Light Dragoons and 17th Lancers). Behind him ride the 11th Hussars (foreground) and the 4th Light Dragoons, with the 8th Hussars to the right rear.

This photograph of the Ordnance wharf at Balaclava in 1855 gives a good idea of the insatiable appetite of siege artillery. Shells are identifiable from roundshot by the circular holes for their fuses.

Horse artillery on the move during the Indian Mutiny.

Felice Beato's photograph shows the skeletons of sepoys still lying in the
Secunderbagh at Lucknow, stormed by the 93rd Highlanders.

'A heavy day in the batteries'. A British siege gun battering the walls of the city
from Delhi Ridge. Incoming fire includes a shell or mortar bomb, its fuse burning.

ABOVE A caricature satirising the alleged sale of commissions by the Duke of York's mistress Mary Anne Clarke is a more general attack on purchase, with rich young gentlemen vaulting over more experienced officers to buy promotion.

ABOVE RIGHT This cruel caricature shows General John Whitelocke being ceremonially degraded (though he was in fact spared this indignity) after his cashiering for failure at Buenos Aires in 1807. The devil helpfully suggests that suicide would be his proper response.

RIGHT An apparently mundane illustration of 1807 throws valuable light on infantry training. On the left, a sergeant instructs two ranks of recruits, in white canvas working tunics, while a fugleman to their front demonstrates the correct positions. Another sergeant is drilling recruits, no doubt emphasising that their feet should be swung so low that the soles of their shoes are not visible. Two officers, both with the cocked hat widely worn by infantry officers until 1812, look on.

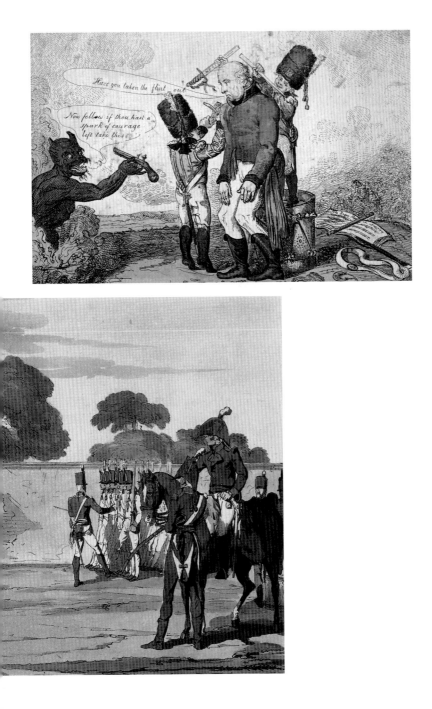

An officer, sergeant and privates of 1ˢᵗ Foot Guards in the Peninsula. The soldiers'
1812 pattern shakos are covered in oilskin, with a waterproof neck-curtain.
Greatcoats were grey, and those of NCOs and men had collars and cuffs the
colour of regimental facings.

A French illustration of Scots regiments in Paris in 1815 shows kilts a good deal shorter than they were actually worn, and hints at the disclosures threatened by bending soldiers.

'Shoot me like a soldier: don't hang me like a dog.' Hanging was regarded as an ignominious end. These sepoys have been hanged for murder at Peshawar in 1850.

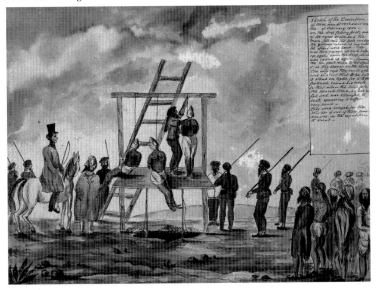

The British revived the old Mughal military punishment of blowing from cannon. Here mutineers have been strapped to the muzzles of guns of the Bengal Horse Artillery and are about to be blown into eternity. In fact many victims faced this dreadful death with remarkable courage.

Uniforms rarely look as smart in photographs as they do in uniform plates, as this photograph of the cookhouse of the 8th Hussars in the Crimea shows.

agony and the poor old Colonel lay on his back, his helmet off and his grey hair stained with blood, calling in a faint voice to Captain Barnard ... How he could speak at all was a puzzle to me for the whole of his stomach lay beside him on the ground as if it had been scooped out of his back, and yet I heard afterwards that he lived a quarter of an hour.[109]

For the last 300 yards the brigade had to deal with canister, metal containers filled with balls disgorged as the tin ruptured on leaving the cannon's muzzle. Private Albert Mitchell saw that it 'brought down men and horses in heaps.'[110]

In the late eighteenth century, French artillery equipment was standardised by Jean Baptiste de Gribeauval, inspector-general of artillery from 1776. His influence spread widely, and the Royal Artillery adopted wheels of uniform size and carriages of standard pattern for guns of the same calibre. Guns were classified by the weight of the shot they fired. For service in the field (siege guns were another matter altogether) they ranged from the derisory 3 pdr, through the 6 pdr and 9 pdr to the 12 pdr. The calibre of howitzers was given in inches, with the 5 in howitzer as the most common.

The artillery manuals of the age show just what a wide variety of pieces were available. My 1801 edition of *The Little Bombardier and Pocket Gunner*, dedicated to 'the junior officers of the Royal Artillery by a brother soldier', lists nine sorts of iron and 24 of brass guns. It also distinguishes four sizes of iron mortar and as many of brass. Mortars were stubby, wide-muzzled weapons which fired explosive bombs: the expression bombproof originates from the masonry and earth roofs put on vulnerable buildings like powder magazines to keep out these unwelcome guests.

Effective ranges varied, but a 12 pdr with 3 degrees of elevation would send its roundshot out to 1,063 yards where it would make 'first graze', whence, unless it fell in mud or swamp, the ball would rise again to achieve 'second graze' 300 yards behind. At this range the gun might hit a target representing a line of infantry with 17 per cent of its shots, a proportion which grew steadily to 87 per cent at 600 yards, the effective range of the field artillery. At close range the canister was murderously effective, with 41 per cent of the balls from a British 6 pdr hitting the target at 400 yards. In real emergencies – for the force of the recoil strained barrel and carriage alike – gunners might fire double canister, or slip a canister on top of a roundshot, which is what Mercer did at Waterloo.

The effect of such fire at close range was appalling. Near Tournai in 1793, the Coldstream Guards were caught by a concealed French battery:

> which commenced the heaviest firing of grape shot ...
> The fire was so sudden that almost every man by one
> impulse fell to the ground – but immediately got up again
> and began a confused fire without orders – The second
> discharge of the French knocked down whole ranks. The
> officers exerted themselves to make the men come to
> charge ... but all was in vain. The soldiers on their knees
> kept on firing and would have remained so till all were
> killed ...[111]

'The discharge of every gun,' wrote Mercer of Waterloo, 'was followed by a fall of men and horses like that of grass before the mower's scythe.'[112] The fire of his guns left such 'heaps of carcasses' that the survivors could not get past them, and he saw how men 'struggled with each other ... using the pommels of their swords' to fight their way out of the chaos. Major General Sir Peregrine Maitland, watching the effect of artillery on French infantry, saw 'fragments of men, Grenadier caps, muskets and belts' thrown up by the impact. A gunner officer remembered seeing 'four or five men and horses piled up on each other like cards, the men not even having been displaced from the saddle, the effect of canister.'

A first-line supply of ammunition – for the 9 pdr 26 rounds of ball and six of canister – was carried in a two-wheeled limber, towed between the team of horses and their gun, and more ammunition followed the battery in caissons. Mercer's troop began the Waterloo campaign with five 9pdrs and a 5in howitzer, supported by nine ammunition wagons, a carriage for spare wheels, a travelling forge, a light cart and a baggage wagon. The guns and howitzer were drawn by eight-horse teams and the ammunition wagons by four.

A 9 pdr like Mercer's was served by five men, while another four kept it provided with ammunition. The No. 1, a sergeant, commanded and aimed the piece. The No. 2, the spongeman, to the right of the barrel, wiped it out with a damp fleece on a wooden staff to extinguish any smouldering debris left by the previous shot. The No. 3, the loader, on the left, then placed the ammunition – usually a serge bag of powder attached to the projectile by a wooden sabot – into the muzzle. The spongeman had now reversed his staff, and rammed the charge home, while the No. 4, the ventsman, standing by the breech, blocked the touch-hole with his leather thumb-stall to prevent a rush of air which might fan any embers which had survived sponging.

If the ventsman was not attentive to his task the spongeman would cuff him with the rammer, for if the charge went off prematurely he stood to lose his hands. Mercer saw a spongeman, Gunner Butterworth, 'one of the greatest pickles in the troop, but . . . a most daring and active soldier' stumble after ramming, just as the piece was fired. He lost both arms at the elbows, and 'raised himself on his stumps, and looked most piteously in my face . . .' Nothing could be done to help him, and he bled to death.[113]

The No. 1, meanwhile, had traversed the gun, using a wooden handspike, and then laid it with the aid of an elevating wheel beneath the breech. The ventsman pricked the charge-bag through the touch-hole, and either filled the hole with finely ground powder, or, after about 1800, inserted a powder-filled quill. The No. 5 fired it on order, by applying a portfire, a length of quick-match on a wooden handle, to the touch-hole. It was important for all members of the detachment to stand well clear as the gun fired, because it would leap back on its wheels, crushing feet as it did so. Before being loaded again the gun would have to be run up, pushed back to where it had started. Mercer's men became too tired to run their guns up, and by the close of the battle they finished up 'in a confused heap, the trails crossing each other, and the whole dangerously near the limbers and ammunition wagons . . .'

At Waterloo Mercer's troop carried out the positional role usually entrusted to field artillery. Horse artillery was designed to accompany cavalry on the move, which is why all its gunners had mounts of their own or rode on limbers. However, its ability to change ground rapidly meant that a commander might use it to shore up a sagging front or take advantage of a fleeing opportunity. Mercer moved up the road towards Quatre Bras against a tide of stragglers, many of whom reported 'Monsieur, tout est perdu! Les Anglais sont abimés, en déroute, abimés, tous, tous, tous!' It was not until he met a wounded Highlander of the 92nd that he received a more objective version. 'Na, na, sir, it's aw a damned lie,' the man assured him: 'they war fechtin' yat an I left 'em; but it's a bludy business, and thar's na saying fat may be the end on't. Oor regiment was nigh clean swept off, and oor Colonel [Cameron of Fassiefern] kilt just as I cam awa'.' The troop stayed at Quatre Bras just long enough for its men to say, as Mercer put it, that they had been in the battle. On the way back, in filthy weather, Lord Uxbridge, commanding the cavalry, sought out Mercer and gave him a typical horse artillery task: he was to give the French advanced guard a round from each gun just as it crossed the nearby crest-line, and then make off smartly.[114] And when the troop galloped cross-country to its position at Waterloo, Wellington exclaimed: 'Ah! That's the way I like to see the horse-artillery move!'

The apotheosis of horse artillery was the performance of Captain Norman Ramsay's troop at Fuentes d'Onōro in 1811. It was ridden down by French cavalry and presumed lost, but onlookers saw a sudden disturbance in the very midst of the French mass.

> Men and horses there closed with confusion and tumult towards one point, a thick dust arose, and loud cries, and the sparkling of blades and the flashing of pistols, indicated some extraordinary occurrence. Suddenly the multitude became violently agitated, an English shout pealed high and clear, the mass was rent asunder, and Norman Ramsay burst forth at the head of his battery, his horses breathing fire, stretched like greyhounds along the plain, the guns bounded behind them like things of no weight, and the mounted gunners followed in close career.[115]

The British army experimented with rockets designed by Sir William Congreve, comptroller of the Woolwich Laboratory. They were used in Wellesley's attack on Copenhagen in 1807, and although they managed to hit that largish target fairly well, their erratic performance prejudiced Wellesley against them. In January 1813 two rocket troops were formally added to the Royal Horse Artillery. They were equipped with 12, 18 and 24 pdr rockets carried in carts, and 6 pdr rockets in saddle holsters: mounted gunners carried bundles of sticks for the 6 pdrs in a small bucket near their offside stirrup.

They did not perform well in the Peninsula, and Wellington declared that he did not want any for the Waterloo campaign. A kindly gunner officer objected that Major Edward Whinyates, the troop commander, was devoted to them, and it would break his heart if he lost them. 'Damn his heart,' snapped Wellington. 'Let my orders be obeyed.' He subsequently relented, and a rocket troop took part in the campaign. Mercer was not hugely impressed. Having watched the first 'fidgety missile' burst squarely under a French gun, he was surprised to see that none of the rest followed its course:

> Most of them, on arriving about the middle of the ascent, took a vertical direction, whilst some actually turned back upon ourselves – and one of these, following me like a squib until its shell exploded, actually put me in more danger than the fire of the enemy throughout the day.[116]

General Sir John Colborne came close to become the most distinguished victim of the rocket when commanding the forces in Canada in 1837 and watching a rocket troop in action. A witness reported that:

> The Ordnance Department imagined, I believe, that rockets would improve like port with keeping; the result was that when it was fired, instead of rising, it fell, and not clearing a wooden fence in front of the troop, broke its long tail short off. The huge head went whirling and twirling, whizzing and fizzing, all over a ploughed field in the most frightful manner. There was a great stampede – Headquarter Staff, Rocket Troop, and all, took fright.[117]

There were no casualties, and Colborne survived to become a peer and a field marshal.

Most artillerymen, officers and soldiers alike, wore uniforms of workmanlike blue with red facings. They shared the general military fashion of the age, shifting from long coats with broad lapels in the eighteenth century, to shorter jackets in the Napoleonic wars and tunics for the Crimea. The Royal Horse Artillery, however, turned out in light dragoon uniform consisting of a blue dolman with red facings and yellow braid (gold for officers) and a fur-crested Tarleton helmet. They did not follow the light dragoons into French-style uniforms in 1812, although they later changed the Tarleton for a hussar-style busby.

CURRENCY OF WAR

WOUNDS AND DEATH are the common currency of war, and it was the task of the combat arms to inflict them with musket, sword and pistol, shot and shell and even – though they rarely succeeded in doing so – with the rocket. However, throughout the period disease killed more soldiers than human agency. We have already seen the lethal nature of stations like the West Indies and the prevalence of cholera in India. But even in the Peninsula the British army lost 24,930 men to disease and 8,889 to enemy fire. In the Crimea 2,255 men were killed in action and 1,847 died of wounds to a shocking 17,225 deaths from disease. Ignorance of the process of infection and appalling sanitary conditions in military hospitals meant that death from infection was the outcome of many wounds and operations.

There were gradual advances in medical science. Petit's screw tourniquet, introduced in 1718, controlled the flow of blood in the femoral artery and made amputation at the thigh possible and amputations below the knee far safer. John Hunter, an army surgeon during the Seven Years' War, argued against blood-letting and the routine enlargement of gunshot wounds, while the French surgeon Pierre-Joseph Desault developed the technique of debridement, the removal of necrotic tissue from infected wounds, a practice whose importance was re-emphasised as recently as the Falklands War of

1982. Some contemporary surgeons, like Claude Pouteau, John Pringle and Alexander Monro believed that there was a relationship between cleanliness and mortality in surgery. Monro even claimed a mortality for major amputations of only 8 per cent, a remarkable figure given that overall mortality rate for hospital surgery in the period was 45–65 per cent. In 1827 George Guthrie, an army surgeon in the Peninsula, published his *Treatise on Gunshot Wounds . . .*, which established the doctrine of primary amputation. Yet the greatest leaps forward came at or after the end of our period, with the discovery of ether in 1846, chloroform in 1847, and Pasteur's work on microbiology and Lister's on antisepsis in the 1860s. Throughout the period a soldier whose leg wound demanded amputation at the thigh was far more likely to die of post-operative infection than to survive it: the death-rate for this operation was 70 per cent at Waterloo and still 63 per cent in the Crimea.

Military medical organisation steadily improved. In the Peninsula, Dr James McGrigor established small regimental hospitals which gave a better prospect of earlier treatment and did his best to ensure that larger hospitals, to which wounded progressed, were efficiently run. Even so they were not pleasant places. Corporal William Wheeler of the 51st was wounded in November 1813 and was first taken to a field hospital in a farm just behind the battle, though warned that he lacked the skill to describe the place, for:

> It would require the genius of Hogarth to perform the task . . . Outside the buildings were a great many wounded soldiers, some drinking and smoking, others rolling about, some half and others mad drunk, while a great many lay stretched out as if dead. Women too who had followed up the rear of the army had forgot they had come up in the laudable pursuit of seeking their husbands, had freely partaken of the damnable potation until that had transformed themselves into something more like fiends than angels of mercy. But for the honour of the sex there were many exceptions. In one place you would see a lovely young woman, supporting the head of her dying husband on her bosom, anxiously watching the last gasp of life, then again your eye would meet with one in bitter anguish,

bewailing her loss, fondly clinging to the cold remains of
all that was dear to her . . .

One of the regimental women was widowed for the third time since
Vitoria, just six months before. Wheeler's wound worsened and, after
he had been admitted to a general hospital, was declared to be
'sluffed' or infected, and he was moved into:

> What we call the incurable ward, none of the other
> patients are allowed to enter this ward as the sluff is infec-
> tious. . . During the five weeks I was in it, what numbers
> I had seen die under the most writhing torture, and their
> places filled again by others, who only come to pass a few
> days in misery, and then to be taken to their last home.
> The bed next mine were occupied by six soldiers, five
> died, the sixth I left in a hopeless state. One of those men
> I knew, he was a sergeant in the 82nd, his wife was nurse
> to the ward, she pricked her finger with a pin left in one
> of the bandages, caught the infection, her finger was first
> amputated, then her hand, the sluff appearing again in
> the stump, she refused to undergo another operation, the
> consequence was she soon died.

Wheeler was lucky. A Spanish doctor treated his wound 'with some
thing like pepper and salt mixed,' and it 'was . . . changed from a
nasty sickly whitebrown colour to a bright red.' Even so he remained
in hospital for six months.[118]

After the war McGrigor did much to improve the status and
professional competence of medical officers. The ratio of medical
officers per combatant increased from one to 145 in the Peninsula
to 1 to 77 in the Crimea. And by the time of the Crimea the army
had a few purpose-built ambulance wagons of the type designed by
the French military surgeon Larrey, and eight stretchers per battalion. But these organisational changes, like the corresponding
advances in medical science, were of a modest and evolutionary
nature: and the challenges they faced were mammoth.[119]

The lethal accuracy of modern weapons has been paralleled by
major scientific advances (the discovery of the sulfa drugs and the
development of blood transfusions chief amongst them), radical
improvements in casualty evacuation so as to make the best use of

the 'golden hour' after wounding, dispersion on the battlefield, and the rediscovery of body armour. Moreover, as the size of the military 'tail' has increased at the expense of its smaller but sharper teeth, so the proportion of soldiers in harm's way has tended to diminish. Since 1865 wars have killed far fewer soldiers as a percentage of the force deployed than was the case before. At the time of the wars of the French Revolution casualties tended to run at about 9 per cent of the winner's total force and 16 per cent of the loser's, but the close-range intensity of the battles of the Napoleonic period raised these figures to 15 per cent and 20 per cent respectively.

These statistics can be no more than general. However, for a chilling view of their practical impact we might consider the battle-field of Waterloo. An area slightly larger than New York's Central Park, or about the combined size of St James's Park, Hyde Park and Green Park in central London, was strewn with perhaps 50,000 casualties. About a third were beyond human help. But to look after the remainder there were in theory 273 British surgeons (but some had become casualties themselves), rather fewer Prussian medical officers, a handful of French doctors and an assortment of medical gentlemen of several nationalities who had travelled to Brussels to lend a hand. The picture is a stark and simple one. Throughout our period any major battle swamped the medical facilities available. Medical science could do little for so many of the wounds inflicted, with such ugly caprice, by the weapons of the age. And too many of those it might have helped lay out on the field until their chances of survival had passed. Lead, black powder and their attendant microbes still held sway over science and organisation.

Musketry was the main casualty-producer, causing over 60 per cent of casualties in most battles and a remarkable 91 per cent of British casualties at Inkerman where the effectiveness of Russian artillery was limited by the fog. An officer of Napier's Regiment told his mother of running the gauntlet of roundshot and musketry at Minden in 1759.

> At the beginning of the action I was almost knock'd off
> my legs by my three right hand Men, who were kill'd and
> drove against me by a cannon ball, the same Ball also
> kill'd two men close to Ward, whose post was in the rear

of my Platoon . . . Some time after I received from a spent
Ball just such a rap as I have frequently from that once
most dreadful weapon, your crooked headed Stick; . . . I
got another of these also on one of my legs, which gave
me about as much pain as would a tap from Miss Mathews's
Fan. The last and greatest misfortune of all fell to the
share of my poor old coat for a musquet ball enter'd into
the right skirt of it and made three holes. I had almost
forgotten to tell you that my Spontoon was shot thro' a
little below my hand; this disabled it, but a French one
now does duty in its room.[120]

He was fortunate, for a musket-ball (accompanied, at close range,
by fragments of wadding and unburned powder) could kill instantly
by hitting skull or abdomen. Roger Lamb, then a corporal in the 9th
Foot, was on Burgoyne's advance to Saratoga in 1777 and saw how
'a man, a short distance on my left, received a ball in his forehead,
which took off the top of his skull.'[121] Rifleman Joseph Cockayne of
the 95th was lifting his canteen to his mouth when a ball went through
his canteen and on into his brain, killing him on the spot; Corporal
William Wheeler was glancing at Sergeant Webster on the field of
Nivelle at the instant he was shot dead 'by a ball entering about an
inch below his breast plate,' and John Cooper's comrade David Wilson, resentful of a recent rebuke, stood up in a line of crouching
men 'and was directly shot through the heart'.

A bullet wound could cause a man to bleed to death quickly. On
Walcheren in 1799 William Surtees' fellow-Northumbrian Thomas
Bamburgh was hit 'just above the ham; he instantly fell, and roared
out most piteously.' Surtees tried to help him from the field but he
could not stand the pain of being moved – the ball had probably
broken a bone – and he soon died. Stomach wounds were particularly
feared. They were often painful when inflicted: Sergeant Frazer of
the 95th gasped out that his wound hurt so much that he could not
bear it, and then died in Benjamin Harris's arms. And if they did
not kill from shock and loss of blood, an almost inevitable slow death
from peritonitis followed. The observant Captain Thomas Browne
saw that men, when hard hit, behaved like birds or animals.

> I have observed a Soldier, mortally wounded, by a shot
> through the head or heart, instead of falling down, elevate
> his Firelock with both hands above his head, & run round
> & round, describing circles before he fell, as one fre-
> quently sees a bird shot in the air... Men, when badly
> wounded, seek the shelter of a stone or a bush, to which
> they betake themselves, before they lie down, for support
> & security, just as birds, or hares do, when in a similar
> state of suffering.[122]

Other musket wounds were serious but, unless infection set in, not necessarily life-threatening. John Colborne was hit by a ball that entered his shoulder, drove part of his epaulette into the wound, and lodged in his arm. The ball was extracted fifteen months later, and although the shoulder-joint was frozen he regained free use of his arm below the elbow. William Keep was wounded on the Nive in 1813. A bullet hit him in the neck, sending blood

> spurting like a fountain from my mouth whilst I was laying
> on my back. The blow was severe, it was like a cart-wheel
> passing over my head, but this was instantaneous only,
> fore all pain ceased, and I was left in full possession of my
> senses, with the warm drops falling upon my face.[123]

At Freeman's Farm in 1777 Captain Bloomfield of the artillery was hit in the face, but the ball passed clean through both cheeks without doing any damage. Balls often described unusual trajectories through the body, and in their efforts to find them with fingers and probes surgeons would encourage their patients to adopt the pos-ition they had been in when hit. Private Henry Oxburn of 7th Fusiliers, crouching as he ran away from the Americans at New Orleans, received a ball above the hip which ran right up his body to finish near his eye. It was successfully extracted, but he rejoined his regiment 'much altered in shape, and not fit for further service.' A surgeon might recommend amputation if a ball broke a limb, for plaster of Paris was not yet available and splints were primitive. Sometimes the wounded man, hoping to keep the limb, only gave his consent to amputation when it was too late. Captain Glanville Evelyn, hit by three American 'bullet shots' near New York on 18

October 1776, at last agreed to have his right leg taken off three weeks later, but died on 6 November, 'much regretted as a gallant officer'.

At extreme range musket balls might do no more than sting – Wheeler was bruised in exactly the same place – 'on the inside of my right knee' – at Waterloo as he had been in Spain. And, like the bullets of later generations, they could be deflected by a variety of possessions from watches to bibles. Ensign Hill of the 28th had a silk handkerchief in his left breast pocket when he was hit at Vitoria in 1813. He was carried away apparently dead, but as William Keep happily recorded: 'Hill's handkerchief that saved his life had nineteen holes in it exactly as if cut with scissors, and the contusion completely blackened his body; but he is now quite recovered.'[124] Even spent balls could kill. One of Brotherton's light dragoons was hit in the corner of the eye by a ball that turned the eyeball in its socket without producing a drop of blood. However, it caused inflammation which killed him.

Artillery fire was another matter. Even a very near miss with a round-shot could cause bruising: in the Peninsula, Captain Carthew of the 39th found his legs go 'black as charcoal' after a ball passed between them. A direct hit could cut a man in two: in 1814 a shot struck Sergeant Major Thorp of the 88th in the chest and 'whirled his remains in the air.' Limbs could be carried clean off. In his first action in 1799 Ensign Colborne saw a man lose his leg: 'The poor fellow screamed so, and seemed in such agony, that I hoped I should never have my leg carried off.'[125] At Waterloo Private Steel of the 73rd lost a foot to a cannon-ball that seemed to be rolling gently along the ground: these were always more dangerous than they seemed. He supported himself on his stump, yelled 'Damn you! I'll serve you out for that,' and fired his musket at the advancing French.

A glancing blow could leave a man dreadfully mangled. Captain Brown of the 77th was standing in the siege-lines before Flushing in 1809, timing the frequency of shots so as to shout warnings to men working in the trenches, when 'he was hit by a cannon ball on the left leg, to which was suspended an elegant sabre, which was shivered to pieces, by which he lost two fingers of the hand resting on the guard . . .' Although he could move the toes on his wounded leg, the surgeons decided to amputate, and he seems to have survived.[126] Sir John Moore caught a cannon-ball obliquely in the chest at Corunna. Colborne saw that: 'the ball had carried away his left breast, broken two ribs, shattered the shoulder, and the arm was scarcely attached to it – the whole of his left side lacerated.'[127] Near Salamanca in 1812 the French brought up artillery and fired on the British camp. Sergeant Maibee of the 51st was on duty in the line, but his wife, preparing his breakfast in camp, 'was in the act of taking some chocolate off the fire when the shot carried away her right arm and breast.' She died at once.[128]

Cornet William Williams of the 11th Light Dragoons was seen stalking off the battlefield of Salamanca with a peculiarly rigid gait. William Napier, commanding the 43rd Light Infantry, at first thought that he was holding a bloody handkerchief to his chest, but then saw that it was in fact a terrible wound. George Hennell tells us that 'a cannonball had taken his right breast off and his arm was smashed to a mummy.' His heart and lungs were clearly visible, but his voice never faltered. He died shortly afterwards in the arms of his son, who had accompanied him to the Peninsula in the hope of obtaining a commission for, as Napier observed, they were not an affluent family.

Shells were more capricious. Sometimes they burst in the air, sending fragments flying. At the Alma, W. H. Russell found 'the rush of shot' appalling and recalled being 'particularly annoyed by the birds, which were flying about distractedly into the smoke, as I thought they were fragments of shell.'[129] Sometimes they lay, with fuses fizzing, long enough for men to take cover or even knock the fuse out. One of George Napier's men, an Irish ex-marine with a taste for drink, belaboured a shell with his shovel and, having rendered it safe, cheerfully presented it to his officer. The first Victoria Cross was won under not dissimilar circumstances: Mate C. D. Lucas RN flung a live Russian shell overboard in June 1854. Sergeant Morris saw a shell fall in front of his battalion's square at Waterloo.

> While the fuse was burning out, we were wondering how many of us it would destroy. When it burst, about seventeen men were either killed or wounded by it; the portion which came to my share, was a piece of rough cast-iron

about the size of a horse-bean, which took up its lodging in my left cheek; the blood ran copiously down inside my clothes, and made me rather uncomfortable.[130]

Some wounds caused secondary injuries to others. A Peninsular soldier was hit full in the mouth by a musket ball, and some of his teeth wounded a Portuguese infantryman twenty yards away. As Ensign Leeke stood with his colours in the square of the 52nd at Waterloo, a man in front of him was decapitated and a fragment of skull hit him on the thumb: it was 'black and sore' next morning. Lieutenant Wray of the 40th was chatting to Captain Fisher at Waterloo when 'his head was blown to atoms' and he was covered with brains. After the Charge of the Light Brigade Sergeant Major Loy Smith was being congratulated on escaping intact by his friend the orderly room sergeant, who said: 'What is this on your busby and jacket?' Loy Smith discovered that it was 'small pieces of flesh' from Private Young, who had been hit as he rode beside him. John Pearman was advancing on the Sikhs at Badowal in 1846 when:

> another ball struck Harry Greenbank in the head. It sounded like a band-box full of feathers flying all over us. He was my front-rank man, and his brains nearly covered me. I had to scrape it off my face, and out of my eyes, and Taf Roberts, my left hand man, was nearly as bad.[131]

This ghastly sound would have been competing with so many others. There was musketry, popping away in distant skirmishes but sounding like rending calico as the infantry slugged it out in line. Cannonballs thrummed overhead, and shells and mortar bombs whistled and groaned. As infantrymen advanced with bayonets fixed and their arms at the shoulder there was a good deal of metalwork for canister and musketry to hit, and the clatter of lead on steel mingled with the dull thud of projectiles which hit human flesh. Hand to hand fighting at Waterloo reminded a British sergeant of a thousand coppersmiths at work. Add the shrieks of the wounded, drumming hooves, shouted orders, the constant sound of drum and bugle and occasional snatches of music from bands and Highland pipes, and the full horror of battle asserts itself.

A wounded man who could walk, or be carried by his friends,

would receive his first attention at the hands of his regimental surgeon or his assistants. Although the principles of triage, the sorting
of casualties by type so that aid can be offered to those most likely
to profit from it, had not been formally adopted, it was often clear
when there was no point in giving treatment: one of Wellington's
ADCs, shot through the abdomen at Waterloo, could hardly speak
from pain, and was simply propped up by knapsacks and died
immediately. At Freeman's Farm in 1777 Lieutenant Harvey of the
62nd, nephew of Burgoyne's adjutant general, was slightly wounded
several times and then badly hit. He was carried to a field hospital,
where it was clear that his case was hopeless. Roger Lamb heard how
'the surgeon recommended him to take a powerful dose of opium,
to avoid a seven or eight hours life of most exquisite torture. This
he immediately assented to.' He barely had strength to mutter to
Lieutenant Colonel Anstruther, his commanding officer: 'Tell my
uncle I died like a soldier . . .'[132] At the other extreme, in 1813 the
28th's assistant surgeon quickly removed the ball from William Keep's
neck, told him that he would get on well, and left him to make his
own way to the rear.

A regiment might establish its own hospital close behind the
firing line, treating men who would recover quickly as well as those
who were unlikely to survive a further journey. But most men with
serious wounds staggered, or were carried by ambulances or country
carts to a general hospital set up in a village or farm complex. In
1812 William Grattan found the whole of the village of Villa Formosa
full of wounded but he eventually discovered the designated hospital.
There were four badly-wounded officers of the 79th in one room:
one of them died as he looked on, but another, shot clean through
the lungs, was destined to recover. In the central courtyard were
about 200 men waiting to have their limbs amputated. 'It would be
difficult to convey any idea of the frightful appearance of these men,'
said Grattan.

> They had been wounded on the 5th, and this was the 7th;
> their limbs were swollen to an enormous size. Some were
> sitting upright against a wall, under the shade of a number
> of chestnut-trees, and many of these were wounded in the
> head as well as limbs. The ghastly countenances of these

> poor fellows presented a dismal sight. The streams of gore,
> which had trickled down their cheeks, were quite hard-
> ened with the sun, and gave their faces a glazed and cop-
> per-coloured hue . . . there they sat, silent and statue like,
> waiting for their turn to be carried to the amputating
> tables.[133]

Grattan went inside, where he found the surgeons, 'stripped to their shirts and bloody.' He was hauled in to help Dr Bell amputate the leg of a man of the 50th. The surgeon 'was one of the best-hearted men I ever met with,' writes Grattan, 'but such is the force of habit that he seemed insensible to the scene which was passing on around him . . .' Bell was munching almonds from his waistcoat pocket, and offered some to Grattan, who was too shocked to eat. There was a huge pit outside to receive bodies: they were taken out, a dozen at a time, and covered with earth until the pit was filled.

The same courage which kept men brave in battle might also help them face the pain of wounds, or of surgery without effective anaesthetic. After Waterloo, Sergeant Michael Connelly of the 95th admonished a wounded man for groaning in the presence of French wounded. 'Hold your tongue, ye blathering devil,' he snapped, 'and don't be after disgracing your country in the teeth of these 'ere furriners by, by dying hard. For God's sake die like a man before these 'ere Frenchers.' Not far away Lord FitzRoy Somerset showed gentlemanly 'bottom' by asking an orderly to bring back his ampu-tated arm as there was a ring on the finger that his wife had given him, and Lord Uxbridge, the morning after having had his leg off, joked with the pretty Marquise d'Assche that he would now only be able to dance with her with a wooden leg.

William Wheeler tells of a Peninsular gunner who elected to have an arm and both damaged legs taken off in a single operation, and was found propped up in bed on his one elbow the following morn-ing, smoking a short black pipe. The foot guards were not to be outdone, as Ensign Gronow tells us. Captain Robert Adair bled to death in the square of 1st Foot Guards at Waterloo, as Surgeon Gilder cut away at his thigh with instruments blunted on the flesh and bone of others, joking: 'Take your time, Mr Carver.' Ensign Somerville Burgess had his leg amputated and refused assistance to the reach the cart that would take him to Brussels, saying: 'I will hop into it.'

Sergeant Thomas Jackson of the Coldstream Guards was wounded in the leg at Bergen-op-Zoom in 1814, captured by the French, and operated on by an English surgeon. He downed a pint of strong liquor, which 'wrought a wonderful effect, and raised up my spirits to an invincible courage.' He declined a blindfold, and chose to be operated on sitting down: one surgeon held his leg while the other applied a tourniquet, quickly cut the flesh around the leg with a scalpel, and then began to saw the bone. 'When the saw was applied,' said Jackson, 'I found it extremely painful; it was worn out. It stuck in the way, as a bad saw would in a green stick.' The surgeon regretted that he had nothing better, cut the bone and then tied off the ligatures. Finally, he drew down flesh to cover the bone, held it together with sticking plaster, and then bandaged it. The whole operation took half an hour.[134]

There were odder injuries. In North America stragglers and deserters risked being scalped or tortured by Indians, a fact upon which Burgoyne's General Orders laid much emphasis. Pro-British Indians found scalping apparently tolerated by British authorities, which led to tensions within Burgoyne's army. German surgeon Julius Wasmus reported that some soldiers were prepared to watch an American prisoner being scalped by Indians after a ritual dance, but others 'happened to come by and were so horrified by this cruelty' that they liberated the unfortunate victim 'who was half dead by then.'[135] The scalping of Jane McCrea, who was engaged to Captain David Jones, serving with one of Burgoyne's loyalist American regiments, 'caused quite an uproar in the army'. Her brother John fought with the rebels, and her family had fled south as Burgoyne approached. Roger Lamb maintained that Jones had hired Indians to ensure her safety, but they quarrelled about the proceeds, and she was shot and then scalped.

And not all wounds were physical. John Colborne, doyen of Peninsula commanding officers, admitted that after a serious wound he was so overwrought as to be unfit for service in the field. 'I was obliged to go; I was fit for nothing,' he said. 'I was so nervous that I used to be obliged to say, 'Give me a glass of wine, I am going to cry.'[136] He mastered himself in front of his men, because he did not want them to think that he was crying because of the pain of his wound. Sir Thomas Picton begged to be allowed not to accompany Wellington on the Waterloo campaign, telling him that: 'I am grown so nervous that when there is any service to be done it works upon my mind so that it is impossible for me to sleep at night. I cannot possibly stand it, and I shall be forced to retire.'

There were more permanent hospitals further down the lines of communication. In the American war the largest British hospital was at Albany, in a building unkindly described by its matron as 'little better than a shed'. In the Crimea there was a general hospital at Balaclava, based on a disused school with two marquees, and later four huts, in front of it. It had a capacity of about 110 men, but regularly held between 200 and 300, and in October 1854 topped 500. In the autumn of 1854 it was in a ghastly state. W.H. Russell wrote that:

> The commonest accessories of a hospital were wanting; there was not the least attention paid to decency or cleanliness – the stench was appalling – the foetid air could barely struggle out to taint the atmosphere, save through the chinks in the walls and roofs, and, for all I could observe, these men died without the least effort to save them . . . The sick appeared to be tended by the sick, the dying by the dying.[137]

Those wounded who survived immediate treatment in the Crimea itself, where it was recognised that those operated on quickly did much better than those whose operations were delayed, went by sea to the hospital at Scutari. Arrangements for embarkation were often poorly supervised, and Mary Seacole, the daughter of a Creole woman and a Scottish soldier, had set up the 'Seacole Hotel' whence she distributed tea to the waiting men. 'She did not spare herself if she could do any good to the suffering soldiers,' wrote Assistant Surgeon Douglas Reid. 'In rain and snow, in storm and tempest, day after day, she was at her self-chosen post, with her stove and kettle . . .'[138] Her hotel was in fact a very substantial hut which offered accommodation, supplies and meals. Although the authorities awarded her the Crimean medal, she was almost bankrupted by the cost of her efforts.

Although the Barrack Hospital at Scutari was in a substantial building loaned by the Turkish authorities, conditions were no better than they would have been at Albany during the American war or Lisbon in the Peninsula. Sarah Anne Terrot was one of the eight nurses selected from the Davenport-based Sellon Order by Florence Nightingale. She found the hospital 'such a scene of dirt and disorder, rags and tumult . . .' Her first task was to nurse a dying soldier's wife, and she saw her patient:

> unnoticed and alone, though the place was covered with beds on the floor miserably dirty, attempts at ragged curtains being put up between them. Some women were lying in child-bed, some rude and noisy, seemingly half-drunk; all dirty, worn-out and squalid looking, not one fresh face to be seen; the very babies were pale and squalid.[139]

Nurse Sarah Anne was immediately impressed by the formidable Miss Nightingale, and played her own steadfast part in the gradual transformation of the hospitals at Scutari, a process which required all Florence Nightingale's energy and political contacts. Many of the orderlies ignored the dying. One man was 'very dirty, covered with wounds, and devoured by lice,' but could get little attention and there were too few nurses to go round. Food was unpalatable, and was often simply laid beside men who were 'in a state of stupor or exhaustion, unconscious of its presence, and even if conscious quite unable to sit up and feed themselves . . .'[140] It was due in no small measure to women like Sarah Anne, whose own health was broken by her efforts there, that the mortality rate at Scutari dropped from 44 per cent to 2 per cent . Yet the place still witnessed the ultimate contradiction between dreams of military glory and human destiny. 'One little lad lingered long,' she wrote. 'One night I found him weeping bitterly, and trying to comfort him, he sobbed out: "I'm going to die, and my father and mother did love me so." '[141]

V

HOME FIRES

MORE LIKE PRISONS

The army is a self-effacing part of contemporary British society, and soldiers are rarely seen in public in uniform: the contrast with Georgian and Victorian Britain could not be more striking. Regular officers and soldiers in uniform were an everyday sight, prominent even during peacetime, and during the Napoleonic wars, their ranks swelled by embodied militia, Yeomanry and Volunteers, they gave the land a bright frosting of scarlet, blue and gold. The newly-commissioned William Thornton Keep joined the 77th in Winchester in 1808. He was immediately aware that this was a garrison town.

> The first objects that struck my attention were some members of the Band in their fanciful apparel and the officers and soldiers passing about, reciprocally saluting as they met, their uniforms corresponding with my own made me feel as if I already belonged to them.[1]

As Keep told his mother, a young officer was a welcome adornment of:

> Assemblies which take place frequently twice a week at one of the principal Inns, where the Belles of Winchester congregate. The price of admission is 3/6d for tea, dancing and cards. The Dowagers chiefly amuse themselves

with the latter. I attend once a week. The brilliancy of the
scene is greatly enhanced by the red coats, I can assure
you, and when the country dances are forming a line of
them has a splendid effect by candlelight.[2]

He hoped that his new coat would arrive soon so that he could cut
'a respectable figure', but begged his mother to be sure that its
facings (the 77th wore yellow) were quite the right shade, as those
of his old coat were 'completely out of uniform'. But all was not
sweetness and light, for he found 'Winton but little enlivened the
presence of the Militia Volunteers, they are a great annoyance to
the sober inhabitants and a great trouble to our Guard, to secure
the drunken and riotous.'[3]

Nowadays young Keep would live in his battalion's officers'
mess, part of the barracks housing the unmarried officers and men
of his battalion. Then he lodged at the Swan Inn, in the High Street,
and was not in the least surprised to do so, because barracks were
relatively rare: the fine neo-classical Peninsula Barracks in Winchester, soon to be home to the Rifle Brigade (and now, in the
inevitable way of things, luxury flats) had not yet been built. In
the eighteenth century most troops were billeted in 'inns, livery
stables, alehouses, victualling houses, and all houses selling brandy,
strong waters, cyder or metheglin by retail to be drunk upon the
premises, and no other.'[4] These words, from the annual Mutiny Acts,
enshrined one of an Englishman's inalienable rights: that soldiers
could not be billeted upon him in his private house save by his prior
consent and with appropriate payment. Billeting on private houses
was legal in Scotland, was practised in Ireland and was a bone of
contention between the British government and its colonists in
North America.

In England, however, billeting in public houses was the norm,
and the practice involved the government inflicting what it regarded
as one criminal class upon another, inn-keepers. Local Justices fixed
the maximum daily rates that were to be charged for food and
accommodation. Bills were to be settled before men were paid, and
paymasters could deduct uncleared debts from officers' arrears or
regimental subsistence funds: if all else failed, they were allowed to
give the innkeeper certificates acknowledging the debt. The area

was so sensitive that any breach of the rules rendered an officer liable to cashiering.

The reason for this concern is not far to seek. In the English Civil War, the billeting of troops on private houses, often at 'free quarter', was deeply resented. Burghers complained that daughters were seduced and sons debauched, and soldiers resented the fact that they were, as a letter from the Council of the Army to the Speaker of the House of Commons observed, 'compelled to grind the Face of the Poor, to take a livelihood from them, who are fitter to receive alms . . .'[5] After the Revocation of the Edict of Nantes, which had granted toleration to French protestants, Louis XIV used billeting as an instrument of religious coercion, quartering troops on Huguenot households. The practice, bitterly remembered in Huguenot history as the *dragonnades* – for dragoons were the Sun King's preferred scourge – has given us the verb 'to dragoon'. It took extraordinary courage for a family to sustain its faith in the daily presence of soldiers who raped, stole and smashed, but could be called off in an instant if their reluctant hosts converted to Catholicism. To the folk-memory of the civil war and suspicions about the religious sympathies of Charles II and James II were added the horror-stories told by the Huguenot refugees who flocked to England in the late seventeenth century.

So battalions found themselves strewn about the inns and ale-houses of English towns, either in permanent quarters, like the London-based guards, or on their way from one garrison to the next, like the 'marching regiments' of foot. In 1726, for instance, 1st Guards, with its two battalions, had nine companies spread about Holborn, two in Clerkenwell, two in St Giles Cripplegate, one each in Spitalfields, Whitechapel, and St Sepulchre without Newgate, one in Shoreditch and Folgate, and one in East Smithfield and St Katherine's. Another ten companies were quartered south of the Thames in Southwark. When the 20th Foot changed quarters from Canterbury to Devizes in May 1756 it was billeted in thirteen towns or villages en route, and as its lieutenant colonel, James Wolfe, observed it ruined half the public houses on its line of march because the villages were simply to small too feed a battalion without 'destruction to themselves'. It was rarely a happy relationship, and men joked that: 'The Angel treats us like devils, and the Rising Sun refuses us light to go to bed by.'

If quartering was a matter of deep suspicion, barracks were no more popular, for they were regarded in England as concentrations of brutal and licentious soldiery, and in both Scotland and Ireland they were seen as nails hammered in by an occupying power to hold down a hostile population. Even in England they were seen by Radical politicians as evidence of the government's intention to coerce the population, and Sir Francis Burdett complained in the Commons that they were intended to enable 'the troops paid by the people to subdue the people'.

There were already a few barracks in the early eighteenth century. In England and Scotland some troops were barracked in castles, and after the conclusion of William's campaign in Ireland in 1691 funds were voted for the building of barracks to secure the country against a potential Jacobite rising. The latter were generally small, with the normal cavalry barracks holding only a troop. More barracks were built, and some old buildings converted, as the eighteenth century went on, but most were small and insanitary. The largest, Fort George, Ardersier, built from 1753, could hold 1,600 men by 1764, and Hilsea Barracks at Portsmouth contained, at least in theory, a full battalion, although in 1740 it was in too poor a state to do so, and when the Norfolk Militia was sent there in 1759, it discovered that smallpox, dysentery and typhus flourished on this marshy site. Another barracks comprised an old three-storey malt-house, the bottom storey with an earth floor and a ceiling 5ft 9ins above it, and the top storey an attic, hot in summer and cold in winter. Cooking had to be done in the barrack rooms, and two men slept in beds packed so tightly that it was hard to make them.

By 1792 an estimated 20,000 men could be housed in forts and barracks in Britain and the Channel Islands. That year Colonel Oliver Delancey was appointed the first barrackmaster-general, and his office was confirmed the following year. On Pitt's instructions he embarked on an extensive programme of barrack building, and although Sir John Fortescue complains that 'he made the most extravagant bargains for land and buildings,' over 200 barracks were eventually built for 146,000 infantry and 17,000 cavalry.[6] Most were small – of the 48 cavalry barracks only two were designed to contain six troops – and were sited as much for 'the maintenance of internal order' and the prevention of smuggling in the absence of an effective police force as for the comfortable housing of soldiers.

The barracks built in the 1790s largely housed the Victorian army, for it was not until after Cardwell's reforms of the 1870s had created country regiments, with two Regular battalions and a permanent depot, that a systematic programme of barrack-building was embarked upon. Many English towns still contain the red-brick barracks of this era – like Roussillon Barracks in Chichester, Le Marchant Barracks in Devizes and Brock Barracks in Reading's Oxford Road their great square keeps still grinning out across the changing townscape.

Barracks were generally laid out as a square, as much to keep soldiers in as the enemy out. The main entrance was protected by a guardroom, where the unit's guard, usually a dozen men and a drummer under the command of a sergeant, was based for its 24-hour stint. The guard was to be fully dressed at all times, with arms and ammunition to hand. At 9.00 each morning the old guard fell in outside the guardroom for inspection by the orderly officer, a subaltern also on a 24-hour duty, and then handed over to the new guard. The orderly officer took the guard reports, giving an account of the occurrences of the past day and night, to the adjutant, and would turn out the guard, to ensure that it was in good order, at least once during his tour.

The guard provided an armed sentry in full dress at the barrack gate: this worthy was enjoined to remain sober and attentive, not to smoke, talk or whistle, and to wait till the end of his two-hour duty before attending to any pressing needs of nature. Regimental customs and practices varied, but as a rule officers in uniform were saluted by the sentry, while general officers, and field officers of the regiment were paid the compliment of having the whole guard turn out and present arms. The guard stopped those without proper authority from entering the barracks, although there were lapses as ladies with urgent emotional or financial interest slipped past. It also prevented soldiers from leaving unless they were properly dressed: indeed, for the first few weeks of a recruit's life it would deny him exit altogether, for he was not allowed out until he was enough of a dandy to 'pass the guard' and be allowed to walk out. Soldiers returning to barracks had to be sufficiently sober to walk past the guardroom: drunkards were confined to the cells behind the guard-room, where they joined offenders awaiting sentence or already undergoing short periods of confinement.

While the guard remained in barracks, there was sometimes a regimental watch that patrolled the town, trying to ensure that there were no clashes between soldiers and civilians, and detaining the inebriate. The watch originated in the seventeenth century in the formal perambulation by an armed party with its drummer who beat tattoo, an instruction for sutlers to 'taptoe', and close the taps of their casks, and then summoned men back to camp or quarters. He started with a warning beat at the watch's first post and ended with a valedictory beat – later the most haunting bugle-call in the military repertoire – at the watch's last post. Thereafter the watch proceeded back to barracks, with the drummer rattling out the retreat, which marked the end of the military day. The procedure was an important one, for few soldiers in the period owned watches, and might easily find themselves out of sight of a clock on a public building like the town hall or an 'Act of Parliament' clock in an ale-house. However, at times of popular unrest it was likely to promote the very disturb-ances it sought to prevent.

The officer's role in the watch was always difficult. It was axio-matic that his presence was important if the watch had to use its arms, and yet there were times when he was best out of the way. Wellington, when commander-in-chief, issued a general order warn-ing superior ranks to take care against 'coming into contact with soldiers overcome by liquor', as the latter might so easily convert the crime of drunkenness into the capital offence of striking a superior. Although this would normally result in the offender being trans-ported to New South Wales, it became so prevalent in the 1840s that three men were shot for it in an eighty-day period at Meerut in 1847.

The working day began when the orderly sergeant entered the barrack room at perhaps 5.00 on a summer's morning or 7.00 in the winter, with his well-rehearsed liturgy:

> By Bob's rattle the sun's burnin' holes in your blankets.
> Rouse about, you insanitary frequenters of the casual ward.
> Turn out, you gutter rats, you unchristened sons of mendi-
> cants. Bless your eyes! Bless your souls![7]

Washing and shaving were perfunctory: in the eighteenth century only the rich or fastidious shaved daily, and it was not until the nineteenth that soldiers were expected to follow suit. By then fashion had simplified their task, for while the army of George III was generally clean-shaven that of Victoria was proudly hirsute. Private Buck Adams of the 7th Dragoons Guards entered his first barrack room in 1843, and was 'at once taken possession of by a huge Irishman who stood 6ft 3 ins. high, not a particle of the upper part of whose face was distinguishable for the amount of hair which covered it.'[8]

   In the eighteenth century moustaches and lovelocks were the hallmark of grenadiers and hussars in continental Europe. When young Marbot joined the French 1st Hussars as a private soldier in 1799 his mentor, an old sergeant, had 'moustaches half a foot long waxed and turned up to his ears, on his temples two long locks of hair plaited, which came from his shako and fell onto his breast . . .' Marbot was too young to grow a moustache, so the sergeant took some blacking 'and with his thumb made two enormous hooks covering my upper lips and reaching almost to my eyes.'[9] The German grenadiers who fought alongside the British in North America wore moustaches, and the substantial German contingent in the 60th made it a spectacularly hairy regiment. By the 1830s moustaches and long, bushy sideburns, leaving only a scrap of chin to shave, were de rigeur in dragoon and lancer regiments: elsewhere, 'shaven chins and upper lips and mutton-chop whiskers were the order of the day.'[10] The virile symbolism of facial hair was not lost on R. S. Surtees' character Mr Jorrocks, the hunting tradesman, who warned:

> Should there be a barracks in the neighbourhood some
> soger officers will most likely mix up, and ride at the
> 'ardest rider amongst them. The dragon soger officer is
> the most dangerous and may be known by the viskers
> under his nose.

According to N. W. Bancroft of the Bengal Horse Artillery, these 'hirsute facial appendages and embellishments were the envy of the men and the distraction of the women of the service.' In January 1844 his unit received orders to cease shaving.

> Great was the rejoicing; razors were consigned to oblivion; the prices of Rowland's macassar; all kinds of abominations known under the generic title of 'hair oil'; the real genuine bear's grease . . . and 'Universal Hair Grower and Restorer' reached fabulous amounts; and yet the demand exceeded the supply.[11]

British soldiers were eventually forbidden to shave the upper lip in the expectation that most would produce a suitable moustache. The link between hairiness and manliness was widely identified, and the nickname for a French First World War soldier, *poilu*, had virile and well as battle-seasoned implications. It was the height of absurdity when an officer was court-martialled for shaving the upper lip in 1916. He did not deny the offence, but pleaded in mitigation that he was an actor in civilian life, and feared that he might find it hard to get work if the removal of his moustache at the war's end left a white mark or caused a rash. The adjutant general in France, Sir Neville Macready, through whose hands the sentence of cashiering passed, had never much liked his own moustache, advised that the sentence should not be confirmed and got the rules changed.

Until the 1760s officers usually wore wigs, in keeping with civilian fashion, although on campaign many wore their own hair cinched back in a short pony-tail or even cropped short. Thereafter their hair was scraped back into a plait and powdered. Officers of fusilier regiments had the plait turned back and fastened to the top of the head with a small comb, while 'the hair at the side of the face, which we called the side locks, was not allowed to grow longer than an inch, & was frizzed and rubbed up with the palm of the hand, before the powder was dusted into it.'[12] Men wore their hair greased, 'clubbed' into a thick queue held by a polished leather strap (adorned with a silver grenade by fusiliers), and powdered. The process took up to an hour, with soldiers taking it in turns to prepare

THE CAMP AT CHOBHAM.

Soldier. "IF YOU PLEASE, SIR, IT'S FIVE O'CLOCK, AND I'VE BROUGHT YOUR SHAVING WATER."

In the summer of 1852, almost 18,000 soldiers were exercised around Chobham in Surrey, an event which attracted enormous public interest. This cartoonist pokes gentle fun at a Household Cavalry officer, accustomed to more comfortable quarters, using his burnished cuirass as a mirror, while his orderly brings him hot water to shave the small unwhiskered area of his face. *Punch* cartoon of 1853.

one another's hair: married men relied on their wives, who often took great pride in their hairdressing, for a wife who was adept at clubbing and powdering was rarely short of suitors if she was widowed. The process was usually completed in the evening so that the hair was ready for the coming day, and with luck, several days to come. John Shipp, who joined the army in 1797, recalled the ritual.

> A large piece of candle-grease was applied first to the sides of my head, and then to the long hair behind. After this, the same operation was gone through with nasty, stinking soap, the man who was dressing me applying his knuckles as often as the soap ... A large pad, or bag filled with sand, was poked into the back of my neck, the hair twisted tightly round it and the whole tied with a leather throng. When thus dressed for parade, the skin of my face was pulled so tight by the bag stuck at the back of my head that it was impossible to so much as to wink an eyelid. Add to this an enormous high stock, which was pushed up under my chin, and felt as still as if I had swallowed a ramrod or the Sergeant's halbert.[13]

Powdering was in theory abolished in 1795, although it continued much longer in some regiments. When powdered hair disappeared the soldier still wore his hair knotted in a queue at his neck. This practice in turn was abolished in 1808, but Thomas Browne says that the queue's disappearance produced a row 'very little short of mutiny'. The regimental wives feared that their appeal would be diminished if they were no longer required to show their skill as hairdressers. The commanding officer ordered the first company to fall in, had benches brought out from the barrack-rooms, made the men sit down on them and then ordered the barbers ('of which there are always plenty in every Regiment') to cut off the queues. The angry wives dared not complain too loudly for fear of being turned out of barracks, and very soon all 'were reconciled to this great improvement'.[14] It took about three hours for a man to prepare himself for a formal parade, a process which included arranging his hair, brushing his hat and uniform, blackening his shoes, scouring his musket and bayonet, polishing his brasswork, pipe-claying all his white leather equipment and heel-balling the black.

Happily this standard of dress was not expected every day. When the day's work proper began at about 5.30 in the summer or 7.30 in the winter the recruit would find himself on the barrack square for most of the day, with an hour for lunch, first mastering foot drill and then going on to march, stepping out so that his foot slid so low over the ground that the instructor could not glimpse the sole of his shoe. His normal pace was 75 steps to the minute, but he was taught to step out at 120 when 'quick march' was ordered, or when he had to carry out the wheeling step as his squad swung like a gate on its hinges. For arms drill, which took them from individual drill to platoon exercise, the recruits followed the fugleman, a trained soldier who stood in front of the squad and carried out the drill movements correctly and to their proper time.

The process was rigorous and repetitious: it might take six months for a man to pass off the square to the sergeant major's satisfaction. Surgeon George Pinckard watched recruits of a West India Regiment being drilled.

> The activity and exertion which are required, to bring such recruits into habits of method and order, are almost beyond belief. Where the whole, being bred up in ignorance and constant toil, are very much upon a parallel with oxen taken from the plough, you will imagine what the most stupid of them must be, who form that select body called the 'awkward squad.' Upon beholding them when they first assemble, it might seem nearly as practicable to teach a party of mules to carry arms.[15]

It was essential that men learnt the vocabulary of close-order battle before they went out on regimental or brigade field-days where their superiors would combine these drills into the more complex phraseology of larger manoeuvres. A sharp young recruit might soon find himself made file-major, almost an unpaid NCO and just a step away from the 'chosen man' who deputised for the corporal and was to become a lance-corporal in the nineteenth century. As file-major John Shipp was able to enjoy 'a good many tricks with my friends, such as filling their pipes with gunpowder, tying their great toes together and crying fire, sewing their shirts to their bedding when asleep, and fifty more.[16] How popular he must have been.

Collective training on an even larger scale took place at camps of instruction set up in wartime at places like Warley and Coxheath

This near-caricature shows three soldiers presenting arms as they train to mount guard in one of the training camps of the 1780s. The left-hand soldier is a 'hatman' from a battalion company, while his two comrades wear the fur cap of the grenadiers, shown here in exaggerated size. Watercolour *en grisaille* by J. C. Escher de Kessickon from a design by William Henry Bunbury.

during the American war and Shorncliffe and Brighton in the Napoleonic period. In 1855 work began on constructing permanent camps, in England at Aldershot on the borders of Hampshire and Surrey, and in Ireland at that 'most delightful station', the Curragh of Kildare. William Keep was invalided out of the 77th in 1809, with recurrent fever contracted on Walcheren, but was well enough to join the 28th two years later. He found the regiment at Berry Head, in Devon, carrying out its last training before embarking for the Peninsula, with:

> ball firing at targets, that is not quite bloodless either, for our faces are sometimes specked and stained with the course powder used by the men around us, particularly in firing blank cartridge in line,
>
> Our ears are becoming accustomed to the sound of volleys close to us, and our visual organs to the smoke that envelops us; and then the charge of bayonets, and formation of hollow squares to resist cavalry foes, and rapid movement into close and open columns, and into line again, all very forcibly representing what we may expect to have to do hereafter.[17]

Officers and men were toughened up by gymnastic training which included 'swimming, lifting cannon balls, climbing precipices, etc.'

Basic training in the cavalry was complicated by the facts that many recruits had never ridden before. When Alexander Somerville joined the Greys in 1831 he had already been a farm labourer, but he found his new lifestyle a shock. Horses were turned out to grass for about four months of the year, but for the remaining eight they had to be groomed and exercised and their tack had to be cleaned. The cavalryman's day was long, and began with morning stables.

> At a quarter to five in the morning the recruits must dress, roll their bedding on the iron bedstead, fold the blankets, the two sheets and the rug so that the colours of the rug shall appear through the folds of the sheets and blankets like streaks of marble. They must take the point of a knife and lay the edges of the fold straight until they look artistical to the eye.
>
> At 5.15 the stable trumpet sounds, and all hasten down to the stables. The litter must be shaken out, and all that is dry tied up, the other cleaned away . . .
>
> If the recruit has not been active in getting downstairs to have his turn on the limited space, others will be there before him [and] if he be not yet beyond the point of having tricks played on him, he may be seen laying out his plaited bands and fancy straw on the stones, horses on each side kicking with their hindfeet within a yard of his head . . . A man tickles one of them to make him prance and strike the stones, or to toss back his litter upon the recruit. As if in a rage, the man professes to command the horse to stand still, and asks if it means to knock Johnny Raw's brains out?[18]

The recruit then changed from stable order into cap, jacket, breeches, boots and spurs for the riding school. He led his horse out, trying to avoid getting his breeches splashed with mire or his jacket flecked with equine saliva: one of Somerville's comrades had his head smashed against the stable door. The instructors in the riding school were not always benign, as the future field-marshal 'Wully' Robertson discovered when he joined the 16th Lancers as a private soldier in 1877. Old soldiers,

addicted to rough behaviour, heavy drinking and hard
swearing ... exacted full deference from the recruit ...
Riding school was the terror of most recruits, few of whom
had ever before been across a horse. For some weeks no
saddle was allowed, no stirrups for some months, and the
chief aim of the instructor or 'rough-rider' was not to give
his pupil confidence but as many falls as possible ...[19]

There was another round of stables at 11.00, then tack-cleaning till
lunch, afternoon's work – foot drill, arms drill and gymnastics till
tea and third stables, followed by more cleaning. An unlucky recruit
might not find his work completed till 9.00, only an hour before
retreat was sounded.

In the early nineteenth century rifles and light infantry used
bugles for the passage of orders in the field and in barracks, and
although line regiments followed suit their drummer, who now
played both bugle and drum, still retained the title of drummer.
Cavalry regiments passed orders with trumpets in barracks and camp
but handier bugles in the field. Calls relayed instructions in peace
and war, and could be given added emphasis by the insertion of a
company or squadron preface and, if several regiments were in ear-
shot, preceded by a regimental call. The system was sophisticated
enough for an adjutant in barracks to be able to summon No 1
Company's orderly sergeant or tell the officers that it was time to
dress for dinner. In the field a cavalry colonel could get his trumpeter
to sound troops half left, slope swords or sling lances, and tell his
brigadier that he was facing a mixture of infantry and horsemen. By
the century's close calls were given words so that soldiers would
remember them, but sadly the words prescribed in *Trumpet and Bugle
Sounds for the Army* were often corrupted. Thus the call for the guard
to fall in was officially:

> Come and do your guard my boys, come and do your guard!
> You've had fourteen nights in bed, so it won't be hard.

But it was speedily converted into:

> Come and do a picket boys, come and do a guard
> You think it's fucking easy but you'll find it's fucking hard.

The soldier who found himself safely back in barracks as retreat sounded was jammed tightly into his barrack room. Two years after the Crimean war a soldier had less than half the allowance of space given to a convict, and even poor-house dormitories, unoccupied in the daytime, had more space per occupant than most barracks. Iron beds were still uncommon: most soldiers slept on the floor on straw palliasses, or in wooden cribs filled with straw. A private of the 15th Hussars found men in the cavalry barracks at Maidstone 'packed . . . so closely that I have seen them sleeping on the tables used for dining, under the tables and in the coal-boxes!'[20] Individual beds were standard by 1820s, but there was sometimes as little as five inches between them, and scarcely more space between them and the communal eating table which ran down the centre of the room.

Men ate, slept, cleaned their kit and 'did everything but drill' in these warrens. Pipe-smoking grew increasingly popular amongst soldiers (officers favoured the cheroot), and in 1842 an officer who entered a room 72 feet long by 36 feet wide found that he could not see any of its 48 occupants because of the smoke. Because many soldiers came from what was patronisingly termed as 'a class very little persuaded of the advantages of ventilation' windows were often blocked up, which was scarcely surprising because even in 1855 it was estimated that the allowance of coal for heating needed to be increased by one-third.

Despite official attempts to give soldiers adequate living space – a General Order of 1845 decreed that new barracks on home stations were to have 450–500 cubic feet per man – barrack rooms remained tightly-packed, with the 196 troopers at Brighton coping with 412 cubic feet and the 44 in Kensington barracks with a meagre 363 each. Barrack hospitals were scarcely better, and when Queen Victoria visited one just after the Crimean War she angrily told Lord Panmure that she found:

> the wards more like prisons than hospitals, the windows so high that no one can look out of them . . . There is no dining room or hall, so that the poor men must have their dinners in the same room in which they sleep, and in which some may be dying, and, at any rate, many suffering, whilst others are at their meals.[21]

The Royal Commission into the Sanitary Condition of the Army, which began its work in 1857, recommended a minimum of 600 cubic feet per man, a suggestion which was calculated, in 1861, to leave a shortfall of more than 32 per cent in existing accommodation. It was not until the Cardwell barracks appeared that the deficiency was made up.

Even in these new barracks the accommodation blocks at first lacked plumbing or sanitation, and men still ate in them. Each room was provided with a large wooden tub – Spooneristically nicknamed the 'sip pot' – which was used as a night urinal. Until the gradual addition, from the 1850s, of 'ablution rooms' – separate wash- and bath-houses adjacent to barrack blocks, the urine tub, rinsed out and filled with water, did duty as wash-basin by those who preferred not to sluice down under the communal pump. Proper urinals were added in the 1880s – they still stand as turret-like additions to the rear entrances of Cardwell barracks, but, according to Sir Evelyn Wood, sometimes became so offensive that they could not be used.

In consequence of all this, barrack rooms were extraordinarily smelly even by the odoriferous standards of the age. Horace Wyndham described 'an indescribable and subtly all-pervading odour of pipe-clay, damp clothing, lamp oil, dish cloths, soft soap and butter and cheese scrapings . . .'[22] One sergeant reported that when entering a barrack room to rouse men in the morning he had first to get the barrack room orderly to open the windows because the place stank of the urine-tub, sour breath and unwashed feet. Things were even worse in the cavalry, where barrack rooms were often thoughtfully placed above the stables, a practice which led an 1861 committee to complain that they were 'saturated throughout with ammonia and organic matter . . .'[23]

When soldiers were billeted on inn-keepers they received 'diet and small beer' from their hosts at contracted prices. In barracks, however, the arrangements resembled those on campaign. Soldiers were issued with rations to a prescribed scale, for which subsistence money was stopped from their pay, and were then responsible for cooking them. Both on campaign and in barracks cooking was carried out by messes, with a soldier appointed to act as cook for a small group of comrades. A cook who let his mess's food get tainted by smoke risked facing a 'company court-martial's a kangaroo court which inevitably sentenced him be cobbed. 'The ceremony,' wrote Captain Thomas Browne, 'is performed by the Soldiers forming two ranks, facing inwards, and making the Cook pass between them, cobbing him well about the head with their foraging caps.'[24] Sometimes fairness in the distribution of rations was ensured by the cook standing with his back to the mess and asking 'Who will have this?' so that his comrades could not see whether they were bidding for meat or gristle. There was usually a close correlation between the mess and the battlefield, for a man slept and ate alongside the men he would fight beside. Soldiers of the age might have been puzzled by phrases like 'small unit cohesion' so dear to modern theorists, but not least among the effects of barrack life was the forging of close and durable relationships.

The scale of rations varied from time to time, and their precise composition would change with local conditions. For much of the Napoleonic period men were entitled to 1lb bread, 1lb of beef, 1 oz of butter or cheese, 1lb pease and 1 oz rice. Amongst the permitted substitutions were 1lb pork for the beef, and troops being transported by sea had a wider variety of items including suet and raisins which enabled them to make varieties of the very popular 'figgy duff'. Bread, nicknamed 'Tommy' or 'Pong,' was usually black or brown, and was sometimes so badly baked that the loaf had a sticky, paste-like interior. Issue beer was barely-alcoholic small beer, brewed largely to make water safe and palatable, rather than the more robust porter men would drink given a chance. Wives on the regimental strength received half-rations, and children a quarter ration. Soldiers were provided with two large copper pans for every eight cavalrymen or twelve infantrymen (more robust iron 'camp kettles' were used in the field), a can for small beer, and two tin mugs to help dole out the food. Each man was issued with a wooden trencher or pewter plate, a bowl and a spoon: many soldiers, then as now, had their own clasp knives which coped with everything from gristly meat to long finger-nails or jammed musket-locks.

Meat was boiled in one copper and potatoes in another, and the predictable result was boiled beef, boiled potatoes and beef broth, sometimes with oatmeal added to the broth to make a thin gruel

called skilly, a product remembered in the words accompanying the
bugle-call for officers' dinner:

> Officers' wives get puddings and pies
> And sergeants' wives get skilly
> But a private's wife gets nothing at all
> To fill her poor little belly.

Breakfast consisted of bread and small beer, with tea becoming popular and affordable as the eighteenth century went on, though sometimes replaced by saloop, an infusion of sassafras, with milk and
sugar. The main meal of beef and potatoes was at midday. Although
a third meal was made obligatory in 1840, this 'tea meal' at around
5.00pm was rarely substantial – one account describes it as 'if anything the same as breakfast' – and soldiers who wanted anything else
had to go into town or buy something from one of the hawkers,
usually ex-soldiers, who were allowed past the guard.

When their soldiers were billeted officers too lived in inns, also
supplied with rations by the inn-keeper but messing together and
paying for extra rations and better drink. They might entertain
civilian friends, returning some of the hospitality they often
received in garrison or on the line of march. By the late eighteenth
century, these informal arrangements had taken on many of the
characteristics of modern officers' messes. Officers had sparsely-
furnished rooms, and lived out of their chests and portmanteaux. In
1808 an old captain in the 23rd Foot, whose eccentricity was attributed
to a blow on the head during a shipwreck, had all his belongings
'spread out upon the Floor, a sort of Alley being left from the door
to his bed.' He maintained that this made it easy to find things and
check his kit: he had 307 items ('coats, waistcoats, fishing rods &
stockings, boots and swords, shoes and sashes') and having them
spread enabled him to count them in a mere ten minutes.[25]

In 1799 the officers of the Inniskilling Dragoons paid 2s 6d a
day to their mess whether they attended it or not.

> A Bottle of wine is reckoned for each officer attending.
> After that portion has been drunk, the officer at the
> bottom of the table signifies it by a hint, and a toast is
> then given, viz, 'Colonels and Corps' – after which an

officer who remains to drink another glass is made to pay an equal proportion for the wine which is drunk in the course of the evening. The Mess hour is 5 o'clock. The present Mess of the Inniskillings consists of about 18 officers. Married men generally live with their families.[26]

Purpose-built officers' messes were included in many of the new barracks, and as officers became less peripatetic so their messes became more elaborate. In 1832 a letter to the *United Services Journal* complained that the practice of requiring officers to pay heavy mess subscriptions 'chiefly for the purpose of accumulating costly articles of Mess Plate, showy but frangible services of china, glass, &c., on a scale, in a style, and of description more savouring of parade and display that suited for the sober use' unreasonably increased their expenses, and counted for nothing when they changed regiments.[27] Eight years later a gentleman who signed himself 'purse-strings' and had a young ward in the infantry complained about the 'Royal or Diplomatic pageantry and feasting' which made mess life so expensive. His ward pointed out that an officer could not refuse to contribute his share of the expense of lavish entertainment, and that his association with 'men of wealth and property' begat 'the habits of expense'. The aggrieved correspondent concluded that young men should not be commissioned unless they had private incomes of £2–300 a year.[28] In practice many regiments made it clear that substantial private incomes were indeed required: in 1815 the colonel of the Greys stipulated that a young gentleman desiring a cornetcy required at least £200 per annum over and above his pay.

The Inniskillings' ration of one bottle of wine per officer was modest: in John Peebles' mess in North America, officers often drank much more than this. Even the hardened William Hickey found the routine toasting, with all present required to drink a bumper – a full glass with no heel-taps – at a military dinner in 1799 to be too much for him. After 22 such bumpers the mess president said that 'everyone might then fill according to his own discretion, and so *discreet* were all the company that we continued to follow the Colonel's example of drinking nothing short of bumpers till two o'clock in the morning.' Hickey described it as the most 'severe debauch' he ever experienced.[29]

When James McGrigor joined the 88th as its surgeon in 1793 there was a drunken row between two officers in the mess: they fought and one was killed. 'This incident took great hold on my mind,' wrote McGrigor, 'and doubtless of life after, by making me cautious . . . to avoid brandy-and-water parties at night.'[30] Hot words at night too often led to cold steel in the morning. An officer was obliged to fight if his honour was impugned, his opponent was a gentleman and no satisfactory apology was forthcoming. Regimental Courts of Honour, ad hoc gatherings of officers usually meeting under a major, took a view of doubtful cases. A wise old major could often persuade his brother officers that a handshake between two hung-over youngsters would settle the matter, but not all Courts of Honour were so forbearing. An officer who declined to fight without an overriding reason might find himself shunned by his comrades, and might simply be banished from his regiment as being unworthy to serve with it. This may be the cause of an entry in Howe's order book in August 1776. 'In consequence of a representation . . . from the officers of the 47th Regt respecting some improper '. . . conduct of Capt Holmes of that Regt, the officer . . .' concerned was suspended from duty and told that he had 'liberty to go to Europe'.

Duelling was a feature of civilian society: one contemporary counted 172 duels in England between 1760 and 1821, with 91 fatalities. That this was an underestimate is beyond question, and the total would certainly have been much higher had it included Ireland, where duelling was so prevalent that a society of Friendly Brothers, sworn to oppose duelling, was formed. Its members wore a knot of green ribbon to show that, though gentlemen, they would neither issue nor receive challenges. The society was organised in local associations known as knots, and soon regiments stationed in Ireland acquired their own groups known as 'marching knots'. The Middlesex Regiment has long been amalgamated, but its marching knot still survives, and both friendly and convivial it is. Although the members of marching knots did not have to be Irish, the Friendly Brothers were well to the fore in celebrating St Patrick's Day in Philadelphia in 1778:

> The Hibernians mounted the shamrock & an Irish Gren-
> adr. personated St Patrick in a Procession thro' the streets
> with a prodigious mob after him – the friendly Brrs. and
> several other Irish Clubs dined together & dedicated the
> day to the St & the Bottle . . .[31]

Gentlemen habitually wore swords with civilian dress until the 1790s, and the small sword, with a simple shell guard and straight blade was the preferred weapon for the duel until the 1770s, when pistols, whose cased, matched pairs became part of the gentlemanly trousseau, began to take over. However, to fight a duel was always to attempt murder, and in 1828 it became a capital offence simply to shoot at another man with intent to harm him. In 1837 this law was modified so that the offence was only capital if a wound was inflicted. In practice the law did not always take its course, for juries tended to view the exchange of sword-thrusts or pistol balls between gentlemen in quite a different light to more sordid scuffles between lesser mortals.

When a Mr Elliot killed a Mr Mirfin in a duel which had resulted from a carriage-crash on Derby day in 1838 the jury at the Old Bailey was unimpressed, in part because neither man had serious claims to gentility. Although Elliot and his second fled abroad, Mirfin's second received a year's penal servitude with hard labour for abetting murder. Yet if duellists were demonstrably gentlemen and the rules of duelling were adhered to, juries often declined to convict. Only two duellists were hanged, in one case because of an apparent breach of the rules of duelling. In 1808 a trial in Ireland centred not upon the unquestioned fact that a duel had taken place, but that the man who fired the fatal shot had donned his spectacles before doing so, and might thus be said to have broken the rules by making excessive preparation.

Great men often put their obligations as gentlemen before their duty to the law. The playwright Richard Brinsley Sheridan fought two duels with Captain Matthews, a married man who was pressing his attentions on the future Mrs Sheridan. The Duke of York fought Colonel Lennox; Wellington duelled with Lord Winchelsea; the fifth Lord Byron killed his cousin Mr Chaworth in a furious set-to with small-swords in the back room of a London club; and Lord

Castlereagh wounded his political rival Mr Canning. John Wilkes, radical politician and militia colonel (his ever-reliable adjutant used to act as his second), fought Lord Talbot after mocking his poor equestrian performance at the coronation of George III, was prevented by police intervention from fighting a duel in Paris with a Scots officer, and was lightly wounded by Samuel Martin, MP for Camelford.

An unusually tragic meeting between two cavalry subalterns took place in London in 1798. Lieutenant Riddle of the Horse Grenadiers fell out with Lieutenant Cunningham of the Greys over a game of cards. A Court of Honour of Riddle's brother officers found that he was not obliged to fight, but Cunningham would not be denied. He grossly insulted Riddle in a club, and then sent a note offering to give him satisfaction. The note was accidentally opened by the officer's father, Sir James Riddle, who resealed it and passed it on. The officers fought at eight paces, having drawn lots as to who should fire first. Riddle shot Cunningham in the chest, but Cunningham remained standing, took deliberate aim – in itself a questionable act, for a gentleman was meant to fire as soon as his pistol was levelled – and shot Riddle in the groin, inflicting a mortal wound. Cunningham was arraigned for manslaughter, but died a week after the duel.

This affair, for all its ghastly outcome, was formal, but many combats were not. In February 1760 there were two fights in Bombay, the first when Commissary Chandler fell out with Conductor Vaus (a senior storekeeper, not strictly speaking a gentleman) over the usual 'disagreeable words'. Chandler hustled things on by waylaying Vaus when he emerged from a sale:

> He demanded satisfaction and desired Vaus immediately to draw, on which they both drew, made some pushes at each other (but before anybody came up to part them, though in the middle of the day and on the open green) Chandler gave Vaus a wound in his right breast which was so deep that it pierced his lungs . . .

Chandler fled to join the Mahrattas, and James Wood, who tells us the story, left Vaus 'in hopes of his recovery.'[32] Less than two weeks later there were high words between Captain Tovey and Captain-

Lieutenant Barrett, both of the Royal Artillery. They drew, and 'after making a few passes Captain Barrett ran Captain Tovey through the sword arm . . . on which the affair was settled, and as it was not a wound of any great consequence no further notice was taken.'[33] 'Further notice' might have ensued because neither of these encounters was a proper duel. There were no seconds, one of whose duties was to try to obtain an apology, and no surgeon. The later was a feature of formal duels, although one civilian duellist, run through the ribs, replied to his seconds' call for the surgeon with a demand for a tailor, as his coat had been ruined.

Officers sometimes found their gentlemanly obligation to fight over matters of honour circumscribed by the constraints of rank, for officers were prohibited from challenging their superiors. Lieutenant Colonel Hervey Aston of the 12th Regiment committed a minor impropriety during a period of absence, and on his return told his officers that he was prepared to meet them one after the other if they wished, as he knew they could not legally challenge him. The major and the senior captain took up his helpful offer. The major's pistol missed fire, and Aston did not shoot. But the captain wounded him mortally. In August 1813 four subalterns of the 100th Foot were found guilty at Winchester of the murder of the fifth in a minor disagreement over clothes. All were sentenced to be cashiered, but the Prince Regent pardoned Ensign McGuire, who had actually fired the shot, presumably on the grounds that he had had no alternative but to fight, while the seconds were culpable for not having done more to prevent the meeting.

The Earl of Cardigan was a snobbish and boorish commanding officer of the 11th Hussars, and after selling his commission in the regiment in 1840 Captain Harvey Tuckett wrote to the *Morning Post* saying that the earl had regularly insulted his officers but avoided a duel because they had been unable to challenge their commanding officer. Cardigan at once challenged Tuckett, and the two men met on Wimbledon Common, where Tuckett was severely wounded. Cardigan exercised his right to trial by his peers, and the prosecution foundered because it failed to prove that the individual shot by the earl was indeed the Harvey Garnett Phipps Tuckett specified in the indictment.

There was much dissatisfaction with the Cardigan verdict, but it was to take another duel, in 1843, to sound the death-knell of military duelling. Lieutenant Monro of the Blues challenged his brother-in-law Lieutenant Colonel Fawcett of the 55th Foot as a result of a row in which, in the presence of a servant, Fawcett had ordered Monro from his house. Fawcett was shot dead and Monro fled abroad. There was a widespread feeling that Fawcett should have apologised for the incident, but great indignation against the government which refused to grant his widow a pension. Although military law was made slightly more stringent as a result of the case, as Sir Robert Peel put it, 'the influence of civilisation' changed attitudes.[34]

When officers were not engaged in the all too closely related activities of drinking and duelling, they rode, walked prodigious distances, shot and hunted. Ensign Howell Gronow of 1st Guards remembered that:

> During the winter of 1813 the Guards were stationed with head-quarters at St. Jean de Luz, and most comfortable we managed to make them ... There were two packs of hounds ... and our Officers went uncommonly straight. Perhaps our best man across country (though sometimes against his will), was the late Colonel [Bacchus] Lascelles, of my Regiment, then, like myself, a mere lad. He rode a horse seventeen hands high, called Bucephalus, which invariably ran away with him; and more than once he nearly capsized Lord Wellington.[35]

Wellington was a keen foxhunter, and followed a pack of hounds known as 'the Peers' hunted by Tom Crane, late of the Coldstream Guards. Wellington wore the sky-blue coat of the Hatfield Hunt, sent him by Lady Salisbury. An officer wrote that:

> When the hounds were out, he was no longer the Commander of the Forces, the General-in-Chief of three nations, the representative of three sovereigns, but a gay, merry country gentleman, who rode at everything, and laughed as loud when he fell himself as when he witnessed the fall of a brother sportsman.[36]

Fanny Duberly attended a race-meeting in the Crimea, and when it ended:

> as the sun was still high, the meeting dispersed for a dog-hunt. I rode with them as far as Karani, and then turned back. I could not join in or countenance in any way a sport that appears to me to be so unsportsmanlike, so cruel, so contrary to all good feelings, as hunting *a dog*.[37]

Some officers played football: Lieutenant Colonel Mainwaring of the 51st encouraged robust tackles, telling his men that there was no rank on the field. Others, especially the Scots, played golf or practised putting the shot or, if there was no suitable shot at hand, putting the stone. Cricket was popular, and battalions often fielded several teams, an all-ranks eleven to take on other battalions, and perhaps an officers' mess team to engage those hirsute sloggers of the sergeants' mess. When the 68th Light Infantry was in Turkey in 1854, waiting to sail for the Crimea, it played cricket in what the scorebook calls 'Sultan's Valley, Asia Minor'. Private Fossy ran through his opponents' batting order like wildfire, taking four wickets. Corporal Jester took another three, including that of Lieutenant Barker, caught and bowled. The fortune of war was less kind to sportsmen: Jester was killed at the Alma and Barker fell at Inkerman. In 1864 the battalion was commanded by Lieutenant Colonel Greer, a notorious flogging colonel but keen cricketer, bowled out for a duck by an agile (if unwise) private in the year's main match.

Many officers read widely: when Lieutenant Colonel Wellesley of the 33rd, the future Duke of Wellington, sailed for India in 1796 he took a prodigious library which included geography, military and diplomatic history, Blackstone's *Commentaries of the Laws of England*, the classics, Johnson's dictionary, a treatise on venereal disease and nine volumes of *Women of Pleasure*. Officers attended theatres if they were to be found within travelling distance, and organised their own masquerades and amateur performances if they were not. Captain Evelyn of the 4th King's Own told a friend that there were 'some very capital performances' in the theatre at Boston. Alas, a topical show, 'The Blockade of Boston' by Lieutenant General Burgoyne was 'most ridiculously interrupted' when a sergeant, who had heard firing outside, rushed in shouting 'Turn out! Turn out! They're at it hammer and tongs' only to have his convincing performance applauded by the delighted audience. Not to be stifled (sergeants seldom are), when the applause died away he yelled: 'What the devil are ye about: if ye won't believe me, ye need only go to the door, and there ye'll hear and see both.'[38]

William Keep wrote from Spain that:

> We have a superb theatre, in the palace of a traitor . . . the walls of the house before the curtain lined with fine tapestry . . . The audience part rising from the orchestra and forming an elevated pit with two stage boxes, one fitted up in great style for the general, the other in imitation, painted very cleverly as if containing spectators, and to complete the effect our Bands furnish musicians for the orchestra, and the scenery wouldn't disgrace a Greenwood and assistants . . .[39]

In the Crimea the rather less prepossessing surroundings of 'the amputating house of the Naval Brigade' became:

THEATRE ROYAL, NAVAL BRIGADE
On Friday Evening 31ˢᵗ of August, will be Performed

DEAF AS A POST

To be followed by

THE SILENT WOMAN

The whole to conclude with a laughable farce, entitled

SLASHER AND CRASHER

Seats to be taken at SEVEN o'clock. Performance to commence
Precisely at EIGHT o'clock
God Save the Queen! Rule Britannia!

The performance was judged a great success, even though what W. H. Russell thought an 'agreeable ballet girl' had to leave early to help work a 68 pdr siege gun bombarding Sevastopol.[40]

Officers' messes regularly gave balls, to which local ladies and gentlemen were invited, and sergeants' messes often followed suit. Dancing did not require ladies, and on campaign officers trod the measure of country dances to the accompaniment of a fiddler or piper. Smaller groups played with cards or dice. Not all games were played for high stakes, and the hours could be passed away pleasantly enough at whist or passdice. Face-pulling contests called grinning matches were played in the mess, and there were sometimes all-ranks contests. And, of course, like the soldiers they commanded, officers fell in love.

DAUGHTERS
OF THE REGIMENT

IN 1855 COLONEL RICHARD GILPIN told the House of Commons that he had just visited the barracks at Weedon, where:

> I saw an unfortunate woman in the barrack with some fifty men, the only accommodation being that between two beds a sort of curtain was set up ... What a position in which to place a woman, especially when her husband is away on duty.[41]

In 1846 William Lucas joined the Inniskilling Dragoons and was dismayed to find that his barrack room contained 18 men, two married men and their wives and, unsurprisingly in a pre-contraception age, seven or eight children. Arthur Trevor Hill of the 33rd thought soldiers' wives 'generally the greatest nuisances,' arrangements in barrack rooms 'revolting to decency' and marriage inevitably resulting in the soldier's family, trying to make too little money stretch too far, finishing up 'naked and starving.'[42] By 1845 the 11th Hussars allocated a single barrack room to its families to avoid the inconveniences of the 'married corner' in a common barrack-room, the practice was taken up by other regiments, and in 1852 a group of guards officers clubbed together to build a hostel for their regimental families. However, it was not until 1860 that the first official married quarters were built.

There were repeated attempts to dissuade soldiers from marrying, and in 1685 it was made an offence to marry without permission. Its granting was no foregone conclusion. In 1727 a soldier in Gibraltar who presumed to ask to wed 'a lady of no good reputation' 'was sent to cool his courage in the black hole for the night, and this morning for breakfast received 100 lashes . . .'[43] After receiving the punishment he renewed his request – 'though his back was like raw head and bloody bones' – and this time 'in consideration of his sufferings, noble merit and undaunted gallantry' was allowed to marry the lady. James Wolfe was steadfastly opposed to the marriage of soldiers, and in 1751 he first warned his officers to discourage the practice as 'the Service suffers by the multitude of women already in the Regiment,' and then told his men than any of them who contracted an unauthorised marriage could expect 'to be proceeded against with the utmost Rigour.'[44]

For much of the period most sergeants and around seven per cent of rank and file were permitted to marry, appearing on the Married Roll of their regiment, and, at the Marquess of Anglesey's conservative estimate, another seven per cent were married unofficially. Only those on the roll – by the 1870s one wife for every eight cavalrymen and every twelve infantrymen – were allowed to live in barracks. There they earned some money by washing for the soldiers and sometimes the officers too. They helped nurse the sick in regimental hospitals in peace and bore a hand with the wounded in war. After the battle of Bunker Hill in 1775 Lieutenant General Thomas Gage directed every regiment to send 'two careful sober Women' to the hospitals. For all the complaints about soldiers' women it is clear that well-conducted regimental women were an asset in barracks. Many preserved their dignity – though it is hard to see how – and often their very presence induced men to behave better. The drum-major's wife in the 22nd was 'a drunken old Irish woman,' but John Shipp owed his survival as a recruit to her, for she rescued him from a hostile group of boy soldiers with a shout of:

Aargh! What are you gazing at, you set of spalpeens, you
be off you set of thieves, or I'll be after breaking some of
your dirty mugs for you. Don't mind them, sure they are
nothing but a set of monkeys just catched. Come here,
honey, and let me see who will lay a finger on you![45]

Simply being on the Married Roll did not entitle a wife to accompany
her regiment overseas. The quota of women allowed to sail varied:
in 1758 ten women per company were authorised to accompany six
regiments of foot sent to the West Indies, but in 1801 the 95th
prescribed only six for every hundred men, inclusive of all NCOs'
wives, and warned that women with more than two children could
never be allowed to go on overseas service. Moreover, women 'of
immoral and drunken character, or who refuse to work for the men'
would not be allowed to remain in the strength even in Britain, but
would be sent to the poor house. Being 'turned out of barracks and
stuck off the list' was the usual penalty for wives repeatedly convicted
of such offences as drunkenness, using obscene language or fighting
in quarters.

Selection of those allowed to sail was by drawing lots of throwing
dice on a drum-head, and there were heart-rending scenes as families
were split up. Joseph Donaldson of the 94th describes how the wife
of one of his comrades, unsuccessful in the ballot, followed him to
the quayside, only to die there with her newborn child. The soldier
did not even have time to bury them. He rarely spoke again, and was
killed in the Peninsula. Other wives managed to smuggle themselves
aboard: in 1845 Pearman saw four 'contraband' wives of the 3rd
Light Dragoons aboard his vessel. Regimental authorities, all too
well aware of the heartache caused by the quota system, were often
pleased to make a welcome virtue of necessity. In 1869 Mrs Johnston
and Mrs Burns stowed away aboard the transport *Flying Foam*. The
former, of the 58th Foot, was 'given room in barracks as she has no
other place to go,' and the latter was simply taken onto the authorised strength of the 107th Foot. Sergeant Anthony Hamilton of the
43rd Light Infantry argued that it was a mistake to take women on
campaign in view of what he had seen on the retreat to Corunna in
the winter of 1808–9. Things were appalling for the men.

But the agonies of the women were still more dreadful to behold. Of these, by some strange neglect, or by some mistaken sentiment of humanity, an unusually large proportion had been suffered to accompany the army. Some of these unhappy creatures were taken in labour on the road, and amidst the storms of sleet and snow gave birth to infants, which, with their mothers, perished as soon as they had seen the light ... Others in the unconquerable energy of maternal love would toil on with one or two children on their backs; till on looking round, they perceived that the hapless objects of their affections were frozen to death.[46]

Regimental women were subject to a discipline scarcely less severe than that which bore upon their men. In 1745 a woman convicted of petty theft, as General Pulteney rather too keenly told the Duke of Cumberland, had 'her tail immediately turned up before the door of the house, where the robbery was committed, and the Drummer of the Regiment tickled her with 100 very good lashes,' and in the Peninsula offending wives received 'a dozen on the bare doup [sic]' from the drum-major's cane.[47] More spectacular was the 1775 case of Winifred McCowen, 'retainer to the camp' tried by General Court Martial for having stolen the town bull of Boston and causing him to be killed. She was:

Found Guilty of the Same and sentenced to be tied to a cart's tail, and thereto to receive 100 lashes on her bare back in different portions in the most public parts of the town and Camp and to be imprisoned three months.[48]

Sometimes wives unwittingly drove their husbands to crime. At Louisbourg in 1747 Private Daniel Buckley was accused of murdering Sergeant John Gorman. He admitted the act but pleaded mitigation because the sergeant had 'been keeping company with and debauching his wife while Buckley was on guard,' and had not given up the affair although he had promised his company commander that he would. John Buckley was sentenced to death but pardoned. Lydia Buckley was drummed out of the fort at the cart's tail, a standard punishment for prostitutes, and then ducked and sent to Boston for trial by the civil authorities.[49]

Even more harrowing was the case of a tall, handsome grenadier of the 61ˢᵗ Foot who visited the camp of the 95ᵗʰ in Spain to try to persuade his wife, who had left him for Sergeant Battersby of the Rifles, to return. Edward Costello was chatting to the sergeant at the time. 'Nelly,' begged the redcoat, 'how can you stoop so low as to seek the protection of such a man as this . . .' 'He treats me better than you do,' she replied. 'Maybe, but why leave your three year old child. I cannot look after her.' When his wife refused to return to him the grenadier bayoneted her and would have killed Battersby too had onlookers not dragged him back. He was sentenced to three months solitary confinement, but was back with his regiment within a month. Both grenadier and sergeant were killed during the campaign. 'Poor creature,' lamented Surtees. 'She was one of the gayest of the females which graced our regimental ball . . . only a short while previous and had often danced with old General Vandeleur on these occasions.'⁵⁰

Women were liable to corporal punishment for some civil offences till 1816, and an earlier generation had not thought it strange for gentlemen to visit the Bridewell to watch the routine whipping of its inmates. The unnamed diarist of the siege of Gibraltar gives one lengthy description of a woman 'for the too frequent bestowing of her favours' being spun in the whirligig – a revolving chair which made the victim sick and incontinent – for an hour, 'the place being well attended.' On another occasion: 'Mrs Malone was committed for proper reasons to the whirligig for two hours: it gave great pleasure to the spectators.'⁵¹ There was quite evidently more to these punishments than the preservation of order, and the enjoyment aroused by their chastisement was not least amongst the many perils of soldiers' wives.

Officers who misbehaved with soldier's wives were treated harshly for two reasons. First, because their offence was seen as a breach of trust, and second, because it demeaned the officer's status. We have already seen Lieutenant Kelly of the 40ᵗʰ sentenced to cashiering for a prolonged affair with a soldier's wife, and in 1814 an officer of the 19ᵗʰ, who had visited a soldier's wife on several occasions was suspended from rank and pay for three months. The leniency of the sentence shocked the General Officer Commanding, who wrote furiously that nothing could more seriously affect an officer's character and reputation or be more injurious to the service.

The offence was a breach of caste. Officers were expected to marry ladies, or at least females who could pass as such. This was a broad definition, and Captain Gronow thought that: 'A pretty girl, a good dancer and a showy rider will have more partners and invitations than Lady Drystick, with her ancient pedigree and aristocratic airs.'[52] Having affairs with serving girls, nursemaids or laundresses was one thing (although their families sometimes became awkward if a little captain appeared on the scene) but marrying them was quite another. Captain Glanville Evelyn of the 4th King's Own had formed an attachment to Peggy Wright, a family servant, while he was home on half-pay. She followed him to North America, and probably tended him after he was mortally wounded in a skirmish near New York in October 1776. He does not refer to her in any of his letters, but his will, made out in Boston on the morning of Bunker Hill, left 'all my worldly substance' to her.[53] However, marriage was evidently a step too far. Even John Peebles, no snob by the standards of his day, simply could not understand why a young officer would marry somebody with neither birth nor wealth. Yet some officers conducted ill-advised marriages and got away with it, often because their wife had the chameleon-like skills required to make the change. Major William Sturt of the 80th married a lady who seemed to have worked in Mrs Porter's establishment in Berkeley Street, patronised by none other than the Duke of Wellington.

Wellington was very much a man of his age. He had a powerful sex drive – a former mistress of Napoleon's found the Duke altogether more satisfactory than the Emperor – and usually satisfied it with married ladies of his own class or 'professional coquettes' like Harriette Wilson and the girls at Mrs Porter's. Unmarried officers who could afford to do so often set up their mistresses in their own establishments, and frequently acknowledged their children. When the future George IV was colonel of the 10th Hussars, most of his officers were said 'to keep their own blood horses and their own girls.' Lieutenant General 'Gentlemanly Johnny' Burgoyne, defeated at Saratoga, lost his wife in 1776. He was a talented playwright, and this – and the general attractiveness of actresses, many of whom formed liaisons with the royal family, aristocrats and army officers – facilitated his relationship with the actress Susan Caulfield, who bore him four children. One of them, John Fox Burgoyne, was commissioned into the Royal Engineers, served in the Peninsula and was chief engineer in the Crimea: he became a baronet and a field marshal, having done altogether better than his father.

Even in the rather primmer Victorian army such arrangements were not unusual. Lizzie Howard was the daughter of a Brighton bootmaker who had run off with the jockey Jem Mason and appeared, rather briefly, on the stage. In 1841 she became the mistress of Major Francis Mountjoy Martyn of 2nd Life Guards, who set her up in a house in St John's Wood and gave her a handsome income, substantially increased when she bore him a son. The arrangement worked smoothly, with the fair Lizzie widely regarded as Martyn's *maitresse en titre*, until she met the future Napoleon III at a reception at Gore House given by Lady Blessington, and fell head over heels in love with him. When he became president of France in 1848 he set her up in a house in the Rue du Cirque, and when he married in 1854 he palmed her off with a title. He never called to bid her farewell, and in 1864, when she was dying, she booked a theatre box at a first night she knew he would be attending, and stared at the Imperial couple throughout the evening.

For the young officer in search of something less permanent there were ladies of easier virtue. Lord Alvanley, commissioned into the Coldstream at the age of fifteen in 1804, was sent to Spain in 1808. His bankers – no less than the regimental agents – requested prompt settlement of a six month's account which included such necessities as:

Lady	£5
Ditto a country girl	£2 2s
One night Mrs Dubois (grande blonde)	£5 5s
Modest Girl	£3 3s
An American Lady	£10 10s
Lately one night with Eliza Farquhar	£3 3s
All night Miss N from the Boarding School, Chelsea	£5 5s[54]

Many of these women must have looked upon the likes of Alvanley with scorn. One prostitute wrote of the military circuit:

The next I met a cornet was
In a regiment of dragoons
I gave him what he didn't like
And stole his silver spoons.

For many prostitutes this life was a downward slope which began with officers in smart St James's and ended with drunken soldiers behind a barrack-wall in Portsmouth, with the decline accelerated once they started giving their gentlemen what they didn't like in the shape of venereal disease.

And yet their motives were not always financial: some simply had a hankering for soldiers. Henry Mayhew interviewed a women working in a barber's shop in Chatham who had begun by having an affair with a recruit, and then taken up with a sergeant, 'which was a cut above a private, and helped me on wonderful.' An officer invited her to become his kept woman, but she refused: 'I was fond of my old associates, and did not like the society of gentlemen; so, when the regiment left Dover I went with them till I was five and twenty.' She then fell in love with a soldier in the Blues, and had stayed with the regiment ever since, 'going from one to the other, never keeping to one long, and not particular as long as I don't get needful.' She regretted not having a house and children, and resented the fact that men held her in scant respect. 'If I have a row with a fellow,' she said, 'he's always the first to taunt me of being what he and his fellows have made me.'[55]

Large garrisons inevitably attracted prostitutes, some of whom had begun their descent after 'long-standing common-law relation-ships' with soldiers. Con Costello's engaging history of the Curragh camp tells the sorry story of the 'wrens', women who lived around the camp in huts made of gorse. One had followed the gunner who had seduced her, but when he heard that she was pregnant he told her to 'go and do like the other women did,' and she gave birth out on the plain. Another girl claimed to have been seduced by an officer in the Rifles, and yet another admitted that 'it wasn't one man that brought me here, but many.' While the older women remained behind to mind the children, the younger ones set off for their trysts with soldiers in uninhabited gorse patches, tricked out in crinolines, petticoats, shoes and stockings. One witness saw one girl coming back drunk from her work, 'her hair streaming down her back, she had scarcely a rag of clothing on . . . [she] made at me with a large jug, intending to be smashed against my skull.'[56] Eventually the authorities were compelled to act, and in 1865 agreed to establish a hospital for the women, and wards in the workhouse in the nearby town of Naas were set apart for them.

The story of the wrens of the Curragh typifies authority's wider battle against prostitution which it saw as not simply immoral, but, because of the high incidence of venereal disease, as a major drain on the army's manpower, with up to one-quarter of its strength being infected in the course of a given year. On one day in 1844 the 63rd Foot found itself with 27 per cent of its soldiers infected, 112 with primary and 15 with secondary syphilis, and 125 with gonorrhoea. 'Hospitals for the reception of diseased women' had been set up in the late eighteenth century, known as lock hospitals from the London Lock Hospital, where prostitutes were confined. The principle, which formed the basis of the short-lived 1864 Contagious Diseases Act, was simple enough. Prostitutes in garrison towns – in 1864 these included Aldershot, Woolwich and Colchester in England and Cork and the Curragh in Ireland – were subject to medical inspection, and any found to be infected were detained in a lock hospital until they were cured. But there was no real evidence that the system worked, as it was impossible to be certain of a 'cure' with the medicine available. Compulsory inspection was deeply resented, especially by what contemporaries termed 'respectable' prostitutes and, there was evidence that some inspectors indulged in practices that were deliberately humiliating. The statistics remain ambivalent. VD amongst British troops was at its lowest in Bengal in 1830, after the lock hospitals were temporarily closed, and in 1808 VD in the 12th Foot more than doubled despite the establishment of a lock hospital. There were always wide regimental variations in VD statistics: in 1833 one RHA battery in Poona had 41 per cent of its men infected, and another had only 13.5 per cent.

In Hindi a *lal kurti* was a red jacket, and in the regimental bazaars of nineteenth century British India lal bazaars, essentially regimental brothels, flourished. Their occupants were subjected to regular medical inspection, and it was argued that this greatly reduced the incidence of venereal disease. Lal bazaars were supervised by an 'Old Bawd,' an experienced procuress who was often a woman of some moment. In 1893 one was described by an Englishwoman as 'a very prosperous person, wearing a good deal of solid gold jewellery ... a fine-looking woman, judging by the native type.' The regiment's orderly-room sergeant wanted to marry her, but the authorities seem to have prevented the match by posting him home. The existence of lal bazaars lead to some interesting requisitions, with 2/Cheshire demanding 'extra attractive women for the regimental bazaar,' claiming that it had only six to service a battalion of 400 men and another six were urgently required: 'Please send young and attractive women.'[57] Do-gooders complained that was scandalously un-British: one, on a fact-finding tour, spotted 'a large formal portrait of "Victoria, Queen of Great Britain and Empress of India"' in 'one of the shops of this market of licensed sin.'[58] The bishop of Calcutta objected to the lal bazaars because it seemed to him that they did indeed reduce VD, and therefore 'made sinning safe.'[59]

Yet there were many who realised that male sexuality was at the very nub of the problem. The Surgeon-General of Bengal recognised that:

> For a young man who cannot marry and who cannot attain the high moral standard required for the repression of physiological natural instincts, there are only two ways of satisfaction, viz masturbation and mercenary love. The former, as is known, leads to diseases of body and mind; the latter, to the fearful dangers of venereal.[60]

There were also suggestions that some soldiers took to 'detestable practices' not because they were inherently homosexual – the army of the age disapproved of homosexuality but was not unduly inquisitive in its pursuit – but simply because there was no safe alternative. The situation was much improved by increasing the permitted proportion of wives to 12 per cent of the rank and file, and better treatment and prevention helped bring VD down to a mere 6.7 per cent of the army in India by 1909.

Officers were less vulnerable, if for no other reason than that their wives were able to accompany their regiments abroad without being subjected to a quota system, and if there was no room aboard the transports they could often afford to pay for a more comfortable passage and join their husbands. It was sometimes a scant privilege. A gay party of officers' wives arrived in Boston in 1775, looking forward to the society of this delightful town, to discover that most had just been widowed at Bunker Hill. Sixty women and children returned to Portsmouth aboard *Charming Nancy* in September, after a voyage in company with 170 sick and wounded 'some without legs, and others without arms' in an 'almost intolerable' stench from their wounds.

Catherine Upton, married to an ensign in the Gibraltar garrison in 1781, found herself in exactly the same position as a soldier's wife, in bed with her husband behind a curtain in a hut full of a hundred men. Mrs Maguire was a regimental daughter of the 4th King's Own, born in Boston within hearing of the gunfire while her father's regiment ascended its calvary on Bunker Hill. She eventually married the regiment's surgeon, and was returning from North America in 1797 aboard the transport *The Three Sisters* when she was taken by a French privateer off Land's End. She knew how important the colours were, and when capture was imminent wrapped them round her flat-irons and dropped them overboard. Mrs Maguire was imprisoned with her young son Francis at Brest, where she bore a daughter. Although Surgeon Maguire transferred to the 69th, Francis was commissioned into the 4th, and died very gallantly with it in the storming of San Sebastian. Mrs Maguire lost her husband from yellow fever, and another son was drowned: she died in 1857, still receiving a pension for husband and two boys.

Magdalene Hall, daughter of the distinguished Scots baronet Sir James Hall of Dunglass, married Colonel Sir William De Lancey after a whirlwind romance in April 1815, just after her twenty-third birthday. De Lancey was appointed Wellington's acting quarter-master-general (in effect his chief of staff) for the Waterloo campaign, and on 8 June Magdalene left England to join him in Brussels. Early on the 'clear refreshing morning' of the 16th she saw the army leave the city, 'the fifes playing alone, and the regiments one after the other marched past, and I saw them melt away through the great gate at the end of the square . . .'[61] Her husband had told her to move to Antwerp, and although she was more than thirty miles from Waterloo she could hear the sound of the battle, a rolling, like the sea at a distance, 'but I kept the windows shut, and tried not to hear.' When her terrified maid announced that the French had taken Brussels and all the other ladies were leaving for England, she replied: 'Well, Emma, you know that if the French were firing at this house I would not move till I was ordered; but you have no such duty, therefore if you like, I daresay, any of the families will allow you to join them.' Emma at once declared that 'tho' she was sure she should have to remain in a French prison for 5 years, she would not leave me.'[62]

On Monday 19 June, the day after the battle, Lady De Lancey first heard that her husband was 'desperately wounded' – a cannon ball had hit him in the back, knocking him off his horse and throwing him several yards – and was then told that he was dead. On the 20th she heard that he was still alive, and set off for the battlefield. When they reached Brussels 'the smell of Gunpowder was very perceptible,' and as they approached Waterloo 'the horses screamed at the smell of corruption, which in places was very offensive.' In the village of Mont St Jean she met an officer who told her that her husband was still alive and might recover, and she found him stronger than she had expected. 'It was a dreadful preparation, . . .' she wrote, 'being told of his death and then finding him alive but it was a sufficient one; for I was now ready to bear whatever might ensue without a murmur.'[63]

Magdalene set about nursing her husband, and found Emma 'of great service . . . her excellent heart and superior judgement were quite a blessing to me.' It was difficult to procure most necessities – a visiting officer left his card and it was immediately converted into a tea-spoon – and on Thursday 22 June Sir William showed the first symptoms of feverishness. Early on the 24th he was in great pain, 'and as I raised him that he might breathe more freely. He looked so *fixed* that I was afraid he was just expiring – His arms were round my neck to raise himself by, and I thought we should both have been killed by the exertion . . .' A surgeon told her that death was now inevitable, and on the night of the 26th she 'sat down to watch the melancholy progress of the water in his chest, which I saw would soon be fatal.' Sir William 'said he wished I would not look so unhappy – I wept – and spoke to me with so much affection. He repeated every endearing expression – he bid me kiss him – he called me his dear Wife . . .' She left the room because she could not bear to see him suffer so, but the surgeon ordered Emma to call her back, and she arrived just before he 'gave a little gulp, as if something was in his throat,' and died. De Lancey was buried on the 28th, and Magdalene visited his grave on 4 July, just before she set off for England: 'That day, *three* months before, I was married.'[64]

The formidable Florentia, wife of Major General Robert Sale, who commanded the 13th Light Infantry in the 1841 invasion of Afghanistan and was knighted for his services, was an altogether more experienced campaigner. Nicknamed 'the grenadier in petticoats', she had sounder military instincts than those left in command of the force after her husband returned to Jellalabad with his brigade. In Kabul her daughter Alexandrina married Lieutenant John Sturt of the Royal Engineers, who was wounded when the Afghans rose against their British-imposed ruler. 'He had been stabbed deeply in the shoulder and side,' wrote Florentia, 'and on the face (the latter wound striking on the bone just missed the temple); he was covered with blood issuing from his mouth, and was unable to articulate . . .'[65] He had soon recovered well enough to return to duty, but was too weak to mount his own horses so borrowed Florentia's pony.

Lady Sale was not impressed by the vacillation and poor leadership displayed by the British commanders.

> There is much reprehensible croaking going on; talk of retreat . . . All this makes a bad impression on the men. Our soldiery like to see their officers bear their part in their privation; it makes them more cheerful; but in going the rounds at night, officers are seldom found with the men. There are those that always stay at their posts on the ramparts, and the men appreciate them as they deserve.[66]

She watched the British-Indian force get badly beaten by the Afghans in November: 'It was very like the scenes depicted in the battles of the Crusades. The enemy rushed on and drove our men before them like a flock of sheep with a wolf at their heels.' When the survivors set off for Jellalabad on 8 January 1842 she found the force 'perfectly disorganised, nearly every man paralysed with cold, so as to be scarcely able to hold his musket or move.'[67]

The retreat was dreadful for the women, most of whom set out in camel panniers which:

> were mixed up with the baggage column in the pass: here they were heavily fired on; many camels were killed. On one camel were, in one [pannier] Mrs Boyd and her youngest boy Hugh; and in the other Mrs Mainwaring and her infant scarcely three months old, and Mrs Anderson's eldest child. This camel was shot. Mrs Boyd got a horse to ride; and her child was put on another behind a man, who being shortly after unfortunately killed, the child was carried off by the Afghans. Mrs Mainwaring, less fortunate, took her own baby in her arms. Mary Anderson was carried off in the confusion . . . Mrs M's sufferings were very great; and she deserves much credit for having preserved her child through these dreadful scenes. She not only had to walk a considerable distance with her child in her arms through deep snow, but had also to pick her way over the bodies of the dead, dying and wounded, both men and cattle, and constantly to cross streams of water, wet up to the knees, and pushed about by men and animals, the enemy keeping up a sharp fire, and several persons being killed close to her. She, however, got safe to camp with her child, but had no opportunity to change her clothes; and I know from experience that it was many days ere my wet habit became thawed, and can carefully appreciate her discomforts.[68]

Worse was to come. Sturt was shot in the abdomen that day, and Florentia herself wounded in arm and wrist. Nearly thirty of them were packed into a tent with no room to turn over, and sepoys and camp followers kept trying to force their way in: many froze to death outside. Sturt died on the 9th, 'still conscious that his wife and I were with him: and we had the sorrowful satisfaction of giving him a Christian burial.'[69] Married men and their families were offered protection by a friendly Afghan chief, and it was in his fort that Florentia heard that only one man of the entire force had managed to reach Jellalabad. It was not until the 19th that the ladies were able to wash properly, for the second time since leaving Kabul six weeks before. 'It was rather a painful process,' she wrote, 'as the cold and the glare of the sun and snow had three times peeled my face, from which the skin came off in strips.'[70] On 10 February she received a box of 'many useful things' from her husband. An officer reported that she was not very generous with her new possessions, and refused to part with even a single needle. But young Mrs Mainwaring 'on receiving a box of useful articles from her husband in Jellalabad, most liberally distributed the contents among the other ladies, who were much in need.'[71]

The Persian widow of Sergeant Deane was 'taken by force' and married to an Afghan nobleman, but had been 'very sincerely attached' to Deane and struck her new husband whenever he sought to exercise his conjugal rights. In contrast, Mrs Wade, the wife of a sergeant:

> changed her attire, threw off the European dress, and adopted the costume of the Mussulmans, and professing to have changed her creed also, consorted with the Nazir of our inveterate enemy . . . Of so incorrect a personage as Mrs Wade I shall only say that she is at Mahommed Shah Khan's fort with her lover.[72]

Florentia rejoined her husband shortly afterwards. He was, however, killed at Mudki fighting the Sikhs, in 1845.

Despite harrowing experiences like this, it is clear that many women undoubtedly preferred the discomforts of campaign, which were at least accompanied by the prospect of living some sort of married life, to the limbo of separation and worry, too often ended by a letter in an unfamiliar hand. 'I have received two balls, one in my groin and the other near the breast,' whispered John Randon from Boston in 1775.

> I am now so weak from loss of blood, that I can hardly dictate these few lines, as a last tribute of my unchangeable love to you. The Surgeons inform me that three hours will be the utmost I can survive.[73]

CARROT AND STICK

SOLDIERS AND, by extension, their wives, were induced to tolerate the squalor of the barrack-room and the discomforts of campaign by the prospect of steady pay. The word soldier has its origin
in the old French *soude*, pay, and the Latin *soldati*, paid men: the
king's shilling given to the recruit was symbolic of a relationship in
which money played a fundamental part. Well might the words of
'Over the Hills and Far Away', as popular in the Napoleonic wars as
it had been when first composed a century before, exhort:

> All gentlemen that have a mind
> to serve the queen that's good and kind
> come 'list and enter into pay . . .

The lure of regular pay and attractive bounties made most recruits
enlist, and many officers who bought their commissions and could
not live on their pay still regarded its prompt arrival as fundamental
to their relationship with the army. Men rarely risked their lives for
money alone, but their sense of value sprang not just from serving
with gallant leaders and good comrades in a brave regiment, but
from being regularly paid.

There were occasional mutinies throughout the period, and these
usually stemmed from what the mutineers regarded as a breach of
trust on the part of the authorities. Wills's Regiment mutinied at

Canterbury in 1713 because soldiers being paid off were dissatisfied 'from the small balances some have due to them, and to the great load of necessaries charged upon them, which has brought others of them into their Captains' debt.' In 1760 a regiment grounded arms at Portsmouth rather than embark for the East Indies, arguing that 'their stoppages were twenty months in arrears, and that they were not to be commanded by their own officers . . .' There was a more serious outbreak at Quebec in 1763, when the commander-in-chief ordered that there would be an extra stoppage of 4d a day for rations. Men of the 15th, 27th and 2/60th first assembled unarmed to protest, but then went back to their barracks, armed themselves, and fired on the governor when he addressed them. Eventually, after he had warned the troops of the risks they ran under the articles of war and stressed 'his fixed resolution, with the assistance of the officers, to oblige them to submit, or perish in the attempt,' order was restored. The mutineers marched between a pair of colours as a symbol of their reintegration into the army and, significantly, nobody seems to have been punished.

In Scotland, the Western Fencibles mutinied in 1779 when Lieutenant Colonel Lord Frederick Campbell bought sporrans from a London tailor, and charged his men 3s 6d for them: they believed that canny local purchase would have had them for 1s 8d. In 1783 two Highland regiments mutinied at Portsmouth rather than sail for the East Indies, but commentators noted that the men behaved with soldierly dignity throughout the proceedings: most attended church, having posted guards to ensure that they were not surprised. It was clear that the dispute was about terms of service, and matters were resolved in the soldiers' favour when a proclamation announced that none of them would be sent on foreign service without re-enlisting – for which a handsome bounty would be paid. There were, of course, less complex reasons for mutiny. In 1795 some Fencibles tried to break into the guardroom in Dumfries to release a prisoner, but were stopped by the firm action of the adjutant and sergeant major. In August 1834 part of the 88th, apparently in drink (alas the Connaughts), ran amok in Chatham, prodding peaceable citizens with their side-arms: the *Maidstone Gazette* confidently reported that there was to be a public meeting on the subject.

Pay differed not simply between ranks but between arms of the service too: guardsmen and cavalrymen received more than line infantrymen. There was one substantial pay-rise in our period, in 1797 when the infantryman's pay went up from 8d to a shilling a day, where it was to remain unaltered for the next seventy years. But up to 6d of the soldier's pay was taken for subsistence, and other deductions were made for regulation uniform (other necessary niceties had to be bought from his enlistment bounty), medical treatment, the upkeep of Chelsea Hospital, breakages, barrack damages and the regimental agent. It was not until 1847 that it was ordered that all soldiers had to receive at least 1d a day regardless of all deductions.

Although British soldiers were better paid than French or Prussian conscripts, they were less well paid than almost any of their countrymen in regular work. One attraction of soldiering in India was that money went very much further: even private soldiers could afford an Indian barber who visited their barracks rooms early in the morning to shave them before first parade. On his first morning in India John Pearman was awakened in his 'large open room . . . only iron and wood rails for walls' by the cry of 'Hot coffee, Sahib', a luxury unknown in England. Drink, too, was cheaper. Pearman wrote that at Ambala in the mid 1840s a bottle of imported ale cost 1 rupee 12 annas (3s 6d) but one anna bought nearly three pints of rum. Paddy Burns, one of the regimental wives, had a tin baby with a wax face, and would gradually fill it up with rum in the canteen, on the pretext of soothing it. She then resold the rum at night, when the canteen was shut, and men 'would pay any amount' for drink. The arrangement made enough money to enable her husband to buy a pub when he left the army.[74]

We have already seen how bounties, their size fluctuating with the scale of the demand, were offered to encourage men to enlist. A cavalryman received £4 14s at the start of the Revolutionary war but only £5 4s after Waterloo and £6 17s 6d in the 1840s. When the Crimea loomed, it rose again to £7 15s 6s in 1854 and £10 the following year. But just as pay was subject to stoppages, so bounty too was lacerated by charges items like shirts, waistcoats, cleaning and, for cavalrymen, grooming kit. Even the hated stock, a leather collar buckled round the neck (and gently shaved to diminish its height, and thus make it more comfortable, by knowing soldiers) had to be paid for. In 1819 a trooper in the 18th Light Dragoons found all these sundries amounted to £5 16s 9d, and in the 1830s their cost actually exceeded his bounty. It was not until 1856 that soldiers were at last given a free issue of this kit on joining.

Soldiers as well as sailors were eligible for prize money based on the value of bullion, cash and similar valuables which were legitimately captured and duly 'condemned' as prizes. These goods were assembled and liquidated by prize agents, and the proceeds were then distributed, through regimental agents, according to a sliding scale which gave a specified number of shares to officers and soldiers according to rank. The system was widely condemned because of the small shares which eventually came to those of junior rank, and the process took years. In 1863 an article in the *United Services Magazine* made much of the fact that a Colonel North MP had forced the War Office to disgorge statistics of prize payment. These showed that the first payment for the 1810 Ile de France campaign was made in 1819, and although Ghuznee was captured in 1839 prize money was not issued till 1848. Sometimes prize goods were sold on the spot and the proceeds distributed promptly. Lieutenant John Shipp was appointed prize agent when one of the Rajah of Nagpore's forts was taken in 1804. He put double sentries on the doors of the womens' quarters, but one immediately left his post and stole two large boxes of jewellery. 'We sold our prize goods by public auction,' wrote Shipp, 'and the sale lasted a whole day, bringing us in a good deal of money.'[75]

There was an unprecedented haul of prize goods during the Indian Mutiny. The war correspondent William Howard Russell watched British soldiers looting the Kaiserbagh soon after its capture.

> From the broken portals issue soldiers laden with loot or plunder. Shawls, rich tapestry, gold and silver brocade, caskets of jewels, arms, splendid dresses. The men are wild with fury and lust for gold – literally drunk with plunder. Some come out with china vases or mirrors, dash them to pieces on the ground, and return to seek more valuable booty. Others are busy gouging out the precious stones

from the stems of pipes, from saddle-cloths, or the hilts
of swords, or butts of pistols and fire arms.[76]

Order was gradually restored, and after the end of operations in
Lucknow, Gordon-Alexander was on guard at the palace, where he
found a room full of:

> Finest Kashmir shawls, silver-mounted and jewelled swords
> and other weapons, a solid gold casket divided into com-
> partments exactly like a British kitchen spice-box, which
> I carried myself, and handed over to the prize agent, each
> compartment being quite full of gems, such as diamonds,
> rubies, sapphires and emeralds . . .

He asked to keep a brass sword-cane as a souvenir, and, canny Scot,
demanded a receipt for it. The prize agent valued that room alone
at £30,000. 'My souvenir of the find,' wrote Gordon-Alexander, was,
perhaps, worth two shillings.'[77]

It was an offence to retain items without handing them over to
the prize agent, and Gordon-Alexander sat on a court-martial which
sentenced two men to be flogged for secreting one or two valuable
Kashmir shawls. However, in India the authorities could rarely prevent a substantial proportion of captured money and valuables from
remaining in private hands. Near Gujerat in 1849 John Pearman
and his mate Johnny Grady found two chests of rupees on a bullock
cart, 'filled our holster-pipes on the saddle' and blew the rest up.
'We made what we could and did very well,' he reflected, 'that is if
we had not spent it in a very foolish way, I mean drink, which takes
away the reason.'[78] Men of regiments marching back from Multan
had so much hidden money – 'round their body, and the waist of
their trousers lined with gold' – that they were repeatedly searched
by their officers and the prize agents. Private Waterfield saw that
'some of them could scarcely walk, for their boots were crammed
with gold mohurs', and his brother, on guard that night, 'had a
good deal of money given him, passing £20 on to Waterfield'.[79] The
officers and men of an artillery company were all placed under
arrest for having buried some treasure, which was never found, and
Armourer Sergeant Williams of the 10th Foot was reduced to the
ranks and flogged for stealing a gold-hilted sword set with diamonds.

The weapon was never recovered, because the soldier to whom it had been entrusted threw it down a well in Lucknow.

The opportunities were rarely as good in Spain, but there was still money to be made. The French paymasters' wagons were captured after Vitoria. Captain Thomas Browne, who had just escaped, wounded, from French hands, was being helped back by a cavalry sergeant, who at once joined the looting, 'filling his pockets, Haversack, boots & the crown of his cap with dollars.' The sergeant then filled Browne's pockets for him, saying 'at all events your Honour if you have got a hard thump today, you have got your pockets well lined with Doubloons.' Browne made £120, and reckoned that the sergeant must have carried off twice as much.[80] The 28th also did well, and William Keep reports that: 'Some of our drummers made a rich harvest, and one little fellow entered the camp (who was only big enough to play upon the triangle) mounted on a French general's charger with holsters and bags full of valuable commodities.'[81] Not all such ventures had happy endings. Sergeant Anthony Hamilton tells of how, during the retreat to Corunna, kegs full of dollars were staved in and rolled down a steep slope. The wife of Corporal Riley of the 43rd Light Infantry:

> So loaded herself with the money that was scattered about, that afterwards, when embarking in Corunna harbour, in trying to get up into the vessel, she had such a weight around her person that she fell between the boat and the ship, and was drowned.[82]

Whether an item was looted, seized as a regimental trophy, or 'legitimately' purchased depended much on the rank and perception of those concerned. Sergeant Pearman jumped on a fine Arab horse to see if he could ride the beast, although its groom begged him not to steal it. The horse ran away with him, but he managed to get it back to camp, where he sold it to Captain Ouvry for two flasks of grog and 100 rupees (about £10). He invested the proceeds in more grog. The 14th Light Dragoons seized King Joseph's silver chamberpot after Vitoria, and the splendid receptacle is still kept in the officers' mess of the regiment's successor, and used, on guest nights, to hold champagne. Most regimental museums possess items like large bronze Burmese bells, and regard them as campaign trophies. It is, however, not hard to sympathise with Pearman who concluded that while officers found souvenirs or received gifts, soldiers looted and were flogged for it.

A final source of income was entirely legitimate. Units serving in India received field allowances called *batta*, and extra *batta* was often awarded to regiments which distinguished themselves. After Sobraon Pearman reported that 'we . . . get twelve moths *batta* and prize money, £7 12s 6d.' The 13th Light Infantry earned widespread approbation by its defence of Jellalabad in 1842. Ensign C.G.C. Stapylton wrote that they were all to have a silver medal, 'also that every regiment in Hindustan shall, on our march down, turn out and present arms to us in review order. They have also granted us six months *batta* which, however, will hardly cover the losses of the officers.'[83]

Pay, allowances, prize money and loot joined other, often less material, motives in encouraging a man to join the army and to stay in it. But where inducement failed, discipline coerced, and the army was subjected to a disciplinary code increasingly seen as severe even by comparison with the civil law of the age. Military punishments were not only demonstrative but, by involving other soldiers as participants and spectators, made them accomplices in the infliction of death or pain. The seventeenth century punishment of running the gauntlet survived in the British army until the middle of the eighteenth. The offender, stripped to the waist, with a sergeant's halberd at his chest to prevent him from breaking into a run, walked between two lines of soldiers armed with sticks who beat him as he passed. A Prussian general observed that in his army a man sentenced to thirty-six runs, spread over three days, usually died under the blows. Another, even more savage punishment which did not survive was the old practice of burning incendiaries alive, on the principle that the punishment was precisely fitted to the crime. A French agent who tried to blow up a magazine in Lille in 1710 was 'slowly burnt to death between two fires with every refinement of cruelty.'[84]

Military offenders were judged by three sorts of courts martial – regimental, district or general – whose jurisdiction and powers of punishment varied. Regimental courts martial could deal only with NCOs and soldiers of the regiment concerned, and officers could be tried only by general court martial. All consisted of panels of officers advised, in the case of district and general courts, by a judge advocate who was a civilian lawyer. Some sentences required confirmation by Horse Guards or by the commander-in-chief of an expeditionary force: his judge advocate general advised him on the legality of the sentence.

Wellington's judge advocate general, Francis Seymour Larpent, has left a journal which throws a fascinating light not only on the administration of justice in the Peninsula army but on life in Wellington's headquarters generally. His journal is full of human tragedies. A good soldier deserted to the Spaniards because his 'honest and faithful' Spanish wife had been turned out of the regiment by his captain. Larpent took down the story in detail and passed it on to Wellington, who pardoned the man 'from the good character of his regiment and that which the Colonel gave him.'[85] A soldier fired his musket through a door, killing a Spanish girl who had just refused to sell him some chestnuts. Larpent thought him guilty of murder, but the court, 'long in doubt', eventually found him guilty only of 'a most disorderly outrage and killing the girl' and gave him 1000 lashes. Corporal MacMorran of the 42nd was mildly rebuked by Lieutenant Dickenson of his company, and shot him through the heart. He was hanged for murder. 'They were both under twenty years of age, I hear,' wrote Larpent,

> and the most promising men in their respective stations. The officer was a man of mild, humane character. The corporal made no defence: it seemed an excess of Scotch pride. It is altogether a very painful business.[86]

Larpent was meticulous in his oversight of courts martial, sending procedurally incorrect papers back for revision, quashing illegal proceedings and advising Wellington on the confirmation of sentences that were legal. Officers who served on courts martial swore, at the commencement of proceedings, to judge fairly and impartially, and announced their findings in reverse seniority to prevent the verdict of the senior officer influencing the opinion of others. In July 1779 John Peebles sat on a general court martial which tried Private John Sutherland of the 64th Foot for desertion. Peebles thought him 'a poor silly creature who tells a simple & consistent story of his being in liquor and losing his way in the night, his greatest fault was in not returning.' However, he was not persuaded that he had formed the intention of deserting – an essential element in the case – and could not reconcile the death sentence to 'justice or humanity'. The business rankled, and on 19 July, the day of Sutherland's execution, he accompanied another member of the court to Major General Vaughan, told him that they could not square the matter with their 'judgement and conscience', and asked to be allowed to tell the commander-in-chief what had happened. They were delighted to hear that the man had already been pardoned, and saw him given this news at the foot of the gallows, where he promptly fainted.[87]

It will come as no surprise to discover that many crimes were drink-related. Drunkenness itself was an offence. It often led to short-term absenteeism which then turned into desertion, and was frequently aggravated when drunken men insulted or struck officers or NCOs, laying themselves open to capital punishment. In October 1847 Robert Waterfield saw a soldier in the East India Company's artillery shot for striking a surgeon while drunk.

> We were all formed up into three sides of a square; a mud bank, made to stop the shot when the troops are at ball practice, formed the fourth side of the square. We had not long been formed up . . . when a young man belonging to the company's artillery . . . was marched into the centre of the square by an escort.
>
> The prisoner's name was Richard Riley Atkins, and his general court-martial was read by the Brigadier in a loud impressive tone . . . after his sentence had been read, which was approved finally by Lord Gough, Commander-in-Chief, the band, funeral procession, firing party and the prisoner with his coffin borne on the shoulders of his comrades marched round the square, the band playing the Dead March . . .
>
> The firing party consisted of twelve men of HM's 32nd Regiment, not one of whom had ever been witness of a military execution before, and now they became the principal actors in this awful drama . . . The words Ready! Present! in a low drawling tone was given, then we heard

the click of the lock, and in a moment they had fired.
The prisoner was perceived to quiver, but steady in a
moment and kneeling erect on the coffin. The Provost
Sergeant rushed up to the prisoner, and with a large pistol
scattered the poor fellow's brains about the plain.

The troops marched past the corpse in open column
of divisions, from thence to their respective barracks . . .[88]

The procedure was much the same for executions by shooting
throughout the period. Often the officer commanding the firing
party would give his orders by signal to spare the blindfolded prisoner's feelings, and sometimes a second squad stood ready to fire
in case the first volley failed to kill the victim.

Desertion was the bane of armies of the age, in barracks and in
the field. At home men often took advantage of the relaxed discipline
on recruiting parties (or even on parties which were themselves sent
in pursuit of deserters) to abscond. The same inn wall might bear
some posters encouraging young men to enlist and others offering
rewards for the apprehension of deserters. In July 1762 a poster
announced that Corporal John Jones had deserted from Lieutenant
Colonel Patrick Tonyn's Regiment at Litchfield. He had been chas-
ing a deserter on the York road, and was described as '22 years, five
Feet three Inches and a half high, black Complexion, dark brown
hair, hazel Eyes . . .' and was wearing a blue coat and riding a bald-
faced black horse. Those desirous of receiving three guineas reward
'over and above what is allowed by Act of Parliament' were invited
to report Jones to the commanding officer or to our old friend the
regimental agent, in this instance John Calcraft Esq, of Channel
Row, Westminster.[89] Some soldiers made a career of deserting after
taking the bounty, but the introduction of branding on the arm,
head or chest with D for deserter or BC for bad character made it
impossible for a man already convicted of desertion or serious
offence to re-enlist. In 1842 the process was made more humane
when a brass instrument mounting a number of adjustable needle
points was used to stamp the letter into the skin: it was made permanent buy rubbing in a mixture of indigo and Indian ink. The practice
was not abolished till 1871.

In the field, desertion was usually a two-way process, as John

Peebles observed on 6 June 1777: 'Deserters coming in as usual & some Rascals deserting from us.'[90] In peacetime it was rarely a capital matter, although a man who repeatedly deserted and re-enlisted might indeed be shot for it. In wartime soldiers who deserted and took service with the enemy were always shot, and even simple desertion in the face of the enemy was likely to end fatally. In August 1813 Larpent thought that the incidence of desertion was 'terrible', but was pleased to record that five out of the sixteen deserters sent for trial by general court martial had so far been shot: 'This will, I think, at least have a good effect on our new reinforcements.'[91]

When Lieutenant George Gleig's regiment formed up to witness an execution in Spain 'you could almost perceive the sort of shudder which ran through the frames of all who were on parade.' Three deserters were marched on and stood in front of their open grave while the sentence was read out. They were then ordered to kneel and were blindfolded. One was then told that he had been pardoned, but 'the poor wretch . . . knelt there as if rooted to the spot . . . till a file of men removed him in a state of insensibility.' After the volley one man sprang into the air while the other fell flat on his face: neither moved thereafter. 'The discharge of the muskets in the face of the culprits,' writes Gleig, 'was followed by a sound as if every man in the division had been stifled for the last five minutes, and now at length drew in his breath.'[92]

It was considered more honourable to be shot than hanged, although given the poor performance of firing parties it is difficult to say whether hanging, which in this era usually killed by strangulation, was actually more pleasant than shooting. Perhaps Burgoyne, as depicted in Shaw's *The Devil's Disciple*, really did have a point when he told a condemned man that they could hang him perfectly decently, but if they tried to shoot him they would bungle it and leave him to the provost-marshal's pistol. Hanging was the penalty inflicted on murderers, some looters used by Wellington to discourage others (one orchard-raider whose mouth remained open after he fought for breath had an apple stuffed in it to make the point), and other unfortunates whose crime was deemed especially low. In 1776 a soldier in Captain Mackenzie's company of the 43rd was ordered: 'To Suffer Death, being hanged by the neck till he is dead, being the most ignominious manner of inflicting the punishment of death, due to so infamous a Crime as Desertion to the Rebels of his Country.' He was hanged in front of the 43rd's camp, and every regiment in garrison sent its guard to watch. Desertion was bad enough, but what earned the man noose rather than volley was the fact that he had taken arms with the Americans.[93]

Hanging was also the penalty for spies, and an officer on military business behind enemy lines in plain clothes risked hanging even if he had his commission with him and could thereby prove his status. The classic instances of the hanging of spies occurred during the American war. In 1780 Major John André, Clinton's adjutant-general, was taking a message to Benedict Arnold, then an American major general, who had agreed to surrender West Point. A misunderstanding led to his capture, in plain clothes, and a court martial sentenced him to hang. André begged to be shot, writing to Washington that: 'Sympathy towards a soldier will surely induce your excellency, and a military tribunal, to adapt the mode of my death to the feelings of a man of honour.' Washington felt unable to alter the sentence. However, André was hanged from a proper gallows, and allowed to stand on his coffin in the cart while the rope was adjusted, declaring: 'I request you, gentlemen, that you will bear witness to the world that I die like a brave man.' He wrote to Clinton on the eve of his execution, saying: 'I have a mother and three sisters, to whom the value of my commission would be an object, as the loss of Grenada has very much affected their income.'[94] Peebles thought that the whole army was 'sorry for the untimely death of that promising young man.'[95]

Four years before, Nathan Hale, schoolteacher turned patriot officer, was apprehended in the British camp at New York with notes on the disposition of British troops hidden under the soles of his shoes. Howe summarily ordered his execution without benefit of court martial, justifying this in general orders by saying that he was a self-confessed spy. The provost marshal treated him barbarously, denying him a bible and tearing up his last letters. He was strung up from an apple tree in front of the artillery park, and his own last words – 'I regret that I have but one life to give for my country' – showed no less courage than André's. Captain MacKenzie of the 23rd Foot thought that:

> He behaved with great composure and resolution. Saying
> he thought it the duty of every good Officer, to obey any
> orders given him by his Commander-in-chief; and desired
> the spectators to be at all times prepared to meet death
> in whatever shape it might appear.[96]

The point was not that Hale was hanged, but that he was treated discourteously before death in a way that André was not. This stemmed from the fact that, at this early stage in the war, the British found it hard to recognise the patriots as legitimate combatants and the Continental congress as a source of proper commissions. Howe had earlier written a letter to 'Mr Washington', which the latter's secretary had declined to receive on the grounds that there was no such person with the army, and a missive to 'George Washington Esq' fared no better. The British Army was not alone in finding it hard to extend to men who it regarded as rebels their rights as soldiers: such reluctance has formed a dismal backdrop to hundreds of rebellions across the centuries.

Although military executions loom large in the letters and diaries of contemporaries, they were in fact much rarer than they appear. Of the 76 death sentences passed on soldiers between 1826 and 1835 (many of them for offences that were capital under civil law) 35 were commuted to transportation. Nevertheless, a soldier had a proportionately greater chance of being executed than a civilian. During a similar period 8000 civilians were sentenced to death, but only one in twenty was actually executed. In the 1830s the Commander-in-chief in India issued repeated warnings that the offence of striking a superior officer was indeed capital, 'and that he should be compelled to put it into execution if the crime was not put a stop to.' The kindly Lieutenant Colonel Hill of the 32nd Foot formed his men into square and cautioned them against the offence 'until the tears ran down his face on the horse's neck.'[97]

An infinitely more common punishment was flogging. It was inflicted for a range of crimes from a capital offence which had not attracted the death sentence, through less serious offences like drunkenness to comparatively trivial misdemeanours such as shaving the top of one's stock or, in one disgraceful case, persistently demanding the return of money borrowed by an officer. Military

Punishment as propaganda, *c.* 1820. The reality was bad enough, but here the artist, with a political point to make, has worsened things by showing the victim tied to a triangle made from sergeants' half-pikes, stark naked rather than stripped to the waist as was the custom. The diced shako-band identifies the 71ˢᵗ (Highland) Light Infantry. A drummer wields the cat, supervised by the drum-major with his baton.

flogging does not stand alone. It must first be judged by the standards of the civilian penology of the age, when there were powerful arguments for punishments which were speedy, public and thus, it was hoped, deterrent. Civilian offenders, like their military countrymen, risked hanging or whipping under the Bloody Code, the name given to the English system of criminal law from 1688 to 1815: there were well over 200 capital offences in 1800. It was not until the late eighteenth century that it was widely suggested that imprisonment should replace many of the penalties prescribed by the Bloody Code. The growth of public and Parliamentary opposition to flogging occurred at precisely that time when civilian practice was changing (though Dr John Keate, headmaster of Eton, birched 80 boys on a single evening in 1832) but that of the military still lagged behind.

Secondly, flogging met military demands for punishment which was prompt, demonstrative and, for it was inflicted by a man's comrades, collective. It usually did not remove the victim from his regiment's strength and, unlike imprisonment, did not allow him to escape from the military service which had often provoked his crime in the first place. Its many defenders, by no means all officers, maintained that the utterly depraved character of a proportion of the military population demanded that the sternest measures were available to keep it in check. Sergeant James Anton of the 42nd Foot attacked 'philanthropists who decry the lash' arguing that it was essential for the protection of the decent majority. Benjamin Harris thought a man was only flogged because of his own fault, and some Victorian soldiers thought it preferable to working the crank or treadmill in a civilian prison. Lieutenant General Sir John Macdonald maintained that a ranker captain had told him that flogging had been the making of him: 'I was never worth a damn until I got 300 lashes.'[98]

Gordon-Alexander thought the abolition of corporal punishment in the army 'a lamentable mistake,' telling of a 'smart, clean brave soldier' in his company of the 93rd Foot who 'when he took to drink developed a murderously violent temper.' Flogging was the only thing that could check him, and yet he did not seem degraded by it. Indeed, echoing an argument sometimes used by other defenders of flogging, Gordon-Alexander argued that flogging was not as terrible as it seemed. This soldier took his fifty lashes and announced: 'Dae ye ca' *that* a flogging? Hoots! I've got many a worse licking frae ma mither.'[99]

The majority of non-commissioned diarists, however, are resolute in their opposition to flogging: Thomas Morris castigated its 'frequency and gross inhumanity.' One of his comrades 'a fine young fellow' sentenced to 300 lashes, seized a musket from the rack in the guardroom and blew his brains out. 'Poor fellow,' wrote Morris. 'He was much esteemed by his comrades, and, I think, on the whole, they were not sorry that he had freed himself from the horrors of the lash.'[100] When Roger Lamb was on his way to North America aboard the transport *Friendship* in 1776 Private Brooks of the 9th Foot jumped overboard, and the ship passed right over him. Miraculously, he appeared in its wake, but swam strongly away from his rescuers. 'The fear of punishment,' wrote Lamb, 'was the cause of this desperate action, as the day before he had stolen a shirt from one of his messmates knapsacks.'[101]

When John Shipp was Regimental Sergeant Major of the 24th Light Dragoons the regiment had one soldier who was always being locked up in the guardroom for minor offences. The man told him that he had been flogged at the behest of the previous RSM, and that the experience had broken his spirit. 'I am of good family,' he said, 'but will never go back to disgrace them by the scars on my back.' He died, dead drunk, three months later. George Loy Smith saw an old soldier flogged in India on the orders of Lord Cardigan for being drunk on guard. Nobody expected the punishment to take place, as the man had completed his service and was about to return to England. He begged Cardigan for mercy, saying: 'I am an old man and just going home to my friends, and should be sorry for such a disgrace to come on me now.' Cardigan had him flogged regardless.[102]

A soldier who was to be flogged in barracks was marched onto the parade ground or inside a large building like a riding school, with the men of his regiment formed up, in full dress, in hollow square. The adjutant read out the sentence and its confirmation, and then turned to the prisoner, ordering: 'Strip, sir.' The prisoner removed his shirt. He was then tied up, an infantryman to a large iron triangle, derived from the traditional pyramid of sergeants' halberds, and a cavalryman to a short ladder made fast to wall or tree. Short whips called cats o' nine tails were already on hand in green baize bags, in charge of the drum major (for infantry units) or the farrier major (for the cavalry). There was a bucket of water and a chair, a hospital orderly, and the regimental surgeon stood close by to monitor the prisoner's condition. When arrangements were complete, the adjutant reported to the colonel, who ordered: 'Proceed.' The first cat was removed from its bag, and a farrier or drummer struck the prisoner with it, with the sergeant major calling out each stroke.

The punishment went on, with floggers being replaced as they grew tired, and cats being exchanged for fresh ones as they became worn or clogged with blood and tissue. Onlookers routinely fainted or vomited, and commanding officers often intervened to stop the punishment after only a few strokes: Tom Plunket of the 95th was spared after 35 of his 350 lashes. Others drew back from the brink. One colonel stepped forward before the farriers set to, saying: 'I know this man to be a good soldier, and am very sorry to see him

Wellington at Waterloo, 1815. It had rained heavily the night before the battle. The Duke, simply dressed in a blue frock coat and black cocked hat, commanded from his horse's back, moving about the field as the battle ebbed and flowed, though he spent much of his time near an elm tree on the main Brussels road.

'Twenty-Eighth, remember Egypt!' The 28th (North Gloucestershire) Regiment in square at Quatre Bras, two days before Waterloo. During this chaotic battle some British battalions were broken by French cavalry, but the 1/28th, encouraged by Sir Thomas Picton to remember its distinguished achievement in Egypt in 1801, held firm.

Although Felix Phillipoteaux exaggerates some aspects of Waterloo, his painting of French *cuirassiers* attacking British squares (here one which apparently includes a Highland and another line regiment) catches essential elements of the battle. Squares were vulnerable to artillery fire and suffered most of their casualties from shot and shell; most British guns (like the battery in the background) were abandoned when the cavalry overran them, their gunners taking refuge in squares to emerge later; and the bravery of the French horsemen impressed even their enemies. 'By God,' said one British officer, 'those fellows deserve Bonaparte: they fight so nobly for him.'

The 44th (East Essex) Regiment was the only British unit involved in that 'signal catastrophe', the retreat from Kabul in 1842. Its survivors made their last stand at Gandamak, where most were killed: however, Captain Soutar, who had wrapped the colours around his body, was spared.

The 3rd (Kings Own) Light Dragoons charging the Sikhs at Chilianwallah, 1849. This inconclusive battle is best known because of the setback suffered by Pope's cavalry brigade, although most British units engaged fought well against their redoubtable opponents.

British misfortunes in the Crimea attracted widespread criticism, not least from the pen of *The Times* correspondent W. W. Russell. But the terrain was inhospitable and communications poor. This lithograph shows the main road leading inland from the British base of Balaclava.

Scotland for Ever! Elizabeth Butler's painting of the Scots Greys at Waterloo is one of the most enduring battlepieces of the nineteenth century. Despite its inaccuracies – some of the horsemen are set on collision courses, and British cavalry probably did not carry standards (their equivalent of infantry regimental colours) into battle at this period – the picture encapsulates 'the speed of the horse, the magnetism of the charge, and the terror of cold steel.'

Paul Sandby's coloured etching shows a familiar sight in the training camps of the 1780s: a prostitute is drummed out of camp in Hyde Park.

A recruiting party at work outside a tavern, c.1790. An officer reviews the latest batch of the king's hard bargains, while his sergeant does his best to make them look like the soldiers they have just become.

A mounted officer of 18th (Royal Irish) Regiment takes the salute, *c.* 1840.
White trousers looked elegant but speedily became grubby. The need for
frequent washing meant that men often wore them damp, and they were
abolished for home service in 1845.

Baggage trailed behind the armies of the age, though enterprising commanders often did their best to reduce it. These illustrations of 1803 give a good
feel for the mix of public and private baggage and with the attendant cloud of
wives and camp followers.

This painting shows Royal Horse Guards, Life Guards and Dragoon Guards in a barrack room in about 1840: soldiers did 'everything but drill' in these rooms.

Florence Nightingale took a party of female nurses to the hospitals at Scutari, destination of many of the wounded from the Crimea. She came, not wholly fairly, to symbolise compassion amid chaos.

come to this. Will any gentlemen pledge his word for his good conduct in future?' The man's troop leader immediately stepped forward. On another occasion, just before the flogging began, a captain spoke up for 'an old Waterloo man, with not a hair between his head and heaven,' saying: 'For God's sake, Colonel, do not flog that old man, and I will be responsible for him for six months.' He was duly spared.[103]

Some commanding officers actually refused to administer flogging. Colonel Sir John Woodford abolished it in the Grenadiers when he commanded, arguing that 'violent punishments suggest violent offences.' Lieutenant Colonel Mainwaring of the 51st was a 'no flogging' commanding officer, but made a rare exception with a man who had deserted when the regiment was under orders to sail. The man was released after receiving 75 of his 500 lashes, and led through the ranks with the worthy colonel shouting: 'soldiers spit on the cowardly poltroon, you should all piss over him were it not too indecent.'[104]

Dozens of accounts testify to the unpleasantness of witnessing flogging, and many soldiers, like Private Waterfield, thought that 'flogging is a disgrace and ought to be erased from the articles of war.' Of the few who wrote about experiencing the cat was Alexander Somerville, who had written anonymously to a Birmingham newspaper in 1831 at the height of the agitation for reform. He was tied up and heard the RSM order: 'Farrier Simpson, you will do your duty.'

> Simpson took the cat as ordered, at least I believe so; I did not see him, but I felt an astounding sensation between the shoulders, under my neck, which went to my toe nails in one direction, my finger nails in another, and stung me to the heart, as if a knife had gone through my body. The sergeant major called in a loud voice 'one.' I felt as if it would be kind of Simpson not to strike in the same place again. He came on again a second time a few inches lower, and then I thought the former stroke was sweet and agreeable compared with that one. The sergeant major counted 'two'. The 'cat' was swung twice round the farrier's head again, and he came on somewhere about the

right shoulder blade, and the loud voice of the reckoner said 'three.'

After 25 strokes Simpson handed over to a youngster who had never flogged before, but had practised on a stable post of sack and saw-dust, and 'gave me some dreadful cuts about the ribs, first on one side and then the other . . .' It was then Simpson's turn once more, and he 'got up among the old sores; the strokes were not so sharp as at first; they were like the blows of heavy weights, but far more painful than the fresh ones . . .' Somerville was spared after a hun-dred strokes, his commanding officer ordering: 'Stop, take him down, he is a young soldier.'[105]

Flogging in peacetime was abolished in 1868, though it was administered on campaign till 1881 and in military prisons till 1907. There was, however, a gradual decrease in its severity. In 1807, after a private in the 54th was sentenced to 1500 lashes, George III decreed that 1000 lashes were 'a sufficient example for any breach of military discipline short of a capital offence.' Larger sentences were still awarded in cases where the offender might otherwise have been executed. Larpent described a 2,000 lash sentence as legal but absurd, because the recipient would only be able to bear six or seven hundred, and there the matter would end. In 1812 regimental courts martial were restricted to 300 lashes. This became the maximum for all courts in 1829, and in 1832 regimental courts were further restricted to 200. The offences which could be punished by flogging were reduced in 1833, and the Mutiny Act of 1836 limited regimen-tal courts martial to 100 lashes, district courts to 150 and general courts to 200. In 1847 a common maximum of 50 lashes was set, and it was reduced to 25 in 1879. In the late 1820s the army was flogging about one in 50 of its soldiers every year, and this had fallen to one in 189 by 1845.

Flogging was a major political issue from the late eighteenth century, and grew ever more contentious as the civilian punishments became, if only relatively, more enlightened. Resolute opposition to flogging earned Cobbett a two-year prison sentence in 1810, but after the passage of the 1832 Reform Bill governments came under increasing pressure to abolish it. In 1832 the radical MP Sir Francis

Burdett told Lord Grey that: 'It is an atrocity which the public will no longer endure.' By 1835 the secretary at war acknowledged that 'the whole subject has arrived at a stage at which it cannot rest,' and a Royal Commission on Military Punishment sat in 1835. Although it recommended that corporal punishment should continue, it was a judgment demonstrably out of sympathy with the weight of public opinion. Lieutenant Colonel John Townshend, commanding the 14th Light Dragoons, had testified to the commission that in Gloucester, where his regiment was quartered, the public became so enraged when flogging was administered that he was obliged to take the regiment four miles outside the town, and even then the mayor intervened. In 1777 the townspeople of Perth were even less forgiving when a soldier's wife dashed forward to try to stop the drummer from flogging her husband. The populace joined in, and although most of the officers escaped unhurt:

> Not so the Adjutant, for he was laid on his belly, in which
> position he was held by some scores of vigorous hands,
> till he got a handsome flogging on the bare posteriors, in
> the presence of thousands, inflicted with an energy that
> would remain imprinted on his memory till the day of his
> death.[106]

Soldiers occasionally died during or after flogging, despite the presence of a surgeon who was to stop the punishment if it seemed to be threatening the victim's life. In 1824 two men of the 21st Foot died after flogging (Assistant Surgeon Freer, in attendance at the punishment, was swiftly dismissed the service by the Duke of York) and in 1835 Private Thomas Ramsay died after receiving 150 lashes at Woolwich. In June 1846 Private John White of the 7th Hussars was awarded 150 lashes by a district court martial sitting at Hounslow. He seemed to recover from the punishment well, but died three weeks later. The death certificate did not link White's death to his flogging, but the clergyman who buried him, who was also a Justice of the Peace, warned the local coroner.

The resultant inquest exposed issues the military authorities would have preferred to have remained hidden. Amongst these were the facts that cavalrymen were flogged by farriers, who were by definition tough, burly men, while infantrymen were flogged by drummers, who were usually less muscular. In justifying the approach taken by his men, Farrier-Major Wilson maintained: 'I give a fair blow. We flog gentler than any other regiment. In the infantry I have seen men receive half-minute strokes to the roll of a drum. That is much more severe punishment.' The notion of such strokes, which would stretch out a man's punishment, was especially offensive to the public. The jury found that White had died from the effects of a severe flogging, and added its 'horror and disgust at the existence of any law among the statutes and regulations of this realm which permits the revolting punishment of flogging to be inflicted on British soldiers . . .'[107] Regulations were changed the following year, and the days of flogging were numbered. But for the soldier of our period it was an ever-present risk, and a punishment which did much to reduce the army's status in the eyes of the society it served. Red coats were one thing, but bloody backs quite another.

VI

FOREIGN FIELDS

CHAIN OF COMMAND

Forces dispatched outside the United Kingdom were placed under command of a general officer formally appointed by the monarch. This gentleman had been selected by the cabinet after recommendation by (and sometimes horse-trading with) the commander-in-chief. Although seniority, as usual, counted for much, this was an area where it was not decisive, because numerous candidates for high command were far too senior. Promotion to major general and above was wholly by seniority, and an officer who reached the rank of lieutenant colonel (by regimental rank or by brevet) would die a general if only he contrived to live long enough: once a general he remained one till he died. Three major generals were promoted lieutenant general in June 1811: all were drawing half-pay as regimental majors, and none had done a day's duty since the American war ended in 1783.

The senior generals on the Army List were as senior in years as rank: in 1808 there was one who had carried his regiment's colours at Culloden 62 years before. There were 518 generals in November 1812, excluding Royal Marines and members of the Royal Family, but only 200 of them were actually employed. In many cases their tasks were scarcely onerous: in 1812 there was one lieutenant general and two major generals who managed to fill their time at Brighton in 1812, and the 27 generals governing and commanding in the West Indies cannot have complained of overwork.

To select the right man to command an expeditionary force the government often chose a comparatively junior officer and invested him with temporary rank. Major General Sir William Howe was given the rank of general after he assumed command in North America: four other major generals stepped up to lieutenant general and seven brigadier generals were advanced to major general. All these new ranks, however, applied 'in America only'. Lieutenant General Sir Arthur Wellesley was so junior when appointed to command in the Peninsula in 1809 that Castlereagh had to struggle to get his appointment through the cabinet. In 1854 Lieutenant General Lord Raglan was given the temporary rank of general to command 'the Forces eastwards of Malta,' though he was to hold his new rank only while so employed. A long and successful campaign would enable a general to inch his way up the Army List, and once he had reached the rank of general a grateful government might, as it did with Wellington and Raglan, appoint him field-marshal, a rank which could not be attained by seniority.

Occasionally the system showed unusual flexibility. Thomas Graham raised the 90th at his own expense in 1794 and gained his colonelcy on the 'raising for rank' principle when he added a second battalion seventeen months later. But he attained this rank so quickly that, under the Duke of York's reforms, it did not count as permanent. It took the dying request of Sir John Moore, who he had served as aide de camp, to gain him promotion to major general with the added concession: 'that you stand among the major generals in the situation you would have held had the lieutenant colonelcy to which you were appointed in February 1794 been a permanent commission.'[1] This gave Graham so much seniority as a major general that he became a lieutenant general just over a year later.

The commander-in-chief was appointed by a 'letter of service', and given instructions by his government. Wellesley, for instance, was warned that: 'The defence of Portugal you will consider the first and most immediate object of your attention.'[2] Lord Newcastle told Raglan that: 'Much must necessarily be left to the exercise of your own judgement and decision on the spot,' but nevertheless stressed that his 'first duty' was to defend Constantinople, and emphasised that no blow struck at the fringes of Russia 'would be so effective for this purpose as the taking of Sevastopol.'[3] These instructions were especially important in an age when communications were lengthy and uncertain. Commanders were often required to act without consulting their government, and until the telegraph was extended to the Crimea in 1855 the latter had no way of changing a commander's orders rapidly: in 1815 Sir Edward Pakenham fought (and was killed) at New Orleans after peace had been signed. It could take a month to cross the Atlantic: HMS *Cerberus* was 34 days out from Spithead when she reached Boston with her trio of major generals – Clinton, Burgoyne, Howe – in 1775. The voyage from Portsmouth to Lisbon lasted some eight days. And the proverbial passage to India might take six months: Major General Wellesley landed in Dover from HMS *Trident* on 10 September 1805, having left Madras on 10 March.

Commanders also needed firm legal and administrative instructions. They were authorised to convene courts-martial, but warned that these had to conform to the Mutiny Act and the Articles of War forwarded by the judge advocate general. In India and North America they could promote, by regimental seniority, to fill vacancies caused by death, but their order-books specified that most promotions were temporary 'till His Majesty's Pleasure be known'. Unfortunately his majesty was not always pleased to ratify a commander's appointments. A general order of Howe's, issued in September 1776, announced that the secretary at war had decided that a recent batch of promotions to posts created by augmentation – that is, newly-created vacancies – was to be superseded by promotions made in London. There must have been some rueful shifting of epaulettes when the order was read out.

The staff officers in a commander's headquarters mirrored those who served the commander-in-chief at Horse Guards. The concept of a chief of staff was unknown in the British army until the close of the period. The quartermaster general (QMG) came closest to it, for his responsibilities included movement, quarters, camps, bivouacs and their defence. The adjutant general (AG) dealt with personnel issues like appointments, transfers and the promulgation of regulations. In the Peninsula, Wellington favoured the QMG, partly because the post's holder for much of the war was Major General George Murray, a far more competent staff officer than Major General Charles Stewart, the AG. Stewart, perhaps trading on his political contacts – he was Castlereagh's half-brother – went so far as to cross Wellington, maintaining that the examination of prisoners of war was nothing to do with the AG. The result was what officers of my generation would call an interview without coffee. 'I was obliged to say that, if he did not at once confess his error, and promise to obey my orders frankly and cordially, I would dismiss him instanter, and send him back to England in arrest,' relates Wellington. 'After a good deal of persuasion he burst out crying, begged my pardon, and hoped I would excuse his intemperance.'[4] In the Crimea, Major General Richard Airey, Raglan's QMG, fulfilled many of the functions of a chief of staff, and his loosely-worded orders bear at least some of the responsibility for launching the Light Brigade down the valley of death.

A commander's two principal staff officers were supported by assistants and deputy assistants: the diarist Thomas Browne was a deputy assistant adjutant general in the Peninsula in 1812–14. All these officers were meant to be on the effective strength of regiments serving in the theatre concerned. There was no obligation for them to have received staff training. Indeed, although there was a rudimentary staff college from 1799, the Senior Department of the Royal Military College, it was not termed the Staff College till late 1857 and took very few students, only 15 in 1858 and 22–23 thereafter. The establishment did not enjoy high repute:

> Regiments were likely to shunt the idle, overtly ambitious or otherwise unwanted officer to Camberley – or at least would not stand in his way – until the Staff College attained such a high reputation that it became rather an honour to have an officer accepted.[5]

Generals had a very strong voice in the appointment of the officers in their headquarters. It fell short of being a controlling interest, however, for Horse Guards sometimes inserted a senior officer in whom it had confidence to hold an inexperienced – or failing – commander's hand, and to replace him if he faltered. In 1807 Wellesley was given command of an expedition against the Danes, with a very steady brigadier called Richard Stewart as his second in command. Wellesley told Croker: 'When the Horse Guards are obliged to employ one of those fellows like me, in whom they have no confidence, they give him what is called a *second in command* – one in whom they do have confidence – a kind of dry nurse.'[6] He paid little attention to Sir Brent Spencer, foisted on him as second in command in the Peninsula, and though he had more regard for Sir Thomas Graham, who succeed Spencer, he never really opened his mind to him. In Raglan's case arrangements were rather different. Growing press criticism of his conduct of the campaign persuaded the government to send out Lieutenant General Sir James Simpson to act in the newly-created post of chief of staff. Both QMG and AG would report to him, and he was to comment on the state of the army not only to Raglan but also to Lord Panmure, Secretary of State for War. When Raglan died shortly afterwards, Simpson took command.

The selection of his military secretary and aides de camp (ADCs) was, in contrast, a matter where a general could do almost as he pleased. These officers were members of his personal staff rather than the army's general headquarters. Many of their duties were purely military: the military secretary dealt with confidential correspondence and assisted his master in the management of his patronage, and the ADCs carried messages and delivered verbal orders on their general's behalf. But others were more personal. They helped arrange everything from ladies to laundry and horses to houses. They were the trusted recipients of confidential information, for the fact that their masters were great men did not prevent them from behaving, at times, like rather ordinary ones. In North America General Howe took up with Elizabeth Lloyd Loring, and the complaisancy of her husband Joshua was encouraged by the fact that he enjoyed a lucrative appointment as commissary of prisoners. All the discretion of the general's well-bred young gentlemen in the matter of domestic arrangements could not prevent the news not so much from leaking, as cascading out. An unnamed 'poet' suggested that

Howe's inactivity during the Philadelphia campaign had warm and
fragrant motives:

> Awake, arouse, Sir Billy,
> There's forage in the plain.
> Ah, leave your little Filly,
> And open the campaign.[7]

The rank of personal staff officers varied. Lord FitzRoy Somerset, the
future Lord Raglan, was appointed Wellington's military secretary on
1 January 1811 as a 22-year-old captain, while Sir John Moore's
senior aide de camp, Colonel Thomas Graham, was 13 years older
than his general. Relatives and the sons of old friends – above all
men with whom the general felt comfortable – were the preferred
choice. Raglan had four relatives as his aides: Major Lord Burghersh
and Captain Poulett Somerset, his nephews, and Captain Nigel Kings-
cote and Lieutenant Somerset Calthorpe, his great nephews. He
added a relative by marriage as assistant military secretary later. In
the Peninsula Lieutenant General 'Daddy' Hill took his brother as
senior ADC, and Major General Andrew Hay had his son.

Some generals liked scamps, brave and competent youngsters
who enjoyed a drink and a good dinner, never stood too much in
awe of them, and provided a relaxing safety-valve. The dashing Harry
Smith of the 95th was too badly wounded, with a ball lodged in his
leg, to do regimental duty, but Sidney Beckwith, his old commanding
officer, then commanding a brigade, asked him: 'Can you be my
ADC?' 'Yes,' replied Smith, 'I can ride and eat.' However, two months
later Smith heard that his old company had lost its captain, and told
Beckwith that he wanted to rejoin it. 'Go and be damned to you,'
said Beckwith, 'but I love you for the desire.' Smith limped off with
an open four-inch wound in his leg, from which the celebrated Staff
Surgeon Morell had tweaked the ball, breaking his forceps in the
process.[8]

Officers like this delivered their orders with more than a little
panache. In 1813 Smith was on the staff of a brigade in the Light
Division, moving up to support the heavily engaged 7th Division at
Vitoria. The 7th Division's commander, Lord Dalhousie, muttered
that he thought that they had better take a village, held by twelve

French guns, and Smith at once galloped off, deaf to the shouts of Dalhousie and his QMG. He found a battalion of the 7th Division and told its commander to support the attack. 'Who are you, sir?' asked the harassed colonel. 'Never mind that,' snapped Smith, 'disobey my Lord's order at your peril.' The village was taken, guns and all.

A new commander, a grenadier temporarily leading one of the Light Division's brigades, ordered the crucial bridge at Vera, the only way a French column could cross the swollen Bidossa, to be held by a picket of an officer and 30 men. Smith, no respecter of persons, warned him frankly: 'We shall repent this before daylight.' The task was given to 2/95th, and Captain Daniel Cadoux, well aware, like so many experienced officers, of what would be likely to happen, offered to take the whole of his company and part of another, and stay with the men himself rather than leave them to a subaltern. When the French attacked, Cadoux and his men held the bridge to the last extremity, but when Cadoux was eventually shot through the head his survivors were forced back and the French crossed with enormous loss: 'such a scene of mortal strife from the fire of fifty men was never witnessed.' 'I wept over his remains with a bursting heart,' wrote Smith, 'as, with his Company who adored him, I consigned to the grave the last external appearance of Daniel Cadoux. His fame can never die.'[9]

But it was not always wise for flamboyant junior officers to use the established principle that they spoke with their general's authority to jolt a sticky commander into activity. Captain Lewis Nolan, 15th Hussars, was ADC to Airey, Raglan's QMG, and he carried the order that initiated the Charge of the Light Brigade. He was briefed by Lord Raglan in person, and sent on his way with the words: 'Tell Lord Lucan the cavalry is to attack immediately!' He hurtled down the escarpment on which Raglan and his staff were situated, and after an altercation with Lucan, apparently pointed out the Russians at the far end of the valley with the words: 'There, my Lord, is your enemy, there are your guns.'

It was in fact Raglan's intention that Lucan should attack Russians which were out of sight of the cavalry in the valley, but Lucan, faced with the convention that Nolan spoke with Raglan's authority, felt compelled to pass on what seemed to him to be an illogical order to Cardigan, commanding the Light Brigade. Cardigan immediately lodged a protest: 'Certainly, sir; but allow me to point out to you that the Russians have a battery in the valley in our front, and batteries and riflemen on each flank.' Lucan agreed. 'I know it,' he replied, 'but Lord Raglan will have it. We have no choice but to obey.[10]

Less flamboyant than aides de camp were 'sketching officers' who accompanied cavalry patrols and sketched the ground: their work did much to compensate for maps which were few in number and generally inaccurate in detail. In January 1775 Frederick MacKenzie wrote that:

> It has been signified to the army that if any Officers of the different Regiments are capable of taking Sketches of a Country. They are to send their names to the Deputy Adjutant general.
>
> I am afraid not many Officers in this Army will be found qualified for this service. It is a branch of military education too little attended or sought after by our Officers, and yet is not only extremely necessary and useful in time of war, but very entertaining and instructive[11]

Sketching officers played a useful role in the Peninsula too, and 'observing officers' pushed deeper, collecting information from inhabitants who were generally hostile to the French. Lieutenant Andrew Leith Hay, working 150 miles behind the lines, even had a proclamation printed and distributed telling the population how the war was really going. He helpfully sent copies to the major French headquarters in Spain. Much useful work was done by Dr Patrick Curtis, rector of the Irish college in Salamanca, described by Tomkinson as 'a superior, quiet sort of person,' who collected information from village *alcades* (mayors) and forwarded it to Wellington. Best known of the observing officers in the Peninsula was Major the Hon Edward Somers Cocks, killed in Wellington's mishandled siege of Burgos in 1812. Wellington always preferred talent with a title to talent without, and the brave, energetic and perceptive young Cocks was one of his favourites: his death affected Wellington deeply. He entered Colonel Frederick Ponsonby's room and paced up and down in silence before he could bring himself to say: 'Cocks is dead.' He was so over-wrought at the funeral that he could not be approached.

The commander and his staff controlled troops who were some-times constituted into regional groupings, as was the case in North America and Indian Mutiny, with His Majesty's Forces in the Caro-linas or the Delhi Field Force, or into divisions which might either be known from the name of their commander or numbered. Conti-nental armies, which existed to fight wars on a far larger scale than the British, adopted the corps organisation during the Napoleonic period, but the corps was not a standard form of British military structure. Wellington formed his army into three corps for the Waterloo campaign, but he fought it in the old way, dealing with it as a single entity and by-passing the corps commanders when it suited him. It was a reflection on the fact that the British army was never really constituted for continental war on a large scale. As late as 1914 the British planned to fight with divisions controlled directly from general headquarters (GHQ), and adopted corps only to con-form with the practice of the French, then their major ally.

Properly-constituted divisions were first used by Wellington. Div-isions of infantry or cavalry, each with their own artillery, were com-manded by lieutenant generals or major generals whose own small staffs reflected higher organisations. Below them came the brigades, groupings of regiments of a single arm. There was no standard organisation for brigades or divisions, but Wellington's army for the Waterloo campaign had two or three brigades per division and three to five battalions per brigade. A divisional commander could expect to command anything between 7,000 (Picton's 5th Division at Waterloo) and 3,000 men (the battered Light Division in the spring of 1813).

There was no consistent policy for the leadership of brigades. They might be commanded by the senior commanding officer of the battalions which comprised them: Colonel Sir William Myers of 7th Fusiliers commanded the Fusilier brigade at Albuera. They might be commanded by a brigadier, or indeed by a major general: Cardi-gan headed the Light Brigade as such. The rank of brigadier or brigadier general (terminology varied with time) was not substantive.

If its holder did not achieve promotion by seniority during the campaign, he would crash back down amongst the colonels or lieutenant colonels when it ended. Brigadier Shelton, unkindly but accurately described by Captain George Lawrence as 'having incapacity written on every feature of his face' did not have a happy time in Afghanistan in 1842, and when the campaign ended he reverted to command the 44th.[12] He might yet have made his way by seniority, but was killed by a fall from his horse in 1845.

A well-regarded brigadier might gain in death the status which had eluded him in life. When the brave and popular Brigadier the Hon Adrian Hope was killed in a headstrong attack on a mud-walled fort in India in 1858 he was accorded the funeral of a general officer:

> The whole division being present on foot – and even the sick and wounded who could walk stole away from the field hospitals to be present. The massed bands of the three Highland regiments played the Dead March, being relieved by the pipers of the three regiments playing 'Lochaber no More' and 'The Flowers of the Forest.' . . . the procession was very imposing, and the wailing of the bagpipes, alternating with the solemn strains of the Dead March was most impressive. Each Highland regiment having its own Presbyterian chaplain, the Rev Mr. Ross, Presbyterian Chaplain of the 42nd Highlanders, read the 90th Psalm, and the Rev. Mr. Cowie, Episcopalian chaplain to the division, the Church of England service. There was hardly a dry eye in that large assemblage.[13]

A brigade commander was assisted, or sometimes steered, by his brigade major. The Hon Henry Clifford was ADC to 'Gentlemanly George' Buller in the Crimea, and shared a tent with the brigade major. They had one of the least talented of the brigadiers, which may have contributed to Clifford's generally low opinion of the conduct of the campaign. He wrote that the Alma, for example, had been won by 'nothing but Bull-Dog Courage and go-ahead bravery . . .'[14] Brigade majors were a key link in the chain of command, for while brigade commanders might be briefed for specific operations, it was the brigade majors ('majors of brigade' to the army in North America) who attended divisional headquarters on a daily basis, taking down in writing the orders which the divisions had received from general headquarters, and passing them on to regimental adjutants.

The stately hierarchy of order books, all kept in a big round copper-plate hands that look surprisingly similar, shows how information on such things as promotions, courts-martial, the timings of major moves, instructions on dress and transport filtered down the chain, starting as general orders and ending by being read out at battalion muster parades. In 1813 William Keep complained that his captain observed 'ridiculous punctilio' in obeying general orders. No sooner was there an order from Wellington that the men's knapsacks should be inspected for unnecessary articles than he began 'to trouble the men by an examination of their packs, often when tired and falling asleep . . .'[15]

No less important were what we would now call passwords, but were then known as paroles and countersigns. These changed daily, applied to the whole force, and were listed in general orders. In North America in late August 1776, for example, they included London and Fontenoy, Guildford and Courtray, Petersfield and Lisle, with the staff officer responsible clearly trying to link towns in England and the Low Counties and so give his audience some crutch for their two-in-the-morning memory. A general who wished to check the progress of his orders could do so simply enough by asking a private soldier what the parole was. If, that is, he could do so safely. In October 1854 Henry Clifford took his divisional commander, Lieutenant General Sir George Brown, along the lines at night, and the pickets of the 19th Foot fired on them without challenging, putting one bullet through Clifford's coat and sending another whining off his sword-hilt. The picket was in error, and Clifford let them know it:

> 'Well, I *am* ashamed to think you English soldiers should behave in such a way, fire without challenging and in such confusion. I should like to give you all 50 lashes, your officer at your head.' . . . They were all in a pretty state of fear, and the Officer (a young Captain who had never been on service before, and his men all young soldiers) was on his post, as pale as death. Sir George and the other

two officers came up, *Thank God* unhurt ... About 30 or 40 shots were fired at us, so you may think our escape was indeed providential ... To my surprise Sir George, who is not very nice in his language when in a rage to my astonishment said nothing, but ordered the officer, more dead than alive, to move down to the ground he ought to have occupied ...[16]

A generation earlier, Thomas Morris, fast asleep on sentry duty at Stralsund in the Baltic, awoke just in time (thanks to an enormous lion which sprang on him in a dream) to give the proper challenge to 'grand rounds' – the field officer of the day and his orderly sergeant.

'Who comes there?' and 'The Grand Round' was the reply. I demanded 'Stand fast, Grand Round; advance sergeant, and give the countersign.' The sergeant advanced a few paces, pronounced the mystic word, and I called out: 'Pass on, Grand Round; all's well!'[17]

Major General Sir Stapleton Cotton, riding into the British lines at Samalanca in 1812, failed to respond to the challenge of an alert two-man sentry post. The sentries fired, and knocked over both Cotton and his orderly dragoon: it was reckoned 'somewhat singular,' given the inaccuracy of musket-fire at night, that both shots should take effect. But it was clearly Cotton's fault, for the sentries had challenged as they should. More than a century later an experienced infantry officer called the risk of being shot by friendly sentries 'a hazard inseparable from war' and it was certainly so in the 18th and 19th centuries: perhaps the most distinguished victim of friendly fire was the Confederate general Stonewall Jackson, mortally wounded on the evening of his greatest triumph at Chancellorsville in 1863.

Throughout the period headquarters was generally written as two words, for that is what it was: the most important of the quarters occupied by an army. Although senior commanders might operate under canvas, they were usually quartered in a private house in town or country, with enough room for staff officers, servants and grooms in the building itself or close nearby, and adequate stabling for the many horses. Generals usually had a small cavalry escort, billeted nearby, which provided local protection and supplied 'orderly dragoons' for the transmission of orders which did not need to go by the hand of ADC. This process was not without its hazards: in 1808 an orderly dragoon carrying an important order got drunk and lost it, consigning a division to two days' unnecessary marching. Operations were often largely seasonal, for it was difficult to move far in winter when there was little forage to be had. Not for nothing does March, when the campaigning season traditionally opened, take its name from the Roman god of war. With his army in winter quarters, a general might make a point of entertaining widely. John Peebles, not a major figure in the chain of command, was entertained at least six times by Clinton when he was commander-in-chief in North America, four times by Cornwallis, and once or more by six other generals. Cornwallis's informal dinners were summed up by Peebles as 'ease and politeness'. Clinton was also a charming host, although on the last occasion Peebles met him he was anxious to emphasise that he was not to blame for Cornwallis's presence at Yorktown.

Wellington was famously informal. He worked from a large marquee, which did duty as sitting and dining room and also enclosed the small tent in which he slept. His cook, James Thornton, operated from a dug-out kitchen topped by a tarpaulin. This could not cope with heavy rain, which reduced the staff to 'cold meat and bread'. When Wellington was on the move this was his staple diet in any event. His Spanish liaison officer, Miguel de Alava, always made a point of asking, before retiring for the night, what time the staff were to move in the morning and what was for dinner: he grew to dread the reply: 'At daylight. Cold meat.'

In more settled times Wellington dined at five or six, never alone or simply with his staff, for any visitors, as well as commanding officers of nearby regiments, were also invited. Thomas Browne thought that: 'The cook was a good one & the wine principally furnished by the Guerrillas . . . & his guests might take as much of it as they pleased.'[18] George Gleig found: 'The conversation . . . most interesting and lively. The Duke himself spoke out upon all subjects with an absence of reserve which sometimes surprised his guests . . . He was rich in anecdote, most of them taking a ludicrous turn, and without any apparent effort put the company very much at their ease.'[19] Wellington was an early riser, with a belief in doing 'the day's work in the day', and so never lingered over dinner, but called for coffee at about 8.30 and guests left as soon as they had drunk it. He would then work for an hour before retiring to change his linen and boots and lie down on 'a sort of Russia leather bed on iron legs' whence he could spring, fully dressed, if he was summoned during the night.

When the army was on the move staff officers dossed down where they could, sometimes being 'regularly billeted' on the inhabitants but often making their own arrangements. In Ciudad Rodrigo Captain Browne entered a priest's house, and told him, in Spanish: 'Hulloa my friend, tumble up, I am cold & wet & hungry – make a good fire – lend me a shirt – give me some meat, & let me lie down in your place.' After due protest the priest cooked him an omelette, much enjoyed despite 'the quantity of garlic that had entered into its composition' and Browne retired to bed in a borrowed shirt with his wet clothes steaming in front of the fire.'[20] On the way to Salamanca the officers of the AG's branch were all billeted in a village church.

> Our horses had entered the Church with ourselves as a
> matter of course. We were seated under an image of the
> Virgin Mary before which a lamp was burning. Our table
> was the Bier, on which the garment of a Priest was spread
> for table cloth, our chairs were the flag stones, which as
> the bier was low, was no inconvenience. Our Canteens &
> tins of grog were before us on this table.[21]

The group was congratulating itself on its comfortable situation when the ADC to Sir Stapleton Cotton, commanding the cavalry, arrived with the unwelcome news that his general required the church as nowhere else could be found. Browne and his comrades duly turned out, not without grumbling, into the dark and drizzly night, and evicted some Spanish muleteers from their places near a fire by the church wall: 'We were soon rolled up in our cloaks and fast asleep.' They were up before first light, looking for the French.

Conditions were a good deal more spartan in the Crimea. W. H.

Russell reported that: 'The oldest soldiers never witnessed nor heard of a campaign in which general officers were obliged to live out in tents in the open field for want of a roof to cover them . . .'[22] Buller's tent blew down in the great storm of 11 November 1854, and Clifford found him 'floundering like a rabbit in a net, the tent on top of him.' By the time Clifford and the brigade major had re-erected the tent, the brigadier was 'so cold he could not stand'. Clifford thought that the conditions were too much for anyone over 50, and indeed some had responded by selling their commissions and going home. 'I look upon it as a duty,' he wrote. 'Every man out here is bound to hold out and exert all his powers, to put up with the great hardships and privations we have to undergo, and to a man hold out to the last.'[23] The brigadier himself was not least amongst Clifford's own hardships.

> 'Clifford! Clifford!' 'Coming Sir! Coming!' 'Do you hear anything like Gunwheels?' 'No, Sir! It is a Commissariat mule-wagon coming up from Balaclava' or 'where is that firing? Is it on *our* front with our Picquets?' 'No, Sir, it is in front of the French' or 'what is that noise I hear like horses galloping?' 'Oh Sir, it is the rain falling on your marquee.'[24]

Even Raglan was not sumptuously housed. He lived in an abandoned farmhouse four miles from Balaclava, working, sleeping and eventually dying in a single room with Airey, the QMG, next door and the rest of the staff in other farm-buildings or outhouses.

Although generals and their staffs lived more comfortably than the men they commanded, they shared the soldier's risks on the day of battle. They were usually within artillery range of the enemy. Wellington thought it ungentlemanly to fire on individuals, and prevented a gunner officer (rash enough to ask permission) from shooting at Napoleon at Waterloo, although one of his howitzer shells seriously wounded his opponent, Marmont, at Salamanca. Wolfe was killed by musketry at Quebec, and Howe survived it by a miracle at Bunker Hill, where he led the infantry attack and emerged with his gaiters spattered with other men's blood. Moore was mortally wounded by a roundshot at Corunna. Major General 'Black Bob'

Craufurd of the Light Division was hit in the spine by a musket-ball at Ciudad Rodrigo and took a week to die, apologising to Wellington for having been one of the 'croakers' who had complained to influential friends in England about the poor progress of the campaign. 'Craufurd talked to me as they do in a novel,' said Wellington later.[25]

Waterloo winnowed Wellington's senior commanders and staff officers. The Prince of Orange, as plucky as he was unpopular, was badly wounded. Picton, who had begged Wellington not to take him on the Waterloo campaign because his nerves were shattered, was shot through the head in front of his division, cursing to the last. Lieutenant General Sir George Cooke of 1st Division was severely wounded. Lord Uxbridge, commanding the cavalry, lost a leg and survived: Colonel Sir Alexander Gordon, the duke's senior ADC, did not. The American-born acting QMG, Sir William De Lancey, whose anxious wife was waiting in Antwerp, was mortally wounded at Wellington's side. Fitz Roy Somerset, his military secretary, lost an arm.

Major General Sir Robert Sale, hero of the 1842 siege of Jellalabad, was killed at Mudki in 1845. At Balaclava Cardigan rode through gusts of canister into the Russian guns. He considered it 'no part of the duties of a general officer to fight the enemy amongst private soldiers,' but would have felt it wrong not to share their risks. At Inkerman, Lieutenant General Sir George Cathcart of 4th Division was killed in the thick of the fighting with the famous last words: 'We are in mess. We must try the bayonet.' White-haired Major General Strangways, commanding the Royal Artillery in the same battle, lost his leg to a roundshot and said to his staff, with exquisite courtesy: 'Would someone have the kindness to help me off my horse?' Told that death was inevitable, he asked to die amongst his gunners. Generals were no safer in the Mutiny. Three successive commanders in chief died of cholera. Wheeler perished in the shambles at Cawnpore, John Nicholson fell sword in hand in the streets of Delhi, Henry Lawrence died painfully in besieged Lucknow and Henry Havelock succumbed to disease after relieving the place. The generals of the age of horse and musket were many things: but they were not, as they themselves would have put it, shy.

THE TROOPER'S
ON THE TIDE

REGIMENTS WARNED for service overseas brought their manpower up to strength as best they could, with drafts from second battalions and the militia, and last-minute recruiting. William Surtees, then in the light company of the 56th Foot, waited in camp on Barham Downs to embark for the Helder with 'the skeleton of our regiment' fleshed out with recruits and militiamen: 'we were all young, and impassioned in the highest degree, and discipline, as might be expected, was far from good.'[26] Regiments marched to their port of embarkation, usually Liverpool, Portsmouth, Southampton and Dover for troops in England, Leith or Greenock for those in Scotland and Queenstown and Cork for those in Ireland. The last leg of the march was done in style, band playing and colours flying. The 7th Fusiliers left Winchester for Portsmouth to embark for the Crimea, 'nearly the whole of the good people of that town marching with us.' The inhabitants of Portsmouth, 'a warm-hearted set,' were no less enthusiastic, and 'with one tremendous cheer we passed on into the dockyard.'[27]

Some youngsters were anxious to cut a figure. Second Lieutenant John Kincaid of 2/95th marched down to Deal to embark for Walcheren in 1809, eager 'to impress the minds of the natives with a suitable notion of the magnitude of my importance by carrying a

345

donkey-load of pistols in my belt and screwing my naturally placid countenance up to a pitch of ferocity beyond what it was calculated to bear.'[28] Like many of his comrades, Surtees had never seen the sea before, and wrote that he would never forget the effect that the sight of it 'and such a number of ships of various sizes and descriptions' had upon him.[29] When William Wheeler set off for Holland in 1809 he was 'in high glee' at the prospect of embarkation, all the more so because the kindly Lieutenant Colonel Mainwaring did not confine the men to barracks before they sailed, as was the custom. Instead, 'the gates were thrown wide open so that the good soldier might make merry and enjoy himself . . . The confidence reposed in us was not in one single instance abused, not one man having deserted.'[30] In the same year Captain Brown of the 77th Regiment, left behind on recruiting duties, gained permission to join his regiment and 'at great expense hired a boat to follow us, and when out at sea we were surprised to be hailed by it, and find that Brown was on board. We took him in and he accompanied us.'[31]

The heart-rending business of selecting the wives who would be allowed to accompany their menfolk might take place on the quay, but wise commanding officers would have seen to this sooner. Sometimes old or unfit officers and men were left behind, formed into an invalid company. In 1808 the 24th, on its way to Martinique, left behind 'Captain Cortlandt, who was married, Lieutenant Griffith, who was an old and infirm subaltern, and Lieut. Treeve, who was just recovering from a severe indisposition.'[32] Regiments were often seen off by their colonels or local dignitaries, and we should not, from our cynical viewpoint, underestimate the importance of this. When the 93rd left for China in 1857 (because there was no telegraph to India they had no idea that the Mutiny had broken out) Queen Victoria and Prince Albert visited Southampton docks. What Gordon-Alexander called 'this gracious and kindly leave-taking' made a great impression on the soldiers, and the words 'I'm thinking the Queen'll be proud of this day's work' were often used as the highlanders hewed their way across history in India.[33]

Men might be embarked on warships, hired transports or, by the 1840s, HM troopships. Large vessels could take a whole battalion, but sometimes men were spread about smaller ships in company groups. The fleet with which Peebles sailed from Greenock to New York in 1776 was divided into two squadrons, one for the 42nd and one for Fraser's Highlanders. 'Eleven ships for our Regt & double that number for Frasers two battalions, and one The Globe for an hospital ship for both Regts.'[34] Transports were armed with two guns apiece in case of attack by American privateers, and companies rehearsed forming up their men in alarm stations, using their rolled hammocks as breastworks. The 16th Light Dragoons made the much shorter crossing from Ramsgate to Ostend in 1815 in small colliers, each holding from ten to 35 horses. William Wheeler sailed for Holland aboard HMS *L'Impetueux*, which he reached by way of a cutter:

> It being the first time I was ever on salty water nothing could be more pleasant; our little cutter skimmed over the waves like a seagull. I had not the least symptom of sea sickness; never did I pass so agreeable a morning. I was on deck at daybrake. We were running close under the land; it was quite a fairy scene. The only thing that disturbed my mind was that I had entered the army. I would have given the world to have been a sailor.[35]

He was less comfortable when he reached the warship, crammed full of officers and men of the 51st Regiment. When a gun was fired to order the troops to turn in:

> I descended the main hatchway, all was darkness, and the deck completely covered with troops. The first step I took off the slips was on some ones leg, the second on an Irishman's face, who swore by – that some tundering tief had murdered him, I made another stride and found that there was nothing but living bodies to walk on . . .[36]

Unfortunately the decks had been newly caulked, and many soldiers found themselves stuck in the pitch. 'It was a fine treat for the blue jackets to see all the lobsters stuck fast on the decks,' recalled Wheeler.

A Guards private who sailed to the Low Counties in 1708 was being rhetorical when he described his voyage as: 'continued destruction in the foretops, the pox above-board, the plague between decks, hell in the forecastle and the devil at the helm.'[37] Nevertheless, disease flourished aboard overcrowded vessels, and a shocking 11 per cent of the men of twelve regiments sent from Great Britain to the West Indies in 1776–1780 died in passage. Soldiers and sailors often fought, their antipathy fostered by traditional friction between 'lobsters' and 'blue bottles', and worsened, like much else, by drink. John Kincaid had just settled into a hammock slung above a companion-way when a marine officer appeared 'and abused his sentry, for not seeing the lights out below, according to orders.' The sentry was replying that the midshipmen would not put them out for him, when the head of one of the culprits, 'illuminated in a red nightcap' appeared, and joined the debate. 'Damn you, Sir, who are you?' asked the marine officer. 'And damn and blast you, Sir, who are you?' responded the midshipman.[38]

There were frequent accidents. Browne's ship was struck by lightning, one man was killed, another had to be discharged as an idiot, and Browne himself, his left arm and breast, given 'a curious shrivelled appearance' had to be rubbed with spirits.[39] Men were often seasick. No sooner were the 7th Fusiliers out of the Solent, bound for the Crimea, than 'some of our fellows appeared as if one good man could beat a dozen of them; they looked in a most pitiable plight. They had not brought their sea legs with them . . .'[40] When the P&O steamship *Himalaya* left Queenstown for the Crimea with the 5th Dragoon Guards aboard the officers began a good dinner but speedily left the table. Only two of them were not ill, and they worked with the few fit soldiers to help the horses cope with the rough weather.

> We . . . were constantly going round the horses tying them
> shorter, and putting those on their legs who had fallen
> from the rough sea and the wet decks. Some got their
> forefeet over the boxes, and we pushed them back by main
> force, for if they had got loose on deck, someone must
> have been hurt. They were actually screaming with fright,
> the canvas covering their heads was cracked by the wind,
> and by flicking them made them much worse. Two horses
> that fell next to each other gave us much trouble, and at
> last we had to cut them out of their boxes, and drag them
> on deck before they could get up.[41]

Sergeant Major Loy Smith was luckier, for his transport left the Downs in fine weather, and soon found itself in company with another containing 3rd Field Battery Royal Artillery. Trumpeters exchanged calls, and the men exchanged three cheers for each other's regiments. Then gunners sent up a rocket, lit a portfire, and sang 'Rule Britannia': the 11th Hussars replied with 'Cheer Boys Cheer.' They were all 'as happy as men could be.'[42]

Loy Smith eventually reached Varna after 'a most delightful voyage of six weeks.' Not only were few voyages quite this pleasant, but many were simply disastrous. Shipwreck imposed a steady drain on manpower. Sometimes it was on a small scale: the 24th Foot lost its grenadier company and band on the way back from Holland in 1796. And sometimes it was on a much greater scale. Over half the 8,200 men sent from Torbay to Spain in 1706 were lost at sea, and in September 1780 the governor of Barbados reported the total loss of his transports and hospital ships in a hurricane.

It is the individual tragedies that catch the eye. In 1816 the transport *Seahorse* was lost off Ireland with 12 officers, 246 men, 71 women and children and 16 of her crew. The best-reported shipwreck of the age was the loss of HM Troopship *Birkenhead* off southwest Africa on 26 February 1852. She was carrying reinforcements and families to the Kaffir War, and had about 638 souls on board. Her master, anxious to complete the journey as quickly as possible, was hugging the coast in calm seas. Off Cape Danger he struck a submerged rock, and the vessel began to sink. The troops were paraded on deck, and those not required to man the pumps or help the families aboard the boats stood steady in rank and file as the ship went down by the head. When the boats were away and the master ordered 'Every man for himself,' Captain Wright of the 91st and Lieutenant Girardot of the 43rd addressed the men, saying that if they swam for the boats they would surely swamp them. The men stood fast. Colour Sergeant John O'Neill of the 91st called it 'simple obedience of orders, standing on deck and slowly sinking, while the women and children got safely away in the boats . . .' Over a hundred of the soldiers eventually got ashore 'after a long and perilous swim 'midst sharks, breakers and seaweeds . . .'

Those fortunate enough to arrive safely were confronted by a world which most of them found unfamiliar, for this was an age when overseas travel was the preserve of the rich. Georgian New England was redolent of home. Granville Evelyn, writing from Boston, thought that: 'This country is very fine, the climate wholesome, and we are all in good health and spirits, and we get plenty of turtle, pineapples and Madeira.' If only 'the good people of this place' did not 'prevent us from getting our quarters, and . . . forbidding all labourers and artificers to work for us . . .' life might indeed have been pleasant.[43] Peebles had already served in North America and had many American friends. The church at Newport Rhode Island was 'very neat . . . with a handsome organ the Gift of Dr Berkley Bishop of Cloyne . . .' Even the local madam, 'Miss Sal Leak' was 'spoke of by everybody in town in a favourable manner for one of her Profession, a well look'd girl about 30 . . .'[44]

India provided the sharpest of shocks. Passengers landing at Madras came ashore in surf-boats, carried the last few yards by the fishermen who manned them or, especially if they were young, female and attractive, by officers from the garrison who turned out to bear a chivalrous hand. Disembarkation at Bombay or Calcutta was more conventional, but many found, like John Pearman, who landed in 1845, that they spent an uneasy first night because of the heat and the noise of the jackals. Robert Waterfield thought that:

> The bustle attendant on a European camp in India was something strange to us all. The constant jabbering of the natives, and the roaring of the camels, together with the elephants and the buffaloes reminds one of the striking contrast there is between India and peaceful England. It's an old saying that there's no stopping a woman's tongue, but the women of Bengal beat all I ever saw, for they will fight, and keep up such a chattering that they may be heard above the din of the Camp.[45]

The British brought dins of their own. The piper of Lieutenant Innes Munro's company of the 73rd Highlanders was not only popular with soldiers and Indians, but attracted large numbers of snakes, which could be 'discovered . . . dancing round his feet while he entertained the soldiers with a few Highland reels.'[46]

Europeans too easily assumed superiority over 'natives'. The servant of a seventeenth-century Englishman Sir Thomas Roe swaggered up to a Mughal nobleman with the cheery greeting 'How now, thou heathen dog?' and at the Mughal court at Delhi Sir Thomas's valet became involved in an affair which his employer referred to in his diary, crossly but evasively, as 'Jones His Lewdnesse'.[47] This sort of conduct set the pattern for much of what followed, although there were many who recognised that their own behaviour rendered them objects of quiet derision. Innes Munro discovered that:

> As Europeans eat any kind of meat, the Indians have been induced to rank them in the 'pariar'[sic] or lowest class of people, and the Gentoos or Malabars tell you that they are obliged of necessity to serve us, they consider themselves of a much more dignified and gentlemanly rank in life than any European. If you should ask a common cooly or porter what cast he is of, he will answer 'the same as master, pariar cast.'[48]

Lieutenant-Fireworker James Wood (holding what was then the lowest commissioned rank in the Royal Artillery) arrived in Bombay on 30 November 1755 after a journey of, as he meticulously recorded in his journal, 15,746 miles which had taken 254 days to complete. He saw many strange sights, not least of them the 'Towers of Silence' on Malabar Hill, where the Parsees exposed their dead to be eaten by birds of prey.

> Nothing can be more shocking than a view of their dead bodies, loathsome and discoloured, some yellow, others green, some with their eyes torn out, some with the flesh torn off their cheeks, holes eaten in several parts of their bodies and their flesh torn off their bones. Some of their skins are hardened by the sun like tanned leather and others picked clean by the vultures etc.

He found the local religions riddled with 'many absurdities'.

> Some of their Brahmins (Gentoo Priets) sit at their pagodas (their place of worship) all day long throwing ashes every now and then over their bodies; one in particular sitting quite naked under the shade of a tree with a

hole bored through the skin of his privy member with a
large ring fixed in the hole. The fellow was much revered
by the married women who prostrate themselves before
him, and take hold of the member devoutly in their hand
and kiss it, while the owner strokes their heads muttering
some prayer for their purification etc[49]

The prevalence and swift onset of disease were shocking. Wood's
journal is punctuated by deaths of his brother officers. On Sunday
29 February 1756 he wrote:

> This morning Lieutenant Bennet of the Company's artil-
> lery died. He was buried in the afternoon. Minute guns
> were fired on his being carried to the grave. Mr Newman,
> Volunteer, was made a lieutenant in his vacancy, by
> Colonel Clive.[50]

A week later he reported 'our men dying very fast with smallpox,'
and by 1 September the three companies of artillery that had landed
the previous November had lost 70 dead, about a quarter of their
strength.

Things improved little over the next century. 'William West of
ours was taken with cholera and died in a few hours,' wrote John
Pearman of the 53rd Foot in 1845, 'and one of the 80th Foot, his
wife and baby, all died in twelve hours, of cholera.'[51] There was
precious little dignity to burial, which was often all too temporary.
The 3rd Light Dragoons were marching a day behind the 53rd and
reached a grove of mango trees where one of the infantrymen had
been buried, 'but the jackals had taken the trouble to get him up
and pick his bones. His head was off his body, and the flesh eaten
off.'[52] In June 1847 Robert Waterfield noted: 'Thermometer 88-90.
Weather continues intensely hot, men crowding the hospital,
numbers die of apoplexy. The intemperate by no means suffer as
one would imagine.'[53]

Acclimatisation was little help. The men of Richard Barter's 75th
were old India hands, but cholera ran through them like flame. On
the way to Delhi, Barter was talking to Captain Dunbar of No.2
Company when the 'smart painstaking young soldier' Lance Corporal Sweeny arrived to report that two men of the company were

dead of cholera and were to be buried at 6.00pm. When Dunbar returned from the funeral, Barter said: 'So there are two more of the old company gone.' Dunbar replied 'Ah! Yes, three more; I buried poor Sweeny with the other two.'[54]

Portugal and Spain presented fewer shocks, although John Aitchison felt obliged to tell his father that 'Spain is by no means like Scotland; and its situation cannot be compared to the situation of our country in the time of the Bruce.'[55] They too contained some unwelcome fauna. John Spencer Cooper's regiment halted for the night near Oropesa, and he recorded that:

> On our march to this place one of the 3rd, or Old Buffs, was stung by a scorpion in the head, and died in consequence. Also, a man of our company, named John Barber, marched a league with a snake in his dress cap. It had crept in during the night . . .[56]

William Wheeler reported that eastern Portugal abounded with:

> lizards of various sorts, some are very beautiful . . . It is curious if a man lies down several of these will come round him, always keeping at a humble distance; they will raise themselves up on their fore feet and stretch up their necks and watch him; if he moves they will scamper away in all directions.[57]

It took time to adjust to the harsh and unfamiliar landscape. William Tomkinson looked back with amusement at his first experience of bivouacking, in 1809.

> This was an event much thought of, and every officer was employed in bringing into use the various inventions recommended in England for such occasions, many of which were found useless, and, again, many essentials had been left behind, from a determination to face the campaign with the fewest number of comforts, whereby many requisites were omitted which were now found indispensable . . . Our surprise at hearing the noise made by the frogs was very great, but quite common in Portugal.[58]

Summers were hot and the winters cold. In May 1811 John Mills of the Coldstream found his first battle, Fuentes de Onōro, so hot that 'in between the firing lemonade was sold.' But the nights were still cold, and his first attempt at building a hut was 'a mistake in architecture' as its entrance faced the prevailing wind. He told his mother that he was 'tanned to the colour of a dark boot top, and my hands from not wearing gloves to two degrees darker than mahogany.'[59] Many officers and men took to holding a leaf between their teeth to shade the lower lip, which otherwise swelled up and burst in the heat. In high summer it was as well to avoid unnecessary movement. 'The evenings, from the heat of the weather, were the pleasantest part of the day,' recalled Tomkinson:

> And at first we did not lie down as soon as we ought, considering the early hour we turned out. We soon learnt to sleep in the day, or at any time – never undressed – and at night all the horses were bridled up, the men sleeping at their heads, and the officers of each troop close to their horses altogether.[60]

There were frequent complaints about the grubbiness of houses and their occupants. Given the state of affairs in Britain at the time this is condemnation indeed, although it no doubt reflects the fact that officers were reduced to living in the sort of accommodation they would never have experienced at home. It was, however, a sergeant who described Lisbon as 'a dung hill from end to end,' and Corporal William Wheeler who thought that the Portuguese were an 'ignorant superstitious, priest-ridden, dirty, lousy set of poor Devils' and their capital a 'dirty stinking City.'[61] Aitchison lamented that in Lisbon the men lived in barracks and 'the officers are billeted, but in such houses that the lowest servant in England would object to.'[62] In 1812 Captain William Webber of the Royal Artillery was happy enough with his billet in a wine merchant's house at Navalmoral, but made the mistake of wandering into the cellar to see grapes being pressed. 'Several baskets of them are thrown into a large tub,' he wrote 'and a dirty fellow with his feet and legs bare, and actually covered with sores unhealed, was treading them and actually extracting the juice which we drink with so much avidity.'[63]

Although the Roman Catholic Relief Act of 1791 had removed some restrictions on catholics, most did not disappear till a broader act of 1829. In the interim, however, several Roman Catholic Officers were able to serve because each session of parliament passed an Indemnifying Act which enabled them to avoid taking oaths which their beliefs would have prohibited. The Irishman Edward Stack, who had actually fought against the British as a French officer in the American war, was even promoted major general in 1808 after declaring that he was 'of the religion that makes general officers.' There were infinitely more Roman Catholics amongst the rank and file, but the army was, broadly, of Protestant beliefs, with a growing number of earnest Methodists.

It is small wonder that many commentators were struck by the prevalence of priests and friars in the Peninsula. Officers commented on the fact that they seemed better fed than the rest of the population, and a surgeon traced, we know not how, nine-tenths of seductions to the clergy. Officers and men alike were drawn to nunneries like moths to a flame. In September 1812 Webber found 'the largest nunnery I ever saw' in Toledo, whose occupants 'were kissing and waving their hands to us and seemed anxious to be liberated from their confinement.' He found it 'a shameful, ridiculous thing that under mistaken notions of religion many poor girls are debarred the only comforts the world can bestow.'[64] Dan Mackinnon of the Coldstream Guards was a notorious practical joker: the great Grimaldi said that if Mackinnon ever donned the clown's costume he would totally eclipse him. Hearing that Wellington was to visit a convent, he got there first and, having shaved off his whiskers, disguised himself as a nun, and peered gravely at his commander-in-chief. Gronow, the source of the tale, suggests that Mackinnon's interest in nuns went rather deeper than merry japes.

Wellington was anxious to avert religious friction. He ordered his men not to enter churches except for the purpose of attending services, though he maintained that none actually did so. 'I have never seen one soldier perform any one act of worship in these Roman Catholic countries,' he affirmed, 'excepting making the sign of the Cross to induce the people of the country to give them wine.'[65] Soldiers who stole from churches were likely to hang for it. 'The two men of the 4th Dragoon Guards who were hung in Leira this day,' wrote Tomkinson on 4 October 1810, 'were caught in a chapel plundering by Lord Wellington.'[66] A soldier of 7th Fusiliers was flogged for stealing two candlesticks from a church. His back festered: John Spencer Cooper saw it 'full of matter, in which were a number of black-headed maggots striving to hide themselves.'[67]

There was a strong thread of Freemasonry in Wellington's army, and in 1810 there was a serious disturbance in Lisbon when British Freemasons had a procession. Wellington immediately issued a general order forbidding: 'an amusement which, however innocent in itself, and allowed by the law of Great Britain, is a violation of the law of this country, and very disagreeable to the people.'[68] Wellington had no misgivings about attending Roman Catholic services himself: on 25 June 1812 he and his staff attended a Te Deum for the victory of Salamanca in its cathedral.

THE PAINFUL FIELD

THROUGHOUT THE PERIOD battle was the exception rather than the rule, and even on active service a man might spend a hundred days marching or waiting for every one spent fighting. Although the procedure for routine marches – say from Lisbon up into Spain, or along the Grand Trunk Road, the umbilical cord of central India – varied, the principle was clear. Regiments, marching along routes outlined by headquarters and usually prescribed in detail by divisions or brigades, would reach their night's halt only after it had been identified by an advanced party, and company locations had been marked out. Regiments generally sent an officer 24 hours ahead of the main body to have its camp-site or quarters pointed out to him by the QMG's staff. Another officer set off early in the morning and rode to meet his comrade, who briefed him on details of accommodation before setting off for the next halt, where he would again receive instructions. Regimental main bodies were preceded by one camp colourman per company, equipped with small camp colours which told company commanders where their men were to halt. Commissaries and butchers were also expected to reach the campsite before the regiment so that cattle would be slaughtered and provisions ready to hand over to quartermasters as they arrived.

When things went according to plan, regiments crossed the land-scape like torrents of well-drilled soldier ants. They first marched to attention, keeping step and dressing until told to march at ease. Straggling was forbidden: a man who wished to fall out to attend to a call of nature had to obtain a ticket from his company commander, and ticketless stragglers risked flogging at the end of the day. In the Peninsula the Light Brigade and its successor the Light Division, kept under the strictest of discipline by Robert Craufurd, would not tolerate women coming up to join the men, but elsewhere wives often came forward from the baggage to help their man with his musket or pack. On the retreat from Corunna tough little Mrs Skiddy – 'as broad as a turtle' – carried the knapsack and musket of her ailing husband Private Donald Skiddy of the 34thFoot, and sometimes even shouldered him.

Officers enjoyed a more liberal existence. Even infantry subalterns, who were not strictly speaking entitled to horses, often rode on the line of march. In 1810 Ensign John Mills, who was clearly exceptionally comfortable for one of his rank, told his parents that his stud consisted of:

> a horse, Docktail, who was taken from the French at Sala-
> monde – a great favourite. Two mule mares – Bess and
> Jenny. Both are very quiet. A small he mule, Turpin; a
> rogue, he carries William. More mules carry the baggage
> and I ride Docktail. My servants consist of William, a pri-
> vate servant, Duckworth, a soldier servant who looks after
> the animals, Joseph, a Portuguese boy under him.[69]

The Light Division halted for five minutes every hour, trying to align its halts with the presence of streams so that the men could fill their canteens.

When men reached their appointed bivouac site they set to work making themselves comfortable.

> Let their feelings of fatigue be great or small, they are no
> sooner suffered to leave the ranks than every man rushes
> to secure whatever comforts the neighbourhood affords
> as likely to contribute to his comforts for the night. Swords
> [sword-bayonets – our informant is a Rifleman] hatchets
> and bill-hooks are to be seen hewing and hacking at every
> tree and bush within reach – huts are quickly reared, fires

are quickly blazing, and while the camp kettle is boiling,
or the pound of beef frying, the tired and happy souls are
found toasting their toes around the cheerful blaze until
the fire has done the needful, when they fall on like men.
The meal finished, they arrange their accoutrements for
any emergency, when they dispose themselves for rest.[70]

On the march the officers messed by companies, and while one
would attend battalion headquarters for orders, another would see
if offal, like heart or liver, could be bought from the butchers, and
might see if he could 'do' the commissary out of a few extra biscuits
or a canteen of brandy. Lieutenant George Gleig and a comrade
had both taken sporting guns to the Peninsula, and 'between us we
mustered a couple of greyhounds, a pointer, and a spaniel; and were
indifferently furnished with fishing-rods and tackle. By the help of
these we calculated on being able, at times, to add something to the
fare allowed us in the way of rations; and the event proved that our
calculations had not been formed upon mistaken grounds.'[71]

In the Peninsula and India regiments began the marching day
early, so as to have it finished before the heat of noonday. Private
Waterfield gives a good account of how things were done in India
in 1849:

> 27 January. The General [call to arms] Beat at 3 o'clock
> a.m. and the moon shone brightly we departed from Mul-
> tan ... We reached camp by half past 7 o'clock, the dis-
> tance being 12 miles 4 furlongs ...
>
> 29 January. Sidapore. 13 miles. General Beat at 2
> o'clock a.m.
>
> [and so on to] 8 February. Cheniote. 25 miles. The
> Regiment commenced its march at midnight.[72]

With timings like this, officers were able to spend much of their
time as 'gentlemen at large ... hunting among the neighbouring
regiments for news, and the neighbouring houses for curiosity ...'[73]
George Gleig recalled settling down to sleep after just such a day in
Portugal.

> This was the first night of my life which I had ever spent
> in so warlike a fashion; and I perfectly recollect, to this

hour, the impression which it made upon me. It was one
of the most exquisite delight ... When I looked around
me again, I saw arms piled up, and glittering in the light
of twenty fires, which were speedily kindled, and cast a
bright glare through the overhanging foliage. I saw men,
enveloped in their great-coats, stretched or sitting around
these fires in wild groups; I heard their merry chat, hearty
and careless laugh; now and then a song or catch chanted
by one or two ...[74]

Gleig was honest enough to say that things had never been quite
the same since. All sorts of things conspired to spoil this charming
fête champêtre. First was the weather. During the retreat from Corunna,
with Moore's army staggering through mountains with the French
close behind, discipline came close to collapse, and even the Light
Brigade, held together by the unyielding Craufurd, was at its last
gasp.

The shoes and boots of our party were now mostly either
destroyed or useless to us from foul roads and long miles,
and many of the men were entirely barefooted ... The
officers were also, for the most part, in as miserable a
plight. They were pallid, way-worn, their feet bleeding, and
their faces overgrown with beards of many days' growth ...
many of the poor fellows, now near sinking with fatigue,
reeled as if in a state of drunkenness ... and we looked
the ghosts of our former selves.[75]

Rifleman Benjamin Harris saw one of his comrades, Joseph Siddown,
freezing to death in the snow in his wife's arms. 'I knew them both,'

OPPOSITE:
Above: This idyllic camp scene from the late eighteenth century shows soldiers'
wives washing while their menfolk, who are wearing a form of light infantry cap,
tend the communal cooking pot.

Below: A soldier's wife dances to the accompaniment of fife, drum and cymbals.
Although the scene owes as much to artistic imagination as reality, the drummers
are correctly shown wearing grenadier caps and jackets with lace chevrons. Black
percussionists, popular for much of the period, usually wore fanciful 'Turkish'
uniforms.

he wrote, 'but it was impossible to help them.' Lieutenant Charles Diggle, in contrast, owed his life to:

> the kind act of a worthy woman, Sally Macan, the wife of a gallant soldier in my company, who, observing me to be falling from the rear from illness and fatigue, whipped off her garters and secured the sole of my boots, which were separating from the upper leathers, and set me on my feet again . . . A year or so after this, I had the opportunity of requiting her kindness by giving her a lift on my horse the morning after she had given birth to a child in the bivouac.[76]

Many soldiers drank to gain a brief respite from the terrible conditions, and, as Thomas Pococke of the 71st saw, 'they lay down intoxicated upon the snow, and slept the sleep of death; or staggering behind, were overtaken and cut down by the merciless French soldiers.'[77]

Hot weather was no kinder. In 1809 Craufurd's Light Brigade marched 42 miles in 22 hours to reach Talavera, though it arrived too late for the battle. 'Our men suffered dreadfully on the route, chiefly from excessive fatigue and the heat of the weather, it being the melting month of July,' wrote Edward Costello. 'The brain fever soon commenced, making fearful ravages in our ranks, and many men dropped by the road-side and died. One day I saw two men of the 52nd, unable to bear their sufferings, actually put a period to their existence by shooting themselves.'[78] The soldier's crushing burden worsened his plight. Costello carried:

> Knapsack and straps, two shirts, two pairs of stockings, one pair of shoes, ditto soles and heels, three brushes, box of blacking, razor, soap-box and strap, and also at the time an extra pair of trousers, a mess-tin, centre-tin and lid, haversack and canteen, greatcoat and blanket, a powder flask filled, a ball bag containing thirty loose balls, a small wooden mallet used to hammer the ball into the muzzle of our rifles; belt and pouch, the latter containing fifty rounds of ammunition, sword-belt and rifle, besides other odds and ends that at all times are required for a service-soldier.

He believed that 400 men of his battalion died within a few months simply because of this overloading, and doubted whether, when the regiment left Spain five years later, any man 'could show a single short or a pair of shoes in his knapsack.'[79]

The 32nd Foot marched from Ambala to Ferozepore in May 1848 more gently, with its baggage close behind and the regimental bhistis (water carriers, like Kipling's Gunga Din) at hand. 'The weather still continues very close and sultry,' wrote Private Waterfield.

> The remaining bhistis keep well up with the column, with a good supply of water. The water is warm and has a sickly taste with it. A great many men bring sickness upon themselves by overloading their stomach with water when on the line of march. I always refrain from smoking my pipe as much as I possibly can, and generally carry a small pebble in my mouth which keeps it moist. I refrain from talking as much as I can, and find myself less fatigued when arrived in camp than most men. I always draw my two drams of ration rum which I find does one good.[80]

Waterfield was in good company, for there was a widespread belief that strong drink helped insulate men against tropical diseases. Captain Robert Percival was convinced that his men did well in Ceylon by 'drinking plenty of arrack and smoking tobacco' while the unlucky natives 'live so abstemiously, few or none of them eating flesh, or drinking anything but water, that once they are seized with exhausting distempers they want strength to resist them, and they usually fall victims.'[81] In Spain a veteran advised Howell Gronow to take a good measure of spirits every morning to ward off disease, and he reported that the panacea worked well, for he never had a day's illness. Thirty-eight pipes of port wine – almost 4,000 gallons – were consumed by the Duke of York's army in Flanders, and 52,000 gallons of Maderia were sent to sustain the patients in hospitals on the Leeward Islands and St Domingo in the Caribbean. Satirical advice to a newly-arrived subaltern included wise medical advice:

> 'Come,' says the Doctor, 'here is Rum and Segars'
> 'This is the way we carry on our wars.'
> 'Here, smoke, my boy, I know 'twill do you good:

'And try this Country Wine, 'twill cool your blood.'[82]

However, real doctors became increasingly convinced that alcohol did more harm than good. William Fergusson, surgeon to the 67th Regiment, saw his battalion set off on a march up country on St. Domingo, and:

> the troops, previous to marching off, were supplied with a full ration of spirits. It was, as might have been foreseen, speedily consumed, and the men marching under a burning sun, through a dry rocky country that furnished no water, fell down at almost every step. Nineteen actually died upon the road, and those who arrived at the end of the march – a distance of about twelve miles – were in a state of exhaustion and distress that cannot be described.[83]

In 1803 regimental surgeons were ordered to give their men less wine, and amongst the recommendations of Henry Marshall's pioneering analysis of medical statistics, carried out in the 1830s, was the reduction of alcohol rations and the introduction of medical reports on the effect of intemperance on soldiers' health. The conviction that alcohol did indeed damage health joined abundant evidence of its effects on discipline to encourage wider reform, and changes in public attitude, and the growing availability of safe and palatable non-alcoholic drinks, all helped promote change.

The Crimean War was the last major conflict in which wives accompanied the British army on campaign. Prior to this there were women and children in camp, on the line of march and sometimes even on the field of battle. Sergeant Roger Lamb was astonished by their hardiness and resolution.

> If war sometimes in bad men, calls forth all the viler passions of our nature, in women it is obverse; it rouses into action an heroism otherwise unknown, an intrepidity almost incompatible with their sex, and arouses all the dormant susceptibilities of their mind.[84]

But life on campaign could be comfortable, especially for officers' ladies. The French Colonel Lejeune, then a prisoner at Elvas, just across the Portuguese border from Badajoz, saw:

An English Captain riding a very fine horse and warding off the sun with a parasol; behind him came his wife very prettily dressed, with a small straw hat, riding on a mule and carrying not only a parasol, but a little black and tan dog on her knee, while she led by a cord a she-goat, to supply her with milk. Beside Madame walked her Irish nurse, carrying in a green silk wrapper a baby, the hope of the family. A grenadier, the Captain's servant, came behind and occasionally poked up the long-eared steed of his mistress with a staff. Last in this procession came a donkey, loaded with much miscellaneous baggage, which included a tea kettle and a cage of canaries; it was guarded by an English servant in livery, mounted on a sturdy cob and carrying a long posting-whip, with which he occasionally made the donkey mend his pace.[85]

Fanny Duberly thought that a lady required a certain establishment to be able to survive the rigours of the field. In the Crimea she was affronted by the brash Mrs Cresswell: 'so dirty, with such uncombed, scurfy hair, such black nails, such a dirty cotton gown . . .' Mrs Cresswell not only addressed the officers as 'Bill and Jack' but had no lady's maid: 'so who empties her slops – or how she manages about etc., etc., – I can't divine.' However, when her husband died of cholera, Fanny's heart went out to her: 'God help and support Mrs Cresswell under a blow that would crush me to the grave – how full of anxiety I am.'[86] Colonel Hodge was not pleased when his second in command brought his wife to share 'his half of our hut . . . a very disgusting *exposé* to put any lady to.' She had no maid, and the sight of 'the *batman* picking the fleas out of Mrs F's drawers' was altogether too much.

George Bell of the 34th describes the other side of the coin, the comet's tail of soldiers' wives:

> averse to all military discipline, they impeded our progress at time, particularly in retreats. They were under no control. They were ordered to the rear or their donkeys would be shot, to stay with the baggage, under the discipline of the Provost Marshal. Despite the warning, next morning they would pick up their belongings and set off, lamenting their bitter fate, ahead of the column, marauding,

preparing their men's meals, before their arrival, plundering the battle-field or searching it for their dead; they were wounded, killed or died of exposure and hunger. Collectively and individually they formed cameos of the Peninsular campaign, a colourful kaleidoscope of the romance and the tragedy, devotion and self-sacrifice, the hardships and endurance of women at war.[87]

There was romance and tragedy aplenty. Harry Smith of the 95th fell in love with Juana Maria, a 14 year old Spanish girl who survived the storm of Badajoz – though her earrings had been ripped from her ears. Despite their difference in religion and the demands of the campaign they married. She became the darling of the Light Division, and was to follow her husband, who called her 'the only thing on earth my life hangs on and clings to', through a lively career in Europe, North America, South Africa and India. When Sir Harry Smith, as he had become, was governor of the Cape, a town in Natal was named after Lady Smith, and was to play its own brave part in the Boer War.

Drum-Major Thorp of the 88th was 'quite a lad', according to Grattan. He too fell in love with a Spanish girl, and her rich and influential father searched the regiment for her. But Thorp had hidden her in the band, blacked-up as a negro cymbal player. As the regiment departed the band struck up a quick march, Thorp flourishing his cane in front it and his lover clashing her cymbals in the ranks. They lived happily together till Thorp, who had been promoted sergeant major and wounded four times, was killed at the very end of the war. His ensign's commission arrived the day afterwards, and the fact that Mrs Thorp was now an officer's widow 'was the means of reconciling her father to the choice she had made.'

James Anton of the 42nd Regiment married his sweetheart Mary, an Edinburgh lass, 'who shared with me all my fortunes over field and flood, in camp and in quarters, in war and in peace, without any unpleasant reflection at her own share of suffering.' They spent their first night in bivouac in a tent with eleven other men. Anton's comrades helped him make a little hut to give Mary more privacy. Although married couples usually fired their huts when their regiments marched, Anton could not bring himself to ignite their 'bower of happiness', and Mary wept at leaving it.[88] Other bowers were anything but happy. When the 7th Fusiliers was waiting to go home from Dauphine Island after the War of 1812, soldiers and their wives slept in improvised huts. An alligator entered one of these and slithered in on top of a woman: her terrified screams frightened the creature off.

But life on the freezing uplands of the Crimea was far worse. Colonel George Bell of the 1st Royal Scots wrote that his men:

> go down to the trenches wet, come back wet, go into hospital tents wet, die the same night, and are buried in their wet blankets next morning! Nine of my good men lay stretched and dead this morning outside one tent, rolled up in their blankets. Look into this tent and observe the household. You see it all in rags about the skirting, and the floor is a thick paste baked nearly dry by the head of the fevered patients. That bundle of dirty, wet blanket rolled up contains a living creature, once a comely useful soldier's wife, now waiting for death to release her from such misery. This nice looking youth is one of my band. That young women, once perhaps the belle of her village, now in rags, but in good health, is eating her dinner, a bit of salt pork, with broken down biscuit pounded into it; a tin plate and iron spoon is all her fortune – 'What is that down there?' – 'O, Sir, that is poor Mrs H—, sitting on her husband's grave; she is always there shivering in the cold.'[89]

Women sometimes followed their men into action. William Surtees, in his first campaign in 1799, saw how:

> A girl, who had followed a grenadier belonging to my regiment when he volunteered out of the militia, accompanied her protector during the whole of this day's operations, and shared equally with him every danger and fatigue to which he was exposed, and no argument could prevail upon her to leave him till the whole business was over, and the battalion to which her sweetheart belonged was sent to the rear at night.[90]

In Spain a harassed subaltern saw a lady on a mule advancing steadily under intermittent fire, and warned her that it was dangerous. She told him sharply to attend to his own affairs: she had a husband before her. In the Crimea 'the hardy Mrs Evans', married to an officer's servant in the 4th King's Own:

> Objected to being left alone at night when her husband was ordered out on picket, and she defied the rules by insisting on going with him. The men got used to accepting her as one of themselves, and now she became more firmly of the regiment by making light of danger.[91]

Usually women said farewell to their menfolk before battle, and hoped to see them safe and sound when it was over. But occasionally they found themselves spectators of the deadly drama played out by their men: Mrs Handcock watched her husband fall mortally wounded leading the 97th to assault the Redan at Sevastopol in June 1855.

William Grattan thought that most soldiers' wives were philosophical about losing a husband, for 'his place was sure to be filled by someone of the company to which he belonged, so the women of our army had little cause of alarm on this head. The worst that could happen to them was the chance of being in a state of widowhood for a week.'[92] Commissary Schaumann, who was given to consoling himself with 'the beauties amongst the soldiers' wives,' records that Mrs Dunn was distraught when her husband was killed with the 68th Foot at Salamanca, but within a week she had settled down with Sergeant George Hubbs of the same company. Thomas Browne declared that some women kept a list of suitors, and rebuffed the tardy: 'Nay, but thou'rt late, as I'm promised to John Edwards first, & to Edward Atkinson next, but when they two be killed off, I'll think of thee.'[93]

Some soldiers argued that they had a moral obligation to look after their comrades' wives, and the marriage of widows was, in a sense, a symbol of small-group cohesion. John Pearman observed that most women widowed in India had remarried soldiers of the regiment within the four-month period that they were allowed to remain 'on the strength' as widows. Some courtships were swift. A cavalry sergeant in India asked a pretty widow to marry him just after her husband's funeral. She burst into tears, not because of the suddenness of the proposal, but because she had just accepted an offer from the corporal who had commanded the firing party at the funeral: the sergeant would have been a better catch.

Yet there was often real and lasting grief. One of Thomas Browne's brother officers told him of 'a young woman running wildly with her hair loose about the spot where the 3rd Division had attacked [at Salamanca]. She was looking about with earnest anxiety & a distracted air amongst the dead . . .'[94] Her husband, the newly-joined Lieutenant Fitzgerald of the 88th, had been killed. Sergeant McDermott of the 85th, 'a fine young Irishman' had a wife of 'unblemished character, and they were accounted the most virtuous and the happiest couple in the regiment.' McDermott was encouraging some recruits under fire when 'a roundshot struck him in the crown of the head and smashed him to atoms.' There was dismay throughout the company, for he was 'a prodigious favourite with all ranks; and all of us then thought of his young wife, so spotless and so completely wrapped up in him. 'O, who will tell Nance of this?' said another non-commissioned officer, his principal companion – 'Poor Nance' cried the soldiers one and all . . .' Mrs McDermott fell into paroxysms when she saw her husband's remains, refused to believe that those tatters of humanity were 'my own handsome, beautiful McDermott,' and had to 'be removed, with gentle violence, to the camp.' After the first shock of grief had passed, she refused to listen to proposals from other suitors, and wanted to go home. 'To her home she was accordingly sent,' writes Gleig. 'We raised her a handsome subscription, every officer and man contributing something; and I have some reason to believe that she is now respectably settled in Cork, though still a widow.'[95]

And women themselves were killed, wounded and captured. William Grattan remembered that two officers of the 11th Light Dragoons were wounded in a cavalry action in 1812: one lost an arm to a sword-cut, and the other had his front teeth knocked out by a musket-ball. But the real casualty of the action was Mrs Howley, 'the black cymbal-man's wife' of the 88th, who was carried off by French lancers. Officers could be replaced, but 'in the entire army such another woman . . . as Mrs Howley could not be found.'

In spite of all this, there was humour too. Grattan was wounded in the chest at Badajoz and helped back to his tent in camp. He found that Mrs Nelly Carsons, wife of his batman, Daniel Carsons, was lying dead drunk on his straw bed. One of his helpers told him: 'Why then sir, the bed's big enough for yees both, and she'll keep you nate and warm, for by the powers, you're kilt with the cold and the loss ov blood.' Grattan was awakened when his companion 'discharging a huge grunt, and putting her hand upon my leg, exclaimed 'Arrah! Dan jewel, what makes you so stiff this morning.'[96] In the Crimea Mrs Smith, wife of the batman to Lieutenant Sinclair of the 93rd, had a brown, weather-beaten face, pleasant hazel eyes, broad shoulders and a motherly bosom. Like many soldiers' wives she made some money by doing laundry, her arms had been strengthened by wringing out the washing. She had a good wash drying on the grass near Balaclava when some Turkish fugitives ran over it. Mrs Smith rose to the occasion, seized one by the collar and began to beat him with a stick. 'Ye cowardly misbelievers' she roared, 'to leave the brave Christian Highlanders to fecht when ye run awa.' The man's comrades, seeking to appease her, addressed her as 'Kokona,' an honorific term. She, however, thought that they were being abusive, and laid about her even more savagely: 'Kokona, indeed! I'll Kokona ye!' She survived the campaign, and for the rest of her life, in garrison in Scotland, was known as 'Kokona Smith'.[97]

Marching and quartering alike required more attention in the presence of the enemy. Light cavalry, with its vedettes and pickets, screened an army at the halt, and infantry regiments facing the enemy maintained double sentries backed by pickets whose strength varied with the threat. The conduct of these outposts reflected the degree of hostility felt towards the enemy. It is a striking fact that for much of history men who have been required to kill one another in the way of duty have often got on well enough as individuals. The relationship between the soldier and his enemy is conditioned by many things, with wider cultural factors like race, class and religion joining short-term issues such as propaganda, atrocity stories and individual attitudes.

The British soldier's span of hostility stretched from the benign to the virulent. Nobody much wanted to fight the Danes, for they were regarded as decent fellows with sensible ideas about drink and a praiseworthy determination to defend their country. When the 23rd Foot beat a unit composed of university students at Copenhagen in 1807 'our sun-burned soldiers really grieved, to see the fair faces and the curling locks of the gallant young opponents, as they lay extended on the ground. They must have resisted gallantly, as some had fallen, from bayonet wounds given by our troops.'[98] At the other extreme were Indian 'mutineers'. Tales of their atrocities were widespread before men even met them: a soldier of the 9th Lancers rode amongst troops approaching Delhi with an English child's foot on his lance, telling all how he had found it. Soldiers were shown the site of the final massacre at Cawnpore. Gordon-Alexander saw how his soldiers entered the yard laughing and chatting, but emerged swearing to have vengeance. A summary civil court sat daily at Cawnpore, and those convicted were first forced to clean up a portion of the blood-stains. It was decreed that: 'the task will be made as revolting to his feelings as possible, and the Provost-Marshal will use his lash in forcing anyone objecting to complete his task.' After this, victims were hanged, and their remains 'buried in the public road' if they were Hindus, or burnt if they were Muslims, in a reversal of the funeral practice of each religion. Colonel Neill of the 93rd wrote that 'one of the leading men rather objected, and was flogged and made to lick part of the blood with his tongue. No doubt this is a strange law, but it suits the occasion well . . .'[99]

When Sir Colin Campbell briefed his officers before the assault on the Sikanderbagh he urged them 'to impress upon the men that they must trust to, and make good use of, the bayonet; further, that with the foe then confronting us, there could be no question of giving quarter.'[100] After his guns had breached the wall, Campbell, on horseback close behind the waiting 93rd, called out to Sergeant Dobbin Lee: 'Do you think the breach is wide enough, Dobbin?' 'Aye Sir Colin, Your Honour,' shouted Lee. 'Let the infantry storm, and we'll soon make short work of the murdering devils.' Not far behind in the hierarchy of hate came the Afghans involved in the murder of the British envoy and the destruction of Elphinstone's army in 1842. When the British re-entered Kabul they destroyed the houses 'of some of the chiefs who had been most obnoxious to us' and blew up the city's great bazaar, where the envoy's remains had been displayed, as 'a lasting token of our vengeance'.[101] The Sikhs, in contrast, were respected as tough fighters, whose tenacious courage had something 'almost British' about it. That did not, however, prevent Sergeant Pearman from scalping 'a very large dead man, near 7 feet high and large with it ... to make a large black plume ...'[102]

Attitudes to patriots in North America were decidedly ambivalent. British officers at first found it hard to regard them as legitimate combatants, and sympathised, naturally enough, with the loyalists. The social round strengthened these ties: John Peebles often stayed with Judge George Ludlow of Queens County, Long Island, whose brother Lieutenant Colonel Gabriel Ludlow commanded the best turned-out battalion of loyalists that he had ever seen. It was increasingly clear to officers like Peebles that their loyal hosts faced ruin if the patriots won. But there was no denying that the latter were often brave enough: the captured garrison of Charleston had 'more appearance of discipline than we have seen formerly and some of their officers decent looking men.'[103] Some British officers found it hard not to see their opponents as fighting for traditional 'English' liberties, and a few, like Captain Lord Edward Fitzgerald of the 19th Foot, badly wounded at Eutaw Springs in September 1781, were driven towards radicalism by the war. Fitzgerald went on to become a leader of the United Irishman, planning an armed insurrection against the army in which he had once served: he died of wounds received when arrested in Dublin in 1798, having mortally wounded one of the officers who detained him. For private soldiers, in North America elsewhere, politics was politics and life on the outpost line was unpleasant enough without complicating it. Peebles admitted that his sentries chatted freely to their American opposite numbers, and he was pleased to find an old friend (and enemy colonel) safe amongst the garrison of Charleston when it surrendered to the British in 1780.

There were even some gentlemanly exchanges between patriots and loyalists. Captain Frederick MacKenzie tells us that when Brigadier General Parsons approached a loyalist garrison on Long Island he summoned it to surrender.

Brigadier Genl Parsons, Commanding officer of the troops of the United American Army, now investing the Enemy's post at Satucket, to prevent the effusion of human blood, requires the immediate surrender of the post. The officers and soldiers who are under their protection shall be entitled to their baggage, and treated with that humanity which prisoners are entitled to. Your answer is desired within ten minutes . . . if your refusal should oblige to the effusion of human blood, you must charge it to your own account.

Lieutenant Colonel Hewlett, the post's commander, asked for half an hour in which to consult his officers, but Parsons would allow him only ten minutes. Hewlett then replied: 'Colonel Hewlett presents his compliments to Genl Parsons, and is determined to defend his post while he has a man left alive.' Having failed to bluff the place into surrender, Parsons sent another note: 'General Parsons' compliments to Colonel Hewlett, and should have been happy to have done him the pleasure of paying him a longer visit, but the extreme heat of the weather prevents him.' With that he departed, leaving the resolute Hewlett alone.[104]

British soldiers often felt great animosity towards the Revolutionary French: the stories of excesses which emerged from France and the brutal behaviour of Revolutionary armies conspired to make for clashes in which common humanity was sometimes submerged by conflicting ideology. Such hostility was rare in the Peninsula, where the adversaries quickly developed a common understanding that although they were obliged to kill one another when some military advantage could be gained by it, purposeless hostility helped nobody. This is a feature of many wars, but it was especially marked in Spain. When no battle was in progress, the front slipped into an unofficial truce. George Gleig chatted to a French officer who had delivered some letters from British prisoners, 'and after gasconading a good deal, both the one and the other, we shook hands and parted the best friends imaginable.'[105] 'Repeated acts of civility passed between the French and us . . .' wrote Kincaid. 'The greyhounds of an officer following a hare, on one occasion ran into their lines, and they very politely returned them.'[106] A company commander in the 95th, told to take a French-held house, walked across and politely asked its garrison to evacuate the premises, thus avoiding a pointless little battle which he, with numbers on his side, was sure to win. The French moved out.

It was understood that outposts did not fire on one another. 'I was one night on piquet,' recalled Kincaid, 'when a ball came from the French sentry . . . and they sent a flag of truce, next morning, to apologise for the accident, saying that it had been done by a stupid fellow of a sentry who imagined that we were advancing on him. We admitted the apology, though we well knew that it had been done by a malicious rather than a stupid fellow . . .'[107] Occasional malice was not one-sided. Towards the end of the war, a corporal in the 95th shot a French officer on outpost duty, and Surtees was 'apprehensive that this would put an end to that good understanding which had hitherto subsisted between the piquets of the two nations, who much regretted the occurrence.'[108] Immediately prior to this some French officers had enjoyed a picnic only a hundred yards from the British pickets, and a village in no-man's-land was pillaged, by British, French and Portuguese, 'in perfect harmony, no one doubting the other on account of his nation or colour.'[109]

Captain Charles Parquin of the French light cavalry confirms the cordiality of relations. His squadron leader wanted to meet some British officers, so Parquin put a bottle of good brandy in his sabreta-che[110] and rode out to the British outposts, waving his handkerchief. Immediately an officer of the 10th Light Dragoons galloped out and asked him what he wanted. 'I have come to ask you and your fellow-officers to share this bottle of brandy with me and my colleagues,' said Parquin, 'before we make contact with each other in a different manner.' They discussed the British dragoons' success in the light cavalry action at Benavente on 29 December 1808, which the French hoped to avenge, and a British officer then asked if somebody could sent a letter to the town of Moulins, for a friend of his was prisoner there. 'Dulimbert, the adjutant of the 13th Chasseurs, whose father was prefect of Moulins, was glad to offer to do so,' records Parquin, 'and the letter was brought to him under a white flag the next day.' The officers had finished the brandy and made a good start on rum brought by the British when some shells fell nearby and broke up the conversation.[111]

Visitors, many of them 'amateurs' – travelling gentlemen who came out to see the war, and were to be known in the Crimea as 'TGs' – could never understand all this. 'I used to be much amused at seeing our naval officers come up from Lisbon riding on mules with huge ship's spy-glasses, like six-pounders, strapped across the backs of their saddles,' said Kincaid. 'Their first question invariably was "who is that fellow there?" pointing to the enemy's sentry close to us, and, on being told that he was a Frenchman. "Then why the devil don't you shoot him." '[112] Amateurs were unpopular precisely because they hoped to witness hostilities in which they were not obliged to participate. Brotherton thought them 'idle gentlemen who must needs try to show their pluck by poking their noses into danger in action (where they had no business to be) till it became too serious to be pleasant, when they immediately decamped and became great objects of derision . . .'[113] When one, the son of 'Mr Gray, the Jeweller,' fell into French hands, the French offered to exchange him for a captured French colonel. 'Lord Wellington sent Mr Gray Jnr. back again,' wrote John Mills of the Coldstream, 'with his respects and they may keep him.'[114]

Perhaps the only regular example of pointless hostility in the Peninsula was the single combat that regularly took place between cavalry officers. Young officers on outpost duty would frequently challenge their opposite numbers, and considered it ungentlemanly to refuse a fight. Thomas Brotherton particularly resented the 'coarse, bullying manner' of one French officer, and immediately charged him, although Brotherton was on a tiny Spanish horse and the Frenchman on a big charger. The Frenchman galloped off, and though Brotherton's attack carried him into the ranks of the French cavalry, 'they did not attempt to cut at me or even interrupt my return to my own troops, but showed me every mark of respect and approval of my conduct . . .'[115]

At Salamanca Brotherton fought a French officer between the opposing skirmishers, who stopped firing to look on. The French-man fought 'with great cunning and skill', and eventually succeeded in cutting one of Brotherton's reins and a finger on his bridle-hand. While the Frenchman delivered this cut, Brotherton 'had the oppor-tunity of making a thrust at his body, which staggered him and he rode off.' An enquiry, sent next day under a flag of truce, found that the blade had entered the Frenchman's stomach and killed him. 'I shall never forget his good-humoured fine countenance,' wrote Brotherton, 'during the whole time we were engaged in this single combat, talking cheerfully and politely to me, as if we were exchanging civilities instead of sabre-cuts.'[116]

In the heat of battle, though, the soldiers on both sides were anything but civilised, although their officers often prevented the worst excesses. Major Charles Napier's experiences at Corunna, where he led the 50th Foot in a counter-attack against a superior French force, are instructive. His men were barely in control when the advance began, and he put them through some arms drill to occupy their attention. Napier gave no formal fire order. Short-sighted and without his spectacles, he asked his men whether they could see their enemies plain enough to hit them: 'Many voices shouted "By Jesus we do!" "Then blaze away!" And such a rolling fire broke out as I have never heard since.'

In the charge that followed his men wanted to bayonet fallen Frenchmen because they thought they were shamming. This form of fugue was not uncommon. Unwounded men sometimes lay flat, almost semi-conscious, until the fortunes of the day were clear: others were rooted to the spot, like the soldiers in a Brunswick square at Waterloo described by Mercer as having fled 'not bodily, to be sure, but spiritually, because their senses seemed to have left them.' Soldiers whose morale was crumbling often indulged in placatory behaviour, visibly 'shrinking' by clustering together in cowering groups and, if they fired at all, firing high so as not to injure men who would shortly be their masters. The idea of bayoneting the helpless was abhorrent to Napier, and telling his men not to waste their time on cowards, he led them on. When his little party was engulfed the four men with him were bayoneted instantly. Napier himself managed to grab his main opponent's musket by the muzzle, diverting its bayonet, and after being clubbed with the musket-butts of others managed to gasp out *je me rends*. By now the fighting in his immediate area was over, and his surrender was accepted.

Thomas Browne was captured when the French rearguard lunged out at its pursuers after Vitoria. His horse was killed and he took a sabre-cut across his head, but his captors 'in all the rage and vexation of a vanquished Army' treated him roughly. Edmund Wheatley, taken semi-conscious at Waterloo, was robbed of his valuables, as was the inevitable routine, and swept along with the retreating French, 'a poor, cast down, bruised captive, exposed to the insults and bravado of thousands of intoxicated and insolent enemies' who eventually stole his shoes and socks. Both Browne and Wheatley were fortunate in that there was a natural break in the action before their capture, and once formally taken prisoner, they were unlikely to be killed out of hand. But neither rank nor placatory behaviour would save a man when his opponent was in an unstoppable killing frenzy often produced by a dangerous cocktail of drink, rage and the desire for revenge. 'I witnessed several of the Imperial Guard who were run through the body apparently without any resistance on their parts,' wrote Ensign Gronow of Waterloo. 'I observed a big Welshman of the name of Hughes, who was six feet seven inches in height, run through with his bayonet and knock down with the butt-end of his firelock, I should think a dozen at least of his opponents.'[117]

The French and British settled down to become good allies in the Crimea. W. H. Russell of *The Times* thought that the French were far better at living in impromptu camps, and greatly admired the music he so often found playing in them. And at the very end of the war he witnessed an encounter which laid the ghosts of the Peninsula The British 2nd Division was drawn up when a badly battered Zouave regiment, which had stormed the strongest point in the Russian defences only days before, came past.

> The instant the leading regiment of Zouaves came up to the spot where our first regiment was placed the men, with one spontaneous burst, rent the air with an English cheer. The French officers drew their swords, and the men dressed up and marched past as if at a review, while regiment after regiment of the Second Division caught up the cry, and at last our men presented arms to their brave comrades of France, the officers on both sides saluted with their swords, and this continued till the last man had marched by.[118]

THE IMMINENT
DEADLY BREACH

S IEGES WERE A FEATURE of the age. Although they lost much
of their importance in Europe from the turn of the eighteenth
century, the British were involved in four – Ciudad Rodrigo, Badajoz,
Burgos and San Sebastian – in the Peninsula. Charleston was
besieged in the American War, Delhi in the Mutiny, and war in the
Crimea revolved around the siege of Sevastopol. Siege warfare
hinged upon the duel between the engineer, who sought to make
his fortifications impregnable, and the gunner, who strove to batter
them down. Troops of other arms usually found themselves extras
in this opera, furnishing the brute manpower required for earth-
moving, provision-hauling and assaults. Men spent day after day in
the trenches, and contemporaries agreed that the sheer, grinding
duration of a siege imposed strains not often encountered in battles
in open field. 'There is no species of duty in which the soldier is
liable to be employed so galling or so disagreeable as a siege,' wrote
George Gleig.

> Not that it is deficient in causes of excitement, which, on
> the contrary, are in hourly operation; but it ties him so
> completely down to the spot, and breaks in so repeatedly
> upon his hours of rest, and exposes him so constantly to
> danger, and that too at times and places where no honour

is to be gained, that we cannot greatly wonder at the feelings of absolute hatred which generally prevail, among the privates at least of a besieging army, against the garrison which does its duty to its country by holding out to the last extremity.[119]

It was a sentiment with which John Deane, who served through the Duke of Marlborough's great siege of Lille in 1708, would have agreed. He wrote that:

this murdering siege, it is thought, has destroyed more than Namure did last year, and those that were the flower of the army. For what was not killed or drownded were spoiled by their hellish inventions, by throwing of bombs, boyling pitch, tar, oyle and brimstone with scalding water and suchlike combustables upon our men from the outworkes, and when our men made any attack. Esspecially the English grenadiers have scarce 6 sound men in a company; likewise many inventions enough to pussele the Devil to contrive, wch would be tedious to relate.[120]

Fortress warfare had been revolutionised in the seventeenth century by the development of the *trace italienne*, to produce works with the characteristic star-shaped plan often associated with the French engineer Vauban. Instead of building high stone walls that were vulnerable to artillery, engineers constructed low defences of earth, revetted with brick or stone, with deep ditches – which might sometimes be flooded – shielding them from direct assault. An essential feature of the new fortification was the bastion, an arrow-head shaped work that jutted out from the line of the main curtain wall to enable guns mounted on it to cover the wall with flanking fire. Other works – ravelins or demi-lunes – sat in front of the main defences. From the attacker's side little could be seen but a gentle slope, the glacis, which fell away into a shallow walk-way protected by sharpened stakes – the covered way and its palisade. An attacker who got this far was on the very edge of the ditch, perhaps sixty feet wide and thirty deep – with the main ramparts beyond it, their cannon firing over a thick earth parapet or through splayed embrasures lined with masonry.

A carelessly held fortress might be grabbed quickly by a coup de main, with attackers bursting in before its gates were shut, or taken by escalade, with stormers climbing ladders mounted in the ditch to pour over the ramparts. Something hopelessly old-fashioned, like a walled palace or mud-walled fort common in India, might be quickly breached by field guns, ready for infantry assault. But a fortress with pretensions to modernity, held by a resolute governor and a determined garrison, demanded a siege. This bloody ritual had rules as regular and mechanical as those of a dance, and was, above all, a giant logistic feat. Robert Waterfield watched the heavy guns and engineers reach Multan on 4 September 1848.

> The Siege Train arrived here this morning, and with it a great number of camp followers, three companies of foot artillery, and one company of Sappers and Miners. The train consisted of 32 pieces of heavy ordnance, 24s and 18s, and a number of mortars etc. . . . What with shell, shot and ammunition wagons, it reached for 7 or 8 miles. First came a bevy of elephants, then the camels in their long irregular line, some falling down under their heavy loads and left to die; others throwing their load and scampering off through the country.[121]

The attacker first secured his own logistic base, the siege park, and took steps to guard against the approach of a relieving army. Albuera was fought because the French sought to raise the siege of Badajoz, and both Inkerman and Balaclava were intended to help raise the siege of Sevastopol. He opened his first line of trenches parallel with the main defence works (the first parallel) just out of effective range of the defender's guns. His engineers then drove zig-zag trenches forward – a process called sapping – until they were ready to open a second parallel. This was equipped – armed in the jargon – with batteries whose guns took on enemy pieces on bastions and curtain, striving to dismount them, knocking them from their carriages by direct hits on their muzzles. The engineers, meanwhile, sapped on to open a third parallel.

If the attacker had the time and the ground was favourable his engineers might now dig a tunnel beneath the defences, creating a chamber which could be packed with explosives and blown. Or he could launch an assault to gain the possession of the covered way. This was where grenadiers had once come into their own, for they would throw their grenades over the palisade and rush the covered way. With the covered way secure and the guns on the ramparts opposite battered into silence, the attacker could now set up his breaching batteries, armed with very heavy guns. These little wonders, thudding away steadily, would batter the masonry at the foot of the wall, opening a long groove – the cannelure. Then came the moment both longed-for and dreaded. The whole mass of the rampart slid gently into the ditch whence it had come when the place was built, leaving the attacker with a practicable breach through which he could enter the fortress. The great Vauban used to come into his own at this moment, scrabbling forward like some great earthy badger to report the breach ripe: '*c'est mûr, c'est bien mûr.*'

The rules of war were clear enough. Once a breach was practicable and indefensible, and its assault imminent, the governor had to surrender or accept that he and his men would receive no quarter, and that the town in his charge would be given over to pillage. The civic fathers would, no doubt, wish to discuss the matter with him, since their property and their daughters' chastity hinged on his decision. The custom was designed to prevent useless slaughter, for once a wall was breached it was unlikely that the garrison could hold out. It also rationalised the fact that soldiers who fought their way through a breach were likely to be more interested in drink, gold and women than magnanimity in victory and a devout *Te Deum*.

Nothing, of course, was certain. Both sides would be using their mortars to drop explosive shells into the town and onto the attacking batteries, and these might score a lucky and decisive hit. The French took Almeida in 1810 when a dribble of powder, left by a leaking cask, was ignited by a mortar bomb and flashed across the square to the church, which was being used as a magazine, and blew it to bits. The defender would mount sorties, trying to get into the attackers' trenches and smash up his equipment. If the sorties could damage the siege guns (the approved method was to double load them, stuff the muzzles with mud, light a long fuse and retire briskly) their action might even be conclusive. The Russians mounted frequent sorties from Sevastopol. On Christmas Eve 1854 Henry Clifford wrote:

> A sad lesson on the necessity of vigilance on outpost duty has been taught us by the loss of four officers taken prisoner in the works in front of out Batteries. One Major of the 50th Regiment and some twenty-seven privates of the same Corps being bayoneted asleep on the same duty a night or two ago.[122]

John Deane described even more serious misfortunes before Tournai in 1708.

> Since the Grand Army has left Tournay the enemy hath been verry bold, and made severall sallyes upon our folkes and killed a great many, they having gott information that our miners were sapping under there mines wth. a designe to cutt of some of ther pipes [tunnels or saps] belonging to their mines. Whereupon they sprung a mine of theres and clowed up and smuthered severall of our workmen and likewise killd. an officer & 28 men that was thereabouts uppon command, and damaged abundance of other men of severall regiments.[123]

A relieving force might compel the attacker to raise the siege. Or the besieger, eating up all the foodstuffs in the surrounding countryside while the garrison lived off well-stocked provision magazines, might simply run out of food.

The siege of Charleston went on in the approved style. John Peebles, familiar, like any self-respecting professional officer of his era, with the terminology, catalogued the progress of the business. On 3 May 1780 he declared 'the Batteries not yet ready, a piece of Sap work in front of 3d Parallel for small arms.' On the 7th the miners drained the ditch, and on the 8th the batteries were ready, and, with 'things in this state of readiness for close attack' the garrison was summoned to surrender, but discussions over terms speedily foundered. On the 9th and 10th Peebles was happy to note that 'we have dismounted & silenced some of their Guns' though 'one of our own 12 pors. is hurt 10 or 12 men kill'd & wounded.' On 11 May he reported 'a superior fire of both Cannon & small arms last night and this morng. before day the Town was set on fire in two other three places.'[124] The governor surrendered on terms that night.

But Charleston was easy by comparison with many other sieges.

Life in the trenches that inched ever closer to the fortifications was often made as unpleasant by weather as by the enemy's fire. 'The trenches being so verry dirty and miserable for the men who could neither sitt nor lye to rest themselves,' wrote John Deane, 'but was obliged to stand all ways come life or death.'[125] In January 1812 Wellington besieged Ciudad Rodrigo in weather so foul that John Mills found that the water in his men's canteens had frozen, and it was painfully hard work digging the parallels in the icy ground. As soon as the trenches were complete they filled with water.

Besieged and besiegers alike worked hard by day and night, with sentries shouting 'shot' when a cannon was fired or 'shell' to warn of an incoming mortar bomb, thus enabling working parties to throw themselves flat. The defenders fired illuminants known as light-balls, or rolled big inflammable 'carcasses', made of wicker-work, rags and pitch, from their walls when they thought that the assault was imminent.

The assault on the breach was usually spearheaded by a party of volunteers known as the Forlorn Hope. Its officers might expect, though they were not guaranteed, a step up in rank if they survived. So keen was the competition for a place amongst the men that in the Peninsula some sergeants fought as temporary privates, and some soldiers offered their comrades as much as £20 for a place in the assault. It was extraordinarily dangerous. Private Wheeler saw Ensign Dyas of the 51st emerge from the assault of Fort San Cristoval at Badajoz in 1811: 'He was without cap, his sword was shot off close to the handle, the sword scabbard was gone, and the laps of his frock coat were perforated with balls.'[126]

Dyas was 'a young officer of great promise, of a most excellent disposition, and beloved by every man on the Corps – an Irishman whose only fortune was his sword . . .' He twice led the regiment's Forlorn Hope, attempting to scale the walls of Fort San Cristobal, pressing his claim to try the second time with the words: 'General Houston, I hope you will not refuse my request because I am determined if you order the fort to be stormed forty times, to lead the advance as long as I have life.'[127] There were only nineteen survivors of the 200 men who launched the second assault. William Wheeler was one of them:

The ladder I was on was broken and down we came all together, men, firelocks, bayonets, in one confused mass, and with us a portion of the wall. After some time the fire slackened, as if the enemy were tired of slaughter . . . As we were retreating down the glacis . . . I had a very narrow escape of being made prisoner, being cut off from my comrades by the party who sallied . . . However, I hit upon an expedient that answered well. I threw myself down by a man who was shot through the head and daubed my white haversack with his blood. I shewed this to the enemy when they ordered me to get up and go into the fort. From the appearance of the blood they must have thought I had a bad wound in the hip, so they left me . . .

All Wheeler's clothes were stolen, but at daybreak he sprinted barefoot for the besiegers' lines. 'My comrades cheered me and I bounded across like a deer, the Devil take the thistles,' he wrote. 'I felt none of them till I was safe behind the battery.'[128]

Dyas was senior ensign and gained his lieutenancy by seniority after the death of another officer in the same attack. However, although recommended for a captaincy, he was overlooked and was too modest to press his claim: he was still only a lieutenant after Waterloo. In 1820 Lieutenant Colonel John Gurwood, who had gained his own captaincy in the Forlorn Hope at Ciudad Rodrigo, recommended Dyas to the adjutant general, who drew the Duke of York's attention to his claim. Dyas was given a captaincy in the Ceylon Regiment, but his health was too poor for him to serve abroad and he retired on half-pay.

Yet there was never a shortage of volunteers for the Forlorn Hope, drawn on by the desire for distinction and promotion. At Ciudad Rodrigo, Major Thompson, commanding the 88th, asked his officers for a volunteer to lead the Forlorn Hope.

Lieutenant William Mackie . . . immediately stepped forward, and dropping his sword[-point in salute] said 'Major Thompson, I am ready for that service.' For once in his life poor old Thomson was affected – Mackie was his own townsman, they had fought together for many years. And when he took hold of his hand and pronounced the words

'God bless you, my boy,' his eye filled, his lip quivered
and there was a faltering in his voice . . .[129]

Mackie was the senior lieutenant, already sure of promotion if there
was a death amongst his seniors that night: it was not self-interest
that drove him. Happily he survived and was promoted. When San
Sebastian was attacked in 1813 there was the usual demand for
volunteers for the Forlorn Hope, and George Hennell reported that
being ordered to furnish two captains, four subalterns and 100 men
for the Forlorn Hope was 'one of the highest honours the division
could have received.' The senior captain of his regiment arrived at
the conference after officers had already volunteered, and the
colonel said: 'Captain Brock, we are to give the storming party at
San Sebastian tonight. Several captains wish to go. Will you allow it,
being senior?' 'No Sir,' replied Brock, 'I will go myself.'

It was the third time that Lieutenant John O'Connell had volunteered. 'When an officer offers on a service of this kind it is done
without any bombast,' says Hennell, 'they look serious and pale . . .
I have just wished them goodbye as they passed . . . as you would
have taken leave of a person going to a play.' O'Connell was killed,
hit in the thigh and then the stomach: Wellington decreed that his
ensigncy should be sold for the benefit of his mother.[130] John Shipp
knew the risks when he volunteered for the Forlorn Hope at Bhurtpore, but had no relatives to worry about and wanted to make his
name. However, he contrasted mens' reflective feelings while they
were awaiting the assault with the excitement that followed:

> why is it that before the storming of a fort, or fighting a
> battle, men are thoughtful, heavy, restless, weighed down
> with care? Why do men on these occasions, ask more fer-
> vently than usual for the divine guidance and protection
> in the approaching conflict . . . For all my poor compre-
> hension may tell tomorrow I may be summoned before
> my maker.

When the gun giving the signal for the Forlorn Hope to form up
was fired, Shipp kissed his favourite pony Apple and his dog Wolf,
and positioned himself at the head of 'that little column of heroes
– twelve volunteers of each of the different corps of the army. You

may believe me when I say that nothing was in my mind but the enthusiasm of the moment, and pride in the post of honour that had been given to me.'[131]

The Forlorn Hope tried to get as close as it could to the breach without being detected, but an alert enemy would be well prepared, with sentries posted to give the alarm, carcasses ready to be lit and guns loaded with canister to sweep the ground the attackers would have to cross. John Shipps' men were very close to the ramparts of Bhurtpore by the time the alarm was raised.

> We were not discovered until we were within fifty paces of the ditch, then a tremendous cannonade broke out, with volleys of musketry and rockets in all directions. The rampart spouted fire like a vast volcano, while the noise of the guns, and the shrill sound of the trumpets, rent the air asunder. Men were rushing about in the strange light on the tops of the walls as busy as ants. It was an awe-inspiring scene, and one, no doubt, sublimely beautiful to any spectator at a sufficient distance ... We got there, but imagine our consternation at finding a perpendicular curtain going down to the water's edge, with no footing on it except here and there pieces of trees, and stones, which had fallen from above. Not more than three men could climb abreast, and if they slipped a watery grave awaited them ... Close on our right was a huge bastion, which the enemy had cleverly hung with dead undergrowth, which, when it was set on fire, lit up the breach as clear as day.[132]

The first attempt at storming Bhurtpore was thwarted by the ditch, so a second attack was accompanied by 'a bamboo bridge ... which was broad enough to take three files of infantry, advancing abreast of each other ... the hundred men in charge of it would be able to hurl it a considerable distance.' In the event, the defenders had let more water into their moat, and the bridge was too short: Shipp regained consciousness after being hit in the face by a bullet, to see 'the famous bamboo bridge floating quietly down the stream.'

Most storms took place at night, in an effort to reduce the effect of the defender's firepower. In 1704 the Allies had attacked the

Schellenberg in broad daylight, and John Deane saw how: 'no sooner did our Forlorn Hope appear than the enemy did throw in their volleys of cannon balls and small shot among them . . . and they being strongly intrenched they killed and mortifyed abundance of our men both officers and souldiers.'[133]

Behind the Forlorn Hopes came the assaulting parties, with the main strength of the attacking battalions behind them. If a storm was supremely dangerous for the Forlorn Hope, it was scarcely less risky even for these follow-up groups: at Badajoz Major O'Hare of the 95th , commanding the Light Division's assaulting party, prophesied that he would be a lieutenant colonel or cold meat before daybreak. Men often went into this danger with cold determination. William Grattan saw the 43rd Light Infantry on its way to the lesser breach at Ciudad Rodrigo:

> Our attention was attracted by the sound of music; we all stood up, and pressed forward to a ridge . . . it would be impossible for me to convey an adequate idea of our feelings when we beheld the 43rd Regiment, preceded by their band, going to storm the left breach; they were in the lightest spirits, but without the slightest appearance of levity in their demeanour – on the contrary, there was a cast of determined severity thrown over their countenances that expressed in legible characters that they knew the sort of service they were about to perform, and had made up their minds to the issue. They had no knapsacks – their firelocks were slung over their shoulders – their shirt collars were open and there was an indescribable *something* about them . . .

The 88th and the 43rd knew one another well, and many of Grattan's comrades stepped forward for a quick handshake as old friends passed. There was no shouting or bravado, and eventually the column wound out of sight: 'the music grew fainter every moment, until at last it died away altogether; they had no drums, and there was a melting sweetness in the sounds that touched the heart.'[134]

The assaulting parties raced for the breach as the Forlorn Hope disappeared into it. John Kincaid, a subaltern of the assaulting party assailing the lesser breach at Ciudad Rodrigo, tells how:

The space between us and the breach became one blaze
of light with their fire-balls, while they lighted us on to
glory, lightened not a few of their lives and limbs; for the
whole glacis was in consequence swept by a well-directed
fire of grape and musketry – and they are the devil's own
brooms; but our gallant fellows walked through it to the
point of attack, with the most determined steadiness . . .[135]

At Badajoz the French exploded a chain of shells in the main breach,
the explosion fired assorted debris in the ditch, and the flames
greatly aided the defenders' shooting. Men who scrambled up the
breach found their way blocked by beams studded with sword-blades.
A rifleman was briefly glimpsed standing on top of one. 'We made
a glorious rush to follow,' remembered Harry Smith of the 95th, 'but
alas in vain. He was knocked over. My old captain, O'Hare, who
commanded the storming party, was killed. All were awfully wounded
except, I do believe, myself and little Freer of the 43rd.'[136]

And at San Sebastian the defenders had placed a mine under
the main breach, but a mortar-bomb burst near its powder-train
and ignited it prematurely. 'It exploded,' writes Gleig, 'while three
hundred grenadiers, the elite of the garrison, stood over it, and
instead of sweeping the storming party into eternity, it only cleared
the way for their advance. It was a spectacle as appalling and grand
as the imagination can conceive, the sight of that explosion.'[137]
Despite this setback the garrison fought on with 'desperate courage',
and fighting went on till nightfall. John Aitchison of 3rd Guards
arrived on top of the breach to find the attackers under heavy musketry from the town and cannon fire from the other fortifications.
'In this situation,' he wrote,

> they were detained nearly half an hour; all the while how-
> ever they were being reinforced, and at length the bugles
> sounding the 'advance' and a hearty 'hurrah' announced
> to the spectators that we had gained an advantage . . .
> From this time our men gained ground gradually but the
> enemy fought desperately in the town and there was still
> a tremendous fire of musketry at three o'clock when I left
> it . . .[138]

Sometimes the attackers carried ladders, either to scale unbreached ramparts or to help with the passage of the ditch. Volunteer George Hennell, in his first battle, went forward with the 3rd Division, heading not for a breach but for a section of wall. 'We all marched in an indirect way towards the town under strict orders that not a whisper should be heard,' he wrote. 'I got a soldier's jacket, and 60 rounds of ammunition and was the right hand man of the second company of the 94th Regiment.' As they climbed the slope towards the wall, 'much crowded as people at a fair' they dropped to their hands and knees and crawled forward across the slippery ground. At this point 'there came a shot from a 24 pounder ... and twelve men sank together with a groan that would have shook to the soul the nerves of the oldest soldier that ever carried a musket ... It swept like a besom all within its range. The next four steps I took were all over this heap.'[139]

When the British attacked the Great Redan at Sevastopol in broad daylight on 17 June 1855 they were assaulting a powerful, unbreached V-shaped defence work, whose defenders stood four deep behind the parapet. There was a 450 yard fire-swept glacis, with a timber barrier, the abbatis, on the attacker's side of the ditch. Although there was no Forlorn Hope, skirmishers of the Rifle Brigade led off with the intention of keeping the defenders under fire while the main attack went in. Behind them came some parties carrying wool-bags to drop into the ditch and others with 18 foot ladders to scale the ramparts. As men carrying the ladders fell under the heavy fire it became harder for their comrades to bear the added weight. Eventually all were lost, although the bluejackets of the Naval Brigade got theirs further forward than any others.

The infantry coming on behind soon fell into disorder, and the loss of some of its best officers, like Colonel Lacy Yea of 7th Fusiliers, took the heart out the of the attack. Captain Hugh Hibbert was in his battalion.

> We had some hundred yards to advance across an open plain with guns loaded with grape and canister shot blazing away into us. As I advanced I thought every second would be my last. I could hardly see for the dust that the grape shot made in ploughing up the ground all around

us – before – behind – and on each side – shells bursting over my head and fellows rolling over right and left. I seemed to bear a charmed life because nothing would hit me! When we got to the abbatis which was at least fifty yards from the Redan the fire was so heavy that no mortals could stand it and there was nothing for it but to retreat as rapidly as possible. In fact we were regularly beaten back and I saw those rascally Russians taking off their caps and jeering at us.[140]

Almost 1500 British soldiers were hit in a scene which, but for the black powder and red jackets, was grimly portentous of the sufferings of their grandsons. Sergeant Timothy Gowing thought it 'almost a miracle how any of the storming columns escaped. My clothing was all cut to pieces – I had no fewer than nine shot-holes through my trousers, coat and cap – but, thank God, I was not touched.'[141]

It was small wonder that discipline sometimes broke down when men fought their way into a fortress. There were three terrible examples in the Peninsula. The morning after Ciudad Rodrigo was taken Wellington saw a group of soldiers with 'scarcely a vestige of uniform . . . Some were dressed in Frenchmen's coats, some in white breeches and huge jack-boots, some with cocked hats and queues; most of their swords were fixed on their rifles, and stuck full of hams, tongues and loaves of bread and not a few were carrying bird cages.' He asked an officer who this band of ruffians might be, and was told that it was the Light Division.[142] Grattan's men staggered back into camp just as bizarrely clad – some had dressed as priests and others as women – and there set about 'drinking like fishes, while their less fortunate comrades at Rodrigo – either hastily flung into an ill-formed grave, writhing under the knife of the surgeon, or in the agonies of death – were unthought of, or unfelt for.'[143]

The siege of Badajoz was a more serious matter than that of Rodrigo: Wellington's army suffered 5,000 casualties, most of them incurred during the storm. Six generals were wounded, four commanding officers killed, and the two hardest-hit regiments, the 43rd and 52nd, respectively lost 347 and 383 officers and men killed and wounded. What followed was also far worse than the sack of Rodrigo. John Cooper of the 7th Fusiliers admitted that 'our maddened fellows rushed into the town by thousands. Wine stores were broken open, and horrible scenes commenced. All order ceased. Plunder was the order of the night. Some got loaded with plate etc; then beastly drunk; and lastly were robbed by others. This lasted until the second day after.'[144] Grattan, too, was shocked to see men:

> turn upon the already too deeply injured females, and tear from them the trinkets that adorned their necks, fingers and ears! And finally they would strip them of their wearing apparel . . . many men were flogged, but although the contrary has been said, none were hanged – yet hundreds deserved it.'[145]

San Sebastian was sacked, as Rodrigo and Badajoz had been. The troops:

> heated already with angry passions, became absolutely mad by intoxication. All order and discipline were abandoned. The officers had not the slightest control over their men . . . Here you would see a drunken fellow whirling a string of watches round his head, and then dashing them against the wall; there another, more provident, stuffing his bosom with such smaller articles as he most prized . . .[146]

CAPTAINS
IN OPEN FIELD

Attacks on fortresses demanded courage and leadership of the highest order: the British army's success at Ciudad Rodrigo and Badajoz and its failure at the Redan point to some fundamental truths. There is no such thing as a theory of combat motivation with universal applicability: national military cultures are often very different, and there is good reason to doubt whether, for example the preferred modern Anglo-American view, which emphasises the importance of small-unit cohesion, can be applied to the Second World War German army on the Russian front, where manpower turbulence often prevented the creation or sustaining of the relationships on which such cohesion depended. John Keegan comes as close to the truth as we shall get when he identifies the trio of coercion, inducement and narcosis, and adds the pervasive influence of the 'big man', who might not necessarily be big in feet and inches or in the rank he wears. But he is 'the person who brings combat alive . . . the star without whom the film is a flop, the diva without whom an opera is only a recital . . .'[147]

Although externally-imposed discipline buttressed the soldier's behaviour in war as in peace, it is clear that lash, noose and firing-party had their limitations for the creation of battlefield morale. Wellington recognised that most soldiers, from time to time, ran away: the good ones came back again, and it was impossible to court-martial them all. In battles across the period, like Bunker Hill at its beginning, Waterloo in the middle or Badli-ki-Serai at its end, men often had opportunities to flinch or fumble, straggle or stumble, and avoid coercion. Tactical change was to make this easier. The French colonel Charles Ardant du Picq, writing in the 1860s, feared that the tendency for infantry to spread out in the face of improving firearms meant that, as he put it, cohesion would lack the sanction of mutual surveillance. In other words, men would no longer be kept brave by the knowledge that their failure would be witnessed by leaders and comrades alike.

In fact, surveillance had always been threatened by the smoke and chaos of the battlefield, and the urgings of officers like Frederick the Great or James Wolfe that men who wavered were to be run through by the officer or NCO behind them had serious practical limitations. I have found no instance of British officers or NCOs applying this lethal sanction in combat, although several of the reverse. 'Fragging,' the murder of officers and NCOs by their own men, is not a new phenomenon. The unpopular major commanding the 14th Foot at Blenheim addressed the regiment before the battle, apologising for his past behaviour and asking that if he had to fall it should be by the enemy's bullets. A grenadier shouted: 'March on, sir; the enemy is before you, and we have something else to do than to think of you now.' The battle over, the major turned to his troops and raised his hat to call for a cheer: he was instantly shot through the head by an unknown marksman. There is a suggestion that Lieutenant Colonel John Cameron of Fassiefern, formidable commander of the 92nd in the Peninsula and the Hundred Days, was shot at Quatre Bras by a bad character he had had flogged not long before, although it is impossible to be certain.

Discipline got men into battle, helped hold them steady in rank and file as long as good order was maintained, and often stopped them from deserting after it. But for what really motivated them in the smoky world of battle we must look elsewhere. At the top of our hierarchy comes a broad sense of national superiority, that very quality that even allies often found exasperating. The squares of English regiments visibly taughtened when Wellington rode round them at Waterloo, saying: 'Stand fast! We must not be beat! What will they say of this in England?' And when Major Rowland Smyth was about to charge the Sikh guns at Aliwal in 1846, he asked for three cheers for the queen: 'There was a terrific burst of cheering in reply, and down we swept upon the guns.'[148] Colour Sergeant McAlister, hard hit and ordered to drop out of the line in the Crimea, refused, saying, 'I've done nothing for old England yet.'

A song of the English civil war spoke of:

> Captains in open field on their foes rushing
> Gentlemen second them, with their pikes pushing . . .

and the principle was well understood. Officers were expected to lead with demonstrative courage. John Shipp, during one of his periods of service in the ranks, told an officer, politely but firmly: 'The words go on don't become [ie befit] an officer, Sir.' The most successful middle-piece commanders told their men precisely what was to be done, and then led them to do it. At Busaco in 1810 Lieutenant Colonel Alexander Wallace addressed the 88th as it awaited the arrival of a French column,

> Now Connaught Rangers, mind what you are going to do; pay attention to what I have so often told you, and when I bring you face to face with those French rascals, drive them down the hill – don't give them the false touch, but push home to the muzzle! I have nothing more to say, and if I had it would be of no use, for in a *minit* or two there'll be such an infernal noise about your ears that you won't be able to hear yourselves.[149]

Major General John Lysaght Pennefather found his brigade under heavy fire at the foot of the Russian-held slope at the Alma in 1854. As a witness reported:

> Pennefather, the bravest of the brave, got fidgetty. He saw his men were suffering, and said, '30th, you had better advance! You will be safer when you are closer under the guns' and, crossing the river (followed by our poor colonel, who behaved nobly during the whole action) he said, in his pure Tipperary accent, 'Come on! My darling fellows, come on!' On they went, opened their fire and

soon waved their colours over the ground which the enemy had abandoned.[150]

Lieutenant Colonel Richard Pattoun, more than sixty years old, led the 32nd to the assault of Multan in 1849. 'Our Colonel was the foremost. Cutting his way sword in hand,' wrote one of his men. After the battle he 'saw our Colonel's body; it lay under, or rather among about a dozen of the enemy . . . It was maimed in several places; his wrist was nearly cut off and on one side of his head was a deep cut. A musket-ball had passed through his body. He looked noble, even in death. The whole regiment lamented his loss.'[151] Such behaviour inspired soldierly emulation. William Grattan saw Private Pollard of Captain Bury's company of the 88th shot though the shoulder at Busaco: 'But seeing his captain, though wounded, continue at the head of his men, he threw off his knapsack and fought beside his officer; but this brave fellow's career of glory was short; a bullet penetrated the plate of his cap, passed through his brain, and he fell dead at Bury's feet.'[152]

If charismatic leadership was one key ingredient of morale, robust paternalism was another. Private Waterfield was no respecter of persons. Indeed, he thought that: 'Colonel Markham gave us plenty of drill and long parades . . .' And then he added:

> But if he was a little hard, as we thought, in that respect, he was the best of commanders in others. He was very passionate at times; he would curse you heartily, in the true Yorkshire style, then all was forgotten by him directly afterwards. He encouraged every kind of amusement, more especially the old but manly game, cricket. Any company wishing to give a ball (which was often done) he would sign and order for that company to get 25 gallons of rum and as much wine as they liked. That is what made the men like Colonel Markham, or as he was sometimes called 'Douglas' or 'Black Fred.'[153]

In the Peninsula, the men of the 51st liked Major Rice. When his favourite piebald horse was shot under him Wheeler recorded that: 'We are all sorry for poor Tom, as he was the Major's pet. The Major is beloved of every man in the corps, so when he is in trouble we all share it with him.'[154]

Poor Tom's demise may have spread rings of sorry in its own right, for officers and soldiers were often sentimental about animals, which touched that streak of gentleness in so many of them. During his voyage to North America John Peebles lamented 'a pig washed overboard, a goat (poor Betsy) drown an 14 fowls...'[155] Several diarists commented on the fact that 'a large white Poodle dog' scoured the battlefield of Salamanca, looking for its master, and eventually found his corpse, where it 'lay down & howled piteously.' Thomas Browne discovered that he had belonged to a French officer who was to have been married to a local lady. He tracked down her house and tried to buy the dog, but 'received the answer, that it would not be parted with.' Ensign Leeke saw a tortoiseshell kitten lying dead in the mud at Waterloo, and suddenly thought of home. The officers' mess of the 8th Hussars had a pet, Jemmy, a wire-haired terrier, in the Crimea. He fell in behind the rear rank and charged down the North Valley, yapping fiercely as he went and emerging slightly wounded. Major Rodolph de Salis had a special collar made to take the four bars of his Crimea medal. He gained another clasp during the Indian Mutiny, but perished in 1858 when swimming the River Chanbal. Even sergeant majors could be tender-hearted. In the Crimea George Loy Smith took over 'a little Tartar chicken' from the RSM of the 10th Hussars. It had been intended as dinner, but became a pet, living in the sergeant-major's tent, coming when he whistled and following him like a dog. Loy Smith made a perch for it on his tent pole, and it lived happily with him.

Some animals were useful. On campaign in India John Shipp admonished a sentry for not challenging in a louder voice. The man said that he did not want to wake his dog. It transpired that the creature was off duty at the moment. He would 'regularly stand his hour and make his round,' waking his master if anyone approached. Shipp noted that he was 'a powerful animal, a kind of Persian hill-greyhound.' Others were less helpful. Shipp teased a tame elephant by giving it bread with Cayenne pepper in it. He forgot all about the incident, and a month later petted the same elephant, which seemed to relish his attentions. But as soon as Shipp's back was turned, it squirted him with dirty water 'and so was revenged for the Cayenne pepper.'

Officers' language was often paternalistic. John Peebles always speaks of his men as 'lads,' and Thomas Pococke of the 71st contrasted the lively behaviour of French officers with that of his own. 'After the first huzza the British officers, restraining their men, still as death. "Steady, lads, steady" is all you hear, and that in an undertone.'[156] Private soldiers and NCOs are not anonymous, faceless extras in officers' diaries of the period, but are often remembered with affection and regard. Colour Sergeant Switzer and Private Lacy of the 32nd helped Lieutenant Belcher defend his colour at Waterloo. Corporal William Hanley of the 14th Light Dragoons gained widespread approbation by capturing a French lieutenant colonel and 27 men with his eight-man patrol in 1812: his officers had a medal struck for him, and presented it on a full-dress parade. Sergeant Major Thorp of the 88th, with his ensigncy literally in the post (it arrived the following day) was killed showing foolhardy courage at Orthez in 1814 by standing in the middle of a group of corpses saying 'now let us see if they can hit me': a cannon ball cut him in half almost immediately.

Sometimes their first names are recorded, although not always to their advantage: Tomkinson tells us that Lieutenant Weyland of his regiment thrashed his farrier, Mic. Mullen, with the flat of his sword for getting drunk, Craufurd, characteristically handing out floggings on the road to Corunna, ordered the drummers to 'begin with Daniel Howans', and Peebles recorded that his company wounded were doing well 'except Wm. MacIntosh who is just dying – Jno. Car holds it out surprisingly . . .'[157] At Waterloo Sergeant Morris's captain was sixty years old, never in battle before, and so badly frightened that 'several times he came to me for a drop of something to keep his spirits up.' He called his sergeant Tom, perhaps hoping to bring more human warmth into a relationship which inverted the more usual one of old NCO and young officer, and had trouble with his pronunciation, saying: 'Tom, Tom, here comes the calvary.' Sadly, the old gentleman was cut in two by a roundshot near the end of the day.

Experienced NCOs often showed a gruff friendliness to young

officers, especially when they seemed to be made of the right stuff. Thomas Brotherton bore the colours of the Coldstream Guards in 1801, as the regiment advanced in line under fire, with men falling fast, and his covering sergeant asked: 'How do you feel, Sir?' Brotherton gave the honest answer – 'Pretty well, but this is not very pleasant!' The sergeant liked the reply, and thereafter 'seemed to take me under his special protection and care ever after . . .'[158] Ensign William Leeke was carrying the colours of the 53rd at Waterloo when he saw something hiss through the corn. A helpful colour sergeant answered his unspoken question: 'That, Mr Leeke, is a cannon-shot, if you never saw one before, Sir.'[159]

Officers were concerned about the figure they cut in the eyes of peers, superiors and subordinates alike. Some, carrying the logic of the duelling-ground to the battlefield, preferred the probability of death to the risk of disgrace. At the very end of the battle of Waterloo, Major Howard of the 10th Hussars was ordered to attack a French infantry regiment. A brother officer warned him that its square was well formed, and the attack unlikely to succeed without the support of other arms. Howard felt, however, that having been given a direct order he could not in conscience refuse, and duly charged the square: he fell amongst the bayonets of the front rank, where a French soldier beat out his brains with the butt of his musket. Conversely, Lieutenant Colonel Lord Portarlington of the 23rd Light Dragoons was in Brussels when the battle started, and only reached the field after his regiment had been heavily engaged. Although he joined in a charge by another regiment, he was finished, and obliged to resign. Officers were anxious that a sensible withdrawal could not be construed as cowardice. When Colonel Charles Windham decided to run back from the forefront of the hopelessly stalled attack on the Redan to get reinforcements, he first found a subaltern and told him: 'Bear witness that I am not in a funk but I will now try to go back to do what I can.' Slurs upon an officer's personal honour were often deeply resented: when Lieutenant Colonel Charles Bevan of the 4th King's Own was unfairly blamed for the escape of the French garrison of Almeida in 1811 he shot himself.

We have already seen the risks entailed in carrying the colours, but there was no shirking their deadly obligation, as William Keep

discovered at Vitoria as his adjutant called forward ensigns by seniority to replace those who were hit.

> At this moment Mr Bridgeland's voice called for me to
> the Colours, and I proceeded directly there and found
> that poor Delmar had been shot through the heart.
>
> In the confusion of the moment a mistake had been
> made and Mr Hill, being junior to me, should have been
> called. This the adjutant discovered, and I returned to my
> company. But I had not been there long when a second
> call was made for me, and I found that Hill had been
> struck in the breast, similar to Delmar, and carried away
> ... I now took the fatal colour and entered into conver-
> sation with Ensign Tatlow, bearing the other.[160]

This anecdote is an interesting reflection of the formality of the age.
Officers referred to one another by name and rank (ensigns/cornets
and lieutenants were 'Mr'), simply by surname, or occasionally by
rank. We might now find calling somebody 'Major' *tout court* rather
Fawltyesque. But when Lord George Paget was making up a long-
standing quarrel with his second in command, Major John Halkett,
who found himself without rum on the morning of the Charge of
the Light Brigade, Paget said: 'Major, I can give you some.' As they
had not been speaking for some time, Halkett might have been just
too sharp, and John much too familiar. Charles Napier's men
shouted 'Major let us fire! at Corunna, and a badly wounded man
implored his help: 'God, my jewel, my own dear major, sure you
won't leave me!' Napier was so upset that he picked the man up,
only to be hit in the leg by a musket-ball as he did so.

The use of a first name implied a close friendship, but was more
common amongst soldiers than officers. For Harry Smith to receive
a 'Well done Harry' from a divisional QMG was praise indeed. When
John Colborne fell out with Major General Sir William Stewart, the
latter announced: 'Well then, in future, Colonel Colborne, I shall
address you only in the most official manner' and henceforth wrote
to him as Dear Sir, not Dear Colonel[161]. The use of 'Sir' in everyday
address did not imply subordination. Private soldiers received the
unwelcome order 'Strip, Sir' from their adjutants before flogging,
and when Lord Paget inquired of an officer lurking in the regimental

baggage 'What are you doing there, Sir?' he was not being in the least polite, and became less so as the conversation went on. Soldiers, especially Irish ones, often called officers 'Your Honour,' and 'Captain darlin'' was not unknown.

There was often a creative tension between commissioned and non-commissioned ranks, with officers behaving well because it was expected of them, and soldiers both following their good example and reinforcing it with courage of their own. What was honour in an abstract sense to an officer was often as tough a bond of mateship to a private. Battlefield performance was in great measure a product of long and close association in barrack-room and bivouac, grog-shop and brothel, with the creation of a small and introspective world with rules all of its own. Benjamin Harris and Rifleman Jock Gillespie had just heard the bugles sound 'Fire and retire' at Vimeiro, and were falling back, firing alternately, as good riflemen ought, when Harris saw his comrade:

> limp along, as though some one had bestowed a violent kick upon his person. However, he didn't give up at first, but continued to load and fire, and make off with the other skirmishers, till we made another stand . . .
>
> Gillespie loaded and fired very sharply, I recollect, seemingly quite affronted at the treatment he had received; but he got weaker and more lame as he did so, and at last was quite unable to continue the game any longer . . . he was floored from loss of blood.[162]

Gillespie had been hit in what contemporaries called 'the ballocks', but was prepared neither to fall out until he fell over, nor, being a sensitive man, to disclose the nature of his wound. A near miss by a roundshot at Badajoz made William Wheeler's head ache, but he felt duty bound to continue his work. 'Had I been working in a place where there was no danger,' he wrote, 'I should certainly have given up, but here I was ashamed to complain, lest any of my comrades should laugh at me.'[163] A soldier of the 95th who helped bandsmen carry wounded to the rear was shunned by his former comrades, and Costello thought that 'no good soldier would venture, under so frivolous a pretext, to expose himself to the indignation of his comrades, excepting for any very extreme cases.'[164] At the Alma, Colin Campbell widened the field in which status could be lost by warning that any soldier who left the ranks to help the wounded would have his name posted up in his parish kirk.

Benjamin Harris observed that:

> It is indeed curious how a man loses or gains caste with his comrades from his behaviour, and how closely he is observed in the field. The officers, too, are commented on and closely observed. Their men are very proud of those who are brave in the field and kind and considerate to the men under them.[165]

In good regiments the process became a virtuous spiral, and a collective fighting spirit, which neither depended on discipline nor required strong leadership, took over. William Tomkinson tells us that his men had 'a general inclination' to charge what was believed to be a French cavalry regiment coming on at the end of the day at Waterloo, but happily turned out to be Prussian. The 7th Fusiliers showed similar spirit at Albuera, although, as John Cooper wrote, 'our Colonel and all the field officers of the brigade' were killed or wounded, 'men were knocked about like skittles but not a step back was taken.'[166] We see the same thing at Badli-ke-Serai, with Richard Barter's men telling him 'we ain't agoing to turn'.

But drafting in new soldiers to replace battle casualties might produce a vicious circle, as cohesion diminished, demanding more charismatic leadership, which increased casualties amongst officers and NCOs. Sometimes the poor performance of regiments can be explained by the fact that their soldiers had not been together long enough to get to know one another, and to have status which would be impaired by cowardice. It is significant that Braddock's two British regiments which broke on the Monongahela had been brought up to strength for the campaign by drafts from other units, and had never really 'bedded down' properly.

In the Crimea casualties severely eroded the fighting spirit of regiments. Captain Thomas Campbell of the 46th Regiment wrote of the Redan that: 'only the officers and the best men ever reached the battle; a good many of the men did not behave well at all. The army does not consist of anything like so fine a set of men as those that fought at Alma and Inkerman.' Captain Gerald Goodlake of the Coldstream Guards made the same point: 'What a lot of funkers they are making in our army; we have lost so many men and so many are wounded that they are always looking out for cover.'[167] 'Do you see that pale-faced thin boy in the rear rank of all,' asked Henry Clifford,

> thinking of his mother and what a fool he was to leave her and take the shilling? He came out ten days ago, light-hearted, thinking what a fine thing it was to be a soldier, going to fight the Russians and take Sevastopol, and how he would get pretty presents from his sisters when Sevastopol was taken ... Poor lad, he has not got much to say now. Seven days out of ten in the trenches, and on Picquet, have taken almost his life out of him ...[168]

Young soldiers looked to more experienced ones for their example. Roger Lamb, then a corporal in the 9th Foot, first came under fire in a skirmish near Quebec in 1776:

> It really appeared to me to be a very serious matter, especially when the bullets came whistling close to our ears. In order to encourage the young soldiers amongst us, some of the veterans who had been well used to this kind of work said 'there is no danger if you hear the sound of the bullet, which is fired against you, you are safe, and after the first charge all your fears will be done away with.' These remarks I found to be perfectly true many a time afterwards.[169]

Lamb's was a common experience. Waiting for battle was hardest, and the first few minutes of combat, when the enemy's fire began to make itself felt, were utterly terrifying. As Timothy Gowing advanced on the Alma he felt 'horribly sick – a cold shivering running through my veins – and I must acknowledge that I felt very uncomfortable.' But this feeling soon passed off, and he began to 'warm to it', aware of the risks he ran but no longer scared of them. 'The fighting now became very exciting,' he remembered, 'our artillery playing over our heads, and we firing and advancing all the time. The smoke was now so great that we could hardly see what we were doing, and our fellows were falling all around; it was a dirty rugged hill.'[170] In his first action Harris became so excited that his captain had to call him by name to order him to settle down.

Religious belief helped many men make the transition from terror to acceptance. Sergeant John Stephenson of 3rd Guards, 'sixteen years a Non-commissioned officer, forty years a Wesleyan class leader' went into battle at Talavera confident that the Lord would save him even if the worst happened, and Christopher Ludlam of the 59th Regiment no longer feared death after he became a committed Christian because 'sudden death would be sudden glory'.[171] Henry Clifford, a Roman Catholic, told his cousin Letty that during the Alma 'I said my prayers the whole time and I received absolution just before going into battle.' Later he wrote that:

> Mr Sheehan the priest is always with my division and I go to him to get absolution just before I go under fire. I am very happy and as well prepared for death as I can make myself. I have so many to pray for me whose prayers must be heard. I have great hope and confidence in the future. Religion is the only thing that can make a man truly composed and cool under fire.[172]

John Shipp believed that most soldiers prayed before action but few admitted it, 'for in general soldiers deride religious comrades.'

Just as the courage of officers and men was mutually supporting, so too one regiment's regard for another stiffened men's courage. The 30th and the 44th Foot had fought together in Spain, and when a detachment of the 30th, making haste to the field of Quatre Bras, passed wounded of the hard-hit 44th, there were shouts of: 'Push on the old three tens – pay 'em for the 44th – you're much wanted, boys – success to you, my darlings.' At Quatre Bras, too, an appeal to past triumph strengthened present valour. The 28th, in square, was already rocked by casualties, when French cavalry bore down on three sides of it. Picton shouted in his powerful voice: 'Twenty-Eighth! Remember Egypt!' He was referring to the occasion when the regiment had won its distinctive back badge at Alexandria fourteen years before. There were probably very few present that day who could remember Egypt, but the appeal to ancient virtue worked, and the regiment stood firm.

Visible appearance had an almost tangible quality. In his first battle William Surtees saw just how formidable a cohesive battalion looked.

> Nothing could surpass the steadiness and fine appearance of the 23rd, on entering into action; but they were all old soldiers, while our two battalions were composed altogether, I may say, of volunteers from the militia, who had as little idea of service in the field, as if newly taken from the plough.[173]

William Napier, a brave and experienced infantry officer before he became a historian, described the impact of formality when the 92nd returned to action after being badly mauled on the Nive in 1814. Colonel Cameron's horse had been shot beneath him, and he led his men forward on foot, with the sole surviving piper playing *Cogadh na sith* (War and Peace). Napier wrote:

> How desperately did the 50th and the Portuguese fight to give time for the 92nd to rally and reform behind St Pierre; how gloriously did that regiment come forth again to charge with their colours flying and their national music playing as if going to a review. This was to understand war. The man who in that moment and immediately after such a repulse thought of such military pomp was indeed a soldier.[174]

Lieutenant Colonel Mainwaring of the 51st Regiment was not alone in attributing an almost talismanic quality to drill. 'I shall never forget him,' wrote William Wheeler,

> He dismounted off his horse, faced us and frequently called the time 'right, left' as he was accustomed to when drilling the regiment. His eccentricity did not leave him, he would now and then call out 'That fellow is out of step, keep step and they cannot hurt us.' Another time he would observe such a one, calling him by name, 'cannot march, mark him for drill, Sergeant Major.' 'I tell you again they cannot hurt us if you are steady, if you get out of time, you will be knocked down.' He was leading his horse and a shot passed under the horse's belly which made him

Although wounded, Piper George Clarke of the 71ˢᵗ continued to play at Vimiero in 1808. There were no gallantry medals at the time, but Clarke was presented with a set of silver-mounted pipes by the Highland Society of London. The regiment was later converted into light infantry when it showed its Scots origins by a broad diced border aorund its caps. We cannot be sure whether it wore kilts or trews (as shown here) at Vimiero.

rear up. 'You are a coward!' he said. 'I will stop your corn three days.'[175]

Major Charles Napier thought that drill helped keep men's minds off worse things. While waiting to attack at Corunna 'I walked up and down before the regiment, and made the men shoulder and order arms twice to occupy their attention, for they were falling fast and seemed uneasy standing under fire.'[176]

A book which has already dwelt a good deal on drink needs add little about its effects in inducing battlefield narcosis. The very term 'Dutch courage' stems from the use of *genever* by British soldiers fighting in the Low Countries in the seventeenth century. There was usually plenty of drink about, both ration rum (or occasionally arrack in India) and privately-procured spirits of a variety of taste and quality. Men drank to dull their senses in a rainy bivouac. On the night before Waterloo Ensign Short's battalion of the Coldstream Guards remained under arms in a middle field but: 'I with another officer had a blanket, and, with a little more gin, we kept up well.'

William Wheeler found that both 'brandy and Hollands' could be bought in the village of Mont St Jean. 'Night came on,' he wrote, 'we were wet to the skin, but having plenty of liquor were, to use an expression of one of my old comrades, "wet and comfortable." '[177]

Drink helped men face battle. Wheeler watched Sergeant Botley serving out rum under fire from a camp kettle near Badajoz, reserving for himself the rations of men who were killed. Major O'Hare of the 95th chatted with Captain Jones of the 52nd as they waited to attack the fortress. O'Hare was (rightly, in the event,) gloomy and fatalistic. 'Tut, tut man,' said Jones, 'I have the same sort of feeling, but I keep it down with a drop of the *cratur*,' and he passed the major his calabash.[178] Sergeant Morris took 'an extra drop of spirits' (he had three canteens of gin) with his old friend Sergeant Burton before Waterloo, and Burton urged him to keep a nip for after the battle. Morris suggested that few of them would be left, but Burton was sure that 'there is no shot made yet for either you or me.' They both survived, and Burton celebrated by slapping Morris on the back with a cry of: 'Out with the grog, Tom.'[179]

Morris noticed that Corporal Shaw of the Life Guards – who became one of the heroes of the battle, hewing down nine French cavalrymen – was drinking gin at midday, and he may well have been totally drunk when he was eventually killed. John Pearman's comrade Jack Marshall 'had been *drinking* for several days' before the battle of Aliwal, and when the fighting was almost over rode off to attack a mounted Sikh. His chum Bill Driver, 'a fine young man, six feet high,' saw that he was bound to get the worst of it and went to help, but Marshall was cut down before Driver could reach him. Driver was killed by a roundshot on his way back, but his horse, as riderless steeds so often did, came back to the regiment.

Drink was easy to come by in India during the Mutiny, and Assistant Surgeon John Henry Sylvester saw it further excite passions which were already dangerously inflamed. 'Country spirit had been found in the village,' he wrote, 'and many of our European soldiery were drunk and committed atrocities among the villagers.'[180] It was harder to obtain in the Crimea, and few British soldiers could match the single-mindedness of a Zouave who sold his boots to buy drink and blacked his feet for the sake of appearances.

For soldiers of a later generation gallantry medals recognised brave deeds, rewarding those who performed them and encouraging others to do likewise. Officers could be knighted for bravery or distinguished service. The Order of the Bath, probably founded in 1399, was reconstituted, in 1813, into three classes, Knights Grand Cross (GCB), Knights Commander (KCB) and Companions (CB). In the recent past military knighthoods were rank-related, often arriving soon after the happy recipient's promotion to lieutenant general. However, in the late 18th and early 19th centuries things were far less predictable. John Colborne, doyen of Peninsula commanding officers, was knighted as a colonel, and the wounded Lieutenant Colonel Sir Robert Macara of 1/42nd might have escaped death at Quatre Bras had French lancers not spotted the star of his KCB and pressed in to kill him. Robert Sale of the 13th Foot already had a KCB when he defended Jellalabad in 1842, and his advancement to GCB was hailed with particular delight because he was still very junior to receive such a high honour.

The CB became a reward for distinguished service in the field, and was usually given to colonels. In February 1855 Edward Cooper Hodge confided to his diary that he expected one, and it duly arrived in August. Hodge pronounced it 'a very handsome jewel', but hoped to get one or two more awards before the war was over. 'I wish I could get the Legion of Honour,' he wrote, 'and a high caste Turkish order.'[181] Hodge's hunger for foreign orders (and he was to be fortunate on both counts) does not reflect the ambivalence shown by other officers. Knighthoods of the Royal Guelphic Order of Hanover (KH) were more readily available than British knighthoods, though their fount was the same, and they were generally well-received. However, in the torrent of foreign orders that followed Allied victory in 1815 Colborne received the Austrian Order of Maria Theresa and the Russian Order of St George from Wellington. He admitted that: 'I took them, saying "They do not give me the least pleasure" but an old colonel who was standing by me said "Colborne, it is my belief that you care for them just as much as other people." Colonel Lygon sent back his Russian Order of St Vladimir (2nd Class), airily declaiming that: 'it would be degrading to the commanding officer of the Life Guards to wear what every officer in the Russian army is entitled to after two years.' 'Won't Colonel Lygon accept it?' asked Wellington. 'Well then, give it to Colonel Somebody-else, who will.'[182]

Officers might also be mentioned in a commander-in-chief's dispatches. As time went on the lists of such mentions grew longer and longer, and sometimes caused offence by including the names of those commended for valuable service alongside those being rewarded for bravery. When he read the gazette for the Alma, Henry Clifford wrote:

> I am surprised . . . that the names of many who were not under fire at the 'Alma' have also been put in; this is a sad mistake, or rather rule, in our service. It takes so much away from the gratification it gives to those who have exposed themselves so much and have been in such great danger to see their names mentioned on equal terms of commendation with those who looked on, and, who, tho' no doubt would have done as well if called upon, were not under fire at all.[183]

There were no gallantry decorations for non-commissioned personnel until the Distinguished Conduct Medal was instituted in 1854, and the Victoria Cross, an all-ranks award for gallantry, was founded two years later, with its first awards being made retrospectively for deeds in the Crimea. Their absence was a source of long-running resentment, especially during the Napoleonic War, when British officers and soldiers often compared French liberality in recognising bravery – the Legion of Honour was widely awarded to all ranks – with the stinginess of their own government. In October 1854 Fanny Duberly told how:

> A rifleman, seeing a shell light in the entrenchment, knocked out the fuse with his rifle. He was mentioned in general orders. I cannot but think it a pity that our service provides no decoration, no distinctive reward of bravery, for such acts as this. If it were only a bit of red rag, the man should have it, and wear it immediately, as an honourable distinction, instead of waiting for a medal that he may never live to obtain, or may only obtain years hence, when it shall have lost half its value.[184]

Individual regiments did their best to compensate for this by striking private medals, like that awarded to William Hanley, or presenting badges, like the embroidered colour given to Corporal Anton Lutz of the Minorca Regiment, who captured a colour of the French 21st Demi-Brigade Légère at Alexandria, and the VS (for 'Valiant Stormer') badges given to survivors of the 52nd's forlorn hopes in the Peninsula.

Even campaign medals were rare in the British army, although the East Indian Company was more generous. Unofficial versions had been issued for the Carib War of 1773 and the defence of Gibraltar in 1779–83. Although generals and field officers received Army Gold Medals and rather fewer Gold Crosses for the Peninsula, it was not until Waterloo that an all-ranks official British campaign medal was issued. This caused almost as much resentment as satisfaction, for many seasoned Peninsula regiments did not fight at Waterloo and emerged medal-less from the Napoleonic wars. There were also immediate difficulties when the medals were issued, as Sergeant Tom Morris remembered:

> One of the men, whose name was Hadly, a shoemaker, a native of Oxford, I put a veto on his receiving it, by informing my captain that the man was my rear-rank man, at Waterloo, and that he ran away to Brussels, and placing his arm in a sling, reported himself wounded; suspicion was excited; he was examined, and had not a scratch upon him ... The captain, having heard my statement, said he should withhold the medal ... The man, ashamed to return to his quarters without the medal ... deserted; he was quickly followed, taken at Oxford among his friends, and was eventually sent to a condemned regiment in Africa for life.[185]

It was not until 1847 that Military and Naval General Service Medals were authorised, bearing bars naming the actions in which the earner had served. By this time, of course, most of the men entitled to the medals were dead: only ten of the veterans of the well-executed cavalry action at Benavente in December 1808 were able to claim their medals. There were twenty-nine bars authorised for the Military

General Service Medal, and fifteen was the maximum number won – by Private Talbot of the 45th and Private Loochstadt of the KGL.

The Crimean medal, again with the names of battles embossed on its bars, was issued while the war was actually in progress, but it did not please everybody. Colonel Hodge thought it 'a vulgar looking thing, with clasps like gin labels. How odd it is, we cannot do things like people of taste. This is a heavy vulgar thing.' He soon returned to a familiar theme. There should be a simple medal, given 'to those who were *under fire* in the trenches and *to no other*. These medals given to all the world are of no value. They are too common.'[186] Common or not, medals usually did gratify those who received them. They were worn most of the time, as the battered edges of so many surviving specimens show. And when they were awarded promptly, their impact was much enhanced. The government of India took pains to present the medals for the defence of Jellalabad and the march on Kabul so that their recipients could recross the Indus 'wearing the honours they have so justly won'. Even long service was not recognised by a medal till 1830, when the Long Service and Good Conduct Medal was instituted. To earn it a soldier had to be of 'irreproachable character' and to have served for 21 years in the infantry or 20 in the cavalry.

For all the occasional cynicism expressed by officers about decorations, there is no doubt that campaign medals and gallantry awards played their own part in the complex web of motivation. Sergeant Major Loy Smith was was 'highly gratified' to receive his Distinguished Conduct Medal on 1 April 1855. It brought him public recognition – the approval of superiors and the envy of peers – for it was awarded on parade in front of the regiment. And there was the royal connection: he refers to it as 'the Victoria Medal', and notes proudly that the Queen's warrant was read out. It was aesthetically pleasing: he thought it a handsome medal with a 'very pretty' ribbon. And what was more, it brought an annuity of £20, enough to pay the rent on a comfortable property. Who shall blame him if a little battlefield narcosis celebrated his investiture?

EPILOGUE

WORTHY
OF REMEMBRANCE

Veterans did not find that they had returned from the wars to a land fit for heroes to live in. In 1719 'An Epistle from a Half-Pay Officer' had summed up the contrast between military glory and post-war poverty.

> Curse on the star, dear Harry, that betrayed
> My choice from law, divinity or trade,
> To turn a rambling brother o' the blade!
> Of all professions sure the worst is war.
> How whimsical our future! How bizarre!
> This week we shine in scarlet and in gold:
> The next, the cloak is pawned – the watch is sold.[1]

Officers often found themselves shunted off on a half-pay. After Waterloo this was 2s 4d a day for infantry lieutenants, 5s for captains and 8s 6d for lieutenant colonels, and there was a small rise in 1830. The plucky George Hennell tried to stay in Regular service by transferring to 2/39th Foot, but it was disbanded in the post-Waterloo retrenchments. There was little Edmund Wheatley could do with his half-pay ensigncy in the KGL and though he married Eliza Brookes, who features so prominently in his journal, and had four daughters, he died abroad in 1841.

Even those who were able to remain in the service often found themselves dogged by relics of their valour. Lieutenant Colonel Charles Vigoureux of the 30th had made his way entirely by bravery, but was incapacitated for four years following a severe wound received at Waterloo and died in 1841 of an illness exacerbated by the fact that the ball which hit him in the battle had lodged near his spine and could not be extracted. Ensign Severus Stretton of the 68th Light Infantry received a musket ball in the back at Vitoria in 1814. He soldiered on, in constant nagging pain, to become lieutenant colonel of militia: the ball eventually worked its way close enough to the surface to be extracted in 1869, 55 years later.

The half-pay officer, sometimes cad and sometimes pauper, left his mark on the literature and history of the age. In 1763 James Boswell sought to play the part and dressed in the approved raffish style in his 'second-mourning suit, in which I had been powdered many months, dirty buckskin breeches and black stockings, a shirt of Lord Eglinton's which I had worn two days, a little round hat with tarnished silver lace belonging to a disbanded officer of the Royal Volunteers.' When a 'little profligate wretch' charged him sixpence and 'allowed me entrance . . . but refused me performance' and then, when he tried to force the issue, called 'more whores and soldiers to her relief' Boswell at once gained the men's sympathy by shouting: 'Brother soldiers . . . should not a half-pay officer r-g-r for sixpence?'[2] Like Thackeray's characters Major Loder ('reeking of cigars and brandy-and-water') and Captain Rook ('with his horse-jockey jokes and prize-ring slang'), the half-pay officer formed part of 'the little colony of English raffs' in most European cities:

> young gentlemen of good family very often, only that the latter disowns them; frequenters of billiard-rooms and estaminets, patrons of foreign races and gambling-tables. They people debtors' prisons – they drink and swagger – they fight and brawl – they run away without paying – they have duels with French and German officers – they cheat Mr Spooner at *écarté* . . . The alternations of splendour and misery which these people undergo are very queer to view.[3]

A half-pay officer prosecuted for debt at the Surrey Assizes in 1801 had 'the manners and appearance of a gentleman' but was wholly destitute. This was 'too often the case with the Officers in the Army, who upon a small pittance are obliged to keep up an appearance of rank to which their incomes are totally inadequate.'[4] Some had no safety-net except the workhouse, and in November 1819 the *Gentleman's Magazine* recorded the death, in the sick ward of the Lambeth Workhouse, of Lieutenant Henry Bowerman, late of the 56th Foot: his two sons, 10 and 12 years old, were both residents of the Norwood Workhouse.

Soldiers often returned to find that they were forgotten men. Private John Ryder served with the 32nd Regiment in India, and came home in 1849 or 1850 to a village near Leicester:

> on arriving there, I went to Mr Goodman's, the public-house near my father's, for I thought it would be better than going in home at once ... I had sent for my father, by an old neighbour, to meet me at the public-house ... In the house were two of my old companions ... We had been at school together and play fellows, but they neither of them knew me. The landlord who brought me the ale had known me from a child, but he did not appear to have the slightest recollection of me ... While I was in talk, my father came in. He looked round, but did not see any one whom he knew, who wanted him. He sat down and I called to him, and said, 'Come, old man, will you have glass of drink?' He looked very hard at me, and came ... The old man had altered much since I had last seen him: he stooped much, and his hair was quite grey ... I said 'You had better have another.' He stood, and I handed him another. He drank it, and thanked me, and was going away when I said, 'Well then, father, so you do not know me.' He was quite overcome ... He knew me then ... The news soon flew. My mother heard it, and came to see me ... she appeared very confused, and said 'Some one said that my boy had come home, but I did not believe it.' I handed her a glass of ale, and told her to drink, and not to think of any such things; and she was going away quite contented, till I called her back and said

'Do you not see him?' but she did not know me then, until I said 'Mother, you ought to know me.' The poor old woman then knew me, and would have fallen to the floor, if she had not been caught. She was some time before she overgot it.[5]

There was no half pay for soldiers, but there were a limited number of places as in-pensioners at the Royal Hospitals at Chelsea and Kilmainham, and a disabled man who seemed, to the hospital's commissioners, to be able to earn some sort of a living was likely to be sent off as an out-pensioner on a daily rate. Sergeant Thomas Jackson, who had lost his leg at Bergen-op-Zoom in 1814, saw the Chelsea board the following year:

When I appeared before the Lords Commissioners of the Board, they eyed me up and down and seemed to consult for a moment, when one of them said, 'Oh, he is a young man, able to get his a living!' No questions asked of me, but at sight I was knocked off with the pitiful reward of a shilling a day – a mighty poor recompense, I thought, for having spent twelve years of the prime of my manhood in the service of my country . . . Having then no more use for my scarlet coat, I set my wife to cut off the lace [round the button holes], and that, together with the chain and tassels which ornamented my cap, she sold for thirty shillings. I then bought myself a suit of plain clothes to hobble my way home with into a new sphere of life among new beings, and, as it were, into a new world again.[6]

Interest was still important. At Waterloo Tom Plunket, the disgraced sergeant of the 95th, was wounded in the head. Discharged and offered only a pension of 6d a day by the Chelsea Board, he joined a line regiment, which was inspected by his old commanding officer, now Major General Sir Sidney Beckwith, who recognised him at once. Plunket told him what had happened, and was bidden to the officers' mess that night and asked to propose a toast: 'Then, Sir, here's to the immortal memory of the poor fellows who fell in the Peninsula, Sir,' said Plunket, and 'the toast was drunk by all with much solemnity.' He was promoted corporal the following day, and

shortly secured, by Beckwith's influence, 1s a day from the Kilmainham board.

But there were many soldiers who were not so lucky, and in 1814
Benjamin Harris saw:

> Thousands of soldiers lining the streets, and lounging
> about the different public-houses with every description
> of wound and casualty incident to modern warfare ...
> The Irishman, shouting and brandishing his crutch; the
> English soldier, reeling with drink; and the Scot, with grave
> and melancholy visage, sitting on the steps of the public-
> house amongst the crowd, listening to the skirl of his
> comrades pipes and thinking of the blue hills of his native
> land.[7]

Sometimes the discharged soldier ended up a beggar, but Henry
Mayhew believed that: 'begging he abhors, and is only drawn to it
as a last resort.' Far more common were beggars who claimed to
have been soldiers, like the 'Crimean veteran' who eventually admitted: 'The Crimea's been a good dodge to many, but it's getting stale:
square coves (i.e. honest folk) is so wide awake.'

The officers and soldiers whose footsteps we have followed
marched off to a variety of destinations. Richard Barter, Thomas
Brotherton, Henry Clifford and Edward Cooper Hodge all became
generals. Thomas Brown gained his KH in 1818 a British knighthood
in 1826. He too became a general, through he declined any commands as such. John Aitchison also enjoyed a fruitful career, becoming a major general in 1845, a knight in 1859 and a full general the
following year. He had decided not to marry until his active soldiering was over, and so it was not until the age of 68 that he married
Ellen Mayhew, by whom he had a son and two daughters – both of
whom died in an accident.

John Peebles sold his commission in 1782, and, after emotional
farewell to his grenadiers of the 42nd, went back to Scotland to marry
his sweetheart Anne and become, probably through the interest of
his father in law, surveyor of customs for the port of Irvine, a post
he held for thirty years. Both Lieutenant Gleig and Ensign Leeke
became clergymen, the former rising to chaplain-general of the

army. William Tomkinson settled down, as a half-pay lieutenant colonel, to live the life of a country gentleman. He sired four sons and two daughters and, despite the rigours of all his campaigning, died in 1872 in his 83rd year.

William Keep went on half pay in 1814 and was granted a pension for his wound. He caused a family scandal by eloping with his fiancée's maid, Anne Coolly: she bore him four daughters, and they lived, apparently happily, in Camden Town until his death at the age of 92 in 1884. William Surtees spent most of his life in uniform, retiring as quartermaster in the 95th in 1826 and dying in his native Corbridge in 1830. Howell Rees Gronow retired as a captain in 1821, stood for parliament twice and spent the rest of his life as a man about town, dying in Paris in 1865 and leaving a set of chatty and informative memoirs.

Robert Waterfield came back from India in 1857, and became a 'house agent' in London, dying in Lambeth in 1897. John Pearman went off 'to drill the Gentleman Cadets' at Sandhurst but, disappointed not to be given a staff appointment at the college, bought himself out of the army in 1852. He became a detective, rose to the rank of chief constable of a small police force, and then went to take charge of the men employed at Eton College. He died in 1908 at the age of 89. Benjamin Harris, who had learnt how to make shoes before he was drafted into the Army of the Reserve in 1802, set up as a cobbler after Waterloo, and told Henry Curling, his amanuensis, that: 'I enjoyed life more on active service than I have ever done since; and as I sit at work in my shop in Richmond Street, Soho, I look back upon that portion of my time spent in the fields of the Peninsula as the only part worthy of remembrance.' Thomas Jackson, in contrast, deeply resented that his wooden leg was 'the coarse joke of the vulgar; and the sport of impudent children . . . In this moody vein of reflection the once gay and glittering Sergeant of the Royal Guards sees and feels a sad reverse . . .'

The citizen armies that fought the two great wars of the 20th century are commemorated on a variety of war memorials from modest village crosses to larger urban statues and cenotaphs. It is pleasing to see that, thanks largely to the efforts of The Friends of War Memorials, many of these are now being rescued from slow decay and abrupt vandalism. All the servicemen and servicewomen who died in the conflicts either have a known grave or are commemorated on a Memorial to the Missing, like the Menin Gate at Ypres or the soaring Thiepval arch which presides over the battlefield of the Somme. The nation, swift to conscript and slow to compensate, did not always give its returning warriors the treatment that their services demanded. But at least it made them a name, and succeeding generations honour it on Remembrance Day: long may they continue to do so.

In contrast, the men that fought at Minden and Waterloo have few memorials. Even Waterloo itself, strongly garrisoned by café proprietors and museum attendants, and so often swamped beneath the sheer weight of tourism, tells much about Napoleon, Wellington and their senior commanders but far less about the men they led. The dead of these battles were usually tumbled half naked into mass graves whose sites are rarely marked, and there was little dignity to the business. After Vimiero, Rifleman Harris wandered about the field, and saw:

> an officer of the 50th Regiment. I knew him by sight, and recognised him as he lay. He was quite dead, and lying on his back. He had been plundered and his clothes were torn open. Three bullet-holes were close together in the pit of his stomach: beside him lay an empty pocket-book, and his epaulette had been pulled from his shoulder.[8]

Officers might have graves or memorials of their own: Captain John Blackman of the Coldstream Guards long lay where he fell in the garden at Hougoumont, and Lieutenant General Sir Thomas Picton and Colonel Sir Alexander Gordon are commemorated near the cross-roads where the main Brussels road crosses Wellington's line south of Waterloo, where they received their death-wounds. Black Bob Craufurd of the Light Division is remembered near the lesser breach at Ciudad Rodrigo, where his men buried him. There are small guards cemeteries at Bayonne, and one now contains a headstone, moved from the wood in which his battalion camped, which remembers Colour Sergeant William Yuill, 3/1st Foot Guards, killed by grape shot on 7 April 1814 and 'beloved by the Regiment in which he served 20 years.'

Sometimes there was good reason for not commemorating a battlefield. We ought not, perhaps, to be surprised that in 2000 the folk of Badajoz refused to allow the Royal Regiment of Fusiliers to erect a memorial to the storming of their city in 1812. And sometimes it has become impolitic or impractical to maintain memorials that once existed. Lucknow was once, as William Dalrymple puts it, 'a vast, open-air, Imperial war memorial, thickly littered with a carapace of cemeteries and spiked cannons, obelisks and rolls of honour.' All this is now hopelessly dilapidated, choked with rubbish and overshadowed by monsoon-stained tower blocks. Graves and memorials in the Crimea were damaged by fighting in the area in the Second World War and many of the former have subsequently been desecrated by scavengers looking for saleable trinkets. A modern memorial built on the field of Inkerman by public subscription in Britain is described by Colonel Patrick Mercer, historian of the battle, as a thing 'of stunning ugliness'. Not all modern constructions are so undignified: in 2001 The Princess of Wales's Royal Regiment erected a fine obelisk at Albuera to commemorate its predecessors, 1/Buffs, 2/31st and 1/57th, which fought so bravely there on 16 May 1811.

There are more frequent memorials in Britain to the officers of the era. Colonel John Cameron of Fassiefern, news of whose death at the head of his regiment at Quatre Bras was recounted by the wounded highlander encountered by Captain Mercer, has an obelisk at Kilmallie. Private Thomas Gardner fought at Waterloo with 1st Life Guards. After leaving the regular army he became drill-sergeant to a Yeomanry regiment, the Furness Cuirassiers, and was killed when he fell from his horse. He has a memorial plaque on an outside wall of Great Urswick Church, and it is unusual to find a ranker so well remembered. There are moments when a memorial has come as an unexpected shock, for the man it commemorates has featured prominently in the memoirs that have formed so much a part of my working life for the past two years and, ridiculously, I know, it is hard to think of him as being dead. I was visiting the parish church in the Buckinghamshire town of Amersham when a marble slab at one end of the nave pulled me up sharply.

SACRED TO THE MEMORY OF
CHARLES EELES ESQ
LATE CAPTAIN IN HIS MAJESTY'S 95th RIFLE REGIMENT,
WHO AFTER SERVING WITH THE BRITISH ARMY THRO'
THE VARIOUS CAMPAIGNS IN THE SPANISH PENINSULA,
TERMINATED HIS GLORIOUS CAREER
ON THE 18th OF JUNE 1815, IN THE 30th YEAR OF HIS AGE.

HE FELL NOBLY IN HIS COUNTRY'S CAUSE ON THE EVER
MEMORABLE FIELD OF WATERLOO.

ESTEEMED, LAMENTED AND BELOVED.

HIS MOTHER, Mrs SABINA EELES,
NEE LAWRENCE DIED AT AMERSHAM IN 1836.

HIS BROTHER, WILLIAM EELES K.H.
COLONEL IN THE RIFLE BRIGADE (OLD 95th)
DIED AT WOOLWICH IN 1838;
WAS AT BUENOS AYRES UNDER WHITELOCK
PENINSULAR CAMPAIGN AND WATERLOO

Charles Eeles features in John Kincaid's description of the officers of 1/95th at the end of the Peninsular War:

> Beckwith with a cork-leg – Pemberton and Manners with a shot each in the knee, making them as stiff as the other's tree one – Loftus Gray with a gash in the lip, and minus a portion of one heel, which made him march to the tune of dot and go one – Smith with a shot in the ankle – Eeles minus a thumb – Johnson, in addition to other shot holes, a stiff elbow, which deprived him of the power of disturbing his friends as a scratcher of Scotch reels upon the violin – Percival with a shot through his lungs – Hope with a grape-shot lacerated leg – George Simmons with his riddled body held together by a pair of stays ... lest a burst of sigh should rend it asunder ...[9]

I had somehow expected Charlie Eeeles to finish up with his dogs, daughters and hunters in the shires, but no: he was tumbled into a grave-pit at Waterloo.

A headstone in the grounds of Winchester Cathedral sums up this forgotten army.

In Memory of Thomas Thetcher

Grenadier in the North Regt of Hants Militia
Who died of a violent Fever
Contracted by Drinking Small Beer when Hot
12th May 1764 aged 26 years . . .

Here sleeps in peace a Hampshire Grenadier
Who caught his death by drinking cold small Beer,
Soldiers be wise from his untimely fall
And when ye're hot drink Strong or none at all . . .

An honest Soldier never is forgot
Whether he Die by Musket or by Pot

Nor should he be.

REFERENCES

Introduction

1 The best sources are Mitchell and Deane *Abstract of British Historical Statistics*, and the 'Economic History Services' interactive website gives useful details of the comparative cost of living year by year. E. W. Gilboy's seminal *Cost of Living and Real Wages in Eighteenth Century England*, is by far the best source for detail. Other useful sources include Lorna Wetherill *Consumer Behaviour and Material Culture in Britain 1670–1760*, G. E. Mingey *Rural Life in Victorian England*, Carole Shamas *The Pre-Industrial Consumer in Britain and America*. Too many of the men who plied their muskets in line and square ended up in the workhouse, and Ian Moore's *Oldchurch – The Workhouse* is a useful study of one such establishment.

The Age of Brown Bess

1 Christopher Hibbert (ed) *A Soldier of the Seventy-First*, London 1976, p. 62.
2 This account of a clash between a British line and a French column in Spain or Portugal in 1808–1814 is a pastiche. I have chosen the 37th (North Hampshire) Regiment because I serve in one of its successors, and my own scarlet mess-kit is faced with its yellow, though any stains come from mellifluous port rather than villainous saltpetre. The components of the story are pillaged from contemporary accounts. The description of the *pas de charge* is Captain Gronow's and its nickname is recalled by Rifleman Harris; Private Thomas Pococke of the

71st Regiment had a narrow escape from a bayonet that stuck in his pack, and knew well that French soldiers often kept valuables (and, interestingly enough, pancakes) in their shakos. The conduct of the British line is founded on contemporary drill-books, although, as H. Dickinson noted in his 1798 *Instructions for Forming a Regiment of Infantry*, 'some trifling deviations...are permitted in most Regiments.' The manner in which our young colonel (who seems to resemble the legendary John Colborne of the 52nd) handled his battalion, and, in particular, his decision to fire by ranks is an issue explored at length later on. And for our young ensign running forward with his colour, under the protecting pike of his covering colour-sergeant, we have Charles Hamilton-Smith's picture, drawn from life, for he was himself a serving officer, of an ensign of the 9th Regiment.
3 Thomas Creevey *The Creevey Papers* (ed John Gore), London 1934 pp. 128–9.
4 Howard L. Blackmore *British Military Firearms, 1650–1850*, London 1994, pp. 45, 132–3.
5 J. A. Houlding *Fit For Service: The Training of the British Army 1715–1795*, Oxford 1981, p. 9.
6 Basil Liddell Hart *The British Way in Warfare*, London 1932, p. 48.
7 Ibid. p. 92.
8 David Chandler (ed) *The Oxford Illustrated History of the British Army*, Oxford 1994, p. 420.
9 Amanda Foreman *Georgiana, Duchess of Devonshire*, London 1998, p. 65.
10 Browne op.cit., p. 5.

11 Peebles op.cit., p. 480.
12 Ibid. p. 483.
13 Jeremy Black *European Warfare 1660–1815*, London 1998, pp. 1–2.
14 David Blomfield (ed) *Lahore to Lucknow: The Indian Mutiny Journal of Arthur Moffat Lang*, London 1992, p. 130.
15 Lt Col William Alexander-Gordon *Reflections of a Highland Subaltern*, London 1889, pp. 118. 113.
16 Reginald Hargreaves *This Happy Breed: Sidelights on Soldiers and Soldiering*, London 1951, p. 42.
17 Sir John Fortescue *Following the Drum*, London 1931, p. 32–3.
18 Ian Fletcher *Bloody Albuera*, London 2000, p. 88.
19 Moyle Sherer *Recollections of the Peninsular*, London 1827, pp. 159–161.
20 Fletcher *Albuera*, p. 93.
21 John Spencer Cooper *Rough Notes of Seven Campaigns*, London 1996, pp. 60–61.
22 Richard Barter *The Siege of Delhi: Mutiny Memories of an Old Officer*, London 1984, pp. 1, 10.
23 Alan Weekes *The Royal Hampshire Regiment*, London 1968, p. 41.
24 J. MacIntire *A Military Treatise on the Discipline of the Marine Forces*, London 1763, p. 174.
25 C. Griesheim quoted in Christopher Duffy *Military Experience in the Age of Reason*, London 1987, p. 113.
26 Bonneville quoted *ibid* p. 102.
27 Richard Holmes *Firing Line*, London 1985, p. 336.
28 Stanbury Thompson (ed) *The Journal of John Gabriel Stedman*, London 1962, p. 105.
29 Ibid pp. 182–3.
30 Robert McHenry (ed) *Webster's American Military Biographies*, New York 1978, p. 410.
31 Allan R. Millett and Peter Maslowski *For the Common Defense: A Military History of the United States of America*, London 1984, pp. 79–80.
32 Richard Holmes (ed) *The Oxford Companion to Military History*, Oxford 2001, p. 504. See also John A. Lynn

The Bayonets of the Republic: Motivation and Tactics in the Army of Revolutionary France, 1791–1794, Boulder, Colo., 1996.
33 Stéphane Audoin-Rouzeau *Les Combattants des Tranchées*, Paris 1986, pp. 61–62.
34 Anon, 'Tactique allemande – le fusil à aiguille at les colonnes de compagnie' in *Spectateur Militaire* 3rd Series No. 4 (1866) pp. 237–8.
35 Jean Morvan *Le Soldat Imperial* (2 vols), Paris 1904, I p. 114.
36 B. T. Jones (trans and ed) *Military Memoirs: Charles Parquin*, London 1969, pp. 178–9.
37 John Brereton *Chain Mail: The History of the Duke of Lancaster's Own Yeomans 1798–1991* , Chippenham ND, p. 7.
38 Gunther E. Rothenburg *Napoleon's Great Adversary: The Archduke Charles and the Austrian Army 1792–1814*, Staplehurst. Kent 1995, p. 33.
39 Ibid. pp. 234–5.
40 Christopher Duffy *The Army of Frederick the Great*, Newton Abbot 1974, p. 91.
41 David Gates *The British Light Infantry Arm c1790–1815*, London 1987, p. 14.
42 *Ibid.*
43 A. Graydon, *Memoirs of a Life chiefly passed in Pennsylvania*, Edinburgh 1822, p. 210.
44 William Surtees *Twenty-Five years in the Rifle Brigade*, London 1973, pp. 16–17.
45 Arthur Bryant *Jackets of Green*, London 1972, pp. 23–25.
46 David Chandler *The Campaigns of Napoleon*, London 1967, p. 155.
47 R. R. Palmer 'Frederick, Guibert, Bülow' in Peter Paret, (ed) *Makers of Modern Strategy*, Oxford 1986, p. 108.
48 Ira D. Gruber, (ed) *John Peebles' American War 1776–1782*, London 1997, p. 106. The light captain is the captain commanding the battalion's light company.
49 'Shillin a Day' in *Rudyard Kipling's*

Verse: Inclusive Edition, London 1933, p. 420.

50 Duffy *The Army of Frederick the Great*, p. 56.

51 Peebles p. 311.

52 W.E. Manners *Some Account of the Military, Political and Social Life of. . .Marquis of Granby*, London 1899, p. 96.

53 Roger Lamb *An Original and Authentic Journal of Occurrences during the late American War. . .*, Dublin 1809, p. 8

54 Alfred Cobban *A History of Modern France* Vol 2, London 1983, p. 183.

55 René Chartrand and Patrice Courcelle *Emigré and Foreign Troops in British Service 1805–15*, Oxford 2000, p. 15.

56 B. H. Liddell Hart (ed) *The Letters of Private Wheeler*, Adlestrop, Gloucesterhsire, 1951, p. 67.

57 Antony Brett-James, (ed) *Edward Costello: The Peninsula and Waterloo Campaigns*, London 1967, p. 108.

58 Christopher Hibbert (ed) *The Wheatley Diary*, London 1964, pp. 8–9.

59 Ibid. p. 70.

60 George Robert Gleig *The Subaltern: A Chronicle of the Peninsular War*, Edinburgh, 1877, p. 277.

61 Cavalié Mercer *Journal of the Waterloo Campaign*, London 1985, p. 14.

62 John H. Gill 'Vermin, Scorpions and Mosquitos: The Rheinbund in the Peninsula' in Ian Fletcher (ed) *The Peninsular War*, Staplehurst, Kent, 1998, p. 73.

63 Peebles p. 10.

64 Roger Norman Buckley (ed) *The Napoleonic War Journal of Captain Thomas Henry Browne*, London 1987, p. 73.

65 Shaun Corkerry 'The recruitment and personnel of the Royal Artillery 1741–1815' unpublished research paper kindly loaned by its author.

66 Michael Glover *Wellington's Army*, Newton Abbot 1977, p. 25.

67 Edward M. Spiers *The Army and Society 1815–1914*, London 1980, pp. 48–9.

68 Harry Hopkins *The Strange Death of Private White*, London 1977, p. 24.

69 Gates op.cit., p. 86.

70 John Wain (ed) *The Journals of James Boswell 1760–1795*, London 1991, p. 22.

71 Stephen Wood *The Scottsh Soldier*, Manchester 1987, p. 76.

72 Frank McLynn, *Crime and Punishment in Eighteenth Century England*, London 1991, p. 221.

73 Richard M. Ketchum *The Battle for Bunker Hill*, London 1963, p. 171.

74 William Grattan *Adventures with the Connaught Rangers 1809–14*, London 1902, p. 146.

75 Ibid. p. 148.

76 Ibid. p. 68.

77 Ibid. p. 84.

78 Ibid. p. 85.

79 George Napier *The Life of General Sir George Napier*, London 1884, pp. 191–5.

80 E. E. P. Tisdall (ed) *Mrs Duberly's Campaigns: An Englishwoman's experiences in the Crimean War and Indian Mutiny*, London 1963, p. 44.

81 Robert A. Richardson (ed) *Nurse Sarah Anne: With Florence Nightingale in the Crimea*, London 1977, p. 105.

82 Ibid. p. 111.

83 Ibid. p. 121.

84 F. G. James *Ireland in the Empire 1688–1770*, Cambridge, Mass. 1973, p. 63.

85 John Brooke *King George III*, London 1972, p. 310.

86 Granby op.cit., p. 89.

87 Thomas Pakenham *The Year of Liberty*, London 1972, p. 17.

88 William Tomkinson *Diary of a Cavalry Officer*, Staplehurst, Kent 1999, p. 115.

89 Liza Pickard *Dr Johnson's London*, London 2000, p. 126–7.

90 Ibid. p. 43.

91 Kenneth O. Morgan (ed) *The Oxford Illustrated History of Britain*, Oxford 1984, p. 427.

92 Ibid. p. 381.

93 McLynn op.cit., p. 219.

94 Ibid. p. 238.

95 William Thom *Rhymes and
Recollections of a Handloom Weaver,*
Glasgow 1845, p. 28.
96 Christopher Hibbert (ed) *Greville's
England,* London 1981, p. 82.
97 Ibid. p. 83.
98 John Selby (ed) *Military Memoirs:
Thomas Morris,* London 1967, p. 109.
99 J. Sturgis (ed) *A Boy in the
Peninsular War: The Services, Adventures
and Experiences of Robert Blakeney,*
London 1899, pp. 263–299.

*All the King's Horses and All the
King's Men*

1 *Manual of Military Law,* London
1914, p. 161.
2 Peebles op.cit., p. 80.
3 Nicholas Bentley (ed) *The
Reminiscences of Captain Gronow,* London
1977, p. 143.
4 Ibid. p. 246.
5 Chandler op.cit., p. 98.
6 Michael Orr *Dettingen,* London
1972, p. 73.
7 Ibid p. 59.
8 Granby op.cit., p. 116.
9 Chandler op.cit., pp. 109–110.
10 Peebles op.cit., p. 482.
11 Greville op.cit., p. 116.
12 W. Baring *Pemberton Battles of the
Crimean War,* London 1962, p. 55.
13 Ibid p. 139.
14 Philip Warner (ed) *The Fields of
War: A Young Cavalryman's Crimea
campaign,* London 1977, p. 86.
15 Pemberton op.cit., p. 181.
16 Ibid. p. 57.
17 Bellamy Partridge *Sir Billy Howe,*
London 1932, pp. 6–7.
18 Mrs Ward 'Recollections of an Old
Soldier, by his Daughter' *United Services
Journal* 1840 Vol II p. 217.
19 Elizabeth Longford *Wellington: Pillar
of the State,* London 1972 , p. 333.
20 Samuel Ancell and 'Jack Careless' *A
Circumstantial Account of the Long and
Tedious Siege of Gibraltar,* Liverpool
1785, p. 58.
21 *Manual of Military Law* p. 14.

22 Philip J. Haythornthwaite *The
Armies of Wellington,* London 1996, p. 8.
23 Ibid. p. 9.
24 Greville op.cit., p. 246.
25 R. E. Scouller *The Armies of Queen
Anne,* Oxford 1966, p. 1.
26 Charles M. Clode *The Military Forces
of the Crown,* London 1869, Vol II
pp. 691–2.
27 Nicholas Bentley (ed) *Russell's
Dispatches from the Crimea,* London
1964, p. 32.
28 Ibid p. 154.
29 Victor Bonham-Carter (ed) *George
Lawson: Surgeon in the Crimea,* London
1968, p. 56.
30 Peebles op.cit., p. 204.
31 John Sweetman Raglan (London
1993, p. 87.
32 Edward E. Curtis *The British Army in
the American Revolution,* Yale 1926,
pp. 41–2.
33 Colonel Havilland Le Mesurier (ed)
*Extracts from some letters of Commissary
General Havilland Le Mesurier. . .*
privately printed, p. 11.
34 K. Fenwick (ed) *A Voice From the
Ranks,* London 1954, p. 76.
35 Haythornthwaite op.cit., p. 121.
36 Colonel H. C. Wylly (ed) *A Cavalry
Officer in the Corunna Campaign,*
London 1913, p. 24.
37 Richard L. Blanco *Wellington's
Surgeon-general: Sir James McGrigor,*
Durham, North Carolina 1974,
p. 17.
38 Ibid.
39 Ibid. p. 179.
40 Ibid. p. 150.
41 Lamb op.cit., p. 297.
42 Morris, op.cit., p. 68.
43 Patrick MacRory (ed) *William
Bryden's Account from the Memory and
Memoranda made on arrival of the retreat
from Cabool in 1842,* London 1969,
p. 167.
44 Matthew Stevens *Hannah Snell: The
Secret Life of a Female Marine,* London
1997.
45 Victor A. Hatley N*orthamptonshire
Militia Lists 1777,* Kettering 1973,
p. xi.

46 Granby op.cit., p. 96.

47 Fortescue *British Army* Vol IV p. 885.

48 Clode II p. 698.

49 Ian Fletcher (ed) *A Guards Officer in the Peninsula: The Peninsular War Letters of John Rous* (London 1992, pp. 5, 76.

50 A. W. Kinglake *The Invasion of the Crimea*, London and Edinburgh 1866–75, Vol V p. 250.

51 Boswell op.cit., p. 205.

52 Houlding op.cit., pp. 115–6.

53 Haythornthwaite op.cit., p. 18.

54 Colonel Firebrace 'On the Errors and Faults in our Military System' *United Services Magazine* 1842 part III p. 373.

55 *United Services Magazine* 1861 Part II p. 261

56 Duffy *Military Experience*, p. 71.

57 Boswell op.cit., p. 127.

58 Houlding op.cit., p. 106.

59 Stephen Wood 'By Dint of Labour and Perseverance: A journal...kept by Lt Col James Adolphus Oughton...', London, *Society for Army Historical Research Special Publication 14*, 1997, pp. 14–17.

60 *Regimental Companion* 1811, quoted in Donald Breeze Mendham Huffer 'The Infantry Officers of the Line of the British Army 1815–1868', Unpublished PhD thesis, University of Birmingham 1995, p. 338. I am grateful for Dr Huffer's scholarly work on the little-known topic of army agents, and much else besides.

61 Huffer op.cit., p. 339.

62 Ibid. p. 368.

63 Ibid. p. 372.

64 Peebles op.cit., p. 74.

65 Ian Fletcher and Ron Poulter *Gentlemen's Sons*, London 1992, p. 220.

66 Mark Adkin *The Charge*, London 2000, p. 192.

67 Surtees op.cit., p. 249.

68 Ibid. p. 118.

69 Surtees p. 231.

70 Blanco op.cit., p. 91.

71 Lawson op.cit., p. 30.

72 B. H. Liddle Hart (ed) *The Letters of Private Wheeler*, London 1993, p. 153.

73 Glover op.cit., p. 130.

74 Ibid. p. 130.

75 Ibid.

76 Ibid. p. 131.

77 Sir George Larpent (ed) *The Private Journal of Judge-Advocate Larpent, attached to the headquarters of Lord Wellington during the Penisular War...*, London 1854, p. 264.

78 Glover op.cit., p. 132.

79 Le Mesurier op.cit., p. 35.

80 Elizabeth Longford *Wellington: The Years of the Sword*, London 1969, p. 243.

81 Arthur Swinson and Donald Scott (eds) *The Memoirs of Private Waterfield, soldier in Her Majesty's 32nd Regiment of Foot...*, London 1968, p. 34.

82 The Marquess of Anglesey (ed) *Sergeant Pearman's Memoirs, being chiefly his account of service with the Third (King's Own) Light Dragoons in India*, London 1968, p. 65.

83 Terrot p. 116.

84 John Edward Wharton Rotton *The Chaplain's Narrative of the Siege of Delhi*, London 1858, p. 121.

85 Barter op.cit., p. 47.

86 Ibid. p. 49.

87 Fortescue *British Army* IV p. 898.

88 E. E. P. Tisdall (ed) *Mrs Duberly's Campaigns: An Englishwoman's experiences in the Crimean War and Indian Mutiny*, London 1963, p. 198.

89 Harris op.cit., p. 109.

90 Victor Neuberg *Gone For a Soldier*, London 1989, p. 28.

91 William Reitzel (ed) *The Autobiography of William Cobbett: The progress of a Plough-Boy to a seat in Parliament*, London 1933, p. 27.

92 Ibid. p. 32.

93 Ibid.

94 Ibid. p. 33.

95 Ibid.

96 Ibid.

97 Gowing op.cit., p. 71.

98 Ibid. p. 80.

99 Barter op.cit., p. 23.

100 The Marquess of Anglesey *A History of the British Cavalry*, London 1973, Vol 1. p. 164

101 George Loy Smith *A Victorian RSM: From India to the Crimea*, London 1987, p. 35.

102 Rex Whitworth (ed) *Gunner at Large: The Diaries of James Wood RA 1746–1765*, London 1998, p. 106.

103 Mercer op. cit., p. 89.

104 Blomfield op.cit., p. 81.

105 Ibid p. 138.

106 Colonel Cyril Field *Old Times Under Arms*, London 1937, p. 3.

Brothers of the Blade

1 Morris op.cit., p. 7.

2 Harris op.cit., p. 1.

3 Glover op.cit., p. 33.

4 C. G. Moore Smith *The Life of John Colborne: Field Marshal Lord Seaton*, London 1903, p. 10.

5 Wheeler op.cit., p. 17.

6 Antony Brett-James (ed) *Edward Costello: The Peninsular and Waterloo Campaigns*, London 1967, p. 8.

7 Houlding op.cit., p. 118.

8 Curtis op.cit., p. 164.

9 Ibid.

10 Field op.cit., p. 59.

11 Ibid p. 61.

12 Ibid. pp. 59–60.

13 Roy Palmer (ed) *The Rambling Soldier*, London 1977, p. 27.

14 D. G. Chandler (ed) *A Journal of Marlborough's Campaign. . .by James Marshall Deane, Private Sentinel in Queen Anne's First Regiment of Foot Guards*, London 1984, p. 7.

15 Ian A. Morrison 'Survival Skills: An Enterprising Highlander in the Low Countries with Marlborough' in Grant G. Simpson (ed) *The Scottish Soldier Abroad*, Edinburgh 1992.

16 Neuberg op.cit., p. 28.

17 Field op.cit., p. 63.

18 Glover op.cit., p. 27

19 Harris op.cit., p. 5.

20 Andrew Crichton, *The Life and Diary of Lieut Col J. Blackadder. Of the Cameronian Regiment . . .*, London 1824, pp. 236, 197.

21 Harris op.cit., p. 5.

22 Harry Hopkins *The Strange Death of Private White*, London 1977, p. 29.

23 Harris op.cit., p. 2.

24 Costello op.cit., p. 24.

25 Waterfield op.cit., p. 3.

26 Ibid.

27 Cobbett op.cit., p. 24.

28 Thomas Bennett, 'Memoirs of a Saddler Sergeant' in Sir John Fortescue *Following the Drum* London 1931.

29 Longford *Years of the Sword*, pp. 321–2.

30 Hopkins op.cit., p. 23.

31 Spiers op.cit., p. 45.

32 Field op.cit., p. 3.

33 Longford *Years of the Sword*, p. 323.

34 Gowing op.cit., p. 2.

35 *Soldier of the Seventy-First* p. 111.

36 Hopkins op.cit., p. 32.

37 Ibid p. 22.

38 Ibid.

39 Ibid.

40 George Robert Gleig *The Subaltern*, London 1972, p. 127.

41 Richard Henry Wollacombe (ed) *With the Guns in the Peninsula: The Peninsular War journal of William Webber*, London 1991, p. 103.

42 Surtees op.cit., pp. 171–83.

43 Wheeler op.cit., p. 34.

44 Soldier of the 71st, p. 33.

45 Costello op.cit., p. 82.

46 Ibid. p. 13.

47 General Sir George Barrow *The Fire of Life*, London 1941, p. 8.

48 Field op.cit., pp. 9–10.

49 Duffy Military Experience. p. 31.

50 Ibid. p. 32.

51 Ibid. p. 31.

52 Keep op.cit., p. 92.

53 Christopher Hibbert *Wellington: A personal history*, London 1998, p. 206.

54 Cooper op.cit., p. 99.

55 Waterfield op.cit., p. 16.

56 Clode op.cit., Vol II p. 608.

57 Huffer op.cit., p. 19.

58 Ibid. p. 20.

59 Nicholas Bentley (ed) *Russell's Dispatches from the Crimea*, London 1966, p. 117.

60 Hansard 3rd series, Vol 136 Cols 1363–4.
61 The Marquess of Anglesey (ed) *Little Hodge: being extracts from the diaries and letters of Colonel Edward Cooper Hodge written during the Crimean War*, London 1971, p. 57.
62 Houlding op.cit., p. 101.
63 Peebles op.cit., p. 113.
64 MS order book 'General Orders by this Excellency the Hon William Howe General and Commander-in-chief . . .' Joint Services Command and Staff College, Watchfield.
65 Ibid.
66 Bryan Perrett (ed) *A Hawk at War: The Peninsular War reminiscences of General Sir Thomas Brotherton*, London 1986, p. 28.
67 Michael Glover (ed) *A Gentleman Volunteer: Letters of George Hennell from the Peninsular War 1812–13*, London 1979, p. 14.
68 ibid p. 49.
69 Houlding op.cit., p. 105.
70 John Shipp *The Path of Glory*, London 1969, p. 51.
71 Ibid. p. 78.
72 Ibid.
73 Huffer op.cit., p. 130.
74 Ibid. p. 134, Hennell op.cit., p. 22.
75 Surtees op.cit., pp. 47–8.
76 Pearman op.cit., pp. 75–6.
77 Brotherton op.cit., p. 45.
78 *Morris*, op.cit., p. 14.
79 Spiers op.cit., p. 5.
80 Byron Farwell *For Queen and Country*, London 1981, p. 57.
81 Harris op.cit., p. 67.
82 Ibid. p. 68.
83 Morris op.cit., p. 51.
84 Tomkinson op.cit., p. 126.
85 Joachim Stocqueler *A personal history of the Horse Guards, 1750–1872*, London 1873, p. 173.
86 Tomkinson op.cit., p. 161.
87 Field-Marshal Sir Evelyn Wood *From Midshipman to Field-Marshal*, London 1906, Vol I pp. 219, 245.
88 *Duffy Military Experience*. p. 41.
89 Stocqueler op.cit., p. 120.
90 Lamb op.cit., p. 436.

Horse, Foot, Guns – and Wounds

1 Gordon-Alexander op.cit., p. 28.
2 Keep op.cit., p. 78.
3 Ian Fletcher (ed) *For King and Country: The Letters and Diaries of John Mills, Coldstream Guards* London 1995, p. 81.
4 Harris op.cit., p.
5 *Soldier of the 71st*, p. 94.
6 Arthur A. Haley (ed) *The Munro Letters*, London 1984, p. 90.
7 Gordon-Alexander op.cit., p. 95.
8 S. A. Cassels (ed) *Peninsular Portrait: The Letters of Captain William Bragge*, London 1963, p. 46.
9 Fletcher *Albuera* p. 92.
10 Grattan op.cit., p. 50.
11 Longford *Years of the Sword* p. 262.
12 Shipp op.cit., p. 141–2.
13 Russell *Crimea*, p. 160.
14 Michael Barthorp and Pierre Turner *The British Army on Campaign 1816–1853*, London 1987, p. 16.
15 Barter op.cit., p. 3.
16 Lang op.cit., p. 45.
17 Gordon-Alexander op.cit., p. 28.
18 Hargreaves op.cit., p. 59.
19 Harris op.cit., pp. 12–13.
20 W. F. K. Thompson (ed) *An Ensign in the Peninsular War*, London 1981, p. 31.
21 Keep op.cit., p. 29.
22 Gleig op.cit., p. 3.
23 Gordon-Alexander op.cit., p. 28.
24 Houlding op.cit., p. 141.
25 Surtees op.cit., p. 20.
26 Marcellin Marbot *The Memoirs of Baron de Marbot*, London 1929, p. 367.
27 Matthew Clay *A Narrative of the Battles of Quatre Bras and Waterloo: with the Defence of Hougoumont*, Bedford 1853, p. 11.
28 Blackmore op.cit., p. 226.
29 Barter op.cit., p. 16,
30 Peter Young (ed) *Richard Atkyns*, London 1967, p. 19.
31 Surtees op.cit., p. 41.
32 Arthur Bryant *Jackets of Green*, London 1972, p. 52.
33 Lamb op.cit., p. 367.

34 Samuel Hutton 'The Life of an Old Soldier' in Palmer *Rambling Soldier*, p. 152.

35 Sherer op.cit., p. 161.

36 Maj Gen H. T. Siborne (ed) *The Waterloo Letters*, London 1891, p. 298.

37 Grattan op.cit., p. 154.

38 Tomkinson op.cit., p. 9.

39 Wheeler op.cit., p. 129.

40 Pension certificate dated 17 July 1840, author's possession.

41 Brian Robson *Swords of the British Army First Edition*, London 1975, p. 106.

42 William Napier *The Life and Opinions of General Sir C. J. Napier*, London 1857, Vol 1 p. 95.

43 Haythornthwaite op.cit., p. 98.

44 J. D. Aylward *The Small-Sword in England*, London 1945, p. 12.

45 Robson op.cit., p. 106.

46 Keep op.cit., p. 38.

47 Henry Clifford <u>Henry Clifford VC: His letters and sketches from the Crimea</u>, London 1956, p. 91.

48 Lang op.cit., pp. 82, 92.

49 Ibid. p. 103.

50 Gordon-Alexander op.cit., p. 95.

51 Barter op.cit., pp. 55–6.

52 Mary C. Lynn *An Eyewitness Account of the American Revolution and New England Life: The Journal of J. F. Wasmus*, Westport Conn., 1990, p. 63.

53 Brotherton op.cit., p. 11.

54 Gordon-Alexander op.cit., p. 3.

55 Barter op.cit., p. 16.

56 William Lawrence *The Autobiography of Sergeant William Lawrence*, Cambridge 1987, p. 210.

57 Morris op.cit., p. 80.

58 Grattan op.cit., p. 90.

59 Morris op. cit., p. 80.

60 Ian Fletcher (ed) *The Peninsular War: Aspects of the Struggle for the Iberian Peninsula*, London 1998, p. 165.

61 Chandler op.cit., p. 348.

62 *Soldier of the 71st*, p. 17.

63 Grattan op.cit., p. 86.

64 Orr op.cit., p. 65.

65 Cooper op.cit., p. 52.

66 Barter op.cit., p. 17.

67 Gleig op.cit., p. 103.

68 Barter op.cit., p. 17.

69 Gronow op.cit., pp. 45. 47.

70 It was not until the appearance of Ian Fletcher's admirable *Galloping at Everything: The British Cavalry in the Peninsular War and at Waterloo* that the balance has been redressed.

71 Anglesey op.cit., I p. 96.

72 Ibid. p. 107.

73 Fortescue op.cit., IV p. 237.

74 Longford *Years of the Sword* p. 275.

75 Sir Charles Oman *History of the Peninsular War*, Oxford 1902, V p. 522.

76 Anglesey op.cit., I p. 280.

77 Granby op.cit., p. 126.

78 Parquin op.cit., p. 143.

79 Tomkinson op.cit., p. 1.

80 ibid. p. 269.

81 Ibid p. 312.

82 Brotherton op.cit., p. 42.

83 Anthony Ludovici (ed) *On the Road with Wellington: The Diary of a War Commissary in the Penisula*, London 1924, p. 219.

84 Loy Smith op.cit., p. 159.

85 *Fields of War*, p. 129.

86 Hodge op.cit., p. 64.

87 Despite being carried, a trifle oddly for an officer of the 95th, by the actor Sean Bean in the *Sharpe* series.

88 Edward Cotton *A Voice From Waterloo*, London 1862, p. 60.

89 Ian Fletcher *Galloping at Everything*, London 2000, p. 141.

90 Parquin op.cit., p. 143.

91 Marbot op.cit., p. 276.

92 Brian Robson *Swords of the British Army: The Regulation Patterns 1788 to 1914* (revised edition) London 1996, p. 22.

93 Simpson op.cit., p. 85.

94 Ibid. p. 30.

95 Ibid. p. 32.

96 'The Charge of the Light Brigade by one who was in it', *Royal United Services Institute Journal* April 1856.

97 Anglesey op.cit., Vol I, p. 100.

98 Surtees op.cit., p. 284.

99 Tomkinson op.cit., p. 312.

100 Barter op.cit., p. 85.

101 H. T. Siborne *Waterloo Letters*, London 1891, p. 62.

102 Tomkinson op.cit., p. 312.
103 Brotherton op.cit., p. 46.
104 A. McKenzie Annand (ed) *Cavalry Surgeon*, London 1971, p. 208.
105 Browne op.cit., p. 136.
106 Anglesey op.cit., Vol 1 p. 264.
107 Clifford op.cit., p. 91.
108 Adkin op.cit., p. 161.
109 Barter op.cit., p. 14.
110 Ibid. p. 160.
111 Black op.cit., p. 175.
112 Mercer op.cit., p. 175.
113 Mercer op.cit., pp. 172–3.
114 Ibid. p. 147.
115 Napier *War in the Peninsula* Vol III p. 519.
116 Mercer op.cit., p. 153.
117 Seaton op.cit., p. 290.
118 Wheeler op.cit., pp. 140, 152.
119 For medical statistics of the period see Richard A. Gabriel and Karen S. Metz *A History of Military Medicine*, London 1992, Vol II passim.
120 Fortescue *Following the Drum* p. 35.
121 Lamb op.cit., p. 143.
122 Browne op.cit., p. 231.
123 Keep op.cit., p. 91.
124 Ibid p. 186.
125 Colborne op.cit., p. 12.
126 Keep op.cit., p. 58.
127 Colborne op.cit., p. 109.
128 Wheeler op.cit., p. 100.
129 Russell *Crimea* p. 86.
130 Morris op.cit., p. 78.
131 Pearman op.cit., p. 35.
132 Lamb op.cit., p. 179.
133 Grattan op.cit., p. 76.
134 Palmer *Rambling Soldier* p. 180.
135 Wasmus op.cit., p. 62.
136 Colborne op.cit., p. 174.
137 Russell *Crimea* p. 154.
138 Victor Bonham-Carter (ed) *George Lawson: Surgeon in the Crimea*, London 1968, p. 157.
139 Terrot op.cit., p. 83.
140 Ibid. p. 153.
141 Ibid p. 121.

Home Fires

1 Keep op.cit., p. 20.
2 Ibid. p. 21.
3 Ibid. p. 23.
4 Scouller op.cit., p. 165.
5 Firth op.cit., p. 218.
6 Fortescue op.cit., Vol IV p. 906.
7 Anglesey op.cit., Vol III p. 53.
8 Ibid. Vol I p. 127.
9 Marbot op.cit., pp. 26, 28.
10 N. W. Bancroft *From Recruit to Staff Sergeant*, London 1979, p. 4.
11 Ibid p. 28.
12 Browne op.cit., p. 114.
13 Shipp op.cit., p. 14.
14 Browne op.cit., pp. 115–6.
15 13 George Pinckard *Notes on the West Indies: Written during the Expedition under the Command of the later General Sir Ralph Abercromby*, London 1806, Vol III p. 188.
16 Shipp op.cit., p. 15.
17 Keep op.cit., p. 82.
18 Alexander Somerville *Autobiography of a Working Man*, London 1967, p. 84.
19 Field Marshal Sir William Robertson *From Private to Field-Marshal*, London 1921, p. 11.
20 Anglesey op.cit., Vol I p. 129.
21 Anglesey op.cit., Vol I pp. 313–4.
22 Ibid. pp. 313–4.
23 Anglesey op.cit., Vol. II p. 314.
24 Browne op.cit., p. 48.
25 Ibid. pp. 112–3.
26 Field op.cit., p. 285.
27 Ibid. p. 289.
28 Ibid.p. 287.
29 Roger Hudson (ed) *The Memoirs of a Georgian Rake: William Hickey*, London 1995, pp. 398–9.
30 Blanco op.cit., p. 24.
31 Peebles op.cit., pp. 169–70.
32 Wood op.cit., p. 144.
33 Ibid
34 Anglesey op.cit., I p. 176.
35 Gronow op.cit., pp. 14–15.
36 Hargreaves op.cit., p. 210.
37 Duberly *Journal* p. 172.
38 G. D. Skull *Memoir and Letters of Captain W. Glanville Evelyn of the 4*[th]

Regiment (King's Own) in North America, New York 1971, pp. 79–80.

39 Keep op.cit., p. 140.

40 Russell *Crimea* p. 244.

41 Hopkins op.cit., p. 29.

42 Haythornthwaite op.cit., p. 126

43 Sir John Fortescue 'Gibraltar Under Siege 1727' in *Following the Drum*, London 1931, p. 17.

44 Colonel Noel T. St John Williams *The Colonel's Lady and Judy O'Grady*, London 1988 , p. 12.

45 Shipp op.cit., p. 12.

46 Anthony Hamilton Hamilton *Campaign with Moore and Wellington during the Peninsular War* (London 1998, pp. 47–8.

47 Williams op.cit., p. 14.

48 Partridge op.cit., p. 17.

49 Williams op.cit., p. 43.

50 Surtees op.cit., p. 158.

51 Fortescue 'Gibraltar' p. 6.

52 Gronow op.cit., p. 262.

53 Evelyn op.cit., p. 90.

54 Williams op.cit., p. 34.

55 Henry Mayhew and Peter Quennell *London's Underground*, London 1969, p. 48.

56 Con Costello *A Most Delightful Station: The British Army and the Curragh of Kildare*, Cork 1996, p. 162.

57 Kenneth Ballhatchet *Race, Sex and Class under the Raj*, London 1980, p. 60.

58 Ibid. p. 125.

59 Ibid. p. 19.

60 Ibid. p. 10.

61 David Miller *Lady De Lancey at Waterloo*, London 2000, p. 108.

62 Ibid p. 109.

63 Ibid pp. 116–7.

64 Ibid p. 130.

65 Patrick MacRory (ed) *Lady Sale: The First Afghan War*, London 1969, p. 14.

66 Ibid p. 51.

67 Ibid. pp. 100–102.

68 Ibid p. 105.

69 Ibid p. 108.

70 Ibid p. 130.

71 Ibid p. 131.

72 Ibid p. 148.

73 Ketchum op.cit., p. 143.

74 Pearman op.cit., p. 61.

75 Shipp op.cit., p. 193.

76 Roger Hudson (ed) *William Russell, Special Correspondent of the Times*, London 1995, p. 139.

77 Gordon-Alexander op.cit., p. 284.

78 Pearman op.cit., p. 108.

79 Waterfield op.cit., p. 89.

80 Browne op.cit., pp. 217–8.

81 Keep op.cit., p. 154.

82 Hamilton op.cit., p. 37.

83 C.G.C Stapylton *The First Afghan War: An Ensign's Account*, Privately printed ND, p. 21.

84 Field op.cit., p. 297.

85 Larpent op.cit., p. 52.

86 Ibid. p. 78.

87 Peebles op.cit., pp. 276–9.

88 Waterfield op.cit., pp. 30–1.

89 Field op.cit., p. 73.

90 Peebles op.cit., p. 115.

91 Larpent op.cit., p. 244.

92 Gleig op.cit., p. 114.

93 Howe's Order Book op.cit.

94 Lamb op.cit., p. 330.

95 Peebles op.cit., p. 411.

96 MacKenzie op.cit., p. 62.

97 Waterfield op.cit., p. xiii.

98 Hopkins op.cit., p. 21.

99 Gordon-Alexander op.cit., p. 6.

100 Morris op.cit., p. 38.

101 Lamb op.cit., p. 66.

102 Loy Smith op.cit., p. 44.

103 Hopkins op.cit., p. 213.

104 Wheeler op.cit., p. 21.

105 Somerville op.cit., p. 105.

106 Field op.cit., p. 42.

107 Hopkins op.cit., pp. 168–181.

Foreign Fields

1 Glover op.cit., p. 147.

2 Longford *Years of the Sword* p. 172.

3 Sweetman op.cit., p. 179.

4 Glover op.cit., pp. 137–8.

5 Brian Bond *The Victorian Army and the Staff College*, London 1972, p. 107.

6 Croker op.cit., Vol I p. 342.

7 Ketchum op.cit., p. 26.

8 C. G. Moore-Smith (ed) *The Autobiography of Lieutenant General Sir Harry Smith*, London 1902, Vol I pp. 33–41.

9 Ibid p. 125.

10 Adkin op.cit., p. 242.

11 MacKenzie op.cit., p. 3.

12 Peter Collister *Hostage in Afghanistan*, London 1999, p. 31.

13 Gordon-Alexander op.cit., p. 302.

14 Clifford op.cit., p. 51.

15 Keep op.cit., p. 122.

16 Clifford op.cit., p. 65.

17 Morris op.cit., p. 16.

18 Browne op.cit., pp. 200–1.

19 Gleig op.cit., pp. 161–2.

20 Browne op.cit., p. 195.

21 Ibid p. 165.

22 Russell *Crimea*, p. 142.

23 Clifford op.cit., p. 99.

24 Ibid p. 106.

25 Longford *Years of the Sword*, p. 266.

26 Surtees op.cit., p. 5.

27 Gowing op.cit., p. 5.

28 Captain Sir John Kincaid *Adventures in the Rifle Brigade*, London 1929, p. 1.

29 Surtees op.cit., p. 6.

30 Wheeler op.cit., p. 23.

31 Keep op.cit., p. 58.

32 Browne op.cit., p. 88.

33 Gordon-Alexander op.cit., p. 9.

34 Peebles op.cit., p. 24.

35 Wheeler op.cit., p. 23.

36 Ibid p. 24.

37 Deane op.cit., p. 55.

38 *Kincaid Adventures* p. 2.

39 Browne op.cit., p. 89.

40 Gowing op.cit., p. 6.

41 Temple Godman op.cit., p. 11.

42 Smith op.cit., pp. 81–2.

43 Evelyn op.cit., pp. 29, 34.

44 Peebles op.cit., pp. 74–6.

45 Waterfield op.cit., p. 25.

46 Munro op.cit., p. 36.

47 Dennis Kincaid *British Social Life in India*, London 1973, p. 21.

48 Munro op.cit., p. 31.

49 Wood op.cit., pp. 95–6.

50 Ibid. p. 103.

51 Pearman op.cit., p. 27.

52 Pearman op.cit., p. 29.

53 Waterfield op.cit., p. 29.

54 Barter op.cit., p. 8.

55 Aitchison op.cit., p. 94.

56 Cooper op.cit., pp. 16–17.

57 Wheeler op.cit., p. 68.

58 Tomkinson op.cit., p. 3.

59 Mills op.cit., p. 33.

60 Tomkinson op.cit., p. 30

61 Wheeler op.cit., p. 49.

62 Aitchison op.cit., p. 32.

63 Webber op.cit., p. 67.

64 Ibid p. 74.

65 Glover op.cit., p. 153.

66 Tomkinson op.cit., p. 48.

67 Cooper op.cit., p. 14.

68 Longford *Years of the Sword* p. 242.

69 Mills op.cit., p. 42.

70 Captain Sir John Kincaid *Random Shots From a Rifleman*, London 1835, p. 46.

71 Gleig op.cit., p. 35.

72 Waterfield op.cit., p. 92.

73 Kincaid *Adventures* p. 33.

74 Gleig op.cit., p. 34.

75 Harris op.cit., p. 85.

76 Glover op.cit., p. 161.

77 *Soldier of the 71ˢᵗ*, p. 33.

78 Costello op.cit., p. 17.

79 Ibid. p. 18.

80 Waterfield op.cit., p. 44.

81 Martin R. Howard 'Red jackets and red noses: alcohol and the British Napoleonic soldier' in *Journal of the Royal Society of Medicine* Vol 93 Jan 2000 p. 38.

82 Ibid p. 40.

83 Ibid. p. 39.

84 Lamb op.cit., p. 185.

85 Sir Charles Oman *Wellington's Army*, London 1912, p. 277.

86 Duberly *Campaigns*, p. 78.

87 George Bell *Soldier's Glory: Rough Notes of an Old Soldier*, London 1956, p. 61.

88 W.H. Fitchett (ed) *Wellington's Men: Some Autobiographies*, London 1976, pp. 237,249.

89 Duberly *Campaigns*, p. 113.

90 Surtees op.cit., p. 28.

91 Piers Compton *Colonel's Lady and Camp Follower: The story of women in the Crimean War*, London 1970, p. 107.

92 Grattan op.cit., p. 146.
93 Browne op.cit., p. 174.
94 Ibid. p. 173.
95 Gleig op.cit., p. 335.
96 Grattan op.cit., p. 213.
97 Compton op.cit., pp. 89–90.
98 Browne op.cit., pp. 51–2.
99 Gordon-Alexander op.cit., p. 39.
100 Ibid. p. 66.
101 Stapylton op.cit., p. 31.
102 Pearman op.cit., p. 48.
103 Peebles op.cit., p. 372.
104 MacKenzie op.cit., p. 175.
105 Gleig op.cit., p. 225.
106 Kincaid *Adventures* p. 26.
107 Ibid p. 27.
108 Surtees op.cit., p. 267.
109 Ibid. p. 263.
110 A flat pouch hanging from the sword-belt.
111 Parquin op.cit., pp. 130–1.
112 Kincaid *Adventures* p. 26.
113 Brotherton op.cit., p. 29.
114 Mills op.cit., p. 46.
115 Ibid,. p. 36.
116 Ibid. p. 51.
117 Gronow op.cit., p. 48.
118 Russell *Crimea*, p. 262.
119 Gleig op.cit., p. 41.
120 Deane op.cit., p. 69.
121 Waterfield op.cit., p. 54.
122 Clifford op.cit., p. 136.
123 Deane op.cit., p. 85.
124 Peebles op.cit., pp. 370–2.
125 Deane op.cit., p. 120.
126 Wheeler op.cit., p. 64.
127 Ibid. p. 279.
128 Ibid.p. 64.
129 Grattan op.cit., p. 147.
130 Hennell op.cit., p. 123, 124, 132.
131 Shipp op.cit., p. 64.
132 Shipp p.cit., p. 66.
133 Deane op.cit., p. 121.
134 Grattan op.cit., pp. 144–5.
135 Kincaid *Adventures* p. 80.
136 Smith op.cit., Vol I pp. 64–5.
137 Gleig op.cit., p. 55.
138 Aitchison op.cit., p. 264.
139 Hennell op.cit., pp. 13–14.
140 Pemberton op.cit., pp. 202–3.
141 Gowing op.cit., p. 91.
142 Ibid p.
143 Grattan op.cit., p. 170–1.
144 Cooper op.cit., p. 76.
145 Grattan op.cit., pp. 211–12.
146 Gleig op.cit., p. 56.
147 John Keegan 'Towards a Theory of Combat Motivation' in Paul Addison and Angus Calder (eds) *Time to Kill*, London 1997, pp. 8–9.
148 Anglesey op.cit., Vol I p. 263.
149 Grattan op.cit., p. 33.
150 Huffer op.cit., p. 165.
151 Ibid p. 167.
152 Grattan op.cit., p. 32.
153 Waterfield op.cit., p. 112.
154 Wheeler op.cit., p. 83.
155 Pebles op.cit., p. 26.
156 Pococke op.cit., p. 60.
157 Peebles op.cit., p. 102.
158 Brotherton op.cit., p. 11.
159 William Leeke *The History of Lord Seaton's Regiment and Autobiography of the Rev. William Leeke*, London 1866, Vol I p. 24.
160 Keep op.cit., p. 160.
161 Colborne op.cit., p. 146.
162 Harris op.cit., p 65.
163 Wheeler op.cit., p. 58.
164 Costello op.cit., p. 53.
165 Harris op.cit., p. 28.
166 Cooper op.cit., p. 60.
167 Pemberton op.cit., p. 206.
168 Clifford op.cit., p. 124.
169 Lamb op.cit., p. 107.
170 Gowing op.cit., p. 16–18.
171 Haythornthwaite op.cit., p. 124.
172 Clifford op.cit., p. 56.
173 Surtees op.cit., p. 25.
174 Napier *War in the Peninsula*, Vol VI p. 409.
175 Wheeler op.cit., p. 56.
176 Napier *Life and Opinions* Vol I p. 95.
177 Ibid p. 170.
178 Costello op.cit., p. 93.
179 Morris op.cit., p. 80.
180 A. McKenzie Annand (ed) *Cavalry Surgeon*, London 1971, p. 75.
181 Hodge op.cit., p. 122.
182 Seaton op.cit., pp. 241–2.
183 Clifford op.cit., p. 77.
184 Duberly op.cit., p. 105.

185 Morris op.cit., p. 105.
186 Hodge op.cit., p. 130.

Epilogue

1 Roger Lonsdale *New Oxford Book of 18ᵗʰ Century Verse* Oxford, 1984, p. 48.
2 Boswell op.cit., p. 247.

3 W. M. Thackeray *Vanity Fair* London, 1848, p. 332.
4 Haythornwaite op.cit., p. 41.
5 Palmer *Rambling Soldier* p. 264.
6 Ibid p. 254.
7 Harris op.cit., p. 124.
8 Ibid.
9 Kincaid *Random Shots* p. 85.

BIBLIOGRAPHY

A comprehensive bibliography of the British army in this period would itself attain the proportions of a book. This lists only those works used by the author in the course of his research. Biographies, memoirs, letters and diaries are listed by the name of their subject, rather than that of their editor.

GENERAL WORKS

Adkin, Mark, *The Charge*, London, 2000.
Anglesey, The Marquess of, *A History of the British Cavalry*, 8 vols, London, 1973–1997.
Audoin-Rouzeau, Stéphane, *Les Combattants des Tranchées*, Paris 1986.
Aylward, J. D., *The Small-Sword in England*, London, 1945.
Ballhatchet, Kenneth, *Race, Sex and Class under the Raj*, London, 1980.
Bamfield, Veronica, *On the Strength: The Story of the British Army Wife*, London, 1974.
Barthorp, Michael, and Turner, Pierre, *The British Army on Campaign 1816–1853*, London, 1987.
Black, Jeremy, *European Warfare 1660–1815*, London, 1998.
Blackmore, Howard L., *British Military Firearms, 1650–1850*, London, 1994.
Bond, Brian, *The Victorian Army and the Staff College*, London, 1972.
Brereton, John, *Chain Mail: The Duke of Lancaster's Own Yeomanry 1798–1991*, Chippenham, ND.
Brooke, John, *King George III*, London, 1972.
Bryant, Arthur, *Jackets of Green*, London, 1972.
Burnett, John, *A History of the Cost of Living*, London, 1969.
Chandler, David, and Beckett, Ian, eds., *The Oxford Illustrated History of the British Army*, Oxford 1994
Chandler, David, *The Campaigns of Napoleon*, London, 1967.
Chartrand, René, and Courcelle, Patrice, *Emigré and Foreign Troops in British Service*, Oxford, 2000.

Clode, Charles M., *The Military Forces of the Crown*, 2 vols, London, 1869.

Cobban, Alfred, *A History of Modern France*, 2 vols, London, 1983.

Collister, Peter, *Hostage in Afghanistan*, London, 1999.

Compton, Piers, *Colonel's Lady and Camp Follower: The Story of Women in the Crimean War*, London, 1970.

Corkerry, Shaun, 'The recruitment and Personnel of the Royal Artillery 1741–1815' Unpublished research paper.

Costello, Con, *A Most Delightful Station: The British Army on the Curragh of Kildare*, Wilton, Cork, 1999.

Curtis, Edward E., *The British Army in the American Revolution*, Yale, 1926.

Duffy, Christopher *Military Experience in the Age of Reason*, London, 1987.

——*The Army of Frederick the Great*, Newton Abbot, 1974.

Farwell, Byron, *For Queen and Country*, London, 1981.

Fletcher, Ian, *Bloody Albuera*, London, 2000.

——*Galloping at Everything: British Cavalry in the Peninsular War and at Waterloo*, London, 2000

Fletcher, Ian, ed., *The Peninsular War: Aspects of the Struggle for the Iberian Peninsular*, Staplehurst, Kent, 1998.

Fletcher, Ian, and Poulter, Ron, *Gentlemen's Sons*, London, 1992.

Fortescue, Sir John *Following the Drum*, London, 1931.

——*History of the British Army*, 13 vols, London, 1899–1930.

Frey, Sylvia R., *The British Soldier in America: A Social History of Military Life in the Revolutionary Period*, Austin, Texas, 1981.

Gabriel, Richard A., and Metz, Karen, *A History of Military Medicine*, 2 vols, London, 1992.

Gates, David, *The British Light Infantry Arm*, London, 1987.

——*The Spanish Ulcer*, London, 1986.

General Orders by His Excellency the Hon William Howe, General and Commander-in-Chief . . . MS Order Book in the library of the Joint Services Command and Staff College, Watchfield.

Gibson, James, *Memoirs of the Brave: A Brief Account of the Battles of the Alma, Balaklava and Inkerman, with Biographies of those Killed* . . ., London, 1989.

Gilboy, E. W., *Cost of Living and Real Wages in Eighteenth Century England*, Harvard, 1934.

Glover, Michael, *Wellington's Army*, Newton Abbot, Devon, 1977.

Guy, Alan J., *Oeconomy and Discipline: Officership and Administration in the British Army, 1714–63*, Manchester, 1984.

Hargreaves, Reginald, *This Happy Breed: Reflections on Soldiers and Soldiering*, London, 1951.

Haythornthwaite, Philip A., *The Armies of Wellington*, London, 1996.

——*British Infantry of the Napoleonic Wars* London, 1987.

Holmes, Richard, *Firing Line*, London, 1985

Hopkins, Harry, *The Strange Death of Private White*, London, 1977.

Houlding, J. A., Fit for Service: The Training of the British Army 1715–1795, Oxford, 1981.

Howard, Martin R., 'Red jackets and red noses: alcohol and the British Napoleonic soldier,' *Journal of the Royal Society of Medicin,e* Vol. 93, January 2000.

Huffer, Donald Breeze Mendham, 'The Infantry officers of the Line of the British Army, 1815–1868,' Unpublished PhD thesis, University of Birmingham, 1995

James, F. G., *Ireland in the Empire 1688–1770*, Cambridge, Mass 1793.

Keegan, John, *The Face of Battle*, London, 1976.

——'Towards a Theory of Combat Motivation' in Addison, Paul, and Calder, Angus, *A Time to Kill*, London, 1997

Ketchem, Richard M., *The Battle for Bunker Hill*, London, 1963.

Kincaid, Dennis, *British Social Life in India*, London, 1973.

Kinglake, A. W., *The Invasion of the Crimea*, 9 vols, London, and Edinburgh, 1866–75.

Lawrence, A. W., ed., *Capitives of Tipu: Survivors' Narratives*, London, 1929.

Lynn, John A., *The Bayonets of the Republic: Motivation and Tactics in the Army of Revolutionary France, 1791–1794*, Boulder, Colo., 1996.

MacIntire, J., *A Military Treatise on the Discipline of the Marine Forces*, London, 1763.

McHenry, Robert, ed., *Webster's American Military Biographies*, New York 1978.

McLynn, Frank, *Crime and Punishment in Eighteenth-Century England*, London, 1991.

Millett, Allan R., and Maslowski, Peter, *For the Common Defense: A Military History of the United States of America*, London, 1984.

Mingey, G. E., *Rural Life in Victorian England*, Gloucester, 1976.

Morgan, Kenneth O., ed., *The Oxford Illustrated History of Britain*, Oxford, 1984.

Manual of Military Law, London, 1914.

Mayhew, Henry, and Quennell, Peter, *London's Underground,* London, 1969.

Morvan, Jean, *Le Soldat Imperial,* 2 vols, Paris, 1904.

Napier, William F. P. *History of the War in the Peninsula . . .,* 6 vols, London, 1835–40.

Neuberg, Victor, *Gone for a Soldier,* London, 1989.

Oman, Sir Charles, *History of the Peninsular War,* 7 vols, Oxford 1902–30.

——*Wellington's Army,* London, 1912.

Orr, Michael, *Dettingen,* London, 1972.

Pakenham, Thomas, *The Year of Liberty,* London, 1972.

Palmer, Roy, ed., *The Rambling Soldier,* London, 1977.

Paret, Peter, ed., *Makers of Modern Strategy,* Oxford 1986.

Pemberton, W. Baring, *Battles of the Crimean War,* London, 1962.

Pickard, Liza, *Dr Johnson's London,* London, 2000.

Robson, Brian, *Swords of the British Army: The Regulation Patterns,* first ed., London, 1975, revised ed., London, 1996.

Rothenburg, Gunther E, *Napoleon's Great Adversary: The Archduke Charles and the Austrian Army 1792–1814,* Staplehurst, Kent 1995.

Scouller, R. E., *The Armies of Queen Anne,* Oxford, 1966.

Shamas, Carole *The Pre-Industrial Consumer in Britain and America,* Oxford, 1990.

Siborne, H. T., *The Waterloo Letters,* London, 1891.

Simpson, Grant G., ed., *The Scottish Soldier Abroad,* Edinburgh, 1992.

Spiers, Edward, *The Army and Society 1815–1914,* London, 1980.

Stocqueler, Joachim, *A Personal History of Horse Guards,* London, 1873.

Strachan, Hew, *Wellington's Legacy: The Reform of the British Army 1815–1854,* Manchester 1984.

Weekes, Alan, *The Royal Hampshire Regiment,* London, 1968.

Williams, Col Noel St J., *The Colonel's Lady and Judy O'Grady,* London, 1988.

Wood, Stephen, *The Scottish Soldier,* Manchester, 1987.

Wyndham, Horace, *Soldiers of the Queen,* London, 1889.

BIOGRAPHIES, MEMOIRS, LETTERS AND DIARIES

Aitchison Thompson, W. F. K., *An Ensign in the Peninsular War,* London, 1981.

Bibliography

ATKYNS Young, Brig Peter, ed., *Military Memoirs: Richard Atkyns*, London, 1967.

Alexander-Gordon, Lt Col W., *Reflections of a Highland Subaltern*, London, 1889.

Bancroft, N. W., *From Recruit to Staff Sergeant*, London, 1979.

Barrow, Lt. General Sir George, *The Fire of Life*, London, 1941.

Barter, Richard, *The Siege of Delhi: Mutiny Memoirs of an Old Officer*, London, 1984.

Bell, George, *Soldier's Glory: Rough Notes of an Old Soldier*, London, 1956.

BLACKADDER Crichton, Andrew, ed., *The Life and Diary of Lieut. Col J. Blackadder, of the Cameronian Regiment . . .*, London, 1824.

BLAKENEY Sturgis J., ed., *A Boy in the Peninsular War: Adventures and Experiences of Robert Blakeney*, London, 1899.

BOSWELL Wain, John, ed., *The Journals of James Boswell 1760–1795*, London, 1991.

BRAGGE Cassels, S. A., ed., *Peninsular Portrait: The Letters of Captain William Bragge*, London, 1963.

BROTHERTON Perrett, Bryan, ed., *A Hawk at War: The Peninsular War reminiscences of General Sir Thomas Brotherton*, London, 1986.

BROWNE Buckley, Roger Norman, ed., *The Napoleonic War Journal of Captain Thomas Henry Browne 1807–1816*, London, 1987.

BRYDEN MacRory, Patrick, ed., *William Bryden's Account from the Memory and Memoranda made on arrival of the retreat from Cabool in 1842*, London, 1969.

BURGOYNE Hargrave, Richard J., *General John Burgoyne*, London, 1983.

Clifford, Henry, *Henry Clifford VC: His letters and sketches from the Crimea*, London, 1956.

COBBETT Reitzel, William, ed., *The autobiography of William Cobbett: The progress of a Plough-Boy to a seat in Parliament*, London, 1933.

COLBORNE Moore-Smith, C. G., *The life of John Colborne: Field Marshal Lord Seaton*, London, 1903.

Cooper, John Spencer, *Rough Notes of Seven Campaigns*, London, 1996.

COSTELLO Brett-James, Antony *Edward Costello: The Peninsular and Waterloo Campaigns*, London, 1967.

Cotton, Edward *A Voice from Waterloo*, London, 1862.

CREEVEY Gore, John, ed., *The Creevey Papers*, London, 1934.

DEANE Chandler, D. G., ed., *A Journal of Marlborough's Campaigns*

... *by James Marshall Deane, Private Sentinel in Queen Anne's First Regiment of Foot Guards*, London, 1984.

DE LANCEY   Miller, David, *Lady De Lancey at Waterloo*, London, 2000.

DEVONSHIRE   Foreman, Amanda, *Georgiana Duchess of Devonshire*, London, 1998.

Duberly, Mrs Henry, *Diary Kept during the Russian War*, London, 1856.

DUBERLY   Tisdall, E. P., ed., *Mrs Duberly's Campaigns: An Englishwoman's experiences in the Crimean War and Indian Mutiny*, London, 1963.

EVELYN   Falls, Cyril, ed., *A Diary of the Crimea by George Palmer Evelyn*, London, 1954.

EVELYN   Skull, G. D., *Memoir and Letters of Captain W. Glanville Evelyn of the 4th Regiment, King's Own. in North America*, New York, 1971.

GOWING   Fenwick, K., ed., *A Voice From the Ranks*, London, 1954.

Gleig, George Robert, *The Subaltern: A Chronicle of the Peninsular War*, Edinburgh, 1877.

GRANBY   Manners, W. E., *Some Account of the Military, Political and Social Life of ... Marquis of Granby*, London, 1899.

GRATTAN   Oman, Sir Charles, ed. *Adventures with the Connaught Rangers 1809–1914, William Grattan Esq late lieutenant Connaught Rangers*, London, 1902.

Graydon, A., *Memoirs of a Life passed chiefly in Pennsylvania*, Edinburgh 1922.

GREVILLE   Hibbert, Christopher, ed., *Greville's England*, London 1981.

GRONOW   Bentley, Nicolas, ed., *The Reminiscences of Captain Gronow*, London, 1977.

Hamilton, Anthony *Hamilton's Campaign with Moore and Wellington during the Peninsular War*, London, 1998.

HARRIS   Hibbert, Christopher, ed., *The Recollections of Rifleman Harris ...*, London, 1985.

HICKEY   Hudson, Roger, ed., *The Memoirs of a Georgian Rake: William Hickey*, London, 1995.

HODGE   Anglesey, The Marquess of, *Little Hodge: being extracts from the letters and diaries of Colonel Edward Cooper Hodge written during the Crimean War*, London, 1971.

Bibliography

HOWE Partridge, Bellamy, *Sir Billy Howe*, London, 1932.

KEEP Fletcher, Ian, ed., *In the Service of the King*, Staplehurst, Kent, 1997.

Kinkaid, Capt Sir John, *Adventures in the Rifle Brigade*, London, 1929.

——*Random Shots from a Rifleman*, London, 1835.

Lamb, Roger, *An Original and Authentic Journal of Occurrences during the late American War* . . ., Dublin, 1809.

LANG David Blomfield, ed., *Lahore to Lucknow: The Indian Mutiny Journal of Arthur Moffat Lang*, London, 1992.

LARPENT Larpent, Sir George, ed. *The Private Journal of Judge-Advocate Larpent, attached to the headquarters of Lord Wellington during the Peninsular War* . . ., London, 1854.

Lawrence, William *The Autobiography of Sergeant William Lawrence*, Cambridge, 1987.

LAWSON Bonham-Carter, Victor, *George Lawson, Surgeon in the Crimea*, London, 1968.

Marbot, Marcellin, *The Memoirs of Baron de Marbot*, London, 1929.

LE MESURIER Le Mesurier, Col Havilland, ed., *Extracts from some letters of Commissary General Havilland Le Mesurier* . . ., Privately printed, ND.

Loy Smith, George *A Victorian RSM: From India to the Crimea*, London, 1987.

MacKenzie, Frederick *Diary of Frederick MacKenzie*, 2 vols, Harvard, 1930.

McGRIGOR Blanco, Richard L., *Wellington's Surgeon General: Sir James McGrigor*, Durham, North Carolina, 1974.

Mercer, General Cavalié *Journal of the Waterloo Campaign*, London, 1985.

MILLS Fletcher, Ian, ed., *For King and Country: The Letters and Diaries of John Mills, Coldstream Guards*, London, 1995.

MORRIS Selby, John, ed., *Military Memoirs: Thomas Morris*, London, 1967.

MUNRO Haley, Arthur, ed., *The Munro Letters: Lieutenant Innes Munro, 71st Regiment*, London, 1984.

NAPIER Napier, William, ed., *The Life and Opinions of General Sir C. J. Napier*, 2 vols, London, 1857.

Napier, General Sir George, *The Life of General Sir George Napier*, London, 1884.

OUGHTON Wood, Stephen, *By dint of Labour and Perseverance: A journal kept by Lt Col James Adolphus Oughton*, London, 1977.

PARQUIN Jones, B. T., ed., *Military Memoirs: Charles Parquin*, London, 1969.

PEARMAN Anglesey, The Marquess of, *Sergeant Pearman's Memoirs, being chiefly his account of service with the Third, King's Own. Light Dragoons in India*, London, 1968.

PEEBLES Ira D. Gruber, ed., *John Peebles' American War 1776–1783*, London, 1997.

Pinckard, George, *Notes on the West Indies: Written during the Expedition under the command of the late General Sir Ralph Abercromby*, 3 vols, London, 1806.

RAGLAN Sweetman, John, *Raglan*, London, 1993.

Roberston, FM Sir William, *From Private to Field-Marshal*, London, 1921.

Rotton, John Edward Wharton, *The Chaplain's Narrative of the Siege of Delhi*, London, 1958.

ROUS Fletcher, Ian, ed., *A Guards Officer in the Peninsula: The Peninsular War letters of John Rous*, London, 1992.

RUSSELL Bentley, Nicholas *Russell's Dispatches from the Crimea*, London, 1964.

——Hudson, Roger, ed., *William Russell, Special Correspondent of The Times*, London, 1995.

RYDER *Memoirs of John Ryder, 32nd Regiment of Foot*, addendum, to Swinson and Scott, eds., *The Memoirs of Private Waterfield*, London, 1968.

SALE MacRory, Patrick, ed., *Lady Sale: The First Afghan War*, London, 1969.

SCHAUMANN Ludovici, Anthony, ed., *On the Road with Wellington: The Diary of a War Commissary in the Peninsula*, London, 1924.

Sherer, Moyle *Recollections of the Peninsula*, London, 1827.

Shipp, John *The Paths of Glory*, London, 1969.

SMITH Moore-Smith, C. G., *The Autobiography of General Sir Harry Smith*, 2 vols, London, 1902.

SNELL Stevens, Matthew, *Hannah Snell: The Secret Life of a Female Marine*, London, 1997.

SOLDIER OF THE 71st, pseud. Thomas Pococke. Christopher Hibbert, ed., *A Soldier of the Seventy-First*, London, 1976.

Somerville, Alexander, *Autobiography of a Working Man*, London, 1967.

Stapylton, Lt Col C. G. C., *The First Afghan War: An Ensign's Account*, Privately printed, ND.

Bibliography

Surtees, William, *Twenty-Five Years in the Rifle Brigade*, London, 1973.

SYLVESTER Annand, A. McKenzie, ed., *Cavalry Surgeon*, London, 1971.

TEMPLE GODMAN Warner, Philip *The Fields of War: A Young Cavalryman's Crimean Campaign*, London, 1977.

TERROT Richardson, Robert A., ed. *Nurse Sarah Anne: With Florence Nightingale in the Crimean War*, London, 1977.

Thom, William *Rhymes and Recollections of a Handloom Weaver*, Glasgow 1845.

Tomkinson, Lt Col William *Diary of a Cavalry Officer*, Staplehurst, Kent 1999.

WASMUS Lynn, Mary C., *An Eyewitness Account of the American Revolution: The Journal of J. F. Wasmus*, Wetsport, Conn., 1990.

WATERFIELD Swinson, Arthur, and Scott, Donald, eds., *The Memoirs of Private Waterfield, Soldier in Her Majesty's 32nd Regiment of Foot*, London, 1968.

WEBBER Wollacombe, Richard Henry, ed., *With the Guns in the Peninsula: The Peninsular war Journal of William Webber*, London, 1991.

WELLINGTON Hibbert, Christopher *Wellington, A Personal History* London, 1998.

Longford, Elizabeth *Wellington: Years of the Sword*, London, 1972.

——*Wellington: Pillar of the State*, London, 1972.

WHEATLEY Hibbert, Christopher, ed., *The Wheatley Diary*, London, 1964.

WHEELER Liddell Hart, B. H., ed., *The Letters of Private Wheeler 1808–1828*, Adlestrop, Gloucestershire, 1951.

WOLFE Wilson, Beckles *The Life and Letters of James Wolfe*, London, 1909.

Wood, Field Marshal Sir Evelyn *From Midshipman to Field Marshal*, London, 1906.

WOOD Whitworth, Rex, ed., *Gunner at Large: The Diaries of James Wood RA 1746–1765*, London, 1998.

ACKNOWLEDGEMENTS

I first met my wife Lizzie over a quarter of a century ago at a military dinner. When I heard her mention the Lines of Torres Vedras, the table shook and the candles flickered. I proposed a fortnight later. I cannot recall publishing a book in which I have not gratefully acknowledged her support, but this time she has done a good deal more than mop fevered brows. She tracked down many of the first-hand accounts on which this book is based, taking notes in a hand which is a great deal better than my own; she read successive drafts and, in the inevitable last-minute scramble, backtracked methodically to find elusive references. It is quite literally true to say that there would have been no book without her. My daughters Jessica and Corinna have had to put up with a father who is often either absent or simply absent-minded: the fact that they have done so for most of their lives only increases his guilt.

Arabella Pike at HarperCollins gave wise editorial direction by reminding me that this was always meant to be a book about people. Colonel John Hughes-Wilson, in the best tradition of the general staff, produced a timely and comprehensive brief on the cost of living during the period. Lieutenant Colonel Chetwynd-Stapylton lent me the unpublished letters and diaries of his ancestor, who served in the 13th Regiment at the siege of Jellalabad in 1842. The librarians and staff of the Prince Consort Library, Aldershot, the Aldershot Public Library, and the libraries at the Royal Military Academy Sandhurst and the Royal Military College of Science were helpful far beyond the bounds of their duty. And like so many scholars who worked in the old, and much-missed, Staff College Library, I owe a particular debt to Mrs Pam Bendall. Finally, I thank the Princess of Wales's Royal Regiment (Queen's and Royal Hampshires) for inviting me to become its colonel, and yet again showing me, from Salisbury Plain to Kosovo, just how right Wellington was to speak of 'that best of all instruments, British infantry.'

INDEX